Town and Gown Rela

Town and Gown Relations

A Handbook of Best Practices

Edited by ROGER L. KEMP

McFarland & Company, Inc., Publishers

Jefferson, North Carolina, and London

ISBN 978-0-7864-6399-2
softcover : acid free paper ∞

LIBRARY OF CONGRESS CATALOGUING DATA ARE AVAILABLE

BRITISH LIBRARY CATALOGUING DATA ARE AVAILABLE

Cover art: Ionic column capital (Dorling Kindersley/Thinkstock)

Manufactured in the United States of America

*McFarland & Company, Inc., Publishers
Box 611, Jefferson, North Carolina 28640
www.mcfarlandpub.com*

To Anika,
the best and the brightest

Acknowledgments

Grateful acknowledgment is made to the following organizations and publishers for granting permission to reprint the material in this volume.

Arizona State University
Center for Cities & Schools
CEOs for Cities
City of Clemson
City of Orange
The College of William & Mary
Colorado State University
DePauw College
Government Finance Officers Association
Initiative for a Competitive Inner City
International City/County Management Association
International Town & Gown Association
League of California Cities
Lincoln Institute of Land Policy
PACE (Philanthropy for Active Civic Engagement)
Systems Support, Inc.
The Trust for Public Land
University of California, Berkeley
University of Minnesota
Urban Habitat
Wesleyan University
World Future Society

Table of Contents

Appendices

Preface

Interactions between local communities and schools have a long history, dating to the early Middle Ages. These interactions are often referred to as town and gown relations. Misunderstandings between these parties can be traced to historical developments and a lack of general understanding of the implications that these developments have on each other. For the twenty-first century college town, a school has a positive economic development impact, directly and indirectly, on the community and for the residents.

Some issues and problems evolved over time since each community and school (the town and gown) have had separate governing bodies with different priorities and loyalties and shared the same limited geographic space. In many cases, public colleges and universities are typically located on state property, and the higher level of government (the state) usually gets its way with what is placed on its property, even though this property resides within a neighborhood that is located within the political boundaries of a municipality, a so-called local government. Also, such educational properties are usually tax exempt, and the owner of the property (the state) does not have to pay property taxes to the city government.

Nowadays, everyone knows the positive employment, economic contributions and impact made by the educational sector on a community, as well as the purchasing power that school officials, faculty and staff, as well as students, have in the neighborhoods where the schools are located. This goes for all levels of educational institutions — from the lowest to the highest levels. While public educational property might not be on the property tax rolls and might not generate property tax revenue to a community, the revenues from the economic impact generated from those folks associated with schools in a given community is very significant. Also, the economic development influence and impact of a school on the neighborhood in which it is located is dramatic.

For these reasons, many cities and schools are forming neighborhood advisory committees, some elected officials have requested students to serve on their governing bodies, and public and school officials have been working together, since they know that it is in their mutual best interests to do to. The same holds true for citizens and students, since they both reside in the same general geographic area, and should make every effort to peacefully coexist, since they share the same neighborhoods, and use the same goods and services provided by the merchants and the governments located within their community.

The goal of this volume is to educate public and school officials as well as citizens and students on evolving state-of-the art relationships and practices that exist between cities and schools. These best practices would include evolving state-of-the-art planning and management practices related to joint efforts to resolve outstanding issues and problems related to these two separate groups. By working together, mutual issues can be resolved amicably before they become community issues or problems.

This volume is divided into four parts for ease of reference. The first part introduces the reader to relevant state-of-the-art topics related

1

to town-gown planning and management practices. The second part, and by design the longest, includes numerous case studies, or best practices, on how local governments and schools are initiating measures to resolve issues and problems, while maintaining acceptable levels of public and educational services to citizens and students. Such practices are critical to maintaining the quality of life in cities and towns and their educational institutions throughout the country.

The third part focuses on the future of the field of town-gown relations. In short, this section provides a summary of the evolving options and best practices available for charting the future relationship between cities and schools, public and schools officials, and citizens and students, in America's cities.

Part IV contains appendices that have been assembled to promote a greater understanding of this dynamic and evolving field, as well as provide resources for officials, citizens and students seeking additional information and resources. Valuable local, state, national, and international online information and resources are provided.

Based on this general conceptual schema, the four parts are highlighted and briefly examined in greater detail below.

Cities and Schools

Part I sets the stage for the latest best practices being used by public and school officials, and citizens and students, in America's cities, and ways cities are coping and negotiating town-gown related problems and issues. These chapters provide an overview of this subject, including cooperative efforts to jointly plan, and set the foundation for the various evolving best practices that are presented in the following section.

Topics include an examination of the measures that should be taken to ensure proper social responsibilities, the opportunities and risks available to city and school officials, creation of sustainable communities, evolving career options and opportunities, and the source of revenues being used to finance municipal and educational services.

These chapters provide the framework and background against which the best city and school practices that have emerged across the United States in recent years are examined. The purpose of providing this information is so the reader can feel comfortable when reviewing the best practices examined in the second section of this volume.

Best Practices

The various cities, towns, communities, and schools examined in Part II, including the states in which they are located, as well as the highlights of the evolving best practices in this dynamic and evolving discipline, form the basis of this section. The relationships that exist between municipal public officials and citizens in communities, as well as school officials and students, are examined in most of these best practice case studies. The cities and schools featured, the states in which they are located, and the best practices that are examined, are shown below categorically in alphabetical order for reference purposes.

These case studies represent an important and significant research effort to obtain a body of knowledge on the best practices available in the dynamic and still evolving relationships that exist between communities and the schools located within them. The best practices section includes an examination of over 40 local governments and their schools, at various educational levels, which are geographically located in nearly one-half of the states in the United States, including some in Canada.

CITIES

Amherst	Gainesville
Aspen	Greencastle
Boston	Hamilton
Bridgewater	Kannapolis
Canton	Kingston
Chapel Hill	Los Angeles
Charlottesville	Mentor
Chicago	Meredith
Cutler Bay	Middletown
Elmira	New York City
Emeryville	Newark

Orange
Phoenix
Pittsburgh
Plano
Portland
Richmond (CA)
Richmond (VA)
Roanoke
Rockland
Sacramento

St. Paul
San Francisco
San Jose
San Pablo
State College
Sugar Land
Tampa
Warrensburgh
Washington, DC
Williamsburg

Schools

Arizona State University
Bridgewater State University
Central Missouri State University
Chapman University
College of William & Mary
Collin College
Columbia University
DePauw University
Elmira College
Emery Unified School District (Georgetown
  University)
Hampshire College
McMaster University
Mentor Public School District
Miami–Dade County Public Schools
Newark Public School District
Northeastern University
Pearl River School
Pennsylvania State University
Plymouth State University
Portland State University
Queen's University
Roanoke City Public Schools
Sacramento City Unified School District
St. Lawrence University
San Jose State University
University of California
University of Florida
University of Houston
University of Illinois
University of Michigan
University of Minnesota
University of North Carolina
University of Pittsburgh
University of South Florida
University of Southern California
University of Virginia

Virginia Commonwealth University
Wesleyan University
West Contra Costa Unified School District

States

Arizona
California
Colorado
Connecticut
Florida
Illinois
Indiana
Massachusetts
Minnesota
Missouri

New Hampshire
New Jersey
New York
North Carolina
Ohio
Oregon
Pennsylvania
Texas
Virginia

Other Jurisdictions

District of Columbia
Ontario

Countries

Canada
United States

Best Practices

Use of dialog to enhance mutual cooperation
  that is jointly beneficial.
Educational activities produce advocates for the
  continuation of research facilities.
City and school cooperation have led to a new
  generation of "college towns."
Communities and schools continue to negotiate
  over the cost of municipal services.
Cities and schools maintain a positive relationship through mutual cooperation.
Positive planning processes are a result of longstanding cooperative relationships.
Some colleges and universities have community relations departments.
Many colleges and schools seek opportunities
  for the resolution of conflicts.
One school provides cities with emergency response vehicles.
Cities and citizens benefit when students learn
  about disaster management.
Some cities work with schools to involve students in the urban planning process.
A town/gown task force is jointly developed by
  a city and a school.

Cities and colleges work together to develop a neighborhood action plan.

Colleges adopt formal policies to strengthen their relationship with the community.

A city and school work together to provide a joint community policing center.

Cities and colleges jointly cooperate to create downtown campuses.

Cities and schools work together to improve neighborhood security for citizens.

Leading cities and schools create programs to train future public managers.

Citizens benefit when school district budgets are reduced.

Some cities work with schools to provide housing for internship programs.

Cities and schools work together to develop long-term neighborhood plans.

Some schools have learned to work with neighborhood groups.

Communities and their schools involve students in planning for parks by their schools.

Cities and schools cooperate and plan for "joint" downtown areas.

Citizens approve new downtown campus for their state university.

Cities and schools are now involving citizens in their planning process.

Cities and their citizens benefit from student internship programs.

City and college officials work together to create a university district plan.

Communities and their colleges cooperate to make student better citizens.

A city and its citizens benefit from their university's investments.

One city develops a "financial plan" to finance its public school system.

A school uses a "business model" to enhance student achievement levels.

A public university prepared model for joint city/school infrastructure planning.

City planning agencies benefit from a university's technology and software.

Citizens benefit from studies linking families and schools to transit development.

One city and university planned, and built, a joint public library.

A city and school form a partnership to revitalize an inner-city neighborhood.

City seeks student representative from university to serve on their city council.

City and college work together on new campus for educational and economic reasons.

One city's citizens benefit from its university bringing more students downtown.

The citizens of cities benefit from their schools economic contributions.

Cities and their schools work together to reduce town-gown tensions.

One city and college form joint neighborhood relations committee.

The Future

Part III examines state-of-the-art and evolving best practice trends and practices that are taking, and will take place in our nation's local governments and the schools located within their respective political boundaries. The topics examined include emerging urban renewal opportunities, as well as how schools and cities are working together to train future citizens and public officials. Other important topics concerning the future of community and educational services include an examination of the conditions of America's educational system and how cities and schools will use technologies to provide and enhance their educational services. Lastly, will municipal and college relations diminish as more schools, at all levels, provide more online off-campus educational opportunities?

These readings reflect the various initiatives and best practices being taken by public and school officials, many times with the assistance of citizens, students, and employees, to improve town-gown relationships. These practices are still evolving, are dynamic in nature, and represent the new focus of public and school officials in cities and schools throughout the nation. Modern town-gown planning practices that achieve these goals are being developed and implemented with greater frequency by officials throughout the nation during the past few years.

This volume represents an important codification of knowledge in this dynamic and evolving field. Many citizens, including the public officials that represent them, are busy dealing with school officials and students on town-gown issues and problems in their respective communities. This research brings together evolving best practices in a field that has been facilitated by recent economic hard times, and which directly impacts the availability of revenues to finance public and educational services in cities throughout America and Canada. It is important that public officials and citizens work together with school officials and students on existing, evolving, and future town-gown issues, positive and negative in nature, as they now exist or arise.

Appendices

This is the first edited reference work on this topic that offers options for public and school officials, as well as citizens and students, to consider and use in their town-gown cooperation and planning practices. To this end, several important reference resources have been assembled. Brief descriptions are highlighted for reference purposes, and to facilitate future research and obtaining relevant information from these valuable resources.

Glossary of Terms for Cities and Schools. Because the dynamic and evolving nature of this field, it was important to codify the existing terms used in the field of town-gown relations. These terms are frequently used by municipal government and school professionals, as well as citizens and students, involved in town-gown relationships. These terms will make it easier for city and school officials, as well as citizens and students, to understand, discuss, and monitor town-gown issues and problems in their respective communities and schools.

Regional Resource Directory. This appendix includes a listing of all of the community governments and schools included in Part II, Best Practices. Readers wishing to follow up on any of the best practices contained in this volume are provided with immediate access to each government and school via its website. In those communities with the council-manager form of government, it is suggested that inquiries and questions be directed to the office

of the city manager. In those cities with the strong-mayor form of government, it is recommended that all inquiries and questions be directed to the office of the mayor. For public schools, inquiries should be addressed to superintendents for school districts, and to the office of the president for colleges and universities. Additional information, including possible personal contacts, may be obtained from these municipal and school website resources.

National Resource Directory. This listing includes all major national professional associations, foundations, membership organizations, and research institutions serving public officials in local governments and schools, professionals in these fields, as well as concerned citizens and students. Many of these organizations focus on various issues and problems relating to community and school relations, and related issues and problems. The website is listed for each major organization and association; these frequently focus on current issues and problems relating to the town-gown field.

International Resource Directory. This appendix assembles a listing of major international associations, research institutions, and resource centers, focusing on issues and problems relating to local governments, including their city and school related issues and problems, and schools and their town-gown related issues and problems. The reader may wish to find out the town-gown issues and problems in other countries, as well as the specific cities and schools that are located within them. These websites provide valuable resources, relevant information, as well as a list of contacts for questions and additional information.

Bibliographic and Reference Sources. Town-gown issues and problems are listed categorically by subject areas that relate to cities and schools, and their town-gown relationships. This information was obtained and summarized from the town-gown knowledge base, The College Town Resource Center, from the International Town & Gown Association (ITGA), which is located in the United States. This website provides the reader with a wealth of information in those subject matter areas listed. Contacts are listed for additional information, as well as the sources for more information on the best practices that are presented on the ITGA website.

Model Agreements and Documents. This appendix resource includes a listing of national model agreements and documents. Agreements generally related to those arrangements negotiated between municipalities and schools for joint planning, the joint discussion of issues and problems, the provision and payment for municipal services, the relationship between the local government and a school, and related city/school agreements. Documents relate to important reports that contain facts relevant to city and school relationships and mutual cooperation on past, present, and future joint issues and problems.

State Municipal League Directory. Most states have a professional municipal association, which serves as a valuable source of information about their state's city governments, including town-gown related issues and problems. State leagues typically have copies of municipal laws, existing policies, and budgets available for public officials and citizens in their state to review. They would also have information on significant town-gown relationships between communities and the schools located within them. The website for each state's municipal league is listed to provide access to these valuable resources, documents, and related sources of online town-gown information.

State Library Directory. Each state has a central state library and information resource center, and each one typically contains copies of state laws and policies concerning their municipal governments as well as the schools within their respective political boundaries. These libraries serve as an excellent resource center for both citizens, students, as well as public city and school officials. The amount of state funds allocated to cities, as well as their schools, is also available. The website for each state library is listed to provide the reader with direct access to these valuable online information resources.

Distance Learning Resources. Distance learning is taking on significant importance in recent years. It connects educational institutions with students throughout the United States, who may wish to take courses towards many online degree programs. This appendix reflects those organizations that provide online distance-learning information and resources to the public from their respective websites. This information was obtained from the U. S. Distance Learning Association and the Distance Learning Resource Network. These distance learning resources are an excellent source of information about online educational trends and opportunities in America.

The editor hopes that the information contained in this volume will assist citizens and students, as well as local public and school officials, and leaders of community organizations, as they attempt to make sense out of the many best practices emerging in the dynamic and evolving field of town-gown relations and the various programs that serve to create and form them. The future of America's municipalities and schools depends upon the proper planning and management of their respective community and school resources through the best state-of-the-art town-gown practices available. It is only through such cooperative processes that outstanding and emerging issues and problems can be appropriately addressed, and joint proactive efforts can be taken to plan for the future of our cities and their schools.

Citizens and students, as well as public and school officials, should not only expect, but demand, that prudent best practice measures be adopted and implemented for their communities in these areas to insure that appropriate cooperative efforts are taken in the future. This will help define and resolve respective services, issues, and problems — both municipal and school — and ensure that the actions taken provide a benefit to all of the residents of a community — citizens and students alike.

It is the goal of this volume to provide a frame of reference and network of resources to assist public and schools officials, as well as citizens and students, to undertake collaborative and joint efforts to resolve outstanding issues and problems, and to agree upon common services and programs, in order to create an improved quality-of-life for the residents of our cities and their educational institutions. Citizens and students should be active and equal partners in the town-gown relations process.

PART I. CITIES AND SCHOOLS

CHAPTER 1

Evolving Relations

Yesim Sungu-Eryilmaz

Globalization has presented cities with many new and persistent challenges, especially during the current economic slowdown. Almost all major metropolitan areas in the United States have been affected by these changes that have either helped them attract new businesses and residents or left them suffering from disinvestment and population loss.

These economic and social changes in cities and neighborhoods have helped to reshape town-gown relationships. In both advancing and declining cities, local governments have recognized the growing importance of colleges and universities as anchor institutions in economic and community development. This represents a shift in the governance paradigm, since governments alone cannot address the complexity of today's urban problems. This new paradigm encourages the creation of partnerships among the public, private, and nonprofit sectors to harness the collective capacity of all players to solve these issues.

Colleges and universities thus have a key role to play with state and local governments and nonprofits in areas as diverse as education and skills training, technology, industrial performance, public health, and social and cultural development (Adams 2003; ICIC and CEOs for Cities 2002).

Economic Development

The importance of universities to their local economies has long been recognized. Among their many economic impacts, the most important ones are enhancing the industry and technology base, employing large numbers of people, and generating revenue for local governments through university expenditures on salaries, goods, and services.

ENHANCING THE INDUSTRY AND TECHNOLOGY BASE

In the evolving knowledge economy, the contribution of the "creative class" is often seen as strategic and valuable for local economic development (Florida 2005; Glaeser 2000). It is clear that institutions of higher education can play an important role in growing, attracting, and retaining knowledge workers (Clark 2003).

Beyond preparing and attracting a qualified workforce to the local economy, institutions of higher education provide technical support and specialized expertise to firms (Bramwell and Wolfe 2008). Changes in academic research and development funding patterns suggest how these university–private sector partnerships have evolved over the last 35 years. While the federal government continues to provide more than 60 percent of funds for academic research

Originally published as "Evolving Town-Gown Relations in Urban Development," *Town-Gown Collaboration in Land Use and Development*, Policy Focus Report, 2009, by the Lincoln Institute of Land Policy, Cambridge, Massachusetts. Reprinted with permission of the publisher.

and development, industry sources contributed 5 percent ($2.1 billion), and state and local government funding provided 6 percent ($2.6 billion) of the total in 2006.

Colleges and universities can enhance the local technological base if firms locate nearby and coordinate their research efforts with those institutions (Varga 2000). In recent years, technoparks or joint university-industry research centers for ongoing, firm-based research and development have expanded dramatically. A growing number of universities have become directly involved in the incubation of newly established scientific and technical companies.

For example, Worcester Polytechnic Institute (WPI) in Massachusetts, joined the Worcester Business Development Corporation in developing Gateway Park, a 12-acre mixed-use development for life sciences and biotech companies and the people who work for them. The project includes five buildings with 500,000 square feet of flexible lab space, plus 241,000 square feet of market-rate loft condominiums, restaurants, and business services, and a plan for graduate student housing on one of the sites.

While many universities support incubators for newly established technical and scientific ventures, some also provide space for large, more mature companies on their campuses. For example, Express Scripts, Inc., a major pharmacy benefits management company with almost $18 billion in annual sales, located its headquarters at University Place/NorthPark, on the campus of the University of Missouri–St. Louis (UMSL). The company's criteria for selecting the UMSL site included the ability to expand and the opportunity to collaborate with a university in developing information technology projects (Herrick 2007).

GENERATING EMPLOYMENT AND SPENDING

Colleges and universities often rank among the largest employers in metropolitan areas. In 1997, these institutions employed more than 2.8 million workers, or more than 2 percent of the total U.S. workforce. Approximately two-thirds are administrative and support staff, and the remaining third are faculty (ICIC and

CEOs for Cities 2002). In some local labor markets, such as Cincinnati, academic institutions surpassed other corporations as the leading employer.

A 1999 survey of the top employers in the nation's 20 largest cities found that educational and medical institutions accounted for more than 50 percent of the jobs generated in four of those cities (Washington, DC, Philadelphia, San Diego, and Baltimore). Moreover, these institutions were also the top employers in every one of the 20 cities, despite differences in the age of the city, its geographic region, population, and other socioeconomic characteristics (Harkavy and Zuckerman 1999).

Universities also generate desirable local economic impacts because they purchase large amounts of goods and services in the local marketplace, and because most of their expenditures are distributed as salaries, which tend to be spent locally. They also generate large amounts of student spending. According to the ICIC (2002, 7), urban university spending on salaries, goods, and services was more than nine times the amount that the federal government spent on urban job creation and business development in 1996.

Although estimating the full multiplier effects of university spending is complex, numerous studies have demonstrated the significance of this economic activity (College and University Impact Portal 2009). These effects, of course, vary by type of university (public or private), form of organization (single campus versus statewide system), and location (metropolitan area versus small town). For example, a recent study by the University of California at San Diego showed that its impact in the city included approximately $2.275 billion in direct and indirect spending, 20,790 direct and indirect jobs, and $1.228 billion in direct and indirect personal income (UC San Diego 2008).

Community Development

Institutions of higher education have established more formal partnerships with their communities in recent years, often providing technical assistance such as neighborhood planning or capacity-building for community-based organizations. For example, Pratt Institute's Center for Community and Environmental Design has developed long-term relationships with a variety of mature CBOs in New York City, facilitated a collaborative planning process with several community partners, and helped to develop joint agendas driven by local stakeholders (Vidal et al. 2002).

The Center for Community Partnerships at the University of Pennsylvania has engaged in efforts to integrate academic work with the needs of the community in West Philadelphia (Strom 2005). Academically based community service (ABCS) is just one of these activities, which is rooted in problem-oriented research and teaching. The university offers approximately 160 ABCS courses in a wide range of disciplines and schools and in a variety of areas such as the environment, health, education, and the arts.

Other university initiatives intended to support community development include skills training (generally in classes for residents), professional services (such as visiting nurses or legal clinics), information technology (such as shared databases or training for CBO staff), and technical assistance to small businesses. These activities have attracted funding from a variety of sources including the Office of University Partnerships at the U.S. Department of Housing and Urban Development (HUD).

Launched in 1994, the Community Outreach Partnerships Centers (COPC) program is HUD's primary vehicle for helping colleges and universities apply their human, intellectual, and institutional resources to the revitalization of distressed communities. In its first decade of operation, the program granted about $45 million to more than 100 colleges and universities for such efforts as job training and counseling to reduce unemployment; resident-backed strategies to spur economic growth and reduce crime; local initiatives to combat housing discrimination and homelessness; mentoring programs for neighborhood youth; and financial and technical assistance for new businesses.

REFERENCES

Adams, Carolyn. 2003. The meds and eds in urban economic development. *Journal of Urban Affairs* 25 (5):571–588.

Bramwell, Allison, and David A. Wolfe. 2008. Universities and regional economic development: The entrepreneurial University of Waterloo. *Research Policy* 37:1175–1187.

Clark, Terry N., ed. 2003. Urban amenities: Lakes, opera, and juice bars — do they drive development? In *The city as an entertainment machine.* New York, NY: JAI Press/Elsevier.

College and University Impact Portal. 2009. Economic impact report listing. *http://www.edu-impact.com/view/reports.*

Florida, Richard. 2005. *The flight of the creative class: The new global competition for talent.* London: HarperCollins.

Glaeser, Edward. 2000. The new economies of urban and regional growth. In *The Oxford Handbook of Economic Geography*, eds. G. L. Clark, M. S. Gertler, and M. P. Feldman. Oxford: Oxford University Press.

Harkavy, Ira, and Harmon Zuckerman. 1999. *Eds and meds: Cities' hidden assets.* Washington, DC: The Brookings Institution.

Herrick, Thaddeus. 2007. Campuses, companies cozy up. *The Wall Street Journal*, July 11.

ICIC (Initiative for a Competitive Inner City) and CEOs for Cities. 2002. *Leveraging colleges and universities for urban economic revitalization: An action agenda.* Chicago, IL: CEOs for Cities.

Strom, Elizabeth. 2005. The political strategies behind university-based development. In Perry and Wiewel 2005, 116–130.

University of California San Diego. 2008. A study of the economic impact and benefits of UC San Diego. *http://ucsdnews.ucsd.edu/EconomicImpact/pdf/.*

Varga, A. 2000. Local academic knowledge transfers and the concentration of economic activity. *Journal of Regional Science* 40 (2):289–309.

Vidal, Avis, Nancy Nye, Christopher Walker, Carlos Manjarrez, Clare Romanik. 2002. Lessons from the community outreach partnership center program. Prepared for the U.S. Department of Housing and Urban Development Office of Policy Development and Research.

CHAPTER 2

Social Responsibilities

Mary Filardo, Jeffrey M. Vincent, Marni Allen *and* Jason Franklin

A New Social Contract

In addition to the primary responsibility of school districts to provide high quality teaching and learning, schools are increasingly being called on to help create and sustain active, healthy communities and vibrant neighborhoods. These new demands suggest a need to examine the relationship between public schools and their community and the need for new policies to guide the school-community relationship. With new policies and practices, public school facilities can become more vibrant public spaces where public education is the primary — but not only — user.

Across the country, school districts are increasing the utilization of their buildings and grounds by extending access to non-school users, particularly during non-school hours. Consequently, both public and private parties are increasingly exploring the possibility of joint development of school buildings and grounds.

However, entities seeking to use school buildings and grounds or partner in their development often find that school districts are difficult partners. Too often, school districts are not governed, managed, or funded to navigate the complexities and opportunities inherent in school joint use and joint development. To help facilitate joint use arrangements, school districts

need a greater understanding of the benefits to an expanded use of our public schools. School districts and the non-school parties interested in access to school buildings and grounds need a common language to address the barriers to and benefits of joint use. To facilitate this, we provide a conceptual framework for the joint use and joint development of PK-12th grade public school buildings and grounds. From the conceptual framework, more robust policy, planning, and management infrastructures can be established.

Specifically, in this chapter we:

- Define a **typology** for joint use and joint development and provide definitions;
- Describe the factors that underlie **demand** for joint use and joint development;
- Present the **benefits** possible from joint use and development; and
- Identify the **challenges** to expand access to and development of public school buildings and grounds.

We propose that a fundamental shift is needed in how we view our public school buildings and grounds; a new social contract for the use of our public school infrastructure.

Originally published as *Joint Use of Public Schools: A Framework for a New Social Contract*, March 2010, by the 21st Century School Fund, Washington, DC, and the Center for Cities & Schools, University of California, Berkeley. Reprinted with permission of the publisher.

Defining Joint Use

With regard to their facilities, a school district's first responsibility is to provide an adequate environment for compulsory elementary and secondary education programs and the administrative functions that support them. Districts must also balance the space and schedule needs of school-sponsored extra-curricular and athletic activities with the demands of the normal school day and calendar. These primary uses for public school buildings and grounds will be referred to as "public education use."

The use of school district controlled, owned, or utilized facilities by a non-district entity is joint use. There are five types of entities that constitute the joint users:

- *Individuals:* Persons, generally residents of a community, who have access to exterior spaces, such as play equipment, athletic fields or courts, and open space for personal use.
- *Civic Groups*: Individuals, groups, or organizations, who seek occasional use of school buildings and grounds for activities or events such as polling stations, community meetings, and special events.
- *Other Public Agencies*: A public agency that is not part of the school district that may offer programs, need to lease space and offer no program connection to the school, and/or may seek joint development with ongoing joint programming.
- *Private Non-Profit Organizations*: The use of school buildings and/or grounds by a non-profit organization such as after-school programs, health clinics, or adult education classes.
- *Private For-Profit Corporations*: The use of school building and/or grounds by a private for-profit corporation, either for education-related work like a private testing service or unrelated work like private offices.

Spaces inside a school dedicated for joint use could either be spaces used part-time by the school and part-time by other users or be dedicated exclusively for use by an outside entity. Joint use is "shared" when the space is used by the school during school hours, a classroom, for example used in an after school program, or "dedicated" when a school space is exclusively available to the outside entity, for example, an after-school office or storage area.

REASONS FOR JOINT USE

Non-school district entities seek joint use of public schools for a myriad of reasons. As public entities, most school districts currently have obligations, in law or in practice, to allow some levels of general public use of grounds for recreation and to support civic uses of public schools, such as voting, community meetings, and special events. The occasional joint use of school buildings and grounds by individuals, groups, or organizations, for individual or community activities or events will be referred to as "civic use."

Public and private entities seek joint use in schools because of the need for the specialized spaces found in school buildings and grounds, as well as the desire of program providers for convenient access to the child, youth, and family populations they serve. School facility use may explicitly connect to the school mission, such as when other agencies or nonprofits offer social services specifically for the families of the schools' students which enable families to provide better home environments to support their children. The joint users providing school-support have intended to advance student achievement, primarily by addressing social, emotional, economic, and health barriers to school success for children. This is joint use for youth development. In joint use for community wellbeing, while the families of students may be welcome, the joint user has the overall community or neighborhood as its focus; for example, a primary care health clinic located in a school. Joint use with a public charter school would be a community-related joint use even if it has an educational mission because, by definition, it is not linked to the school in which it may be co-located, and because it would be open to students from the entire community.

Finally, there is joint use, either shared or dedicated where the user seeks no relationship with the school or its families but desires access to the location and space in the school. This is real estate joint use. For example, some churches regularly use school auditoria for services and government agencies sometimes locate offices in under-utilized schools.

Related to each of these types of joint use is an interest in joint development. Joint development of new or existing public school facilities enables the site, building plan and design to better support the joint use of the building and land. Successful joint development requires the public education, civic, school, community and real estate users to collaboratively articulate a vision, develop a plan for design, agree on a schedule, and agree on how building and site costs will be paid for and maintained. Ongoing joint use agreements are necessarily a part of joint development agreements. Other public agencies, as well as private developers, may be interested in joint development — particularly of school property in desirable locations given their size, scale, amenities and/or proximity. Public agencies may be interested in locating affordable housing, recreation centers, libraries or elder service centers on school sites. Private developers may be seeking to take advantage of existing public infrastructure to address pent-up demand for housing, commercial, or retail space not already available. Similar to joint use, joint development may be school, community, or real estate driven.

Few states or school districts have adequate policies, guidelines, budgets, plans, expertise, or governance systems to take full advantage of the complex landscape of joint use and joint development possibilities. Current policies and guidelines often leave school district staff unprepared to navigate the competing pressures or requirements for extensive joint use of their facilities, or to evaluate and engage in joint development. In the absence of adequate policy infrastructure, getting access to public school buildings or grounds for non-school use can be difficult or even impossible — especially for non-district organized programs and services. Not harnessing joint use and development strategies to achieve mutually-beneficial development or programming is a missed opportunity for schools and communities.

Factors Driving Demand

Demographic patterns, housing, community character and wealth, and school district capital infrastructure combine to drive the demand for joint use and joint development of public school buildings and grounds.

DEMOGRAPHIC PATTERNS

Demographic patterns affect the enrollment in schools and thereby the needs that the school district has to meet. Our country's public schools are one of the most utilized public assets in our communities. On most weekdays, there are nearly 55 million students and staff in public schools; about one-sixth of the total U.S. population. Nearly 90 percent of all school-age children are enrolled in public schools. This concentration of school children and facilities in communities throughout the country creates an opportunity to expand both the reach of direct service provision and the utilization of centralized recreational and educational spaces to a larger group of users.

Not just the number of students a school district serves, but the economic condition of their families and the neighborhoods they come from affect the demand for joint use and the ability of school districts to respond to these demands.

First, fewer families today have children, and those that do tend to not have as many as in the past. In 1960, 47 percent of all households had children under 18 years old. By contrast, in 2008, only 31 percent of all households had children.[1]

These trends relate to school facilities by lessening school space demands during school hours and potentially weakening public support for educational issues. Fewer school-age children in communities result in steady or declining enrollments, thereby reducing demand for school space by students. Consequently, in communities with fewer school-age children there is often space within schools that is under-utilized and so could be available for joint use. However, when fewer families in a community have children, voters may be less likely to support taxes to fund education, particularly costly expenses such as capital programs.

Second, because of the country's overall population growth, U.S. public school enrollment has increased in recent years and continues to do so, even though the share of households with children has declined since the 1960s and the number of children in each household is down. In the decade between 1995 and 2004, public school enrollment increased more than it did between the 30 years previous from 1965 to 1995. Public school enrollment is projected to increase by 2 million students by 2015 (from 2009 projected enrollment).[2] Where enrollments are rising, crowding is often a problem. In crowded schools, the building and grounds are so intensely used by the school and students that it is difficult for non-school users to get access to the fully utilized space, even after school hours, as extracurricular and athletic activities fill up the school after hours and on weekends. Additionally, joint development is difficult, if not impossible, because school sizes tend to be large to support high enrollments and so added use on the site cannot be accommodated.

Finally, demographic changes have led to entrenched patterns of poverty concentration in some schools, but not others.[3] Schools differ greatly in the types of students they serve, creating different demands and challenges to ensuring educational quality. The effects of the last half-century of metropolitan expansion and demographic change have increased racial and economic segregation, with poverty often concentrated in older neighborhoods and their schools.[4] In many urban centers, the proportion of school-age children is low and the children in the public schools are from low-income families living in distressed neighborhoods.[5] Schools in low-income communities are under enormous pressure to not only educate children but also to battle conditions of poverty such as the lack of health care, poor nutrition, and little homework or other educational support or enrichment from families.[6]

To assist their students, some schools provide services to address these challenges, often partnering with community-based organizations and other public agencies to run programs inside schools. These "out-of-school interventions" can be seen in "Full-Service Schools," the "Community School" model, and the Bea-

con Initiative, altering the space use demands inside schools.[7] In schools serving children from low-income families, the demand by non-profit service providers is high, in part driven by foundation funding to provide academic supports. For example, San Francisco Unified School District, which has approximately 70 percent of its more than 55,000 students eligible for free or reduced priced lunch, has more than 400 non-profit organizations operating programs in one or more of the city's 134 public schools.

HOUSING AND COMMUNITY DEVELOPMENT

The density of housing and the character of the neighborhood and community affect the need and demand for joint use. Nationally, in the 2007–2008 school year, elementary and secondary public school students were enrolled in about 97,196 public schools in 17,899 school districts, including 4,561 public charter schools.[8] Public schools, particularly those built before the 1970s, tend to be located in residential neighborhoods, close to the children, youth and families they serve.

Schools located in the center of dense neighborhoods with suitable housing for families will likely face the most demands for joint use, both school-support and community-related joint use. However, even where schools are more distant from population centers, they will be in demand for joint use, primarily school-support joint use as they provide a desirable concentration of children to serve for afterschool and other enrichment programs.

With significant amounts of the high density public housing that dominated cities for the past half-century being abandoned, demolished, or redeveloped under the banner of urban redevelopment, public schools in many urban areas that were once extremely overcrowded have experienced significant enrollment declines.[9] For example, a public elementary school in Washington, DC that packed in nearly 1,000 students in 1968, currently enrolls a comfortable 350 students. In the past decade, many deteriorated housing units were torn down and not rebuilt, or redevelopment programs such as federally-supported HOPE VI and other local initiatives led to the construction of mixed-income housing that was less affordable or appealing to families. These changes in housing composition have directly impacted local public school enrollment shifts. A 2006 study by the Urban Institute looking at housing patterns and public school enrollment in Washington, DC, found that housing density and type of housing has a major effect on composition of the household. Existing single-family homes in the District of Columbia had 46 public school children per hundred homes; multi-unit rental housing had 27 children per 100 units; and condos had 7 children per 100 units. Housing and neighborhood redevelopment decisions on affordability and type of housing will affect school enrollments.

In urban and suburban communities where households once included more families with children and more children in each family, the utilization of schools necessarily declines. This has been offset somewhat by the expansion of early childhood education.

Half-day kindergarten, while still a fixture in some communities, is essentially gone in most urban school districts, replaced not only by full-day kindergarten, but also all-day pre-kindergarten and even the expansion of public pre-school for three-year-olds. This has been possible, in part, because of the presence of unused space in school buildings where the number of school age children has declined. These underutilized school spaces also serve as potential sites for the expansion of school-support joint use, as well as community-related joint use, especially for the location of services such as adult education, job training, or sports leagues that can enhance opportunities and outcomes for under-privileged communities.

On the flip side, in new growth communities, developers are typically required to set aside land for public schools and other public infrastructure. The location of the school within the development will have a significant effect on how much demand there will be for joint use. The National Association of Realtors has been a proponent of joint development and joint use as a way to limit the acreage requirement for how much land must be provided by the developer for public schools or other public

amenities. Minimizing acreage for new schools enables developers to generate more income from the private development

Low-density development, particularly with the declining number of children per household, means students typically must be bused to school to fully enroll a school to capacity. Once bussing has been incorporated into its operations, longer bus rides for students are of marginal concern to school districts. To support schools with larger enrollments, which generate some economies of scale in staffing and operations, districts will extend travel time for students.

These longer travel times have negative educational and health outcomes for students, with the increased transit time to and from school reducing the time available to students for academic and recreational activities. When students and families live far from school, long travel distances make it less likely that the school will serve as an appealing site for joint use activities, as it is not conveniently located as a school located in a densely-populated community.

SCHOOL DISTRICT CAPITAL INVESTMENTS

There are more public school buildings than any other public facility in the United States; the buildings contain an estimated 6.6 billion square feet of space on more than 1 million acres of land.[10] Schools have highly desirable spaces for joint use, such as meeting rooms, auditoria, gymnasia, swimming pools, playgrounds, and sports fields, and in the decade between 1994 and 2005 about $500 billion was spent by school districts on new school construction and building improvements.[11] About half of this was spent on new construction and additions, but the other $250 billion was spent on improvements to existing facilities.

The condition and design of public school buildings and grounds affect the demand for their use by individuals, civic, other agency, non-profit and for profit users.

Various sources have documented the widespread prevalence of poor quality public school facilities.[12] When a school has no air conditioning, poor ventilation and temperature control, or limited natural light, the demand for this space is minimal. School-support users may seek it, because the students they are serving are in these spaces during the day, but demand by civic, community or real estate users is minimal. However, as public school districts and their communities have improved the conditions of their schools, the buildings and grounds have become more desirable.

With recent capital investment, new schools have been built with modern amenities to meet current codes, such as the Americans with Disabilities Act, air quality, and security standards. The capital spending was also used to make improvements to existing schools. Bond referenda are often promoted based on the possibility that there will be civic and community joint use opportunities with the new or improved facility. The prospect of community use helps secure support for the tax increases required to repay the school construction bonds. Thus, in more and more communities, there is an expectation that these newly improved spaces will be available for community use.

Taken together, these complex and intertwined demographic, housing, and financial conditions pose enormous challenges for public school districts, but they must be addressed for schools to meet their basic responsibilities. Extensive state and local laws exist related to enrollment, school utilization, site selection, and school planning, design and construction. However, the existing state and local laws generally address public education use only. There are few state or local policy roadmaps for other types of joint use or development. The result is that joint use and joint development are being applied on an ad-hoc basis, with strategies differing from district to district, from school to school and from time to time. However, the demands to increase programs, services, and amenities within our schools through joint use strategies will only grow, and the need for fiscal efficiencies in asset and land management will also persist.

Benefits of Joint Use

Demographic shifts, changing housing patterns, and new school capital investments present an unprecedented opportunity to reshape the ways local government and schools work together to provide for the people who depend on them and the resources they manage. This is especially important for low-income, low-resource urban communities who disproportionately struggle to meet community needs.

The macro changes described above create a variety of needs in different local communities. Recently, policy leaders, educators, and advocates have increasingly turned to the joint use of public schools to assist in remedying numerous local concerns. Coming from a variety of perspectives, each brings a unique rationale for joint use of school facilities. Interest in joint development or joint use is from the public, private for-profit and non-profit sectors.

BETTER SCHOOLS

Joint use strategies can directly enhance a school's curriculum-related activities. For example, schools and local partners have developed museums and libraries connected to schools that students use in their coursework. The joint use partnership brings a resource to the school that would otherwise be unavailable. Joint use strategies can also bring in partners involved in the trades to run hands-on Career and Technical Education (CTE) programs for students. Joint use of schools should be seen as an opportunity to enhance school quality.

Helping to ensure that all children are ready to learn is another way that joint use can improve educational quality. Evidence shows that children need basic physical, emotional and psychological needs met to succeed in school.[13] Numerous education-driven initiatives work to increase the resources and services available to address the needs of the whole child. Schools typically bring in outside community-based organizations or city or county agencies to provide health, educational enrichment and other services inside schools. Joint use of public school facilities is at the heart of the full-service community school model.

Under community school strategies, public schools serve as community "hubs," bringing together many partners to offer a range of support services and opportunities to children, youth, families and communities. These include medical, social, and other services. While these full-service schools tend to be found in disadvantaged communities that serve predominately low-income students, in many schools throughout the nation there are after-school programs that help families from all income levels.

In school districts with a high proportion of children from low-income families, the increased needs of many school-aged children and youth mean there is growing demand for public spaces for non-school, district-related activities to provide services to a high need population of children and families. As previously mentioned, there are more than 400 outside agency and non-profit entities with some sort of program partnership with San Francisco Unified School District. The vast majority of these organizations and agencies provide their programs on school grounds.

CHILD AND COMMUNITY HEALTH

Childhood and adolescent obesity has risen to alarming rates across the country, more than doubling in the last 20 years from 6.5 percent to 17 percent of children by 2003.[14] While many factors contribute to the increasing childhood obesity rates, declines in physical activity appear to be a large part of the equation. Physical activity is one of the best predictors for chronic disease and obesity, and establishing a regular physically active lifestyle at a young age is a preventative strategy for combating the onset of illness, disease, and especially obesity.[15] Increasing rates of sedentary leisure activities and vehicle use does not encourage physically active lifestyles, especially for children.[16] Additionally, many neighborhoods lack pedestrian infrastructure and/or do not have public open spaces such as parks or social common areas that incorporate physical activity into everyday life. In other cases, existing outdoor spaces may be deemed or perceived as unsafe or unfit for use. Also, many parents do not permit unsupervised play in crime-ridden communities and are often unable to provide this supervision themselves. As a result, children not attending afterschool programs stay inside watching TV and playing video games.

Research has documented the importance of the school as a primary factor in obesity prevention, arguing that obesity, poor nutrition, and physical inactivity directly increase risk for poor academic achievement but also that "schools are unique in their ability to promote physical activity and increase energy expenditure."[17]

While many communities lack spaces for physical activity, there is a growing interest in joint use of public school buildings and grounds to fill this void. Spaces such as fields, gyms, or playgrounds, represent "modifiable factors in the physical environment;" opening them can directly increase access to recreation space, especially outdoor green spaces, translating into increased opportunities to participate in physical activities. In searching for ways to increase healthy physical and social habits of both children and adults, public health advocates have identified these public infrastructure assets — public school buildings and grounds — as places that can and should play an important role in increasing physical activity not only among children and adolescents but also contributing to healthier communities.[18] In some communities neighborhood schools may be one of few places where children can be involved in active play.

"COMPLETE" COMMUNITIES

There is also new demand for underutilized or closed school buildings and grounds, particularly in urban areas that have lost families, but increased population by attracting singles into more dense, city households. This demand — from both the private and non-profit sectors — for access to school buildings and grounds for development of private housing, commercial or retail development, or where there are substantial numbers of charter schools, for non-district school use has increased in land-limited cities like Washington, DC, Pittsburgh, San Francisco, and Seattle.

Smart growth advocates are fostering a new conversation around the idea of creating "complete communities." Complete communities provide a variety of homes, jobs, shops, services and amenities close to rail stations, ferry terminals, or bus stops.[19] People then have the option to walk, bicycle, or take transit rather than drive a car to run errands, visit friends, exercise, or get to work. Among the benefits are that complete communities:

- Provide choices: a range of housing options available for people with different needs;
- Encourage accessibility: people can walk, bike, or take transit for short trips and for commuting;
- Offer connections: people are linked to jobs, health care, parks, services, and stores;
- Promote health: encourage physical activity and enhance the quality of life for individuals, families, communities, and the environment;
- Improve social and economic equity: meeting the needs of current and future residents; and
- Improve educational options and experiences through innovations in school planning and design.

The joint use of school facilities becomes one of many strategies in creating complete communities. Because schools (especially elementary schools) are frequently located within residential neighborhoods, sharing their facilities means more activities at single locations, with more people having easy access, thereby reducing the need to drive from place to place for different activities. Jointly using schools promotes reduced transportation demand and increased physical activity for children, families, and communities.[20]

ENVIRONMENTAL BENEFITS

The prevalence of schools and the number of students, teachers, and staff traveling to and from them everyday (about one-sixth of the country's population), as well as their often community-central locations, means that they should be integrated into strategies aimed at reducing carbon emissions and conserving land.[21] In urban areas for example, schools contribute to much-needed green space and can amplify efforts to support healthy environments if planned and designed to do so. Using school grounds as public parks and recreation areas can help preserve other natural habitats. Joint planning and design with conservation as a pri-

ority can show the value of reuse and adaptation of schools within existing communities. Maintaining underutilized schools in central locations and bringing in non-school users can preserve centrally-located community assets, reduce driving distances to other activities, and concentrate the use of energy for utilities in a single site that is fully utilized.

FISCAL EFFICIENCY

Government is always challenged to do more with limited public resources. Responsible public agencies look for innovative ways to efficiently use the resources they do have. Local governments and school districts serve the same families and communities; using the public school as the location for community health centers, swimming pools, libraries, or other public amenities or services, can thereby reduce overall public land assets, capital funds, and total operating costs required. However, this increased use may appear to burden school districts, which are under constant budget pressure for school operations and for facility improvements. More often than not, they defer maintenance and repairs and life-cycle system replacements until they are emergencies and so are reluctant to intensify use of public school buildings and grounds, unless explicitly required to do so. However, as more service and program providers seek to locate in or secure dedicated access to school facilities for their programs, school districts have the opportunity to raise revenue from these users to offset costs for utilities, security, maintenance and repair, and even capital and administrative costs associated with facilities. When school buildings are under-utilized, a paying joint use arrangement, with either a public or private partner, can make continued operation of the school building fiscally possible where it might not otherwise have been so.

Overcoming Challenges

The wide array of benefits associated with joint use, coupled with the demographic and housing changes described above, lead to the idea of increasing and expanding the use of our public school infrastructure for a wider variety of users to meet a broad range of community and educational needs. However, there are significant challenges to its widespread implementation. These include:

- Under funding for utilities, maintenance, repair, custodial and security costs that increase with higher facility utilization;
- Lack of staff support to local schools to manage the requirements of collaboration, space sharing, and communication between multiple users;
- Spaces poorly designed to accommodate different users;
- Poor risk management support for student safety and building security; and
- Inadequate decision-making processes for allocating access to buildings and grounds.

These challenges are significant, but there are many cases where school districts and communities overcome these obstacles and jointly utilize their facilities. However, for the full benefits of joint use to be realized, communities need to develop a new social contract with public school districts on the use of public school infrastructure. Central to this idea is that school districts need not have exclusive rights to public school buildings and grounds, and that joint use and joint development should be common practice in communities.

On the school district side of the contract, this means explicit buy-in by school districts to maximize joint use and to enable joint development where appropriate and then to define criteria, decision-making processes, and cost for the allocation of joint use and development opportunities. On the community side of the contract, it means understanding and paying for the real operating and capital cost of using public school buildings and grounds. However, if this change in vision and practice is to occur, then the governance, policy, budgeting, management, planning, and design of our public school facilities will need to change to support this shift in public school facility use. Without this, we will face a "tragedy of the commons" with our public schools, where the burden of so many community use demands will degrade the asset such that its value is seriously reduced to all.

To secure the potential shared benefits of joint use and joint development, a policy and operational framework is needed. Our public school facilities and grounds should be governed, planned, designed, managed, and funded to support their intensive use and joint development where appropriate. Until these explicit governmental systems and support are in place, school districts will likely remain limited and/or hesitant partners in joint use and joint development.

It will take a system of supports and regulation for the health, community development, education, and other community benefits to be maximized. However, once the new social contract and its policy and practice underpinnings are in place, the potential of joint use and joint development to improve the lives of children, youth, families and residents — particularly in low wealth communities — will be unleashed.

NOTES

1. U.S. Census Bureau, Current Population Survey, March and Annual Social and Economic Supplements, 2008 and earlier.

2. U.S. Deptartment of Education, National Center for Education Statistics (2009). Digest of Education Statistics, 2008 (NCES 2009-020), Table 3.

3. Orfield, Gary, and Chungmei Lee. 2005. Why Segregation Matters: Poverty and Educational Inequality. Cambridge, MA: The Civil Rights Project, Harvard University.

4. Orfield, Myron. 2002. *American Metropolitics: The New Suburban Reality*. Washington, DC: Brookings Institution Press; McKoy, Deborah L., and Jeffrey M. Vincent. 2008. Housing and Education: The Inextricable Link. In *Segregation: The Rising Costs for America*, edited by James H. Carr and Nandinee K. Kutty. New York: Routledge; Briggs, Xavier De Sousa. 2005. *The Geography of Opportunity: Race and Housing Choice in Metropolitan America*. Washington, DC: Brookings Institute Press.

5. U.S. Department of Education, National Center for Education Statistics, Common Core of Data (CCD), "Public Elementary/ Secondary School Locale Code File," 2003–04, and "Public Elementary/Secondary School Universe Survey," 2003–04.

6. Rothstein, Richard. 2004. *Class and Schools: Using Social, Economic, and Educational Reform to Close the Black-White Achievement Gap*. Washington, DC: Economic Policy Institute.

7. Dryfoos, Joy, Jane Quinn, and Carol Barkin. 2005. *Community Schools in Action: Lessons from a Decade of Practice*. Oxford: Oxford University Press; Blank, Martin J. Atelia Melville, and Bela P. Shah. 2003. Making the Difference: Research and Practice in Community Schools. Washington, DC: Coalition for Community Schools; LaFleur, Jennifer, Christina A. Russell, Troy A. Scott, and Elizabeth R. Reisner,

2009. Evaluation of the Beacon Community Centers Middle School Initiative: Report on the First Year. New York: Policy Studies Associates, Inc.

8. U.S. Department of Education, National Center for Education Statistics, Common Core of Data (CCD), " Public Elementary/Secondary School Universe Survey," 2007–08.

9. McKoy, Deborah L., and Jeffrey M. Vincent. 2008. Housing and Education: The Inextricable Link. In *Segregation: The Rising Costs for America*, edited by James H. Carr and Nandinee K. Kutty. New York: Routledge.

10. Filardo, Mary. 2008. Good Buildings, Better Schools: An economic stimulus opportunity with long-term benefits. Washington, DC: Economic Policy Institute.

11. Filardo, Mary, Jeffrey M. Vincent, Ping Sung, and Travis Stein. 2006. Growth and Disparity: A Decade of U.S. Public School Construction. Washington, DC: Building Educational Success Together.

12. For a summary, see: Filardo, Mary. 2008. Good Buildings, Better Schools: An economic stimulus opportunity with long-term benefits. Washington, DC: Economic Policy Institute.

13. Rothstein, Richard. 2004. *Class and Schools: Using Social, Economic, and Educational Reform to Close the Black-White Achievement Gap*. Washington, DC: Economic Policy Institute.

14. Ogden Cynthia L., Margaret D. Carroll, Katherine M. Flegal. 2008. High Body Mass Index for Age Among U.S. Children and Adolescents, 2003–2006. Journal of the American Medical Association. 299(20): 2401–2405.

15. Muller, Manfred J. Physical activity and diet in 5 to 7 years old children. *Public Health Nutrition*. 999(2): 443–444.

16. French, Simon A., Mary Story, Robert W. Jeffery. 2001. Environmental influences on eating and physical activity. *Annual Review of Public Health*. 22: 309–335.

17. Story Mary, Karen M. Kaphingst, Simon A. French. 2006. The Role of Schools in Obesity Prevention. *Future of Children*. 16(1): 109–142.

18. Ashe Marice, Lisa M. Feldstein, Samatha Graff, Randolph Kline, Deborah Pinkas, Leslie Zellers. 2007. Local Venues for Change: Legal Strategies for Healthy Environments. Journal of Law, Medicine, & Ethics. (Spring Symposium): 138–147.

19. Association of Bay Area Governments. 2009. www.bayareavision.org/initiatives/PDFs/FOCUS_Brochure_12-08.pdf.

20. Cooper, Tamar, and Jeffrey M. Vincent. 2008. Joint Use Partnerships in California: Strategies to Enhance Schools and Communities. Berkeley, CA: Center for Cities & Schools.

21. Ewing, Reid and William Greene. 2003. Travel and Environmental Implications of School Siting. Washington, DC: U.S. Environmental Protection Agency.

CHAPTER 3

Opportunities and Risks

Paree Roper

A safe and well-run aquatic facility can be a source of pride as well as a revenue generator for a community. As the visible face of local government, a manager deals with the high expectations for service that citizens demand and works hard to enhance the quality of life for citizens who are served. Risk management is a discipline that affects every single department within an entity — whether it is safety, insurance coverage, workers' compensation, or special events.

Risk management, however, is about more than just safety and insurance. Managers can use it as a tool for setting goals and responding to the various wants and needs of a community. This article examines some of the safety and liability issues to consider when building, renovating, or maintaining swimming pools and other aquatic facilities.

Safety, Liability, and Insurance Issues

Risk management: a strategy developed to reduce or control the chance of harm or loss; the process of identifying, evaluating, selecting, and implementing actions to eliminate or reduce harm. — Definition from the Public Risk Management Association (PRIMA) glossary.

Swimming is one of the most popular sports in America. Such athletes as Michael Phelps have raised the profile of aquatics even higher with record-breaking Olympic wins and greater attention paid to issues like swimsuit aerodynamics. Facilities have also undergone tremendous changes — gone are the days when a community could dig a hole, put in a pool, and call it a job well done.

In today's world, constituents want variety. Age-appropriate components and equipment that accommodates people with various levels of ability must be considered when designing, building, or renovating a pool or aquatic facility. In any given community, one may find shallow water and beach areas for youngsters, therapy pools for seniors, competition swimming for the future Olympians, and such features as water slides and special areas for inner tubes and floating. Entities can also include pavilions for social events and attractive aesthetics as drawing cards for customers.

With all these potential needs and demands to consider, the key is to think of risk management in terms of a *strategy*. By using a strategy of consciously understanding inherent risks of an issue, more data become available and better choices can be made. This is by no means asking managers to become risk managers per se — unless it is part of their job description — but it does imply that a manager should learn to think like a risk manager and add this element to a professional skill set.

Many managers confront this typical scenario: A city's pool is crumbling and needs up-

Originally published as "Risk and Opportunity at Public Schools," *Public Management*, Vol. 91, No. 11, December 2009, by the International City/County Management Association, Washington, DC. Reprinted with permission of the publisher.

grading, so a renovation project is announced. Input from the community indicates that some citizens want diving platforms. Other citizens would like to see wading pools for young children. Some want the facility to have features similar to the water park in a neighboring city.

As the renovation project moves along, the finance staff makes everyone aware of what the city can afford. Other staff members review the contracts and bids. Still others are involved with the construction. It is decided that diving platforms, a waterslide, and a wading beach will be a part of the newly renovated facility.

The plans are ready to be drawn, but— hold on a second!— is there anything that could pose a potential problem for the local government in the future, even with all the good planning that was put into this process? This is where risk management comes in: by providing an additional level of discernment. Here are some potential issues:

COMPLIANCE WITH LAWS AND CODES

Over the years, requirements for such items as pool depths, diving boards, and safety equipment have changed dramatically. Most architects and contractors are aware of these changes, but it never hurts to ask questions about pool specifications. The Association of Pool and Spa Professionals has a standard (*ANSI/NSPI-1 2003 Standard for Public Swimming Pools*) that is viewed as a benchmark, but it is not the only one.

Several organizations, including the Fédération Internationale de Natation Amateur (FINA), USA Swim Team, and the American Public Health Association have operating and design standards for pools and aquatic facilities. These standards are voluntary, but if a community is compliant with the provisions of these groups, it carries a great deal of weight when defending against claims and lawsuits.

Although most of these standards are voluntary, federal, state, and local laws and codes are not. Lawsuits are a known occupational hazard for city and county managers, and noncompliance can put an entity in the position of defending against accusations of negligence.

One important example of federal legis-

lation related to pool safety that passed recently is the Virginia Graeme Baker Pool and Spa Safety Act. The law is named for the granddaughter of former secretary of state James A. Baker III, who died in a spa after the suction of a drain trapped her under water. Under the law, all public pools and spas must have proper drain covers (compliant with the ASME/ANSI A112.19.8-2007 standard) installed and a second anti-entrapment system installed where a single main drain exists.

Public pools and spas that operate year round were to comply by December 19, 2008, and seasonal public pools and spas that are currently closed must be in compliance with the law on the day they reopen. As is the case with many laws and regulations, state-specific codes may call for more stringent safety requirements. A comprehensive resource that contains information on all 50 states is provided by the National Swimming Pool Foundation at www.nspf.com/Codes_Links.html#USState.

In addition to compliance with safety laws and regulations are concerns about accessibility. The Americans with Disabilities Act (ADA) requires newly constructed or renovated government facilities, places of public accommodation, and commercial facilities to be accessible to and usable by individuals with disabilities. Swimming pools, wading pools, and spas are some of the facilities that fall under ADA, and the ADA Accessibility Guidelines standard applies. Access routes to and from such supporting elements of the facility as toilets and parking and bathing areas are also required.

LOSS CONTROL

The operation of a safe aquatic facility takes many well-trained and conscientious people. Risk managers, safety specialists, and pool personnel have the responsibility of making sure the facility is maintained, inspected, and operated according to the laws and regulations that apply. A manager needs a global view of what is happening. This can be done through an annual report that summarizes how the facility fared during the fiscal year.

In many jurisdictions, these reports focus (and rightfully so) on the revenues and expenses that occurred during the period. To get a more comprehensive look at what happened, ask for a report that includes:

- Data on claims filed.
- Vandalism expenses.
- Training costs for lifeguards and pool personnel.
- Emergency equipment needs and costs.

The report should also include a review of the facility's emergency plan and its components. Proactive risk management plans show the local government's intentions when it comes to reducing potential liability. These plans can also provide effective defenses as well as deterrents to litigation. Components of the plan should include:

- Safety rules and regulations for the facility.
- Emergency procedures.
- Description of supervision and how supervision is maintained.
- Safety inspection records.
- Security.
- Potential problems in areas with high safety risks such as the pool deck, locker rooms, ladders, and parking lots.
- Safety and rescue equipment available.

Safety and loss control are not just the province of the risk manager and the safety spe-

cialist. As the local government manager, your words and actions can have an unmatched impact. You have the power to set a positive tone of safety that reaches all citizens. When promoting new or renovated aquatic facilities, remember to discuss the safety-related aspects of the facility in news interviews, panels, and forums.

In a Nutshell

"Professional local government managers seek continually to improve their capabilities. Renewing themselves through lifelong learning, managers acquire new expertise and develop their leadership skills to build better communities..." — Excerpt from ICMA 2008 Strategic Plan

Risk management is probably not the number one issue that crosses a manager's desk every day, but it does provide a problem-solving tool, especially for aquatics. A good risk management program is not a cost center; it helps save money, time and lives.

In these times when managers are being asked to perform miracles and then some, a solid knowledge of risk management techniques can provide managers with a powerful edge.

CHAPTER 4

Land

Yesim Sungu-Eryilmaz

Colleges and universities are among the largest landowners and developers in urban areas. To fulfill their mission, these institutions often become involved in land development at the campus edge, whether to construct new dormitories and research facilities or to offset neighborhood decline. Their activities usually have an immediate impact on the neighborhood and even on the entire city.

When the use of urban land for university purposes competes with its use for local priorities, conflicts inevitably arise. A variety of stakeholders — ranging from local governments to nearby residents — may mobilize to counter university land development for reasons related to social and economic concerns, quality of life in the neighborhood, the planning and design process, and loss of property tax revenue.

This policy focus report lays out the competing interests affected by university land use and development activities, and highlights some approaches that have and have not worked in solving conflicts between institutions and their communities. These approaches, of course, have the most potential for success when they balance academic and community needs through a participatory and inclusive planning process.

Institutions of higher education have entered a new era of community engagement. While once functioning mainly as enclaves of intellectual pursuit, colleges and universities today play a much broader role in the eco-

nomic, social, and physical development of their host cities and neighborhoods. They have become key institutions, often termed anchor institutions, in their communities through their economic impacts on employment, spending, and workforce development, as well as through their ability to attract new businesses and highly skilled individuals and to revitalize adjacent neighborhoods.

This evolving situation presents new challenges and opportunities for town-gown partnerships. Because most of these institutions have substantial fixed assets and are not likely to relocate, the need for effective collaboration is increasing. At the same time these institutions must achieve their missions in a highly competitive environment and in a period of extreme fiscal pressure.

Colleges and universities must seek to be "fully vested" urban anchor institutions, not only by advancing the goals of academia, but also by coordinating their place-based strategies with the interests of the city and the community. When land use and development conflicts are avoided or resolved amicably, both universities and communities can reap the benefits of the resources that each has to offer.

Institutions of higher education vary greatly, from community colleges, to small private and public liberal arts colleges, to large private and public research universities. The United States has a long history of small liberal

Originally published as "Executive Summary, The City, Land, and the University," *Town-Gown Collaboration in Land Use and Development*, Policy Focus Report, 2009, by the Lincoln Institute of Land Policy, Cambridge, Massachusetts. Reprinted with permission of the publisher.

arts colleges and large land grant universities located in rural settings. Today, however, an average of 82 percent of all degree-granting public and private institutions are located in urban areas, and in 28 of the 50 states, the percentage is greater than the national average.

Moreover, institutions of higher education in most states are more urbanized than their populations. Even in the very rural states throughout the Midwest and South, colleges and universities are more highly urbanized than the overall population. Among the six states where these institutions are less urbanized than the state population, the population shares in five of these states (California, Florida, Hawaii, Maryland, and New Jersey) exceed the U.S. average of 79 percent.

Until fairly recently, most urban colleges and universities remained enclaves of intellectual pursuit that seldom collaborated with surrounding neighborhoods and host cities to address common problems. This situation was the result of distinct and exclusive interests, missions, and practices. But over the last 20 years, town-gown relationships have undergone a sea change that reflects a greater university interest in working actively with local governments, businesses, and community-based organizations (CBOs).

New language included in university mission statements provides evidence of this shift, such as "engagement," "partnership," and "reciprocity" (Perry 2008). Portland State University ("for excellence in … community engagement"), Northeastern University ("commitment to … urban engagement"), and the University of Maryland ("engage the University more fully in … collaborative partnership") are just a few of the institutions that explicitly make strong community relations part of their missions.

This new practice comes in response to external pressures, including criticism that universities receive public support but ignore the interests and concerns of their host communities (Mayfield 2001). This shift also reflects internal changes in academia, especially those based on enlightened self-interest (Benson, Puckett, and Harkavy 2007). By their nature,

colleges and universities are dynamic and constantly challenged by changes in political economy, funding, demographics, communities, and educational theory and practice. This dynamism has led institutions to expand their roles in society and to improve their relations with their neighbors and their cities as a whole.

Despite a new period of collaboration among higher education, local government, businesses, and community organizations, town-gown conflicts still exist. The friction is perhaps most apparent in land use and development processes at the edge of campuses. Indeed, competition for the use of urban land between university activities and neighborhood or citywide purposes has led to frequent conflicts over the last 20 years, and may be increasing in some places.

The competing interests of the university, the neighborhood, and the city have three implications. First, even in the era of the engaged university, land use and development processes at the campus edge will repeatedly put town-gown relations to the test. Second, nearly all real estate activities of universities and colleges are multifaceted and have multiple stakeholders, including residents, businesses, and local governments. Third, land uses at the campus edge have become a crucial element in both the physical and socioeconomic character of cities and neighborhoods.

REFERENCES

Benson, Lee, John L. Puckett, and Ira Harkavy, 2007. *Dewey's dream: Universities and democracies in an age of education reform.* Philadelphia, PA: Temple University Press.

Mayfield, Loomis, 2001. Town and gown in America: Some historical and institutional issues of the engaged university. *Education for Health* 14 (2):231–240.

Perry, David C., 2008. Changing the research paradigm: From applied to engaged. Paper presented at University as Civic Partner Conference, February 14–16, 2008, Phoenix, AZ.

EDITOR'S NOTE

For more information about what works, and what doesn't work, in the field of university land use and development practices, maps that show the ratio of university vs. state populations, and a table that shows town-gown conflicts over urban land use over time, refer to the website of the Lincoln Institute of Land Policy, which is listed in Appendix C.

CHAPTER 5

Sustainable Communities

Deborah McKoy

Background

California has been implementing new policy initiatives and making tremendous financial investments in improving educational quality and in making our cities and regions more livable and economically sound. Although schools and community quality are intricately connected, rarely do we connect policies across these sectors to leverage "win-wins" for communities and schools. This forum begins that process by building on recent statewide activities including the passage of Senate Bill 375, the creation of the Strategic Growth Council (SGC) the federal Sustainable Housing and Communities Program, the Senate Select Committee on School Facilities, and the California Department of Education's new vision and guiding principles for school facilities that enhance achievement for all students.

Convened August 31, 2010, the half-day roundtable brought together a diverse set of state, regional, and local policy leaders to discuss promising strategies for connecting schools to the creation of healthy, sustainable communities in California. Structured as a "public research" event, participants discussed issues, pointed out challenges, and identified policy and implementation opportunities. In this report, we summarize the speakers' presentations and provide a set of key state policy recommendations developed from the Roundtable discussion.

Introduction

High quality schools play a critical role in the communities where they are located. As Californians, we care about our schools and spend an enormous amount of public funds on school infrastructure. As a member of the Strategic Growth Council, I think that connecting with educators and making the sound infrastructure decisions that simultaneously support schools and communities is essential. Facilitating this discussion is a promising project for the SGC.[1]

With this cross-sector gathering of policy leaders, professionals and practitioners, we hope to forge a lively discussion on the critical importance of connecting education to our state's smart growth planning and development. The UC Berkeley Center for Cities & Schools is proud to partner with the Strategic Growth Council and the California Department of Education on this roundtable aimed at sharing insights, experiences, and opportunities to learn from each other and forge new understanding and identifying shared goals and future potential for collaboration. The afternoon is organized in two parts. First there will be a panel discussion from key leaders in educational policy and regional planning. Next will be facilitated small group discussions aimed at identifying the priorities and recommendations among participants.[2]

Originally published as "Smart Schools for Sustainable Communities: Aligning Sustainable Communities Planning and Public Education in California," *State Policy Roundtable*, November 2010, by the Center for Cities & Schools, University of California, Berkeley. Reprinted with permission of the publisher.

25

New Federal Partnerships for Sustainable Communities

New federal initiatives are aimed at promoting sustainable communities planning across the country. In particular, the EPA, HUD, and DOT Partnership for Sustainable Communities has developed six Livability Principles: (1) enhance economic competitiveness; (2) coordinate and leverage federal investments; (3) value communities and neighborhoods; (4) support existing communities; (5) promote equitable, affordable housing; and (6) provide more transportation choices. Public schools play an important role in all of these principles.

Most fundamentally, children need safe places to get the best education possible. But EPA also sees other benefits related to schools, including health benefits of walking and biking to school; reduced travel-to-school emissions from automobiles and buses; and reduced transportation costs. School siting in particular plays an important role in realizing these benefits. A question that arises in many communities is: how do we incorporate planning for school facilities into our community plans? Unfortunately, there are barriers to doing so at all levels of government. To help address this, EPA will soon release "Voluntary School Siting Guidelines" in partnership with the U.S. Department of Education as mandated by the Energy Independence Security Act of 2007.[3]

California Policy Panel: High Quality Schools in Healthy, Sustainable Communities

PUBLIC SCHOOLS ARE PUBLIC INFRASTRUCTURE

A nexus of issues drives our conversation today: (a) sustainable communities planning, (b) ensuring healthy children and healthy communities; and (c) ensuring high quality educational environments. Each currently has its own policy momentum in California. There is a common-held belief that high quality schools are cornerstones of sustainable, healthy communities and that high quality educational op-

portunities result in improved community and economic vitality. The key question is how do we enhance community sustainability and structure educational opportunity for all young people? I'd like to suggest that these cannot be mutually exclusive, but are intrinsically linked if we are to improve quality of life for all Californians.

Our public schools are public infrastructure. California has about 1,000 school districts with about 8,200 K–12 schools on an estimated 125,000 acres of land. Our schools are community gathering spaces and most neighborhoods have them. Counting students and staff in our schools, one in six Californians travel to and from a school everyday. Since 1996, more than $35 billion in state school construction and modernization funds have been made available; coupled with local bonds, the total is more than $80 billion. In fact, K–12 infrastructure funds are the largest share of state infrastructure investment; between 1972 and 2006 about 35 percent of $178 billion in statewide infrastructure funds went to schools. To effectively meet the state planning priorities of strengthening the economy, protecting the environment, and promoting health and safety for all, we must coordinate and leverage our infrastructure funds (see Government Code 65041.1), including schools.[4]

PLANNING FOR A SUSTAINABLE BAY AREA: WHAT DO REGIONAL POLICIES MEAN FOR SCHOOLS?

ABAG's regional planning process works to promote sustainability and transit-oriented development. We are especially interested in how our Priority Development Areas (PDAs) relate to schools and school quality. In particular, we have been working closely with the Center for Cities & Schools on: (1) expanding the conversation about sustainable regional growth to include educational stakeholders; (2) assessing the role schools and school districts play in regional land use planning; and (3) fostering links between city and school governance to support infill development. We are pursuing activities that create "complete communities" in our PDAs: housing for residents of all income levels; good access to quality education and jobs; increased walking, bicycling, and transit ridership; decreased auto use; local services and shopping; clean air; and access to open space.

Between 2000 and 2006, overall public school enrollment has decreased in the Bay Area by about 2.6 percent. However, more recently we have seen pre-primary enrollment grow by 8 percent, with the largest increases in San Francisco, San Mateo, and Marin Counties. While conventional wisdom holds that the number of children in the inner bay area will decline, we're not so sure. One of the deciding factors about where these families will live is what their school options are. People in our PDAs are having children, but will they move as the children grow up? If so, this may undermine our regional growth goals.[5]

Ensuring High Quality School Environments: A Policy Overview

I am pleased to discuss the current school facilities policy environment at the state level and how it is designed to ensure high quality schools across the state.

My presentation will:

1. First, provide some perspective about how much school building occurs in California and the role of local districts, often called local educational agencies (LEAs). The more than 1,000 public school districts across the state each make their own facility decisions under widely varying circumstances.

2. Second, I will review key challenges school districts face as they plan for their facilities. I will also describe school infrastructure funding sources and provide an overview of the key state agencies that the districts must navigate to build and renovate schools in California.

3. Third, I will describe the work of my staff at CDE's School Facilities Planning Division and our priorities, especially pointing out how they align with key elements of smart growth.

I wish to state clearly that the CDE is very interested in doing an even better job of encouraging smart growth, while staying true to our mission of ensuring that new schools are safe, appropriate educational environments for all students. Cross-sector discussions like this aid in such an endeavor.[6]

Aligning Infrastructure Investment for Sustainable Communities: Goals, Policies, and Strategies

OPR is defined by statute as the comprehensive state planning agency for California. It is responsible for formulating long-range goals and policies for land use, population growth and distribution, urban expansion, and resource conservation. It is also required to provide technical assistance and advice on land use planning and CEQA to state, regional and local governments. OPR is part of the Strategic Growth Council, which is charged with developing policies and coordinating investment strategies to encourage the development of sustainable communities.

High quality education is of huge importance to the people of California. Because of this, the quality and location of schools has a huge impact on development patterns and community economic development, as well as quality of life for residents. For example, targeted school sitting can revitalize urban areas and encourage urban infill. It can promote active living by allowing children to safely bike and walk to school and reduce greenhouse gas emissions by reducing the number and length of car trips that are required to drive children back and forth to school. Targeted investments in school facilities can also reduce community infrastructure costs.

While there are multiple benefits to coordinating school investments there are also multiple agencies that have a piece of the puzzle for sitting, building and administering schools. This can result in tensions between the state, city and county governments and school districts. We need to find a way to all work together to create incentives to put schools were communities and the state reap the greatest benefits economically, environmentally and create the best future for the children of California.[7]

Challenges, Recommendations and Next Steps

Below is a summary analysis of the main challenges and recommendations generated by this roundtable discussion. In general, there was agreement that high quality schools play important roles in ensuring healthy, sustainable communities, but also that community conditions and land use patterns play important roles to ensuring healthy, sustainable schools. The question at hand was how to change current practices to bring different sectors together to work in more collaborative and mutually beneficial ways.

CHALLENGES

Challenge # 1: Local Regional Agency Silos. *Local/regional governments and school districts in California are autonomous entities that too seldom collaborate on school and community planning, missing many opportunities for "win-wins."*

Local agencies tend to have very different cultures, language, and planning timelines — and frequently have adversarial relationships — all of which greatly hinder collaboration. Due to the historic nature of local schools being largely autonomous, local agency staffs have little capacity to forge successful cross-sector partnerships. One core challenge, particularly from a regional planning perspective, is that school district geographic boundaries rarely match those of other local/regional planning entities. So a school district may overlap with multiple municipalities, or vice versa.

Challenge # 2: State Policy Gaps and Obstacles. *California state policy provides very few requirements and/or incentives for local governments and school districts to work together.*

Changes in state policy over time have eroded what structures did exist for local planning collaboration. In particular, 1998's Senate Bill 50, which established a new state school facility funding program, reversed the prior *Mira/Hart/Murietta* Appellate Court decisions, significantly decreasing local agency cooperative planning requirements. Today, regional planning agencies and cities have few requirements to plan with or for school districts, and school districts do not need to obtain city or county approval of new school sites and can override local zoning ordinances. Prior to SB 50, coordination was arguably more common, especially in working together to ensure adequate public school facilities along with development. Additionally, state oversight of school infrastructure approvals and funding is spread over multiple state agencies, creating various logistical challenges.

Challenge # 3: Current funding structure deters school modernization. *State and local school infrastructure funding is biased against existing schools.*

Current school facilities funding policies make reinvesting in existing schools through modernization and expansion more challenging than building new facilities. As a result, inequities persist in facilities funding and in the physical conditions of schools across the state. This bias does not align to the state's planning priorities that include "promot[ing] infill development and equity by rehabilitating, maintaining, and improving existing infrastructure… (Government Code 65041.1[a])."

RECOMMENDATIONS

Recommendation # 1: *Consider including Department of Education (CDE) as a member of the Strategic Growth Council.*

Given the SGC's intent to coordinate state infrastructure investment, the absence of school infrastructure stakeholders leads to missed opportunities. CDE should be invited to participate in the SGC's Infrastructure Working Group and other relevant SGC activities. CDE and SGC should continue to collaborate on improving collaboration around school funding and siting.

- *Lever:* Provide assistance to CDE's newly formed Policy and Standards Unit in the School Facilities Planning Division in its upcoming review of Title 5 in the Education Code
- *Lever:* Utilize the Health in All Policies (HiAP) process to engage CDE.

Recommendation # 2: *Analyze school infrastructure funding patterns.*

To accurately understand how California's recent school infrastructure funds have been spent, conduct detailed assessment of the usage of both state and local funds in recent years: how much was spent? What was the source of funds? What projects were funded? Which school districts and schools received funding? How do these patterns relate to the state's planning priorities, SGC goals, climate change goals, and educational goals?

Recommendation # 3: *Use the next state-wide school construction bond to prioritize modernization of existing schools.*

To address the ongoing capital needs of school districts across the state, there is likely to be a statewide school construction bond brought forth for 2012. In that process, the guidelines for the usage of those funds will be decided in the legislature. Bond language should be proposed that links to the state's planning priorities. Specifically, the bond funds should be prioritized for: existing schools, areas targeted for increased development in the regional sustainable communities strategies, and existing schools deemed to be in the worst physical condition.

Recommendation # 4: *Establish state policy structures, mandates, and incentives for local planning collaboration.*

This requires a detailed understanding of current state codes and how they might be updated and/or strengthened. Doing so is complex. Below are three specific strategies that could lead to greater local agency collaboration.

- *Lever:* Link Regional Plans, General Plans, and School Facilities Master Plans. SGC and CDE should (minimally) make a formal joint recommendation that MPOs, municipalities, and school districts collaborate on land use and infrastructure planning.
- *Lever:* Increase Safe Routes to School (SRTS) funding. SRTS funds work to ensure complete streets around schools. Complete streets are streets that are designed for safe biking and walking, as well as automobile use. This helps meet the state goals of reducing vehicle miles traveled and greenhouse gas emissions. Currently, SRTS funding only goes towards existing schools. An opportunity exists to allow SRTS proj-

ects to also develop complete streets around new school sites.
- *Lever:* Support Innovative Pilot Schools. Use state school construction funds to support "pilot" projects, including funding collaborative siting and planning phases, infill schools, joint use facilities, and retrofitting existing buildings into schools. Pilot projects may have freedom from some state school facility design standards to foster experimentation with new practices and solutions.
- *Lever:* The State Allocation Board (SAB) should consider formally adopting the tenants of Government Codes 65041.1 and 65042 that outline the state's planning priorities and instruct all state agencies to support them.

Recommendation # 5: *Provide technical assistance and build the capacity of local agencies to collaborate.*

State agencies should take a lead role in providing the tools, information, and examples of best practices for localities.

- *Lever:* Conduct trainings and develop information for legislators on public school infrastructure planning policy and funding.
- *Lever:* Conduct trainings and develop information for school districts (superintendents, school boards, and school facilities planners) on the state's planning priorities and how school infrastructure can be planned and implemented in accordance with SB 375 and the regional planning processes.
- *Lever:* Disseminate best practices of new/modernized schools that uphold both the state's planning priorities and CDE's vision and guiding principles for school environments.
- *Lever:* Encourage regional MPOs to provide their detailed demographic analysis to school districts to foster collaboration based on uniform data/information.

Recommendation # 6: *Engage students and schools in sustainable communities planning.*

Sustainable communities' processes should connect to California's growing environmental education programs, including CDE's work in establishing more than 60 "Green Career Academies" in high schools throughout the state. Inspired and funded by AB 519, Green Academies are growing statewide to create school and industry partnerships that "focus on clean technology and energy businesses and provide skilled workforces for the products and services for energy or water conservation, or both, renewable energy, pollution reduction, or other technologies that improve the environment in furtherance of state environmental laws." (AB 519).

NOTES

1. Bob Fisher, member, California Strategic Growth Council, State of California, Sacramento.

2. Deborah McKoy, executive director, Center for Cities & Schools, University of California, Berkeley.

3. Matthew Dalbey, Smart Growth Program, Office of Policy, Economics, and Innovation, U.S. Environmental Protection Agency, Washington, DC.

4. Jeff Vincent, deputy director, Center for Cities & Schools, University of California, Berkeley.

5. Kenneth Kirkey, planning director, Association of Bay Area Governments, Oakland, California.

6. Kathleen Moore, director, School Facilities Planning Division, Department of Education, State of California, Sacramento.

7. Julia Lave Johnston, deputy director, Planning Policy, Governor's Office of Planning and Research, State of California, Sacramento.

EDITOR'S NOTE

To see a list of the 44 participants in this program, by name and agency, please refer to the website of the Center for Cities & Schools, University of California, Berkeley, which is listed in Appendix C.

CHAPTER 6

Career Alternatives

Laurence Sprecher

There never was a local government manager who didn't at one time or another reflect that "…maybe I'd be happier doing something else!" Whether the cause was a particularly disastrous council meeting, the realization that you had been away from home four evenings in a row last week, a meeting with a former colleague who is happy in a new and different career, or just plain curiosity — all of us have thought about making a change. Few actually have followed up on the impulse.

The typical career path in local government management is a curiously linear one. You start out at the bottom, perhaps as a student intern. After your first job as an administrative assistant or another entrance-level staff person, you move on to an assistant manager position or perhaps to that of city manager in a small town. Then you become a city manager in a larger city, or a county manager, and move up through a series of constantly bigger communities.

Now, it's true that there are many variations on this theme, but it is the most common progression. There are a couple of problems connected with this pattern. One is that as you move up the ladder, the number of cities available becomes steadily smaller, and the number of serious competitors grow steadily larger. The other is that you develop "tunnel vision" and begin to see local government management as your only possible career path.

There is, however, an amazingly broad array of alternative career opportunities available to managers. Because most managers are focused on the traditional career path, they seldom give these alternatives serious consideration. The purpose of this chapter, then, is to examine a number of these options in the hope that one or more of them might interest a manager considering pursuing another career.

A Reasonable Alternative

The choice nearest at hand is one that few managers have ever considered: a position as assistant manager. Psychologically at least, this appears to be a step backward. Why would someone, having climbed to the top of the ladder, want to step down one rung?

Maybe for a lot of reasons! Many managers genuinely enjoy and are good at the administrative aspects of management. They like budgeting, organizing, coordinating, and so on. They are "POSCORB people." They don't enjoy nearly as much those parts of the manager's job that entail dealing with community politics, engaging in a dialogue with numerous publics, selling the locality's programs to the citizens, and talking with the media. These are "outside" activities, and they are "inside" people.

On the other hand, a number of mana-

Originally published as "Career Alternatives for Managers: The Choice is Yours," *Public Management*, Vol. 82, No. 6, June 2000, by the International City/County Management Association, Washington, DC. Reprinted with permission of the publisher.

gers, especially in mid-sized and large communities, find that they do not have time to do both the inside and the outside jobs well. They enjoy the public aspects of the position and would be happy to have someone else take charge of the day-to-day administration of the organization.

When you consider an assistant manager position, though, you should make sure that the manager genuinely intends to hand over the direct administration of substantial portions of the organization to you. Nothing could be worse than finding out after you are on board that the manager is unable or unwilling to keep his or her hands off the wheel.

More Alternatives

Another option is the management of special districts. Many managers don't like to think about special districts, but they are a fact of life, and they are not going away. Many special districts, especially medium-size ones, have found that they can no longer depend on appointing managers who have come up through the rank and welcome outside applicants. And most managers have had experience in managing utilities, for instance. There is something intriguing about managing an organization like a utility whose revenue is guaranteed and whose policy board only meets once a month for two hours.

Yet another possible alternative change, for city managers, is to county administration. The roles and responsibilities of counties vary immensely from state to state. In some states, counties are general-purpose local governments that provide all of the municipal services plus a lot of others. In other states, counties are merely administrative arms of the state. In some, a great difference exists between the roles and responsibilities of urban counties and those of rural ones.

Whatever their status, a growing number of counties have created county administrator positions with responsibilities similar to those of city managers. A fair number of city managers have moved over to county administration and have found the work challenging and re-

warding. Burke Raymond served as city manager in four cities before becoming the county administrator of Jackson County, Oregon, where he recently retired after 13 challenging and satisfying years.

Former municipal managers are certainly in a better position than most to understand the motivations of and to work successfully with the city managers in their counties. The relationship between a county administrator and a full-time governing body, however, often is different from a relationship between a city manager and a part-time council. If you are considering this move and want more information, you might want to attend one of the county administrators' sessions at the next ICMA annual conference. County administration is a real growth area within the field of local government management.

State and Federal Positions

The next step up in the hierarchy is state government. Opportunities for management positions in state government vary considerably from state to state. In some states, management appointments are a matter of political patronage, while in others, a tradition exists of promoting from within or hiring only managers with previous experience in state government.

Many state agencies, particularly the more progressive ones, have hired a number of former city managers. In Oregon, for example, the executive department, general services, human resources, water resources, and the Oregon Liquor Control Commission have each, at one time or another, been led by former city managers. All of these departments, it should be noted, perform functions with which city or county administrators are familiar.

As a state manager, I found that once a state budget had been adopted, I had considerably more freedom to manage within the limits of that budget than I had had as a city manager. Besides, there is a certain attraction to an organization whose policy board only meets part of the time. In some states, the legislature is in session for only a few months of the year.

Then there is, of course, the U.S. government. At one time, in the golden years of the 1960s and '70s, the Department of Housing and Urban Development actively sought city managers to staff programs both in Washington and at the regional level, but this is no longer the case because a large proportion of federal funding now is routed through state governments.

There remain numerous opportunities, however, for managers who are looking for federal employment to find openings in lower- and middle-management and management-technician positions, where the skills of city managers are immediately applicable. The nice thing about the federal government is that federal offices are located throughout the United States, which means that managers who want to change careers can continue to live where they are, if they want or need to.

It is possible for generalist managers and technicians to move from one federal organization to the other, and with good salaries and fringes, too. To research positions that are available, you may visit a variety of federal Web sites. For the manager who wants to pursue an alternate career without relocating, the federal government may offer the chance to do just that.

Yet Further Options

Management of non-for-profit organizations will be one of the hottest growth areas for the next decade. Not only are NFPOs proliferating, but also more and more activities formerly carried out by local governments now are being performed by NFPOs.

Too, existing organizations have discovered that they need managers with real experience and management skills, not just knowledge and skills in the area(s) in which the organization operates. NFPOs tend to provide services that appeal to many managers' strong desire benefit the public or in some way improve the human condition.

The staffs of state municipal leagues contain a number of former city or county managers. In fact, many league directors have come from the profession: Jim Miller, the executive director of the League of Minnesota Cities, for instance, is a former city manager. Many state leagues also keep a roster of former city or county managers who are interested in serving as interim managers. Some managers have developed nearly full-time careers as interim managers. The executive director of your state's municipal league probably is the best person to question on this possibility.

A career alternative that has been selected by a large number of local government managers is that of consulting. Basically, a manager can follow one of two paths. One is to join the staff of an existing consulting firm. A large number of these firms exist, ranging from gigantic international corporations to the much smaller companies that may serve a region, a sate, or even an urban area. All of them regularly recruit staff from the ranks of practicing managers; they pay well and tend to reward good performance. The downside is that you will travel a lot and work long hours, and you will be expected to bring in new business. Among the best sources of information on opportunities in consulting would be some of the consultants who have worked for you.

The other path is simple. Declare yourself a consultant, and go out and look for work. You will be surprised at the number of your colleagues who may have assignments for you. They can trust you because they know you and your abilities. Besides, you will cost a whole lot less than your big competitors. You also will be in a position to take on simple, short-term projects that they cannot afford to touch.

I ran my own consulting company for seven years, made enough money to raise six kids, handled many challenging assignments, and traveled to a lot of interesting places. The biggest drawback of being a sole proprietor, however, is that you have to spend more time than you might like in looking for future work. If you want to find out more about this option, talk to some of the people who are doing it.

Managers Make Excellent Teachers

Then there is higher education. Not many people realize how many former managers have entered the world of higher education. Here, there are three paths you might follow.

The first would be, of course, a teaching job. The conventional wisdom is that you need a doctorate to teach at the university level, and it is true that a Ph.D. or a D.P.A. is certainly not a hindrance to getting a teaching job, but there are a substantial number of people out there teaching without one of these degrees than you might expect.

If you are going to teach with just a master's degree — and I taught at the graduate level for more than 20 years without a Ph.D. — you do need to demonstrate ability and to gain experience. One of the best ways to rack up this experience is to teach as an adjunct professor, for which you will not need a doctorate. If you do a good job, your employer will keep you on, thus allowing you to gain experience and demonstrate competence. If you don't have a college or university in your area, try your luck at teaching management or government classes at a community college.

A second path in higher education would be to obtain an administration position. Most colleges and universities have come to realize that the things that make people great academicians do not necessarily make them good managers. A significant number of former managers have proven themselves successful as vice presidents of administration or as the holders of positions with similar titles. George Hanbury was the city manager of Fort Lauderdale before becoming vice president for administration at Nova University. Some people acquire a doctorate before coming on board, but most do not.

The third path within higher education would involve joining the staff of one of the institutes of local government service, or similar establishments offered by the local branches of state universities as staffs of consultants and trainers who provide services to local governments. Here, experience and ability are definitely more important than the degree(s) you possess.

Private Sector Possibilities

Last, but certainly not least, is the private sector, or the for-profit organization, including businesses that are big, medium-sized, and small. If you are interested in going into business for yourself, you need to seek the help of one of the variety of agencies, both public and private, that exist to help startups. You also can benefit from talking with people who have built successful businesses in the area that interests you. If your aim is to manage in the private sector, then you need to start thinking carefully about what you want to do, with whom, and where.

I happen to believe that ICMA really does stand for "I can manage anything." I believe that most managers have the skills and experience to succeed as managers in the private sector. I spent 10 years there before entering city management, and I have returned to the private sector both as a manager and as a consultant since then.

I have seen few private management situations that approached the complexity and difficult of the world that a typical local government manager faces every day. It's a different world with different rules, but management skills are definitely transferable. A thoughtful account of these differences was included in the June 1999 issue of *PM*, in an article entitled "Public or Private Sector Work: The Eternal Question," by Dave Millheim.

Part of the reason that our profession lacks a good feel for the success of former managers in the private sector is that we don't have a tracking system with which to gain this understanding. When a manager leaves the public sector, he or she seems to disappear over the horizon. A few outstanding successes have been noted, like that of Ted Tedesco, a manager and an ICMA president who went on to become a vice president of American Airlines. But such an example, while inspiring, strikes most managers as well beyond their reach.

The success of former managers in the private sector frequently goes unrecorded. One reason is that managers often hesitate to seek an alternative career because they feel that once they leave city or county management, they will never be able to return. There is nothing to indicate that this is so. I personally know a fairly large number of managers who have quit the profession and returned to it later. In many cases, they returned, not because they failed in an alternative career but because they found that they missed local government management.

Councils can find the idea of hiring a manager who has experience beyond city management an attractive one. The manager who hired me for my first city management position told me that the 10 years I had spent in aerospace gave me a leg-up over the other candidates.

Numerous Opportunities

The purpose of this chapter has been to make city and county managers more aware of the many opportunities that are open to them. How you choose the career change to pursue and how you pursue it are points that will have to be discussed in a future *PM* article. In the meantime, if any of the career alternatives covered in this article seem interesting to you, I suggest that you seek people on your preferred career path and ask them for information. There are few things that people like to do so much as to talk about what they do and how they like it. If you decide you are interested in an alternative career, the next questions are which career and how to pursue it.

CHAPTER 7

Revenues

Anthony Flint

The public finance crisis for local and state governments keeps rolling along, a bit like a slow-motion train wreck. Harrisburg, Pa., is on the brink of bankruptcy. In California, police departments say they must cut back on enforcement of certain crimes. Pensions and health care continue to wreak havoc on municipal budgets everywhere.

Meanwhile, the mood of the country is against new taxes, while several states have placed caps on property taxes. And as anyone who has balanced a home budget knows, it's simply unsustainable to have expenditures going out outpace revenues coming in.

Against this backdrop comes heightened interest in collecting payments in lieu of taxes, or PILOTs, from charitable nonprofit organizations such as private colleges and universities, hospitals and medical centers, and cultural institutions that are exempt from paying property taxes in all 50 states and the District of Columbia. Currently, at least 117 municipalities across 18 states have PILOT programs in place; 82 of those cities and town are in Massachusetts. Boston has one of the longest standing and most revenue-productive programs in the U.S., and Cambridge, home to MIT and Harvard, has the oldest, dating back to the 1920s. New Haven and Yale University have worked out another model program.

The basic idea is that while these nonprofits are by law — and in several states mandated by state constitutions — tax-exempt, they might reasonably be asked to make a voluntary contribution that is a fraction of what they would pay if they paid property taxes. The payments typically constitute a very small percentage of overall revenues collected by municipalities. Boston's collection of $15.7 million in the 2009 fiscal year, for example, amounted to .66 percent of the total city budget that year.

Meanwhile, in recent years, other cities have been getting into the PILOTs business, primarily in the Northeast and Mid-Atlantic, but also in the Midwest, plus North Carolina, Georgia, Montana, and California. But the process has been uneven, ad-hoc and often contentious, according to Daphne Kenyon and Adam Langley, authors of "Payments in Lieu of Taxes: Balancing Municipal and Nonprofit Interests," published by the Lincoln Institute of Land Policy.

Some cities and town have been more aggressive than others as they seek revenue from nonprofits. Pittsburgh, Princeton, and Providence tried to establish a controversial "tuition tax," and some state legislatures have contemplated an "endowment tax" on higher education institutions as well. In New Hampshire, the town of Peterborough challenged the tax-exempt status of the MacDowell Colony, founded in 1907 to promote the arts and including an artists-in-residence program. Selectmen argued that all but one of the artists were from out of state, failing to meet the requirement that residents of New Hampshire be admitted to a

Originally published as "Cities Look to Non-Profits as Cash Source," *Town & Gown Network*, December 6, 2010, by Colorado State University, Fort Collins. Reprinted with permission of the publisher.

charity's benefits. Having gotten the institution's attention, they proposed a PILOT program, which the MacDowell Colony refused. The New Hampshire Supreme Court ruled against the selectmen, leaving nothing but hard feelings all around.

Municipalities have also of course increasingly relied on charging user fees that can help pay for basic public services, from police and fire protection to streets and their maintenance or garbage collection. Legal challenges abound in this area as well.

The better approach, the report's author say, is to first decide if a PILOT program is appropriate, then collaborate with nonprofits to structure the program so it's reasonable, predictable, and transparent — all as part of a town-gown partnership that is mutually beneficial. Cities can set a target based on the cost of public services directly benefiting nonprofits, and use the assessed value of tax-exempt property or square footage to calculate suggested contributions. Boston's goal is that nonprofits contribute 25 percent of what they would pay if they were not tax exempt.

"PILOTs can provide crucial revenue for certain municipalities, and are one way to make non profits pay for the public services they consume," Kenyon and Langley say. "However, PILOTs are often haphazard, secretive, and calculated in an ad hoc manner that results in widely varying payments among similar nonprofits. In addition, a municipality's attempt to collect PILOTs can prompt a battle with nonprofits and lead to years of contentious, costly, and unproductive litigation."

Even in Boston's model program, there are wide disparities in what institutions contribute: Boston University leads the way with $4.8 million, followed by Harvard University with $1.9 million. Boston College contributes $293,251, and Northeastern University a mere $30,157. Boston Mayor Thomas M. Menino launched a PILOT Task Force to revamp the program and collect more revenue in a more even way from nonprofits. City Councilor Stephen Murphy says he hopes a phased-in expansion of the program will bring in $40 million per year in five years.

There are big themes at work here that go to the core of U.S. cities and their continued vitality. So-called "eds and meds"— higher education institutions and often related health care medical centers — are an economic engine for many cities, more resilient during recessions. They employ thousands of local residents and support and spin off all kinds of economic activity. But when they expand, more and more land goes off the tax rolls, while they continue to consume the services that cities provide.

Baltimore is an especially interesting case. The city recruited nonprofits to locate there as an economic development strategy — marketing the location as less expensive than Washington, D.C. but still close-by — but ended up being a victim of its own success, in terms of tax-exempt property. A PILOT program had to be established.

Luring businesses with tax breaks and incentives is a tried and true practice in the for-profit world. But tax-exempt status for nonprofits isn't a loophole or a subsidy, says Richard Doherty, president of the Association of Independent Colleges and Universities of Massachusetts. It was established going back some 200 years because nonprofits provide essential services that government does not. Many institutions provide community benefits in many ways, in the public education system or by revitalizing parks and public space, which does not get calculated sufficiently in setting PILOTs contributions.

The role of nonprofits in cities should not be underestimated, says Doherty, who suggests that they are responsible for billions in economic activity. He's against a one-size-fits-all, systematic or formula-based approach, and favors the Connecticut and Rhode Island systems, where the state reimburses cities and towns for some of the property tax revenues they don't collect from nonprofits. Those reimbursements are partial, however, and in hard times are easily cut from state budgets — which brings us right back to the fundamental problem of state and local governments going broke.

It's no surprise that public employee unions are beginning to take particular interest in PILOTs. And nonprofits of all kinds may have some reason to be worried. As cities assess the practice of collecting payments in lieu of taxes, some are starting to look at secondary schools as well as colleges and universities, museums, and even churches. It's possible only soup kitch- ens, which are charitable nonprofit organi- zations like the rest, can feel comfortable that it's with them that municipalities might draw the line.

PART II.
BEST PRACTICES

CHAPTER 8

Amherst and Hampshire College Work Together to Enhance the Entire Community

Gregory S. Prince, Jr.

"How do you build a relationship between an institution and the community in which it lives, in all of its forms?" This is a topic that I have struggled with for more than the 14 years I've been at Hampshire; building these relationships is an incredibly interesting process. I'm going to describe some of the salient points that have influenced the way I work on Hampshire's community relations. It is not coherent. It does not start with a grand design. Rather, it's inductive, based on my experiences and my observations. In addition, this interaction, this back and forth between thoughts and actions, between the college and the community, has been an important part of my own ongoing education about this critical topic.

This process for me began when I worked at Dartmouth College for 19 years. One of the things I found extraordinary at Dartmouth, which is so different from Hampshire, is that Dartmouth is taxed like any other institution, for profit or not, in the state. Because New Hampshire does not have the income tax or the sales tax, the town of Hanover is permitted to impose a property tax on all nonacademic facilities at the college. This tax policy has been in effect for decades, so it is an accepted part of

life. People struggle over all the same issues that any academic community faces, but the conversation in town meetings is quite different when the college is paying just like anybody else. Granted, in Hanover tax dollars go to the schools where the faculty send their own children, so they have a vested interest. But, I saw a relationship between the college and the community that I found very healthy.

When I came to Hampshire College in 1989, everyone was talking about PILOTS (payments in lieu of taxes). I hadn't thought much about PILOTS until I found out that the University of Massachusetts was making these payments to the town, and the town manager wanted Hampshire and Amherst College to start paying as well. So I learned to talk about PILOTS, but I felt there was something intrinsically shortsighted about the arrangement because it was based on a very narrow conversation about money and not about needs. Both Hampshire and Amherst colleges have made contributions to the town of Amherst for certain items, but we have not called them PILOTS, and we have not made them on a regular basis. Now, I am not saying that when a college or university does make a payment in

Originally published as "Principles for College and Community Interactions," *Land Lines*, Vol. 15, No. 3, July 2003, by the Lincoln Institute of Land Policy, Cambridge, Massachusetts. Reprinted with permission of the publisher.

lieu of taxes to a city it is necessarily a sign of an unhealthy relationship. All too often, however, the negotiations about what universities and colleges ought to pay to their host communities focus on the cost of police protection or snow removal, for example, rather than what it means to be part of a community with the rights and obligations that accompany citizenship, what are some of the critical needs of the community, and which ones could the institution most effectively address.

As I tried to figure out how to change the conversation, I wanted all of us to understand that we were having a dialogue. That is, when I'm having a conversation at Hampshire about the town, or with the town about Hampshire, I need to acknowledge that UMass and Amherst College are also part of the conversation. Wherever possible, we try to make sure that all three of us are communicating with the town; admittedly, this four-way conversation is complicated. I found in the process that the real discussion was about how to build sustainable communities. At Amherst College or UMass, sustainability is viewed differently than at Hampshire, a 33-year-old institution with little endowment. We need to figure out how to sustain our college over the long term within these different, complicated relationships. The PILOT conversation never seemed to quite get at that issue, so we've tried to expand it.

Broadening the Conversation

Two very different sets of experiences influenced my thinking about how to broaden and enrich the conversation with the community.

URBAN CONFERENCES

When I first arrived at Hampshire, I received a phone call from the chief counsel for the Transit Police in New York City, whom I had taught years before. He asked if Hampshire College would host a conference in association with the International Association of Chiefs of Police, bringing together representatives from several large urban communities. My first question was, "Great, but why Hampshire?" The

response was that at that time, in 1989, people like Lee Brown (former police commissioner in New York City and now mayor of Houston) and Bill Bratton (former police chief of Boston and New York City, and now police chief of Los Angeles) felt that America had lost its cities but didn't know it, and they were trying to figure out how to talk about it. They wanted to meet at Hampshire because it was the last place in the United States one would think would work directly with the police. The partnership that emerged between Hampshire and the International Association of Chiefs of Police did send a signal, and people noticed.

The conference brought together not just law enforcement officials but also the heads of all the major departments of ten major U.S. cities. Los Angeles dropped out at the last minute because of the Rodney King incident, but Atlanta, Boston, Chicago, New Haven, New York City, Phoenix, Seattle, Springfield and Tulsa were involved in the first group; other cities attended subsequent meetings. The police chiefs did not want mayors to come, because they wanted free and open discussion across professions and across cities. Because Hampshire paid for the conference, we were able to bring students into the process.

Among the most important outcomes of these conferences over several years was the creation of a forum for people involved in community schools, community policing, community health and other areas who never had a chance to converse, and that included the Hampshire students who contributed to an intergenerational discourse. In the first conference, we divided all the participants into groups, mixing professions and cities, and we gave them a four-block area of a fictitious city. Each group had three hours to write a proposal to a foundation on how they would use those city blocks to restore or revive the most problematic part of the city. They had access to unlimited funds, but out of the process came two critical principles that actually had very little to do with money and had everything to do with how people talk to one another and collaborate: (1) the need to have conversations across professions and across community boundaries; and (2) the need for every older adult committee or commission to have a younger counterpart organization. Guess who thought that one up? The students wanted to find a way to generate networks and initiate conversations in which common plans could be developed; they understood that no plan was going to succeed without that kind of cross-generational ownership. They came away with the realization that there is no single answer to what gets done; what is most important is how it gets done. Having conversations across boundaries, be they professional, historic, generational or institutional, may be the core value and core practice of community building.

We had three of these conferences over three years, and I think they had a profound effect on the strategic ways that people like Bratton and Brown and other law enforcement officers and community leaders changed their communities. These same principles of open conversation should be built back into relationships between colleges and universities and their communities. It's not just about PILOTS or taxes. It's about how you generate a conversation so that everybody is part of the process, respects the outcome and is committed to the sustainability of the community.

CULTURAL VILLAGE

The second set of experiences also began in my first year at Hampshire, a lovely campus of 1,200 students surrounded by 800 acres of farmland in Amherst, a small New England town in the western part of the state. Amherst also hosts the University of Massachusetts, a major state land-grant university with over 20,000 students, and Amherst College, with 1,600 students. A bus system links the colleges with the town, but many students complained that they were "in a little teenage encampment." They wanted older adults and more activity around them so they could feel more connected to the community.

As I talked with people in the town and attended meetings on economic development issues, I learned that Amherst was fairly hostile to development. Lack of development intensified the feeling among town leaders that PILOTS were the possible recourse. As I began to understand that perceptions, strategies and concerns about development underlay the conversation about PILOTS, I began to look at land. Could land possibly help the community, since Hampshire had an abundance of land relative to available cash? Our land actually held the seeds for new possibilities in the form of creating a "cultural village."

After many years of planning and negotiating, the grounds of Hampshire College are now being transformed into a center for nonprofit cultural and educational institutions that create more activity for the students and more economic activity for the town. The National Yiddish Book Center became the first new development when, in the early 1990s, it was looking for a new home. The center's director, Aaron Lansky, is a Hampshire alumnus and he wanted to stay in Amherst where he had started the center. It took six years to persuade the boards of the college and the center to agree, but the center now has an absolutely gorgeous building with 40,000 volumes in the library. It runs tremendous events, bringing people together from all over the world. Hampshire College didn't pay for it; the Book Center paid for it. But its building, its facilities, its activities and its staff are on our campus, enriching our life, putting people into our dining room, creating a more interesting intellectual environment for our students, creating economic activity for the town, and not using land that could otherwise be taxed.

The second member of the cultural village, the Eric Carle Museum of Picture Book Art, opened in the fall of 2002. One may well ask, "What does it do for Hampshire College to be the site of the first picture-book art museum in the U.S.?" The 40,000-square-foot building sits on land that Hampshire donated, but Eric Carle, the author of *The Very Hungry Caterpillar*, endowed the museum. It employs 18 people, including some of our students. So we're enriching the faculty and cultural resources for our students, and the town of Amherst gets a large museum to sustain its economic base while limiting environmental impact on its land resources. Only 25,000 museum-goers were expected in the first year, but more than 40,000 attended in the first four months, bringing vitality to both the town and the college.

Intergenerational Viewpoints

These two experiences — developing the cultural village and learning from the urban conferences years before — make me feel that even though Hampshire is in a rural area, the principles that have guided community outreach are replicable even for large universities in urban environments. The key is to generate a conversation that crosses boundaries and in so doing weakens those boundaries. The process is ongoing and has led to many interesting new conversations.

Recently the town of Amherst approached me about developing open space on the edge of the campus for a commercial village center. The area now houses a well-known farm stand, but the town wanted to expand the amount of commercial activity. Through open conversation with the community, college trustees, students and residents, the land was purchased and given to Hampshire with the proviso that it be used to generate income to support the college. At the first public hearing on what to do with the land, we invited the entire community. All ages were present. A group of Hampshire students came to the meeting intending to argue against development; they wanted the area kept as open space. However, the first citizens to speak were in their 70s and 80s; they tore us apart about how terrible it would be to develop this area and how they had bought their apartments nearby because of this open beautiful land. In truth, their retirement community had been built while I was the president of the college, so I knew it, too, had been built on open land. Their attitude was, "we're here and now we don't want any more development." The students understood these arguments, but found themselves thinking about how they wanted to behave when they were 75 years old. They didn't want to imagine themselves as being opposed to growth and change, so this intergenerational conversation made a difference in their attitudes. Talks have continued and the plan is still in development, with a target date of spring 2004 to present it at town meeting.

Principles of Sustainability

Developing the cultural village and new developments in academic curricula converged to make sustainability an increasingly important issue. Suddenly, the cultural village was also becoming a laboratory. When the faculty, in response to issues in the cultural village, proposed seeking funds to do a sustainable campus plan focusing on the natural environment, I suggested that the most important principle in the plan be sustaining Hampshire College. My statement generated a very constructive conversation about what sustainability should mean for Hampshire. Let me summarize the principles that we developed.

1. The core goal in planning for the college must be the school's long-term sustainability as an educational institution committed to providing students with the most constructively transforming liberal arts education possible.

2. In pursuing the first goal, the college must strive for human sustainability — for maintaining and enriching our capacity to live well together, for providing for the economic well-being of those who work at the college, and for nurturing their creative spirit and sense of fulfillment that comes from working at the college.

3. In pursuing the educational and social goals, we must recognize the fundamental relationship between the goals and the physical environment, and strive to achieve the sustainability of that physical environment to the greatest extent possible.

4. In pursuing the core goals of sustaining the college as an educational institution, we must strive to ensure that as an institution, independent of what its graduates accomplish, what we do makes a difference locally, nationally and internationally. Success in achieving the first three goals will ensure that we take a significant step in achieving the fourth goal. In effect, our primary aim is to provide the best education we can. We must model the behavior we expect of our graduates.

5. In pursuing educational and social sustainability, we must encourage entrepreneurial activity, invention and innovation, even if it entails the risk of failure.

6. In sustaining the human spirit of the college community, economic needs must be met, but with the recognition that we must also offer a meaningful mission, a stimulating and creative intellectual environment, and a supportive and enriching physical environment.

7. In seeking to create a sustainable, healthy and enriching social environment, the practical must be balanced with the artistic, the physical and rational with the contemplative, the values of individualism with those of community, and the needs of the college with those of the larger community.

8. In seeking to create a sustainable physical environment, efficient use of energy should be the highest priority, followed by other resource uses and resource disposal. Appropriate land use must be made another high priority. In maintaining the physical plant, we should consider the ease and efficiency of maintenance in terms of those who perform the work, as well as the level of resources needed to carry it out.

9. Wherever possible, physical infrastructure changes should include visible demonstration or interactive educational displays designed to educate about sustainability.

10. The cost of innovations in programs or in the physical environment should include the endowment required to ensure that those who follow us will not be burdened with their maintenance. The projects should be designed so they can be converted to other uses, removed or terminated.

The Board of Trustees reviewed the ten principles of sustainability, then challenged us on how we will interpret and implement them. In the process of working on these tasks, additional guidelines began to emerge:

1. Process is important: conversation and explorations can uncover interests as opposed to positions.

2. Geography matters. It may not be destiny, but it has a great deal to do with it and how you have to build and grow.

3. Focus on the culture, the economy and the environment comprehensively, not as separate subjects in conversations and plans, and involve them early.

4. Involve the community.

5. Involve young people, especially high school students, in any community planning.

6. Promote interdependence.

While these guidelines answer some questions, I struggle with other questions. One of particular importance to me currently is the issue of contiguity. Do our endeavors need to be within our current campus or town or can we successfully move into other communities? The five colleges in the region (Amherst, Hampshire, Mt. Holyoke, Smith and UMass) already work together on many joint programs and all of us have done a great deal of work in Holyoke, a small city about 15 miles south of Amherst that exemplifies all the problems of urban America.

We spent a lot of time trying to encourage UMass to move its art department to an old warehouse in Holyoke. We felt it would be a major boost to the community, but it looks as though it will not happen for equally legitimate reasons. Moving an academic department geographically from the rest of the academic community will increase intellectual isolation and fragmentation. Other ideas include building a five-college dormitory in Holyoke, and that possibility raises equally complex questions related to contiguity and community citizenship.

In both projects the issue is contiguity. Must you always maintain your place as a central, unbroken whole, or can you move outside of your special place? That's the challenge. I think Hampshire has to somehow build a presence in Holyoke. We have made a huge investment there already, and I believe the city has incredible potential. I think we have to face the issue of opening ourselves up physically, not just maintaining the boundaries of our space but carrying ourselves outside of the institution as well. But others resist. What is exciting is the conversation and the process of engaging all of the related communities in that dialogue.

CHAPTER 9

Aspen and Partners from the University of Michigan and Other Schools Protect Research Lab

Joshua Zaffos

Almost an hour before dawn on the summer solstice, Johannes Foufopoulos is scurrying around his cabin at the Rocky Mountain Biological Laboratory — a 245-acre mountain field station at nearly 9,500-feet elevation in the central Colorado Rockies. Foufopoulos, a University of Michigan natural resources professor, gulps a few cups of coffee and some bread with vegetable spread. Out the door at 5 A.M., he is soon hiking along a slope of rock scree, willows, and rivulets of meltwater at the foot of Gothic Mountain.

With Foufopoulos are Courtney Murdock, a doctoral student he advises, and Morgan Graham, a summer research assistant — each carrying two nine-foot-long rods of metal rebar. Where there's a break in the willows, Foufopoulos works a rod into the rocky earth, and Murdock and Graham produce a loosely rolled black nylon mist net.

When unfurled and fastened between the rods, the net will appear as fine as mist to birds, which will then be trapped in flight. The furled nets, say the researchers, resemble the slick, jet-black moustache of Hall of Fame baseball pitcher Rollie Fingers, leading them to name all their field sites after famous major leaguers — Babe Ruth, Catfish Hunter, and this site, which they call Andre Dawson, after Murdock's favorite Cub player from her youth in Chicago.

These researchers are interested in the diseases of birds, such as avian malaria and West Nile virus, which can be passed to humans. Such research could cast light on the spread of virulent "bird" flu to human beings and the emergence of global bird-flu pandemics.

"We want to try to understand which factors determine disease presence," says Foufopoulos, "and predict how habitat change-from global warming, for example-is going to affect prevalence over the landscape."

"The Most Productive Lab in North America"

The Rocky Mountain Biological Lab (RMBL, pronounced "rumble" by locals) is uniquely suited to such experiments. The lab is headquartered at a former mining camp called Gothic, on a steep dirt road between the ski towns of Aspen and Crested Butte, which are separated by Schofield Pass. Encompassing and surrounding the field campus is a nearly pristine region of wildflower meadows, towering peaks, waterfalls, and mountainside forests known as the High Elk Corridor, because herds

Originally published as "High on Science," *Land & People*, Vol. 18, No. 1, Spring 2006, by the Trust for Public Land, San Francisco, California. Reprinted with permission of the publisher. Sign up for a complimentary issue of *Land & People* magazine by visiting tpl.org/freemag.

of elk pass through this part of the Elk Mountains between the Maroon Bells-Snowmass Wilderness to the north and the Raggeds Wilderness to the south.

"It's one of the most beautiful places in the county, and it's an area people are using more and more for recreation these days," says Jim Starr, an attorney and Gunnison County commissioner, who also sits on the board of the Crested Butte Land Trust. Each year thousands of tourists and nature lovers drive up from Crested Butte or Aspen to check out waist-high wildflowers, marmots and hummingbirds, waterfalls and peaks; to backpack into one of the adjacent national forest wilderness areas; to photograph the old mill at the historic town of Crystal (one of the West's most photographed spots); or to ride mountain bikes on the corridor's many miles of trail.

But the corridor is susceptible to development because scattered amid its public land are thousands of acres of privately owned mining claims. Because of these private lands, the development of new trophy homes, cabins, and roads threatens the corridor's value for recreation and environmental protection — not to mention its status as one of the nation's preeminent outdoor laboratories.

RMBL was founded in 1928 as an independent, nonprofit research station. In the years since, its scientists have published over 1,000 papers, and the lab has gained a reputation as one of the finest places on earth to conduct long-term environmental experiments. Noted scientists who have worked here include Paul Ehrlich, author of *The Population Bomb*, and Michael Soulé, a founder of the discipline of conservation biology.

One big reason for this is the wide range of elevations within easy reach of the lab. Four different ecological biomes converge within the High Elk Corridor. "You have access to so many habitats," says Foufopoulos, whose own study sites range between 7,000 and 14,000 feet.

Because of its relatively pristine environment and 75 years of research records, RMBL is also the perfect place for studying how humans have changed and are changing the planet, says Ian Billick, the lab's director. Arriving first in 1988 to take a field ecology course,

Billick went on to do his own research, complete a Ph.D., and eventually teach the same ecology class he once took as a student. He became the director in 2001; along the way he met his wife, a fellow researcher at the lab. "It's really a place by scientists, of scientists, for scientists," Billick says.

Today approximately 160 researchers converge on the lab for the three-month summer research season. Among them are senior scientists, graduate students, research assistants, a few dozen college kids, and laboratory staff. A few RMBL employees stay the winter to look after the buildings, enduring an average snowfall of 450 inches. During the summers, the staff coordinates the logistics for the scientists but lets them figure out for themselves the research they'll conduct.

Most of what scientists know about plant pollination derives from research at the lab. Research on acid rain here led directly to revisions in the Clean Air Act to alleviate air pollution in Western regions. The lab was one of the first places where scientists noted shrinking amphibian populations that were ultimately recognized as part of a global decline. RMBL research on climate change is cited regularly as scientists and policy makers assess the impacts of global warming.

"This is probably the most productive lab in North America in terms of terrestrial ecological research," says David Inouye, a professor at the University of Maryland, who first arrived at RMBL in 1973 to study plant ecology. That year he set up four-foot-square plots at Gothic and throughout the High Elk to study which plants occurred and when they flowered. More than three decades later, Inouye is able to predict when the first wildflowers — such as larkspur and glacier lilies — will bloom and how many to expect. Changes to the abundance and timing of the flowers, says Inouye, are the result of fluctuations within regional climatic patterns as well as global warming.

From Mining to Mist Nets

As he walks between study plots, Inouye examines the ground for bumblebees pollinating the flowers and for rusty, square nails turned out of the soil each spring by gophers-nails left over from the buildings constructed here when mining ruled the High Elk Corridor.

That mining history is the reason why the High Elk's environment, recreation, and value to science are now endangered. After silver was discovered here in the 1880s, towns and mining camps such as Gothic, Crystal, and Schofield sprang up on either side of Schofield Pass. But silver mining boomed and went bust within a few decades. Miners left behind their cabins — some since restored by RMBL — and almost 6,000 acres of mining claims that remained private when surrounding land was added to the national forest system early in the last century.

"Mining created a real crazy quilt of land-ownership," says Doug Robotham, Colorado state director of The Trust for Public Land, which has been acquiring former mining claims in the High Elk Corridor for conservation by White River National Forest. The large number of widely scattered private parcels also makes it harder to decide which lands to protect.

In response, TPL staff launched an effort in 2000 to analyze the inholdings. TPL has prioritized 2,500 acres for protection in partnership with regional land trusts and conservation groups, the U.S. Forest Service, and local governments and businesses.

The goal is to take a landownership pattern that made sense for a 19th-century mining economy and retool it for a 21st-century economy dominated by tourism. Today the High Elk is valued not for silver but for its wildflowers, waterfalls, wide-open views, and value to science.

"It's absolutely wonderful that TPL has taken on the project just because of the sheer numbers of parcels and landowners," says lab director Ian Billick. He describes how development could damage the "tools" of the research — by which he means the yellow-bellied marmots, broad-tailed hummingbirds, Mormon fritillary butterflies, and scarlet gilia wildflowers. To protect the experiments it is not enough to protect researchers' study sites or the land inside the boundaries of the lab. The entire landscape must be protected. "When we lose

unique habitats, that means the scientists lose the tools," Billick says.

Already, visitors to the area have intentionally or inadvertently disturbed research sites. Houses and entry roadways on former mining claims would impact sensitive ecosystems that have been monitored for 75 years. Increased human occupation near the research sites would bring pets, invasive plants, and scavenger species such as magpies and crows, which can disrupt native species and wildlife.

"The more this valley becomes clogged with skiers and snowmobiles and dirt on the road from human presence, the more difficult it is to get useful information for my scientific research," says John Harte, a professor from the University of California, Berkeley, who has worked at RMBL since 1977. Harte uses infrared heat lamps to artificially warm mountain meadows by an extra two degrees centigrade, simulating climatic conditions as they might develop under global warming a century from now.

Back at their study site, researchers Foufopoulos, Murdock, and Graham delicately extract an American robin and a warbling vireo from the mist nets. They clamp a light metal band to one leg of each bird so that they or other researchers can identify it in the future. They also weigh and measure each bird, prick it beneath its wing to draw two tiny tubes of blood, and then release it. Later they will analyze the blood samples to judge the bird's nutrition, hormone levels, and immune functions. The percentage of red blood cells in the sample indicates the presence of avian malaria and enables the researchers to compare the health of infected and uninfected birds.

Like the other RMBL scientists, Foufopoulos hopes that the conservation effort under way here will succeed, protecting the area for recreation and research. Currently, TPL and its partners are halfway to the goal of protecting 2,500 of the 6,000 private acres within the corridor. Funding for the effort includes $2.25 million secured by the Colorado congressional delegation from the federal Land and Water Conservation Fund. Additional support has come from the Great Outdoors Colorado Trust Fund, Gunnison County, the Crested Butte

Land Trust, RMBL, Crested Butte Mountain Resort, and private donors who want to help preserve the High Elk's natural and cultural history. Parcels protected include public trailheads, scenic vistas, and places of scientific importance.

"This is a key area valued for its scenic beauty and habitat," says Don Carroll, deputy supervisor of White River National Forest. "If TPL hadn't acted, there's no doubt we would have seen development here. It is so important to protect areas that offer such important research opportunities. As a government agency entrusted with managing the public's land, the Forest Service also needs access to reliable information derived from sound research."

Completion of the project will be great for the scientists, of course, and for the hikers, backpackers, photographers, picnickers, and others who seek out the corridor for its wildflowers, views, and wildlife. But it will be good news as well for all of us who want hard evidence about the future effects of global warming, diseases that pass from birds to humans, and other RMBL research topics.

"There are very few places in the world where you've had the accumulation of knowledge we've had here," says lab director Ian Billick. "This is going to be one of the places where we really understand what's going on."

CHAPTER 10

Boston, Northeastern University and Other Cities and Schools Are Building "Collegetowns"

James Martin *and* James E. Samels

Here is an easy question to lead off with, a soft lob down the middle for *University Business* sluggers: What do the following cities and towns have in common: Amherst, Cambridge, Berkeley, Huntsville, Madison, Ann Arbor, Princeton, Chapel Hill, and Palo Alto?

If you don't have the answer by now, then you're not likely to recognize the new generation of "collegetowns" emerging from coast to coast. These proactive, creative partnerships are major economic and workforce development drivers, and importantly, key players in urban renaissance. In fact, American colleges and universities are now partnering with municipalities to create a new set of downtown strategic alliances, focused on enriching the educational, cultural, and civic fabric of their towns.

There was a time when host cities and towns revered colleges and universities as beacons of higher learning. Places like Cambridge with Harvard and MIT, and New Haven with Yale, boasted about their world-class destination status.

Over time, however, the proliferation of tax-exempt campuses, occupying choice properties and drawing heavily on police, fire, and emergency medical services, sowed seeds of discontent in town/gown relationships. Cities and towns justifiably expected pilot payments (pay-ment in lieu of taxes), a reasonable contribution for municipal services in lieu of tax revenues. Simultaneously, colleges and universities pointed to special civic commitments, scholarships, public school collaboration, and job creation.

What came next was a spate of taxation cases that called for full and fair evaluation and eventually led to the taxpayers' revolt of propositions 13 in California and 2 in Massachusetts. Sadly, cities and colleges soon turned to litigation and legislation to settle their differences — a far cry from the collegial and bucolic settings of typical collegetowns. Over the last decade, new municipal officials and campus leaders have started fresh conversations dedicated to mutual growth.

Town/Gown Win-Wins

In Boston, higher ed–city hall relationships hit a new low when student drinking and rowdiness after a Red Sox game led to the death of a college student at the hands of a Boston Police Riot Squad in 2004. Today, these adversarial town/gown relations have changed for the better with Boston Mayor Thomas Menino and Northeastern University President Richard Freeland penning an advertorial in *The Chron-*

Originally published as "'Collegetowns' Popping Up All Over," *College Town Topics*, April 2006, by the International Town and Gown Association, Clemson University, Clemson, South Carolina. Reprinted with permission of the publisher.

icle of Higher Education entitled "Town-Gown Relationships: A New Model Emerges." In that piece, Menino and Freeland envision a new age of higher education municipal partnerships aimed at promoting Greater Boston's undisputed global marker as the Athens of higher education.

In 2007, Binghamton University (N.Y.) will partner with nearby Broome Community College to establish an Education and Community Development Center. As currently envisioned, the new center will offer needed programs such as a master's degree in Public Administration and a master's in Social Work, helping area residents further their education while contributing to the revitalization of downtown Binghamton. "Binghamton University is at the center of much of the change we see taking place in our community," says President Lois B. DeFleur. "Our vitality is dependent on the vitality of the city and region."

Envision, if you will, the historic whaling seaport of New London, Conn., a rising collegetown anchored by the prospect of co-locating a U.S. Coast Guard museum and archives with a professional and graduate school.

Significantly, this vision also conceives of an adjacent destination resort, quality hotel, and conference center, along with new housing, upscale retail, and other complementary community uses. An interesting note is that the smallest institution in town, Mitchell College, played a key leadership role in collaborating with the New London Development Corporation, the U.S. Coast Guard Academy, and the City of New London. Mitchell President Mary Ellen Jukoski, Academy Superintendent Rear Admiral James Van Sice, and NLDC President Michel Joplin are all involved in transforming this historic whaling village into a new seaport collegetown on the Connecticut shore.

In the city where what happens there, stays there — "viva Las Vegas" — the Community College of Southern Nevada is collaborating with the University of Nevada, Las Vegas; Nevada State College; and the city to develop seamless lifelong learning pathways in places like Cheyenne, West Charleston, and Henderson. CCSN President Richard Carpenter notes

with pride that these partnerships provide a critical workforce development capacity to support the indigenous industries of tourism, gaming, and hospitality management.

Recognizing that collegetowns must offer affordable higher education and housing, and quality healthcare, Warren County Community College (N.J.) is collaborating with the Hackettstown Regional Medical Center to build a new state-of-the-art health science education center on the campus of the hospital — a campus capital outlay initiative aimed at making Warren and Hackettstown great places to visit, play, stay, and learn.

Finally, take a look at Trinity College in Hartford: Its collegetown initiative has achieved national recognition. With the completion of its Learning Corridor model, the institution helped displace crack houses with new public schools, affordable housing, a community-based public health organization, and public television and radio. Former Trinity President Evan Dobelle reflects on how the Learning Corridor has had a transformative impact on the surrounding community, while offering wonderful service learning, teaching, and research opportunities for Trinity students, faculty, and staff.

Michael Rudden, a senior city planner at the architectural firm Saratoga Associates, believes town/gown relationships can move from "stress" to "success" when both the community and institutions develop and achieve goals collaboratively. Early on in the planning process, Saratoga assisted the City of Fitchburg, Mass., and Fitchburg State College in developing a "Main Street revitalization" plan. Later, when planning for a new recreation-fitness center, Fitchburg State College chose a blighted downtown neighborhood at the edge of the main campus. This coincided with the mutual goal of revitalizing the college and the downtown by physically, economically, and culturally linking the campus with the city.

Collegetowns of Today and Tomorrow

So, what do *UB* readers need to know about the characteristics of contemporary collegetowns that will make these locales so special and noteworthy?

Modern collegetowns often have strategic downtown locations away from the main campus — in industrial, science, and technology parks, and at schools and neighborhood health centers.

Collegetowns co-locate bookstores and continuing education centers alongside cybercafes, gourmet food courts, and fitness, wellness, and edutainment centers.

Modern collegetowns reduce the rate of public school attrition, teenage pregnancy, substance abuse, and alcohol abuse by helping to create community aspiration and civic commitment to make downtowns more attractive, vibrant, and, most importantly, more livable.

Contemporary collegetowns co-locate intermodal transportation centers for convenient transport between their downtown learning centers and the main campuses.

Collegetowns create new fine, visual, and performing arts venues and the kind of cultural diversity that beckons both tourists and neighbors.

In publications as diverse as *Forbes, AARP The Magazine, Living Southern Style,* and *Outdoors Magazine,* we see common themes of promoting collegetowns as great places to settle. After all, many baby boomers are now empty nesters looking for upscale townhouses on the edge of a growing campus and just down the street from a growing medical center.

What is really intriguing about nascent collegetown trends is the deployment of a campus-style presence as a critical tool for urban redevelopment and civic enrichment. In his seminal urban planning treatise *The City in History,* Lewis Mumford reminds us that a city's history will be written not in the façades of great skyscrapers, but in the education and culture of its people. Today and tomorrow, *UB* readers may find a new collegetown springing up near their own schools and hometowns.

CHAPTER 11

Bridgewater and Other Cities Seek More Revenues from Bridgewater University and Other Schools

Christine Legere

Two college towns south of Boston say they're fed up with providing municipal services to help educational institutions in their communities without getting substantial tax payments in return.

But officials in Easton and Bridgewater are apparently running into an ivory wall. Unlike in Milton, where the positive relationship between Curry College and the town keeps channels of communication open, the discussion for more dollars than small yearly "gifts" for Easton and Bridgewater has recently taken the form of angry accusations.

Easton hosts Stonehill College, a Catholic school that owns 375 local acres. The institution is afforded double protection from local taxation, as both a religious and educational institution. Stonehill, in the past, provided an annual $20,000 "gift" to the town in lieu of taxes. "But now we get nothing," said Easton Town Administrator David Colton.

Down the road in Bridgewater, officials are also bemoaning Bridgewater State University's not paying for its impact on the local infrastructure. The school, which owns 198 acres locally, had provided a $50,000 annual gift in recent years, but stopped last year due to fiscal constraints.

Even when given, local officials complain, such gifts have failed to cover municipal expenses in either town for the services rendered.

Colton said a past Department of Revenue report estimated that Stonehill's properties would generate about $700,000 in local taxes were they not exempt. Deciding to pursue a portion of that, the Easton town administrator contacted Stonehill officials in April 2008.

"I gave them some indication of what I thought their financial impact was to the town," Colton said. "I came up with $70,000, based on the Fire Department, which is the biggest cost."

The college and town established a joint committee to review costs and impacts, but so far that hasn't produced the bigger contribution sought by Easton. "We met a few times, and the college said they'd take it under advisement," Colton said. "The next year, they sent the $20,000 with no comment otherwise."

Since then, the town-gown relationship has further soured. Easton fined Stonehill $55,000 in fall 2009 for starting a major construction project without a building permit. The college paid the fine, but has since sued the town to get the money back. Meanwhile, it has also halted its $20,000 gift.

Recent comments by Stonehill spokesman

Originally published as "Towns Asking More of Colleges, Bridgewater, Easton Lobbying," *Town & Gown Network*, April 11, 2011, by Colorado State University, Fort Collins. Reprinted with permission of the publisher.

Martin McGovern made it clear college officials are also unhappy.

"As a tax-exempt organization, the college has a long and generous record of supporting the town with annual gifts," McGovern said. "At the moment, that process is stalled by an excessive and arbitrary permit penalty. Until that case is settled, we're not in a position of providing an annual gift."

Easton selectmen chairwoman Colleen Corona said she believes Stonehill should come to the table with more and the two sides should settle the matter.

"We've seen more and more communities talk to colleges within their borders, and we've seen colleges increase their amounts to the towns," Corona said. "We'd like to do the same."

Colton, on the other hand, said he believes such discussion is futile. "Being a person who doesn't enjoy banging his head against the wall, I'll wait for a change in leadership" at the college, he said.

Meanwhile, Bridgewater State University president Dana Mohler-Faria last week jointly announced the restoration of the University's $50,000 gift with Bridgewater Town Manager Troy Clarkson and state Representative Angelo D'Emilia, a Bridgewater Republican, and promptly served up more hard feelings locally.

The announcement incensed Bridgewater's town councilors because they had been left out of mitigation discussions, and it put an even greater strain on the Town Council's tense relationship with Clarkson.

Town Councilor Peter Riordan called the $50,000 "crumbs" compared with the cost of services provided to the university by Bridgewater. A mitigation subcommittee of councilors had been formed a few months ago to pursue increased payments from all three state facilities in Bridgewater: the university, a prison complex, and an MBTA station.

The subcommittee, chaired by Riordan, will meet with prison representatives next week, but has yet to secure a meeting date with university officials.

"The term 'gift' is ridiculous," Riordan said. "How can you 'gift' something you were responsible for in the first place? And the $50,000 doesn't cover police, fire, and other resources they use. They don't want to face up to their financial responsibility to their host community."

The university uses the town's water and sewer system and pays user fees at the same rate as residents. But local officials said the town's treatment plant is in need of an upgrade due to the rapid expansion of the university in recent years.

The university should bear some of the capital costs, said Town Councilor Kristy Colon, who also serves on the mitigation committee.

Councilors said they want to hammer out a written contract that adequately reflects the impact of the college on the system.

Clarkson said university officials have agreed "to sit down and put a permanent plan in place."

But mitigation subcommittee members said they want to hear that for themselves.

Bridgewater State University officials did not return calls for comment.

Some communities have managed to maintain good town-gown ties. In Milton, Town Administrator Kevin Mearn said the town and Curry College have a mutually beneficial relationship.

In Norton, Wheaton College and its host community have historically supported each other with a "handshake" agreement, said selectmen chairman Robert Kimball. The college pays $19,500 annually in lieu of taxes, along with about $112,000 annually for noneducational holdings, which are not tax-exempt.

Kimball said he would like to pursue a more formal agreement with Wheaton.

"Unfortunately right now, the economy is as bad for them as it is for us," he said. "We brought it up last year, and we'll talk again."

CHAPTER 12

Canton and St. Lawrence University Work Together to Maintain a Positive Relationship

Daniel F. Sullivan

I have loved St. Lawrence University and the Canton community from the very first time I saw it in the fall of 1960 when I visited as a prospective student. The university, located in the heart of New York State, owes its founding in 1856 to community leaders who, in collaboration with the Universalist Church, "lit a candle in the wilderness that will never be extinguished." The university and the Canton community have, as a result, an interdependent relationship that is like — but also very different from — the typical "town-gown" pairing.

Today the university is among St. Lawrence County's largest employers, and we realize that critical to our success as a university is a healthy, attractive, and vital town of Canton with excellent K–12 schools, high-quality health care, attractive housing, affordable day care, and a growing tax base.

We are committed to working closely with Canton's business and government leaders to strengthen our community in strategic and sustainable ways. Thankfully, because of our good work together, our neighbors view us as a true partner and not the proverbial pound gorilla. They have seen how we have added financial resources and an improved quality of life to the community.

In 1997, St. Lawrence University's Board of Trustees dedicated $1 million to our first strategic and sustainable community effort, known as the Canton Initiative. Four years later, the board voted to add another $1 million to this initiative.

The goals of the ongoing initiative are:

To invest in and stimulate others to invest in properties within a defined enterprise zone so as to improve the physical attractiveness of the zone and promote its economic enhancement.

To increase directly the tax base of the village and town of Canton through investment, development, and/or divestiture of tax-exempt university property.

To establish and maintain a "partnership" spirit between the university and the Canton community as we pursue projects of mutual advantage together.

Some of the Canton Initiative projects we have completed include:

Preservation and renovation of several historic buildings to house over a dozen new retail businesses, service businesses, and restaurants.

Support of our local Habitat for Humanity chapter, to allow construction of new, energy-efficient Habitat houses. As the owners

Originally published as "Sustaining a Town-Gown Relationship," *Town & Gown Network*, July 11, 2011, by Colorado State University, Fort Collins. Reprinted with permission of the publisher.

pay back the funds, the money will be used to construct additional houses.

Support of a major cleanup project at the site of an old service station and the restoration of a village park.

Support of a planned restoration of an old grist mill that will become a cultural history center.

Support of the construction costs of a new fire station for the community.

Support of a major renovation to the historic public library, a partner serving elementary and middle school children and village residents of all ages.

As we continue to consider co-investments such as I have described, the Canton Initiative Board of Advisors, drawn from our community as well as from the university, suggested to us that what we were doing was not enough to sustain long-term, healthy growth for our community.

Growth and Challenge

We have also begun to see dramatic growth in our own competitiveness over several years, with record numbers of applications to St. Lawrence in the past two cycles. It is likely that the number of St. Lawrence faculty and staff will grow as we become even more competitive. This will increase the demand for housing in and near Canton.

Thus, the community's interest in a somewhat larger population base coupled with our expectation that we will enlarge our employee rolls have inspired a new project, Coming Home, that seeks to bring 100 new families to the region. While some of these families will be those of newly added employees, many of them

will also be our own alumni who already understand the benefits of living in a historic residential village that has two universities (Canton is also home to one of the 64 State University of New York campuses) and almost unlimited outdoor recreational opportunities, regional and Canadian cultural attractions, and great people.

We are seeking partnership with a developer on a variety of Canton Initiative/Coming Home investments that would encourage young alumni with families and those of retirement age to return to the area. Central to our plans is the opportunity to build residences that are sustainable in design and environmental sensitivity. Three such homes are in the final stages of site plan review, and we hope to begin construction this year.

We also serve as a role model for sustainability efforts in other ways, having created one of the first environmental studies programs in the nation over 30 years ago. Just recently our board of trustees voted "environmental sustainability" as a core university value. And we're seeing this value in practice as we prepare to open our Johnson Hall of Science. The two-building complex features an innovative "green" design, and both construction techniques and materials are state-of-the-art with regard to environmental sensitivity. The project has employed hundreds of local workers, who are being trained in sustainable construction and who are working with sustainable materials.

St. Lawrence's Canton Initiative and Coming Home projects are proving that town and gown can work together and that growth and sustainability can be mutually achievable goals. All of this is good news for New York's North Country.

CHAPTER 13

Chapel Hill and the University of North Carolina Cooperate on a Positive Planning Process

Roger Stancil *and* Mary Jane Nirdlinger

The theme of the 2009 ICMA Conference in Montreal was "Leading Communities to Success in the New Global Economy." ICMA Executive Director Bob O'Neill facilitated a session on Peter Block's book, *Community: The Structure of Belonging.* Block's work is about bringing people together and initiating conversations that make a difference using the six principles he identifies: invitation, possibility, ownership, dissent, commitment, and gifts.

At the same conference, David Suzuki talked about sustainable development and the state of the environment. His focus was on the unique human attributes of foresight, memory, and the ability to change. But can we really change? And can it last for more than one project?

On June 22, 2009, it took the Chapel Hill, North Carolina, town council about 20 minutes to approve a 20-year development agreement with the University of North Carolina for a new, three-million-square-foot addition to its campus. Just a year earlier, this would have seemed impossible. What made it happen? The Montreal conference offers a framework for reviewing this planning venture between the town and the university.

Residents of Chapel Hill like to think of their hometown as the village at the edge of the

Research Triangle. The home of the Tar Heels is also home to more than 50,000 residents and a sizable student population with a long tradition of community activism. It's no surprise that the university's plan to develop its 1,000-acre property in the middle of town was a source of contention between town and gown.

For nearly 20 years, the development of this property had been the focus of planning efforts, citizen reviews, political scrutiny, and cross words. Both sides had claimed sustainability as a shared goal, but sustainability often took a backseat to conflicts about traffic impacts, the community's need for affordable housing, land preservation, and density.

When the university's need for new research and expansion space brought the parties to the negotiating table again in 2008, in the form of a chancellor-appointed leadership advisory committee (LAC), the same conflicts emerged. The time was right for something new, and a changeover in town leadership helped pave the way.

The council had recently hired me as the town manager, and I saw an opportunity to approach old arguments from a new angle. Town and university staffs met to identify lessons learned from past interactions, forge a new con-

Originally published as "A Sustainable Interest in the New Global Economy," *Public Management*, Vol. 92, No. 5, June 2010, by the International City/County Management Association, Washington, DC. Reprinted with permission of the publisher.

nection based on what had gone well, and learn from what had not gone so well. The focus was on identifying shared interests and trying to put aside the well-worn arguments of the past.

Town staff worked closely with Jack Evans, executive director of Carolina North for UNC, Chapel Hill, to fashion a new approach to negotiating an agreement. With Evans's concurrence, the town engaged David Owens, a land-use planning expert and faculty member at the UNC School of Government, to be a neutral adviser to the town.

These new players had another new tool to work with: a firm deadline. June 2009 represented a key time in the town's and the university's evolution, when turnover in leadership was expected on the town council and on the university's board of trustees.

With Dr. Owens's cautiously optimistic declaration that the deadline was "achievable, but not easy," we agreed to begin negotiating from interests, not positions. This required a process that would support the goal, and a joint staff working group was formed. This group of 12 key staff leaders from the university and the town met weekly to hash out the structure of the agreement with Dr. Owens and to shape the joint staff work and public process that would ultimately lead to the adoption of the development agreement. It was a fast, unpredictable, 10-month process, and full of hurdles.

The university's new plan for the property looked to innovative site design and high-performance buildings to meet its commitment to build what UNC–Chapel Hill Chancellor James Moeser had called "a model of sustainability." The town had also been moving toward greater sustainability with its recent construction of a new operations facility, enhancement of stormwater management, and council-led land use planning that encourages higher-density infill growth in the community. As the two parties began to negotiate through a list of more than 20 topics, sustainability rose to the surface as a key interest, sometimes guiding the parties away from their earlier positions.

During the public meetings between the council and the board of trustees, things sometimes still got edgy. One stridently disputed issue was how much and with what level of cer-

tainty would the university preserve open space on the parcel. During the earlier LAC sessions, trustees had agreed to limit development to 250 acres for 50 years, but they refused to create easements or perpetual protections that limited the university's ability to use the land in the future.

At one joint meeting, councilmembers and university trustees squared off with the familiar "preserve it" versus "absolutely not" argument. In the past, this kind of exchange would have halted the discussions and led to both parties retreating into mutual distrust. Why didn't that happen this time?

The joint staff group had invited the community into the conversation at all levels. They could talk to the trustees and councilmembers; they could meet with the staffs and consultants. There were meetings on topics the community cared about, including renewable energy sources, transportation impacts, and forest management. Meeting records were online, and the open nature of the process kept everyone aware of what was at stake, what the trade-offs between competing interests were, and where compromises or concessions were made.

As the joint staff group built a base of shared goals by working with the community, the staffs, and the leadership, a new sense of collaboration emerged. Issues were becoming more interconnected through the development agreement, and everyone was beginning to see the relationship between stream preservation and density, between a successful mixed-use campus and lower traffic impacts.

A summary of the highlights of the major steps involved in this planning process are presented below. They include the costs involved, the contents of the development agreement, and the steps involved in this positive planning process. These items are presented categorically.

What Did It Cost?

- Application fee of $35,786, paid by the University of North Carolina at Chapel Hill.
- Standard rezoning application fee based on the size of the property to be rezoned.
- Development agreement fee of $300,000,

paid by the university and based on actual time spent by town employees on the agreement. This amount ended up being close to the standard per-square-foot of development calculation used for special use permits in Chapel Hill.

• Consultant fee of $46,037, paid by the town to the UNC School of Government.

What Went into the Development Agreement?

• Zoning map amendment (rezoning).
• Land use management ordinance text amendment.
• Development agreement.
• Transportation impact analysis.
• Fiscal impact analysis.
• University design guidelines for Carolina North.
• Ecological assessment of Carolina North.
• Campus master plan.
• Meetings between September 25, 2008, and June 22, 2009.
  — Council-trustee work sessions (11).
  — Regular council meetings (11).
  — Public information and comment meetings (9).
  — Joint staff meetings (bi-weekly or weekly).
  — Town advisory board meetings (some joint) (15).
  — Public hearing (1).

Working Together

Interested-based collaboration is helping the town of Chapel Hill operate differently in several other ways:

• Developing a way-finding system for vehicles and pedestrians.
• Holding conversations on public art.
• Developing short-range transit planning.
• Implementing new development review technology.
• Finding new partnerships for economic development.
• Continuing economic development.

This focus on the future of the community helped the staffs and the leadership grapple with the long-term horizon of the agreement. Some areas were identified for permanent preservation, and other areas allowed disturbances for utilities and trails. Housing had to be provided, but on a timeline that worked with the university's capital planning process. Traffic impacts would be mitigated, and extra incentives are built in for better-than-expected alternative transportation targets.

The public discussed interim agreements, and the community had real opportunities to shape the final agreement. Residents who participated in the discussions were encouraged to contribute their ideas. Not everything was included in the final draft, but such pieces as the campus-to-campus bike trail requirement were a direct result of community participation. As the development agreement took shape, the working group added provisions for continuing public participation.

A clearly voiced interest in a sustainable future became the focus for nearly every part of the agreement. Although at times people disagreed about priorities or implementation strategies, everyone was able to continue seeing the agreement as an interrelated series of sustainable conditions. No single position became the trigger for failure.

The final agreement is a living document incorporated into the town's established public participation and planning processes. Both parties have committed long-term resources in this shared vision of a sustainable future. The result is an accumulation of gifts to the future.

After working on such a complex project for so long, the staffs found that the habit of looking for shared interests and mutual goals carried over into other areas of common interest.

Chapel Hill and UNC are seeking ways to support and encourage more collaborative work. A debrief of the staffs identified opportunities for shared development of new collaboration skills. The staffs are working together to sustain the new relationship, and, judging by the conversations about bike connections and transportation impacts, things are moving along.

CHAPTER 14

Charlottesville and the University of Virginia Work Together to Solve Community Problems

Tracy Clemmons

The University of Virginia is the driving force behind much of the economic and social structure around Charlottesville. But there is more than meets the eye in the town-and-gown relationship; some good, some not so good.

How a university and the community get along is an issue of some debate. It all depends on your perspective, and what you think about the t-word. UVA students and folks who just live in town cheer together at football games, walk the corner together, and on the surface everything seems peachy. Underneath, some say this town-gown relationship is frayed.

"You can sense the animosity between the two," said UVA alumnae Tiffany Monroe. "It's always there."

Animosity, that is, between some students and "townies," as they are known. Monroe has lived in Charlottesville all her life, and she graduated from UVA last May. She says it was early in her first year when she heard students refer to the people in her community as townies.

"They're sort of treated as second class citizens within their own community," she said. "Because let's be honest, they were here first. It's seen as offensive. It's really seen as offensive."

Ike Anderson grew up in Charlottesville. He agrees that the strain is there.

"For the longest time, it was kind of taboo to even associate yourself with UVA students," said Anderson.

But he bucked that and joined X-Tasee, a UVA dance crew. He says he is not offended when students use the word townie, or when they exclude them from their activities.

"You go to the school, I live in the town," he said. "I don't think it's anything that's degrading. It's too much to say Charlottesville resident. Townie just makes it cooler, I guess, in a sense."

Not every student falls into that category, but it is enough to raise red flags. The university, as a whole and as a student body, has worked to smooth that relationship over.

"The vast majority of our students not only respect the local community, but they contribute dramatically to it," stated UVA Executive Vice President Leonard Sandridge. "They participate in what goes on. They want to be part of helping in the areas where they can."

Fourth-year Marnie Coons volunteers with Madison House. She says ever-increasing volunteer efforts have helped improve the relationship between the students and the people who live nearby.

"Students don't just volunteer once and then come back to UVA," Coons explained.

Originally published as "Town-Gown Relations in Charlottesville, Virginia," *Town & Gown Network*, May 4, 2010, by Colorado State University, Fort Collins, Colorado. Reprinted with permission of the publisher.

"They volunteer at the same place every week. So they're really able to foster a relationship with the community partner there. They're able to foster a relationship with the people they're working with."

The university's Community Relations Department also works to improve town-gown relations. Director Ida Lee Wooten has been there for ten years.

"I have seen the use of the word townie decline dramatically," she stated. "And I honestly believe it's because there are so many ongoing programs out in the community through which UVA students and faculty are working hand in hand to address current community needs."

That has been a top priority for outgoing president John Casteen over his 20 years in office. Early in his tenure, the university worked with the city on redesigning Main Street.

"Leonard Sandridge and I were going to neighborhood meetings to see what we could do to contribute to that, and what the city could do to make things easier for us," he recalled.

Casteen says the trolley that takes students and townspeople between grounds and downtown is the symbol of that effort. The university and the city of Charlottesville fund that jointly.

"The reason we do it is that for us, it's good for students to be in the downtown mall," Casteen explained. "For the city, it's a way to take students there to spend their money and to enjoy what the city really is."

Sandridge says looking for ways to improve the large-scale relationship between the university, the city of Charlottesville, and Albemarle County is always on their mind.

"Our attempt is to make sure that we work cooperatively with the city and the county so that we avoid surprises, that we participate in solving problems where we can," he asserted.

But there is still tension below the surface between students and townspeople that individuals from both sides want to see fixed. Tiffany Monroe says the first step is figuring out why the strain exists in the first place.

"I think a lot of it is lack of knowledge," she said. "And if you would just sit and spend time with the community and partake in ac-tivities with the community, you would see that it's not all that it looks to be on the outside."

"With my dance crew X-Tasee, that's one of our missions, is bridging that gap between Charlottesville and UVA," added Anderson.

"It's difficult because students are only here for four years, and there might be the sentiment that, 'How much of a difference can I make if I'm only here for four years?'" said Coons.

As he leaves his post, President Casteen is reflective on the difference his four years, five times over, have made.

"I think and I hope it has improved steadily," he said. "And I hope it's done it on a person to person basis. One person from the local neighborhoods, one person from the university forming a relationship and out of that, discovering common interests and common purposes."

Continued improvement to the town-gown relationship will certainly be something to keep an eye on in the future, especially as new UVA President Teresa Sullivan prepares to take the helm.

UVA's Local Economic Impact

A news release from the University of Virginia, titled "U.Va. Brings in More Than $1 Billion Locally, Generates More Than $600 Million From Out-of-State Sources," describes in detail state-wide, regional, and local economic impact of the University of Virginia. The local impact is highlight below:

- Student spending in the Charlottesville area totaled $211.9 million in fiscal 2005.
- Spending by U.Va. visitors totaled $122.1 million in 2005 based on 1.6 million visitor-days. Visitors included: visitors of faculty and staff, students' visitors, athletic-event season-ticket holders, Medical Center outpatients and patients' families, conference attendees, attendees at Alumni Association events, prospective students and their parents, participants in the executive education programs run by the Darden School, participants in continuing medical educa-

tion programs, presenters and attendees at the Virginia Festival of the Book, attendees at the Virginia Film Festival and participants in executive development programs run by the School of Continuing and Professional Studies.

• For every dollar attributable to the University that is spent locally, because of the multiplier effect, the ultimate local spending generated is $1.45.

• The University is the largest single employer in the Charlottesville metropolitan area, with 19,487 employees, or one-fifth of the area's total non-farm payroll employment of 95,300, in 2005.

• The U.Va. Medical Center cared for 86,021 local residents on an outpatient basis in fiscal year 2005. In addition, the Medical Center provided a significant amount of indigent care to local residents: $11.8 million of inpatient care and $15.8 million of outpatient care.

• As a tax-exempt institution of higher education, the University pays no property taxes on real estate holdings used for academic operations. In 2005, however, the University of Virginia Foundation, a component unit of the University, paid $189,694 in real estate taxes to the city of Charlottesville and $1,149,487 to Albemarle County for properties such as the Boar's Head Inn and research park buildings not used for academic purposes.

• Taxable real estate owned or rented by faculty, staff and students in the city of Charlottesville and Albemarle County was valued at $3.3 billion in 2005 and yielded $28.3 million in property tax revenues, divided nearly equally between the two localities.

For the study, the authors defined the "local area" as the Charlottesville Metropolitan Statistical Area (MSA), which has a population of 187,100, and includes the city of Charlottesville, and the counties of Albemarle, Fluvanna, Greene and Nelson.

EDITOR'S NOTE

A complete copy of the news release is available online from the website of the Office of Public Affairs, the University of Virginia, which is listed in Appendix B.

CHAPTER 15

Chicago and the University of Illinois Revitalize Inner-City Neighborhoods

David C. Perry, Wim Wiewel *and* Carrie Menendez

For most its history the American university has been treated as an enclave — a scientific and reflective ivory tower removed from the subjective turmoil of the city. More recently the university has come to be viewed by many public officials and analysts as a driver of overall urban development (CEOs for Cities 2007). University leaders often represent their institutions as "engaged" with "urban agendas" (Kellogg Commission 1999).

By 1996 there were nearly 2,000 universities and colleges in the cores of U.S. cities, and their combined budgets comprised nearly 70 percent of the more than $200 billion spent annually by universities nationwide. Put another way, urban universities were spending about $136 billion on salaries, goods, and services, which is more than nine times what the federal government spends in cities on job and economic development (ICIC and CEOs for Cities 2002, 7). Universities consistently rank among the top employers in metropolitan areas, and are among the largest and most permanent land and building owners. It is estimated that, using original purchase price as a reference, urban colleges and universities own more than $100 billion in fixed assets (ICIC and CEOs for Cities 2002, 8).

As impressive as these data are, they do not represent all of the activity or value of universities and other place-based or anchor insti-

tutions in cities, such as hospitals, civic foundations, and public utilities. These institutions are most successful as catalysts for urban change when they are fully engaged in the collective capacity of civic leaders to achieve the multiple interests of cities and communities, as a well as universities (Perry and Wiewel 2005).

Anchoring Urban Change

Our previous studies of urban anchor institutions have centered on the land or real estate practices of urban universities (Perry and Wiewel 2005; Wiewel and Perry 2008). Here we continue to use universities as the institutional lens through which to conduct a national study, but we expand the focus, seeking to address the following question: In different types of metropolitan areas, how do institutions of higher education work with the government, business, and community/civic sectors to mutually define and shape (i.e., "anchor") individual and collective interests in regard to planning and community development?

This chapter presents two cases of institutional collaboration that represent two types of cities: a global command and control center (Chicago) and a declining industrial city (Baltimore). Both have large and vigorous higher education sectors, strong community organiza-

Originally published as "The University's Role in Urban Development: From Enclave to Anchor Institution," *Land Lines*, Vol. 21, No. 3, July 2009, by the Lincoln Institute of Land Policy, Cambridge, Massachusetts. Reprinted with permission of the publisher.

tions, an organized business sector, and significant issues of local and metropolitan governance. Both also are good examples of how cities differ in the ways they benefit from place-based, multiple, and often contested relationships among anchor institutions that produce the processes of development.

Global Cities: The Case of Chicago

The geographic center of the Chicago economy and its emergence as a global, knowledge-based, command and control center for most of the past hundred years has been the Loop (Abu Lughod 1999; Sassen 2003). This downtown business district surrounded by a circuit of train tracks is the centerpiece of the city's diverse economy: financial markets; business services; corporate headquarters; transport linkages; vibrant universities; public-private partnerships; dynamic immigrant communities; and new professionals (Cortright 2006).

A core element of this geo-economic, Loop-centered strategy has been the development of key educational anchors (Cohen and Taylor 2000). In the western area of the Loop, the University of Illinois at Chicago (UIC) is the primary institution; and in the economically challenged South Loop, a mix of public and private universities and colleges make up an academic corridor.

UIC's South Campus/University Village project has transformed a depressed, albeit historically well-known, area of immigrant landing, Southside Chicago blues, and the internationally renowned Hull House and Maxwell Street Market. Now the neighborhood is a $700 million mixed-use area including university buildings, private residential development, and mixed lease/ownership retail and commercial ventures.

The entire project could not have occurred without the collaborative efforts of the mayor, city planners, and private developers, along with university and community organization buy-in, as well as university land banking and real estate development. Ironically, while the university was the anchor of development, al-

most everyone connected with the project suggests that it was the leadership of the city — from the political vision of the mayor to the technical capabilities of the planners — that created the institutional glue that made the project work. While the university was purchasing the land, the city was substantially driving the process through regulations, eminent domain, and its own prior ownership of land parcels.

Harkening back to the city's comprehensive plan from the 1960s, the current mayor, Richard M. Daley, continued his father's legacy to support an urban campus — viewing the university as a key institutional anchor driving the expansion of downtown-centered urban development. The city sold its land near the university via quitclaim deeds, and agreed to vacate certain streets, move the historic Maxwell Street Market, and undertake street improvements through the largest tax increment financing (TIF) district in history. In turn, the university agreed to finance the land use analysis and moving of the Market, thus becoming the public lightening rod for the community and historic displacement that such development represented (Weber, Theodore, and Hoch 2005).

Even after these actions had targeted the land for development, UIC still could not control the fiscal needs of the entire South Campus project through its own investment, and had to sell up to 40 percent of the property to private developers (Landek 2008). In some ways this collaboration was foreordained by the increasing scale of the project — almost 87 acres by the time the city and university were ready to proceed with development. By turning the area into a TIF district, the city contributed to renovation of the infrastructure and rationalization of the street grid for what quickly became one of the largest mixed-use development projects of any university in the nation.

In the end, the university could be credited with developing an integrated academic, residential, recreational, and commercial complex. It included housing for more than 1,500 students, 930 units of private residential housing, academic offices, 40 retail establishments, parking facilities, and athletics fields. In 1999 the total development cost was estimated at $600 million, although that figure ballooned to more than $700 million, of which UIC had invested $50 million in land acquisition, infrastructure, and other facilities. Through the issuance of tax-exempt and taxable bonds in 1999, 2000, and 2003, the university provided an additional $83 million to complete land acquisition and infrastructure improvements.

The university maintains ownership of almost 60 percent of the land and properties, and has been credited with turning the once-forbidding south edge of the campus into an attractive residential university setting. The process has contributed to enhanced university-community relations, workforce training, and service contracting, mediated by a 12-member community council that continues to meet with the university's vice chancellor for external affairs.

On the other hand, the university contributed to the destruction of the vernacular architecture of the historic immigrant entry point of the Midwest — the Maxwell Street Market and neighborhood. The university also stimulated advancing gentrification in the Near West Side and Pilsen neighborhoods of West Loop Chicago.

As a result, many community activists would disagree with the positive assessment of the city-university collaboration that is at the heart of Mayor Daley's strategic extension of universities as sources of Loop development. They would argue that, just as the original development of the UIC campus in the 1960s displaced thousands and erased important elements of Chicago's immigrant heritage in the past, the South Campus project displaced community members and businesses, removed the original site of the Maxwell Street and South Water Markets, disrupted retailers, and spread gentrification to surrounding neighborhoods.

It would be incorrect to lay these trends fully at the feet of the university, but the mix of anchor-driven collaborations that brought about the expansion of the Loop's Near West Side certainly contributed to the mixed-use urban development practices of the contemporary university and to displacement and gentrification as well.

Declining Cities: The Case of Baltimore

Institutions of higher education in Baltimore boast campuses that are not only hubs of knowledge and social interaction, but also centers of employment and ongoing construction. In 2005, research and development funding at many of the city's academic institutions amounted to $1.9 billion of investment in regional economic growth overall, and continued growth in high technology, education, and health services in particular. Despite this success, Greater Baltimore faces many of the challenges common to declining cities.

The East Baltimore Revitalization Initiative is a 10 to15 year effort to invest $1.8 billion to redevelop the 88-acre Middle East neighborhood adjacent to the Johns Hopkins Medical Institutions. Even though it was initiated by the city government under Mayor Martin O'Malley in 2001, the project received considerable skepticism and fear from many neighborhood residents, based on a history of tense relations with the medical complex.

It is hard to imagine a greater contrast between an anchor institution and its neighborhood than between the wealth and power of Johns Hopkins and the deprivation of one of Baltimore's worst neighborhoods. Through extensive discussions and negotiations, and ample funding from the Annie E. Casey Foundation and others, most issues have been resolved and the project is now managed by a quasi-public corporation, East Baltimore Development, Inc. (EBDI). The project is expected to create 2 million square feet of commercial and biotechnology research space, 2,200 new and renovated housing units, a new school, transit stops, and 4,000 to 6,000 new jobs.

The Middle East is a low-income neighborhood whose population is 90 percent African American and has a high unemployment rate. It is located about one mile from Baltimore's Inner Harbor, and immediately north of the Johns Hopkins Medical Institutions. Johns Hopkins has been in that location for more than a century, and is the largest private employer in Baltimore and in the state.

In the early 2000s, one of every four Middle East housing units was abandoned, more than in any other of Baltimore's 55 neighborhoods, and more than four times the citywide average (Baltimore Neighborhood Indicators Alliance 2005). Johns Hopkins owned many of these failing properties, but did little to maintain them or engage the neighborhood, even after several violent crimes were committed against Hopkins students and staff in 1992 (Hummel 2007, 2).

In 1994 the area was designated a federal Empowerment Zone, entitling it to significant federal funds for renewal. The Historic East Baltimore Community Action Coalition (HEBCAC), with representatives from the city, state, Johns Hopkins, and various community organizations, secured funds to lead the revitalization of the area. Their efforts focused on housing rehabilitation, but by late 2000 they had rehabilitated only 46 homes and used less than one-third of the $34.1 million in available federal funding (Hummel 2007, 26–27).

Dissatisfied with the slow-moving, community-based HEBCAC, Mayor O'Malley argued for the city to take over the project. The tension between the mayor and the community was eased with the establishment of a multi-institutional intermediary, the East Baltimore Development Corporation, with a board composed of three mayoral and one gubernatorial appointees, two members appointed by Johns Hopkins, two members from the community, three at-large members, and six city and state officials serving ex-officio. This model met the mayor's desire for control, and Johns Hopkins' desire not to be in the lead. The Goldseker Foundation agreed to provide $750,000 as startup funding for staffing. Deputy Mayor Laurie Schwartz left City Hall to become interim director.

Several local foundations joined Goldseker in sustaining this effort, the most important being the Annie E. Casey Foundation. Foundation President Doug Nelson was initially skeptical of the city's need for control and Johns Hopkins' lack of community interest. He agreed that Casey would provide up to $33 million and play an active role only if the effort would help with relocation, family assistance, job training, and other social services. Com-

bined with the federal funding still available from the original Empowerment Zone and significant new funding from Johns Hopkins and city and state government, the project became well-positioned for success.

This case is interesting because it took a multi-institutional intermediary to serve as the locus for the extensive negotiations and final resolution regarding payment of relocation benefits to residents; management of the demolition process; the preference given to local and minority contractors; the role of the private developer in the project; and the nature of ancillary services being provided by EBDI.

The relocation benefits, funded from a $21 million loan from the U.S. Department of Housing and Urban Development and $5 million from Casey and Johns Hopkins, were considerable: $109,133 per homeowner, in addition to the average $30,450 purchase price (Hummel 2007, 31). According to survey data, the majority of households described their relocation experience as positive and believed they were better off after the move (Abt Associates 2008). This was only possible because of the extraordinary involvement of institutions with a strong interest in the project's success and very deep pockets. This case study makes clear that it is possible to accomplish successful displacement and redevelopment if investors do not need financial returns, or at least not within any normal economic timeframe.

Johns Hopkins University and its Medical Center had several motivations for involvement. The conditions around the medical complex were continuing to deteriorate. While relocation was considered several times over the decades, the Medical Center represents a multibillion dollar investment in plant and equipment that would be extremely difficult to replicate; in addition, the political ramifications of such a move would be enormous.

For EBDI, the physical redevelopment aspects of the project were only part of a broad range of its activities serving Middle East and parts of the entire East Baltimore community. In a neighborhood where in 2007 more than 40 percent of adults were not in the labor force at all and 14 percent were unemployed, EBDI facilitated job referrals for almost 475 residents, and supportive family services and educational programs for more than 300 residents, assisted by the Casey Foundation, Johns Hopkins, and public agencies.

By early 2008, 723 private properties had been acquired and demolished, and approximately 400 households had been relocated. Two new residential rental buildings have been completed, with a total of 152 units. Per the agreements developed between EBDI and the original residents, those who were displaced had the right of first refusal to return to the community. In the building for the elderly, developed by the Shelter Group, 45 percent of the units have been rented to returning residents (Shea 2008).

There is a compelling logic to the East Baltimore Revitalization Initiative from an economic, social, political, institutional, and planning perspective. Given Johns Hopkins' role as the largest medical center and private employer in Maryland, and given the state's emphasis on biotechnology development, it is not surprising that redevelopment would focus around this niche, although a purely residential and mixed-use approach also would have been possible if the university's biotech interests had moved outside of the city.

Conclusions

These case studies show that urban changes in Chicago and Baltimore did not result from the singular activities of universities. They are the outcomes of ongoing relationships between universities and multiple institutions and stakeholders. It is this process of relationship building to develop the city in mutually agreeable ways that is the major lesson. Several key features of institutional collaboration can frame the study of other cities.

- **Leadership.** In each city success was directly related to the role of a mayor, university president, or foundation leader, either directly or by assigning responsibility for their vision.
- **Resources.** Success is directly equated with resources, their institutionalization or sustainability, and the ability of public, civic,

or private institutions to leverage them collaboratively.
- **Organizations.** Almost every example of the processes we are studying requires new or intermediary organizations of representation, resistance, accommodation, or development.
- **Expertise.** Each of the case studies required prodigious amounts of expertise in collective capacity building — whether in the reorganization of land around Johns Hopkins University or the multi-institutional development of the UIC South Campus expansion.

These two cases demonstrate a clear set of competitive differences or even conflicting interests among the key institutional actors that need to be identified both as part of the self-interested definition of the institutions and as potential opportunities for conflict resolution. University, government, and community actors all played prominent roles in both case studies. Civic foundation capital was more clearly a driving force in the declining industrial city of Baltimore, while private sector capital was critical in the globalizing city of Chicago.

After conducting these pilot studies, we believe even more strongly in the saliency of examining other cases to increase knowledge about the nature of the institutional relationships that produce the critical contributions of anchor institutions.

REFERENCES

Abt Associates. 2008. *East Baltimore Neighborhood Revitalization: Phase I — Baseline Summary Report 2001–2005.* Cambridge, MA: Abt Associates.

Abu-Lughod, Janet L. 1999. *New York, Chicago, and Los Angeles: America's Global Cities.* Minneapolis: University of Minnesota Press.

Baltimore Neighborhood Indicators Alliance. 2005. *Vital Signs 3.* Baltimore: University of Baltimore.

CEOs for Cities. 2007. *City Anchors: Leveraging Anchor Institutions for Urban Success.* Chicago: CEOs for Cities.

Cohen A., and E. Taylor. 2000. *American Pharaoh: Mayor Richard J. Daley: His Battle for Chicago and the Nation.* New York: Little Brown.

Cortright, J. 2006. *City Vital: New Measures of Success for Cities.* Chicago: CEOs for Cities.

Hummel, Phillip A. 2007. *East Side Story: The East Baltimore Development Initiative.* Maryland Legal History Publications. Paper 11. *http://digitalcommons.law.umaryland.edu/mlh_pubs/11*

Initiative for a Competitive Inner City (ICIC) and CEOs

for Cities. 2002. *Leveraging Colleges and Universities for Urban Economic Development: An Action Agenda.* Boston: CEOs for Cities.

Kellogg Commission on Higher Education. 1999. The engaged institution. *www.nasulgc.org/Kellogg/kellogg.htm.*

Landek, Michael, Associate Vice Chancellor for Student Affairs, University of Illinois at Chicago, personal interview, May 14, 2008.

Perry, David C., and Wim Wiewel, eds. 2005. *The University as Urban Developer: Case Studies and Analysis.* New York: M.E. Sharpe.

Perry, David C., Wim Wiewel, and Carrie Menendez. 2009. *The City, Communities, and Universities: 360 Degrees of Planning and Development.* Working Paper. Cambridge, MA: Lincoln Institute of Land Policy.

Sassen, Saskia. 2003. A global city. In Madigan, Charles, ed. *Global Chicago.* Chicago: University of Illinois Press.

Shea, Christopher, chief real estate officer, East Baltimore Development Initiative, personal interview, January 28, 2008.

Weber, Rachel, Nik Theodore, and Charles Hoch. 2005. *Private Choices and Public Obligations: Ethics of University Real Estate Development.* In Perry and Wiewel 2005.

Wiewel, Wim, and David C. Perry, eds. 2008. *Global Universities and Urban Development: Case Studies and Analysis.* New York: M.E. Sharpe.

CHAPTER 16

Cutler Bay and Miami–Dade County Public Schools Create Emergency Response Vehicles

Steven Alexander

Here in the town of Cutler Bay, Florida, a newly incorporated municipality some 10 miles south of Miami, Florida, we're all too familiar with natural disasters. When Hurricane Andrew — at the time the costliest natural disaster in our nation's history — raged through South Florida in 1992, our area was among the hardest hit. Cutler Bay is near the Atlantic coast and most of the town lies in flood-prone areas, so when the tidal surge came, much of our town was swept away.

Thousands of residents lost their homes, and most of us suffered through the sweltering summer without electricity for many weeks. Sixteen years later, we're still completing our recovery. In fact, the devastation from Hurricane Andrew and the slow, painful rebuilding was one of the catalysts that mobilized our town to incorporate two-and-a-half years ago.

Then, in 2005, only a few months after residents voted to become an independent town, Hurricane Katrina blasted through Florida, devastated New Orleans, and destroyed many areas on the Gulf of Mexico. Once again, we lost electricity for weeks. And with more than 20 inches of rain accumulated in some neighborhoods, first responders were unable to reach the people who needed help or even to transport basic supplies like water and ice to our neighbors in need.

Being Prepared

Some hard lessons were learned from those disasters: to be prepared and to be resourceful. This year, we were ready for whatever the hurricane season might literally throw at us. That's because the town's director of public works, Ralph Casals, and I recognized the need for emergency response vehicles that could make it through floods to carry supplies to residents or transport evacuated residents in the event of a catastrophe.

We first looked into purchasing emergency response vehicles that could be used in a large-scale emergency situations like a natural disaster or terrorist attack. Unfortunately, the cost was prohibitive. These types of vehicles can cost upward of $300,000 each and can sit idle for most of the year. Maintaining the vehicles is wildly expensive, not to mention the cost of depreciation.

After some creative brainstorming, Ralph Casals and I identified some alternative vehicles we might be able to use as emergency response tools. As the possibility of using surplus school

Originally published as "Rolling Relief: How Cutler Bay Turned Surplus School Buses into Emergency Response Vehicles," *Public Management*, Vol. 91, No. 1, January/February 2009, by the International City/County Management Association, Washington, DC. Reprinted with permission of the publisher.

buses as a flexible platform for that purpose emerged from our discussions, we decided to consult partnering government agencies with which we have a mutual interest in being fully prepared for emergencies. Fortunately, Cutler Bay's former Miami–Dade County school board representative, Evelyn Greer, knew of the availability of five surplus school buses. After inspecting the buses, we realized that they sit much higher off of the ground than any other vehicle we had considered. With their extra-high platforms, all buses could pass through the flood waters other vehicles typically struggled with as well as traverse other obstacles in the roads like tree branches and detritus remaining after a storm.

What's more, the buses have ample room for emergency personnel and large equipment that pickup trucks can't accommodate. If residents need to be evacuated, the buses can safely transport plenty of people in one trip, avoiding the trouble and danger of sending trucks and utility vehicles back and forth through inclement weather or treacherous areas.

After negotiating with the Cutler Bay school board, we reached an accord that exemplifies the ideal professional courtesy between government agencies. With the agreement that Cutler Bay wouldn't "flip" the school buses — sell them at a profit — the town purchased five school buses, which typically auction for $15,000 to $25,000 each, for a mere $10 each. Of course, the town had to ensure adequate money for converting the buses once they were in the town's possession, and we found a creative way to free up funds for that purpose.

Every year, the public works department applies for grants from the federal government for emergency management, many of which require the town to match the funds received. For each of the grants applied for, the town has had to provide for the same amount in the budget in case it was awarded the grant. The town, however, didn't always receive the grant requested. Thus, contingency monies were in the budget reserved for those grants, and surplus funds were directed toward retrofitting the buses.

Buses Made Ready

With the buses and conversion funds in the town's possession, it was time to plan the management of these newly acquired assets. The public works department was assigned responsibility for housing and maintaining the buses. It was decided, however, that the buses would be made available to other town departments to ensure that the entire town got the best use out of them and that they wouldn't sit idle during most of the year.

Parks and recreation, for instance, had been using them for field trips, and the schools are using them for after-school programs. They've also been used at special events where traffic-directing supplies like barricades are needed.

It was also necessary to ensure that a broad range of town staff members could use these vehicles to maximize the effectiveness of responding to a disaster. Public works and parks and recreation employees have achieved certification with commercial licenses to operate the buses, and the police department staff can do so too. Ralph Casals will soon earn his license, too.

We also had to figure out how to retrofit the buses to best serve the town's needs. First, it was obvious that plenty of cargo space was needed. Second, the buses needed to be able to safely transport emergency responders as well as citizens. Third, in accordance with the town's commitment to environmental sustainability, we wanted to minimize the pollution that these huge vehicles might produce.

With these needs in mind, we got down to business. Luckily, our work was made easier by the fact that, although the buses were old, the school board had kept them in great shape. The interiors and the seats were in excellent condition, and the engines were well maintained.

With that, converting the buses was relatively simple and quite inexpensive. Moving toward our administration's goal of becoming more "green," we retrofitted the buses to run on biodiesel fuel. Most of the seats were torn out to provide cargo space although some seats were left in place to carry passengers securely.

After painting the interiors and exteriors with the same durable mold-resistant paint used to paint airplanes, which was generously donated by a Cutler Bay resident and saved us thousands and thousands of dollars, we supplied the buses with portable generators, chain saws, traffic cones, stop signs, and barricades.

If a hurricane is heading toward Cutler Bay, the staff plans to stock buses with such other emergency supplies as water, food, blankets, tarps, and plywood to distribute to residents. With the abundance of space provided by the roomy 70-passenger and 20-passenger buses, we can transport the same volume of cargo that would require several pickup trucks, saving staff time in a situation when minutes are precious.

All this was completed in some 90 days. The buses were converted by the first week in August, just as the hurricane season was heating up. We've faced four-plus hurricane threats as of the date this was written, and we are grateful that danger has been avoided so far. After testing the buses and rehearsing their deployment with several practice runs, however, town staff feel fully prepared for whatever might come our way. It is our hope, though, that we only get to use the buses for parades and town celebrations.

Citizen Reaction

Civic leaders have been proud to receive an overwhelmingly positive response to the new buses from residents who, after the struggles of hurricane seasons past, like the feeling of preparedness and the appearance of the buses, too! We often peer out our office windows and see citizens posing by the buses for pictures.

I'm a career public servant who's worked in local government for more than two decades. Over the years, I've watched with admiration as my colleagues in other regions implement thorough and careful emergency plans and with horror when the absence of planning leads to catastrophic devastation, including the destruction and havoc in New Orleans after Hurricane Katrina ravaged the Gulf Coast and the levees failed.

And, of course, the recent images of the devastation in Haiti and Cuba from Hurricanes Gustav and Ike strike close to home for us in Cutler Bay, reminding us of the day when many people lost everything to Hurricane Andrew. We've thankfully taken several lessons to heart: that preparation is paramount, and that creativity in using the town's limited funds can serve the town better than blindly spending taxpayer money.

The surplus buses outside my office window are striking reminders of how resourcefulness-and the collaboration of government agencies — can save money, time, trouble, and even lives when a fast and effective response matters most.

CHAPTER 17

Elmira Benefits from Elmira College Students Learning About Disaster Management

Adam Prestopnik

Earlier this year, students in a graduate level disaster management course at Elmira College had the opportunity to speak with Holly Harrington, special assistant to the director of the office of public affairs at the U.S. Nuclear Regulatory Commission. The focus of this conversation was not, however, nuclear power. Rather, students were given the opportunity to learn, in depth, about one aspect of Holly's former position with the Federal Emergency Management Agency (FEMA); the creation of *FEMA for Kids*.

It is understood that anyone can be affected by a disaster, but children require special attention when it comes to explaining disasters and disaster mitigation. In 1996 Holly was given the task of creating an interactive website, to be used both at home and in the classroom, the mission of which was to educate children about disasters. Although originally designed for children in grades 3–4, the site eventually included sections that covered Kindergarten to fourth grade and is even used occasionally with older children. The main goal of the site is to educate children on what disasters are, why they happen, and what the children themselves can do to prepare for and mitigate disasters. From the moment one logs on, the appeal to children is evident ranging from Herman, the hermit crab in search

of a disaster proof shell, stories, a section for games, and an opportunity to become a Disaster Action Kid who knows how to survive and prepare for a disaster. The site even offers trading cards, modeled on baseball cards, which display rescue dogs used in various parts of the country.

The site has more sobering aspects as well, including a section of photographs of disaster damage containing straight-forward captions that explain what has occurred in plain, easy to understand language, and an interactive map of the United States that allows children to learn about possible disasters in their areas. A conscious decision was made to allow pictures of destroyed homes and cities, but not include injured or killed people or animals in any of the uploaded content.

According to Holly the site has gone through several changes since its first inception. Originally *FEMA for Kids* was to be called FEMA for School. This idea, however, was scrapped in favor of the current name that refrains from labeling the site as a purely classroom resource. The site also led to instructions pertaining to children being included in press releases. The need for this had always been evident but it was not until *FEMA for Kids* that it became easy to communicate to children on an understandable level during disasters.

Originally published as "Preparing Children for Disasters," *Disaster Recovery Journal*, Vol. 22, No. 4, Fall 2009, by Systems Support, Inc., Arnold, Missouri. Reprinted with permission of the publisher.

70

Other changes included the addition of terrorism to the *FEMA for Kids* site. Before the terrorist attacks of Sept. 11, 2001, *FEMA for Kids* was focused solely on natural disasters. After such a prevalent attack however, it became necessary to give terrorism a real presence on the site. Holly recalls how on 9/11 repeated footage of aircraft flying into the twin towers caused children to think that the event was being repeated all over the country because they did not understand that they were seeing recurring footage. Although a request from the government ended the replaying within half an hour, it was evident that children, regrettably, needed to be educated about terrorism as well as natural disasters.

Although the main goal of the site was instruction for children, there was a second motivation behind beginning *FEMA for Kids*. Adults in the United States seemed reluctant to heed advice pertaining to disaster mitigation, and it was hoped that if children were well versed in disaster preparedness they might convince their parents. This was envisioned as being similar to the way in which children sometimes remind their parents to wear a seatbelt or hound them to stop smoking. The site could both educate children and hopefully work towards changing bad habits in their parents.

FEMA for Kids had to appeal to all races and creeds across the nation, and therefore the illustrations on the site are either cartoon animals or very ambiguous in terms of ethnicity. Additionally it was understood that in 1996, when the site was released, many families would not have internet access at home. Therefore the site content was distributed on CD, and the stories contained therein were distributed in book form as well.

Since its inception, *FEMA for Kids* has been used in homes and classrooms across the nation to educate children and their families on disaster preparedness, mitigation and recovery.

FEMA for Kids can be accessed at http://www.fema.gov/kids/.

This Federal government website is accessible 24–7 to citizens of all ages. This FEMA website lists a four (4) step plan for young people to prepare for emergencies, either natural or man-made. These steps include:

1. Know the Facts
2. Make a Plan
3. Build a Kit
4. Get Involved

There are also three (3) additional sections of this website dedicated to:

1. Graduate from Readiness U!
2. Fun and Games
3. Parents and Teachers

Several resources and policies are also highlighted on this *FEMA for Kids* website. They include the following links:

1. FEMA Website
2. DHS Website
3. Disaster Assistance
4. Citizen Corps
5. USA.gov
6. Freedom of Information Act
7. No FEAR Act Data
8. Community and State Information
9. Equal Opportunity Data
10. Privacy Policy
11. Accessibility

This information is also available in a dozen different languages. For different languages, all you have to do is click on a "language" link.

Young people can also follow FEMA for Kids on the following five (5) websites:

1. Facebook
2. Twitter
3. Email Sign-Up
4. FEMA YouTube
5. FEMA Blog

Lastly, and possibly most importantly, this website lists the following eight (8) types of disasters contained in their "readiness" website database:

1. Hurricanes
2. Winter Storms
3. Floods
4. Earthquakes
5. Tornados
6. Wildfires
7. Biological Threats
8. Pandemic

Some cities even have *Localized Ready Programs* for young people to sign-up and attend. If you wish to see where these programs are located throughout the nation, click on this website menu link. Also, any questions can be directed right to FEMA officials via the "Contact Us" link on their website!

CHAPTER 18

Emeryville and the Emery Unified School District Jointly Improve the Quality of Life

Deborah L. McKoy, Ariel H. Bierbaum *and* Jeffrey M. Vincent

The U.S. Secretary of Housing and Urban Development's (HUD) Secretary Shaun Donovan has made it clear that advancing "social and economic justice" in our nation's cities will require "building communities in a more integrated and inclusive way." Transforming distressed neighborhoods into vibrant and desirable communities necessitates more than housing redevelopment: "a HOPE VI development that is surrounded by disinvestment, by failing schools or by other distressed housing has virtually no chance of truly succeeding." HUD realizes that it must link "housing interventions more closely with intensive school reform and early childhood innovations." In the Obama administration, HUD is now "standing shoulder-to-shoulder" with the Department of Education. As a result, federal policy is catching up with local practice: "Example after example in communities across the country has shown us that the correlation between successful housing and good schools is not just a theory — it's practice."[1]

These major developments make it clear that uniting urban planning and educational reform for transformative change is no longer a radical idea but a practical imperative; one that promises to move us as a nation from pockets of positive change to sustainable systems of opportunity that serve all families.

For the past five years, UC Berkeley's *Center for Cities & Schools* (CC&S) has worked to both integrate urban planning, educational reform, and policymaking and include youth and other marginalized groups in local and regional efforts aimed at building healthy, equitable and sustainable communities. Our work is built upon a three-legged stool for effective city-school collaboration: (1) leverage bricks and mortar investments for innovative built environments; (2) implement and align systemically grounded innovations in education; and (3) institutionalize innovations in collaborative policymaking.

CC&S's *PLUS* (Planning and Learning United for Systemic Change) *Leadership Initiative* has been a major engine of such work. PLUS is a multi-year initiative designed to prepare current and future educational, community, and civic leaders in the San Francisco Bay Area region; develop collaborative, mutually-beneficial policies and practices; and to facilitate comprehensive systems-change across city government and school districts. PLUS aims to

Originally published as "The Mechanics of City-School Initiatives: Transforming Neighborhoods of Distress and Disrepair into Neighborhoods of Choice and Promise," *Policy Brief Report*, November 2009, by the Center for Cities & Schools, University of California, Berkeley. Reprinted with permission of the publisher.

achieve equitable, positive outcomes for all students, families, and communities.

This policy brief introduces HUD and others to our evidence-based framework for action: the *10 PLUS Mechanics of Change*. Grounded in lessons learned from both nationally recognized policies and practices and the hard-won results of Bay Area initiatives, our *10 PLUS Mechanics of Change* explain the nuts and bolts of city-school district initiatives for community and school transformation. We illustrate the tools and strategies in our framework by describing the experience of three PLUS collaborations. The brief ends with a set of recommendations for how HUD and other agencies can support local and regional efforts to transform neighborhoods of distress and despair into neighborhoods of choice and promise.

Building an Evidence-Based Foundation from Nationally Recognized Policies and Practices

In this section we survey a number of nationally recognized policies and practices that have influenced both CC&S's thinking and the work of PLUS participants. In doing so, we establish an evidence-based foundation for our *10 PLUS Mechanics of Change*.

- **From Local Approach to National Model: The Harlem Children's Zone.** Geoffrey Canada, founder and CEO of the acclaimed nonprofit organization Harlem Children's Zone (HCZ), is now leading much of the national conversation on the importance of pursuing a "place-based" approach coupled with "people-based" strategies for educational improvement that expands beyond elementary school to students' and families' entire lives. Canada and HCZ are committed to do "whatever it takes" to provide all children in Harlem with the resources and support they need to succeed from before birth through college. With an annual budget of nearly $60 million, HCZ serves more than 10,000 young people in a 97-block neighborhood of Harlem

by offering essential services and support systems to parents, students and families. The Obama administration's proposed "Promise Neighborhoods" initiative in the U.S. Department of Education aims to replicate the success of the HCZ in poverty-stricken areas of twenty U.S. cities.[2] Neighborhoods of promise are future oriented: they invest in and leverage all resources today in order to create new opportunities for residents and their children tomorrow.

- **Community Schools and Full Service Schools** offer a model of school and community improvement through increasing resources and services to address the needs of the "whole child" to better prepare them to succeed in school. Common strategies include providing medical, social, and other services *inside* schools, creating what has come to be known as "full-service" or "community" schools. The Coalition for Community Schools, a national research and advocacy organization, has made tremendous strides in creating community schools in underserved neighborhoods all across the country. As the Coalition notes, "[The community school's] integrated focus on academics, health and social services, youth and community development, and community engagement leads to improved student learning, stronger families and healthier communities."[3] John Sugiyama, Superintendent of Emery Unified School District and PLUS participant, explains what this model has meant to his team: "The Emeryville Center of Community Life really takes 'community schools' to the next level. It's not about building or renovating schools and creating spaces for a variety of other services to come in to support the education of the children. It's really about creating a true community center that is designed to provide a rainbow of services to all residents in the community. In this sense it's not about a physical facility per se; it's really about the concept of how you transform a community to really meet the needs of the entire community and to really impact the quality of life."

- **P-16 ("preschool through college") educational** strategies aim to close the ever-widening achievement gap.[4] Governors in seventeen states have established P-16 Councils to foster "unprecedented collaboration between all segments of the business community, higher education, and the K–12 system" in an effort to align the K–12 system with higher education systems and the current needs of the workforce to promote better articulation amongst all stakeholders."[5] Philanthropies such as the MacArthur Foundation in Illinois and Education Quest Foundation in Nebraska have funded the development of high quality childcare and preschool programs that support an individual's learning trajectory from "birth to college."[6] The P-16 movement is an important reminder that families will choose to stay in neighborhoods that provide lifelong trajectories of educational opportunity for their children and that other families will choose to move into neighborhoods that promise as much.

- **Career and Technical Education (CTE)—** *combining preparation for both college and careers*—builds on more than two decades of research and policies. High schools no longer track some students directly into entry-level work; instead, preparing all students for postsecondary education is a nearly universal goal. CTE is a strategy that prepares students for college while at the same time supports the development of work-related skills and connects students to learning opportunities in communities and workplaces outside of school through internships, apprenticeships, career academies, and other innovative strategies.[7] In addition to support from federal, state, and local educational agencies, many large foundations have recently made CTE a top priority. For example, the Irvine Foundation has invested more than $11 million in ten school districts to develop "multiple pathways" across California. The multiple pathways approach to high school education combines academic learning and career skills to give students the intellectual and real-world experience they need for success in college, career, and life.[8] CC&S's own award winning Y-PLAN (Youth-Plan, Learn, Act, Now) initiative, a university-community partnership at UC Berkeley,[9] and the national Youth Leadership by Design Initiative, a HUD program from 1999 to 2005 modeled on Y-PLAN, build on many of the same principles behind CTE.

- **Smart Growth & Regional Equity** movements offer insight to school and neighborhood improvement from a broader scale. Smart growth emerged out of a history of "public planning and development policies that encouraged rapid, low-density suburban growth, often at the expense of central cities, older suburbs, rural communities, and their low-income residents."[10] The smart growth movement has set forth a community and regional land use framework for curbing suburban sprawl through more dense and efficient land use planning, emphasizing reinvestment in cities and inner suburban communities with existing infrastructure. Smart growth advocates focus on creating a mix of housing types, multi-modal transportation, and retail in all communities to encourage walking and bicycling and preserve open space. Increasingly, the smart growth movement has also focused on the role of schools in metropolitan growth and on how designing neighborhood-oriented schools can foster healthier neighborhoods and more robust school-community connections. The regional equity movement provides a framework that enhances the efforts of smart growth advocates and aims to redirect regional, state, and federal growth management policies through a lens of social and economic justice for low income communities and communities of color. PolicyLink, a national think tank and leader of the movement, notes that at its core, "regional equity seeks to ensure that individuals and families in all communities can participate in and benefit from economic growth and activity throughout the metropolitan region — including access to high-performing schools, decent affordable housing located in attractive neighbor-hoods, living wage jobs, and proximity to transit and important amenities, such as supermarkets and parks."[11] Leaders like Doug Shoemaker, Director of the San Francisco Mayor's Office of Housing, un-derstand that innovation on the local level is not enough: "there is a profound need to have a conversation at the regional level ... but our systems of governance don't provide us with the opportunity to have that conversation." Smart growth and re-gional equity provide such a framework to focus on regional dynamics of growth and equity.

- **School-Oriented Community Develop-ment** is a bricks-and-mortar strategy that prioritizes the rehabilitation and/or new construction of schools as a centerpiece to new housing development, making it more appealing to a mix of residents. Several leading affordable housing developers such as McCormick, Baron, and Salazar in con-junction with their nationally recognized nonprofit arm, Urban Strategies, have uti-lized the national HOPE VI program to focus specifically on the redevelopment of elementary schools as a means to create vi-brant mixed-income housing communities in a number of cities including St. Louis and Atlanta. The nonprofit organization Enterprise Community Partners (ECP) has documented many of these successes — providing "existing proofs" that housing redevelopment and education can have a positive, mutually beneficial relationship.[12] This movement highlights the importance of inviting the private sector to participate in integrated initiatives.

- **Schools as Centers of Community.** Devel-oped largely by nationally recognized ur-ban planners and designers, this approach to planning strategically locates schools in neighborhoods so that they are easy to get to and act as central public spaces for events and community building. A school's convenient location for families and com-munities enables more walking and bicy-cling to school and likely also means that more people can come to the school to ac-cess services, programs, and/or activities housed there. In effect, the schools as cen-ter of community concept combines the ideas of smart growth advocates about effi-cient land use with the service provision perspective of community schools.[13] The BEST collaborative, funded by the Ford Foundation, provides model policies for building high performing school facilities in all communities. The schools as centers of community movement is an important example of how planning and community development practice is increasingly aware of the complex and reciprocal relations be-tween the built environment and learning opportunities.

Having surveyed some of the develop-ments that have been especially influential on our thinking, we now introduce the three city-public school initiatives partnering with the PLUS Leadership Initiative to illustrate our framework for action. While based in the Bay Area, these initiatives and communities reflect many common challenges and socio-economic contexts identified in neighborhoods with con-centrated poverty across the nation.

Innovative City-School District Partnerships from the PLUS Leadership Initiative

The PLUS Leadership Initiative is a multi-year effort sponsored by the Walter and Elise Haas Fund, the Stuart Foundation, and the national BEST Collaborative. PLUS lever-ages the resources of CC&S and the Graduate School of Education, Department of City and Regional Planning, and Haas School of Business Center for Nonprofit and Public Lead-ership at UC Berkeley to support innovative city-school initiatives. Now in its fifth year, PLUS is not a "model" program offering itself for replication, but rather a strategy that aims to facilitate and document comprehensive sys-tems-change. The diverse experiences — suc-cesses and setbacks — of participating city-school district teams have grounded and refined CC&S's framework for action. While PLUS involves a growing number of teams throughout the Bay Area region, the following descriptions feature three initiatives that represent a diverse range of small and large urban districts, cities and socio-economic contexts.

The Emeryville Center of Community Life (ECCL) in Emeryville, California, aspires to be a "21st-century urban place where we will play, learn, grow, and come together as a community. By offering a variety of educational, recreational, cultural, and social opportunities, as well as services and programs that support lifelong learning and healthy lifestyles, the Center will transform the quality of life of all Emeryville citizens."[14] Emeryville is a 1.2 square mile, bustling urban city of about 10,000 residents in the heart of the San Francisco Bay Area, wedged between Berkeley, Oakland, and the Bay. While the city boasts tremendous resources from large companies such as Pixar and Novartis, city leaders and residents refer to the "two Emeryvilles," describing a great divide between the newer, wealthier "loft dwellers" and longer-standing residents, primarily families of color who reside in older homes in the lower income areas.

Emery Unified School District (EUSD) serves about 800 students at its two schools — Anna Yates Elementary and Emery Secondary School. By contrast to the relative wealth of the city overall, approximately 80 percent of EUSD students qualify for free or reduced-price meals. Likewise, while the City is quite racially diverse, EUSD is 89 percent students of color, with the majority of students identifying as Black or African American. Working to get past a recent state takeover for fiscal mismanagement and low academic performance, EUSD is seeking to improve its educational system significantly by becoming a far more integral part of the city revitalization efforts and is improving academically in the process. The Emeryville Center of Community Life is a project that has and continues to be jointly visioned, planned, developed, funded, and managed by the City and the District.

The Nystrom United Revitalization Effort (NURVE) in Richmond, CA, is a collaborative effort of more than a dozen key city stakeholders spearheaded by Bay Area Local Initiatives Support Corporation (LISC). Partners include the City of Richmond, Richmond Housing Authority (RHA), Richmond Children's Foundation (RCF), West Contra Costa Unified School District (WCCUSD), local neighborhood councils, and community residents. Launched in 2001, NURVE aims to revitalize the economy and improve quality of life in the area surrounding the Nystrom Elementary School and Dr. Martin Luther King, Jr. Community Center and Park (Santa Fe and Coronado neighborhoods) through over $218 million in capital building projects, programming and community partnerships, and greater connections between stakeholders. The area was historically a site of great industrial, economic, and social progress during World War II — and home to the nation's first child care center built to support women ship yard workers, better known as "Rosie the Riveters." Today, Nystrom is one of the poorest communities in California with a high school graduation rate of only 28 percent. Despite the odds, NURVE is bringing the community together to improve conditions for all residents to succeed in school and beyond through the development of district supported elementary- and high- charter schools, the renovation of the local Nystrom public elementary school, 210 units of affordable housing, new recreational park space and rehabilitated community center.

The HOPE SF Initiative in San Francisco, CA, seeks to transform San Francisco's most distressed public housing sites into vibrant, thriving communities. Modeled on the national HOPE VI initiative, San Francisco is revitalizing eight of the most distressed public housing developments in the city into mixed-income developments that include new affordable and market-rate homes, as well as parks and other public amenities for residents and neighbors alike. Launched in 2007 by Mayor Gavin Newsom, and now driven by the Mayor's Office of Housing and the San Francisco Housing Authority, HOPE SF represents a unique opportunity to take a systemic approach to educational improvement and housing redevelopment, aiming to lift housing, security, and educational quality for all students and families. The initiative recognizes that all families need and deserve the opportunity to have safe, high quality housing and neighborhoods and good educational options. They also recognize that creating vibrant and successful mixed-income communities requires high quality educational options for all families. To this end, city leaders are working with the San Francisco Unified School District (SFUSD) to create vibrant communities for all of San Francisco's families, starting with the Hunters View revitalization, the first HOPE SF site located in the Bay View/Hunters Point neighborhood.

10 PLUS Mechanics of Change

After five years of research and collaborative practice with PLUS city-school district teams, CC&S has identified a set of recommendations and related tools and strategies that can be used in the difficult yet necessary work of building communities in more integrated and inclusive ways. We present the elements of the framework in a particular order, but in practice they are often overlapping, flexible, and iterative. Systemic change ultimately depends on adapting, aligning, and implementing strategies in response to needs and circumstances of each city and local educational agencies and organizations.

Recommendation One

Cultivate visionary leadership at all levels, across all agencies, and identify a "champion" to harness ideas, energy, and concerns, and mobilize collective resources.

Leadership among all stakeholders is essential and requires time and cultivation. Further, a designated entity or person capable of offering a united voice is critical to effective collaboration. Many leaders may intuitively know greater collaboration would be beneficial, however, both the decades and history of isolated, "silo" practices of civic and educational professionals and agencies and the need to invest in planning and preparation should not be underestimated.

TOOLS AND STRATEGIES

Third-party intermediaries can play im-

portant roles to build capacity (e.g., conducting training, coaching, professional development; establishing regional learning networks; and/or situating local work in broader national contexts through research and documentation).

Recommendation Two

Create and formally adopt a shared vision for the collective future of urban revitalization and education.

An explicit and public vision statement provides the basis of a "story" from which all stakeholders can work and allows for consistent communication of goals across silos. The formal adoption of that vision by governing bodies (e.g., boards of education and city councils) ensures the sustainability of and commitment to that shared mission.

TOOLS AND STRATEGIES

Integrated master planning and joint grant writing create forums for stakeholders to work together, identify the win-win early on, lay out a plan for work moving forward, and grapple with important questions to formalize the shared vision and mission for future collaborative work.

Recommendation Three

Maximize all physical infrastructure and resources.

Strategic, coordinated capital investments are needed to foster good urban design that enhances safety while maximizing connectivity and access. Coordinated capital investments can also leverage physical improvements to local school facilities as part of larger redevelopment strategies.

TOOLS AND STRATEGIES

Integrated master plans provide a framework for optimizing physical infrastructure and point to specific implementation strategies such as, joint use of school and community facilities, the strategic co-location of programming, and quality urban design that promotes safe physical paths between facilities and foster connectivity.

Recommendation Four

Create formal agreements that hold the shared vision, articulate mutual accountability, and ensure sustainable collaboration.

Formal written agreements are the vehicle to sustain the vision, ideas, and agreements crafted among partners amidst constant political change, including the all-too-frequent leadership and staff turnover in public agencies. Agreements evolve and must be updated over the life of the project, formalizing planning, implementation, and maintenance phases across physical development and programming/service provision.

TOOLS AND STRATEGIES

A variety of formal, binding and nonbinding agreements are available for cross agency collaboration and serve a range of purposes, depending on the local context.

- **Memorandum of Understanding (MOU)** is a very general term that describes almost any written agreement between multiple parties. It "is not meant to be binding and it does not hinder the parties from bargaining with a third party."[15]
- **Joint Use Agreement** is a type of MOU and is specific to facilitating joint construction, operation, and maintenance of a facility.[16]
- **Joint Powers Authority** is the creation of an entirely new public agency that combines the powers of both parties and allows for greater independence.

Recommendation Five

Establish a robust interagency communications strategy that aligns internal communications, shared decisionmaking, and interagency data systems.

Sharing information across educational, planning, and redevelopment agencies can be tremendously challenging and frustrating, and yet ongoing and updated information is critical for collaborative policymaking. Specifically, data sharing can be challenging given issues of confidentiality, disparate tracking methods, and different technology. Despite this, all agencies must be empowered with the most updated and complete data to make informed, data-drive policy decisions.

TOOLS AND STRATEGIES

A clear communication strategy that includes working groups, task forces, and/or joint committees is critical for ongoing information sharing and ongoing collaboration. Information technologies (e.g., online project management software) and shared or aligned data system, such as SchoolPower, are ways that city agencies and districts can track data in a single system.

Recommendation Six

Provide comprehensive social service support systems that are aligned to educational needs and opportunities.

Across the nation, researchers and practitioners are recognizing the need for aligned education and social service systems that address all needs of the child — twenty-four hours a day, seven days a week — throughout their lifetime. Access to high quality education, mental and physical health services, after-school programming, academic enrichment, and cultural activities are critical to success of children and families.

TOOLS AND STRATEGIES

Access to these services can happen through a number of venues — *in and off* of a school site. For example, a school may partner with a county health department to bring a mobile health/eye clinic to school sites. Local community-based organizations and city and county agencies may have services and programming for students adjacent to or nearby the school building. Finally, some schools adopt a full-service or community-school model, whereby a range of social and health services are housed in the school building itself.

Recommendation Seven

Prepare all students for college and future careers.

In far too many low-income communities of color, college-going rates are low — and graduation rates even lower. Special attention to creating a "college-going culture," providing rigorous and relevant curriculum, and supports for students from pre-school through college are critical to ensuring the success of all students.

TOOLS AND STRATEGIES

Leverage existing evidence-based educational reform strategies and investments that prepare students for college and career-oriented trajectories. Work with local schools and district to ensure that curriculum content aligns with college requirements and that all students gain access to high quality elementary, middle and high school opportunities. Partnering with local universities and implementing "P-16" initiatives are other opportunities for connecting young people to college and career.[17]

Recommendation Eight

Engage children and youth authentically in the policymaking and planning for the revitalization of their neighborhoods.

Young people offer unique and important perspectives and insights into what makes a joyful, healthy, and vibrant place to live and learn. Further, engagement in real public policy questions cultivates young people as civic leaders and exposes them to new college and career opportunities. Such engagement also leads to greater levels of ownership and "buy in" to redevelopment efforts as young people are often more than 50 percent of a community and too often feel alienated from such processes. Finally, this kind of engagement provides academically rigorous educational experiences and can be connected to young people's schoolwork and college preparation.

TOOLS AND STRATEGIES

Initiatives such as Y-PLAN, a nationally recognized university-community collaborative to engage youth in city planning and development, among other national projects, offer (1) authentic problems for young people to grapple with; (2) opportunities for shared decisionmaking with adults; and (3) success for individuals and institutions, which ensure sustained involvement.

Recommendation Nine

Coordinate a consistent external communications strategy to the public.

Once a shared vision is established, it is essential to communicate agreed upon strategies and detailed plans to the broader community to gain buy-in, maintain public accountability, and sustain support. Materials and outreach strategies much reach diverse people — teachers, parents, residents, business owners, young people, etc.— in multiple venues and locations.

TOOLS AND STRATEGIES

Leverage existing lines of communication across agencies to multiple constituencies — e.g., housing developers can outreach to local parent-teacher associations (PTAs), while schools and districts can outreach to tenant associations. Interactive websites, regular newsletters, and well-advertised accessible public meetings provide avenues for transparency and feedback with city leaders.

Recommendation Ten

Incorporate ongoing research and assessment to guarantee a constantly improving and transparent system.

Evaluations must inform the whole process and not simply provide post-project feedback. Outcomes should be defined collaboratively and reinforce the interconnectedness of the project while also addressing traditional indicators of success (e.g., promotion and graduation rates). Finally, assessments should focus not only on discrete tangibles but also on process and relationships as benchmarks of success.

TOOLS AND STRATEGIES

On-going formative and summative evaluations by university partners, firms, or nonprofit intermediaries and cross agency internal assessment systems will support ongoing collaborative work. Most importantly, on-going assessments can hold diverse stakeholders mutually accountable to one another and identify areas for improvement to stakeholders and the public. For example, each of these three case studies have partnered with the PLUS Leadership Initiative and prioritized documenting the processes and outcomes.

Conclusion: Places, People, and Policies

We stand at a unique and historic crossroads, calling us to move beyond strategies that foster isolated pockets of positive change and toward the creation of sustainable systems of opportunity that serve all families.

As described in this brief, the work of CC&S proceeds from the recognition that the relationship between the conditions for learning and the vitality of neighborhoods is a two-way street. Both educators and city leaders in urban revitalization must recognize their mutual impact and collective power to structure success for all young people and families in and outside of school. While charter schools and other local and community innovations increasingly offer exciting alternatives to traditional education, the fact remains that they only account for 2.4 percent of our nation's school children. This being the case, systemic change ultimately depends on redoubling our efforts to inspire and hold accountable the local schools and districts that are responsible for educating 86 percent of our nation's children.[18]

To this end, we propose that local and national policymakers build on lessons learned from coast to coast — from the Harlem Children's Zone to the San Francisco Bay Area city-school partnerships to the many innovative and important initiatives in between. The *10 PLUS Mechanics of Change* provides a framework of action that can inform the work of cities and school districts seeking to move past the national conversations into local action.

With the complex and reciprocal relations between places, people, and policies in mind,

we conclude this brief by suggesting how HUD and other federal agencies can encourage and support city-school initiatives and align their work to the three-legged stool of effective city-school collaboration.

LEVERAGE BRICKS AND MORTAR INVESTMENTS FOR INNOVATIVE BUILT ENVIRONMENTS

The federal government can incentivize city and school leaders to break from decades of isolated practices and policies and come together to think in new ways about how educational and community facilities and environments can provide physical and social pathways to opportunity for all residents. Education does not stop at the gates of schools; our physical neighborhood environments structure access to learning opportunities and set the conditions for all students to be prepared and ready to learn. Innovative and strategic land use decisions among diverse stakeholders make this possible.

What HUD Can Do

- Support local integrated master planning processes to align goals and strategies.
- Prioritize projects that incorporate the joint use of school and community facilities to increase educational supports, physical activity, and community programs/amenities.

ALIGN FUTURE REDEVELOPMENT TO SYSTEMATICALLY GROUNDED INNOVATIONS IN EDUCATION

After a century of "tinkering toward utopia" in educational reform, communities and their school districts are starting to embrace the idea that preparing all students to succeed in the 21st century requires both local innovations and system-level changes that reflect the fact that learning happens before, during, and after school bells rings.[19] A student's ability to do well in his or her education demands that he or she has the right conditions for learning — both in and outside of school buildings. All students need and deserve an education that is engaging, rigorous, and relevant, starting in preschool (or before) and extending all the way through college.

What HUD Can Do

- Ensure all Federal Notice of Funding Availability (NOFA) and subsequent applications align with priorities of Department of Education funding to a) maximize local coordination with traditional and alternative education systems and b) leverage local educational foundation support to schools and districts.
- Require local social service plans that are aligned to educational goals and district-wide resources and service provision.
- Support innovative planning and development processes that authentically incorporate young people and educational stakeholders.

INSTITUTIONALIZE INNOVATIONS THROUGH COLLABORATIVE POLICYMAKING

Ultimately, a transformation in the paradigm of cities and schools requires systemic change, but this change is a function not just of the individual capacities within our public agencies. As Oakland Superintendent Anthony Smith says, "It's not just a personal responsibility or an institutional responsibility, it's a system responsibility." This calls on all individual actors — leadership, staff, and community leaders alike to become clear and passionate about changing the status quo, to break down the silos that currently structure policies and policymaking practice, and to have the courage to make mistakes and keep trying to get it right.

What HUD Can Do

- Fund ongoing formative and summative assessments that incorporate aligned benchmarks of educational and neighborhood improvement.
- Support local capacity-building for leadership to learn how to work collaboratively and develop mutually beneficial policies and practices.
- Fund local collaborations with demonstrated capacity of shared agreements, governance

structures, and mutually beneficial policies and practices while inspiring new partnerships through planning grants.

NOTES

1. From "Prepared remarks for Secretary of Housing and Urban Development Shaun Donovan at the Brookings Institution Metropolitan Policy Program's Discussion — 'From Despair to Hope: Two HUD Secretaries on Urban Revitalization and Opportunity,'" located at www.hud.gov/news/speeches/2009-07-14.cfm.

2. Promise Neighborhoods: Recommendations for a National Children's Anti Poverty Program Inspired by the Harlem Children's Zone®, PolicyLink and Harlem Children's Zone (2009).

3. Coalition website http://www.communityschools.org/index.php?option=content&task=view&id=6&Itemid=27. Additional information on community schools: Martin J. Blank, Atelia Melville, and Bela P. Shah, *Making the Difference: Research and Practice in Community Schools* (Washington, DC: Coalition for Community Schools, 2003); James G. Cibulka and William J. Kritek, eds. *Coordination Among Schools, Families, and Communities: Prospects for Educational Reform* (Albany: State University of New York Press, 1996); Robert L. Crowson and William L. Boyd, Coordinated Services for Children: Designing Arks for Storms and Seas Unknown, *American Journal of Education* 101 (1993): 140–179; Joy Dryfoos, Jane Quinn, and Carol Barkin, *Community Schools in Action: Lessons from a Decade of Practice* (Oxford: Oxford University Press, 2005); Joy Dryfoos, *Full Service: A Revolution in Health and Social Services for Children, Youth and Families* (San Francisco: Jossey Bass, 1994).

4. "By bringing everyone to the table and coordinating the efforts of many groups throughout the community, P-16 councils (consisting of representatives from education, business, government, and the community) have achieved successes that no institution could have realized acting on its own. By taking a data driven and student centered approach, P-16 teams have implemented academically rich curricula and common approaches to professional development. They also have identified institutional barriers and formulated creative strategies to smooth the transition from elementary to middle school, middle to high school, and high school to college." Dennis McGrath, *Convergence as Strategy and as Model: Linking P-16 Education Reform and Economic Development* (Knowledge Works Foundation, Ohio, 2008).

5. *Executive Summary: A Framework for Closing California's Academic Achievement Gap*, California Department of Education (2008), p. 5.

6. For more information on linking childcare and economic development see: http://www.lincc childcare.com/Content/10005/resources.html.

7. For more information on the evolution of CTE and related research see: J. Oakes and M. Saunders, eds., *Beyond Tracking* (Harvard Education Press, 2008); D. Stern and D. Wagner, eds, *International Perspectives on the School-to-Work Transition* (Cresskill, NJ: Hampton Press, 1999). D. Stern, N. Finkelstein, J. R. Stone III, J. Latting, and C. Dornsife, *School to Work: Research on Programs in the United States* (London and Washington: Falmer Press, 1995); D. Stern, M. Raby, and C. Dayton, *Career Academies: Partnerships for Reconstructing American High School* (San Francisco: Jossey Bass, 1992).

8. See Irvine Foundation — http://www.irvine.org/grant making/grantmaking-programs/youth/multiplepathways.

9. Deborah L. McKoy and Jeffrey M. Vincent, Engaging Schools in Urban Revitalization: The YPLAN (Youth — Plan, Learn, Act, Now!), *Journal of Planning Education and Research* 26 (2007): 389 403, 2007.

10. Funders' Network for Smart Growth and Livable Communities, *Regional Equity and Smart Growth: Opportunities for Advancing Social and Economic Justice in America* (2004), p. 1. Additional references on smart growth and schools include: Constance E. Beaumont with Elizabeth G. Pianca, *Historic Neighborhood Schools in the Age of Sprawl: Why Johnny Can't Walk to School* (Washington, DC: National Trust for Historic Preservation, 2002); Council of Educational Facility Planners International, Inc., and U.S. Environmental Protection Agency, *Schools for Successful Communities: An Element of Smart Growth* (Scottsdale, AZ: Council of Educational Facility Planners International, 2004); Reid Ewing and William Greene, *Travel and Environmental Implications of School Siting* (Washington, DC: U.S. Environmental Protection Agency, 2003). Local Government Commission, *New Schools for Older Neighborhoods: Strategies for Building Our Communities' Most Important Assets* (Washington DC: National Association of Realtors, 2002).

11. *Regional Equity and Smart Growth*, p. 1.

12. Jill Khadduri, Heather Schwartz, and Jennifer Turnham, "Reconnecting Schools and Neighborhoods: An Introduction to School Centered Community Revitalization" (Enterprise Community Partners, 2007). Additional references include: Paul C. Brophy, *Making the School Housing Connection Work: A Briefing Paper for the Enterprise Foundation's Real Estate Leadership Council* (Columbia, MD: The Enterprise Foundation, 2004); Connie Chung, Connecting Public Schools to Community Development, *Communities & Banking*, Winter (2005), 10–16; Jill Khadduri, Jennifer Turnham, Anne Chase, and Heather Schwartz, *Case Studies Exploring the Potential Relationship Between Schools and Neighborhood Revitalization. Prepared for Office of Public Housing, U.S. Department of Housing and Urban Development* (Cambridge, MA: Abt Associates, Inc., 2003); and Tony Proscio, *Schools and Community and Development: Erasing the Boundaries* (Columbia, MD: The Enterprise Foundation, 2004).

13. See *Smart Schools, Smart Growth: Investing in Education Facilities and Stronger Communities*, a joint working paper by Policy Analysis for California Education and Center for Cities & Schools (2009); Deborah L. McKoy and Jeffrey M. Vincent, Housing and Education: The Inextricable Link, in James Carr and Nandinee Kutty, eds., *Segregation: The Rising Costs for America* (Routledge, 2008); Richard W. Riley,

"Schools as Centers of Community," Speech delivered to the American Institute of Architects annual meeting, Washington, D.C., October 13, 1999. Available online: http://www.ed.gov/Speeches/10 -1999/991013.html; and Steven Bingler, *What If ... New Schools, Better Neighborhoods, More Livable Communities* (Los Angeles: The Metropolitan Forum Project and New Schools, Better Neighborhoods, 1999).

14. http://www.emerycenter.org/html/background/index _background.html.

15. Byron Garner, *Blacks Law Dictionary*, 8th Edition (2004).

16. Tom Rizzuti, Tom Silva, and Mel Roop, *Joint Use Agreements: A How To Guide*. California Association of School Business Officials, Sacramento, CA (1997).

17. From ConnectEd's website and the Coalition for Multiple Pathways http://www.connectedcalifornia.org/coalition/.

18. According to recent National Center for Education Statistics data, of school aged children in the US, 88 percent attend public school. Of those students, 2.4 percent attend a public charter school. See http://nces.ed.gov/.

19. David Tyack and Larry Cuban, *Tinkering toward Utopia: A Century of Public School Reform* (Harvard University Press, 1995).

Editor's Notes

1. Under the ten recommendations listed in the section titled "10 Plus Mechanics of Change," there is a subsection titled "Tools and Strategies." The actual *Policy Brief Report* lists examples of the tools and strategies used for those projects where these programs were implemented. They include additional details about the programs implemented in the city of Emeryville, the city of Richmond, and the city of San Francisco. This information is available in detail in the entire report on the Center for Cities & Schools' website, which is listed in Appendix C. When at the website, click on the menu category titled "Publications," and this report is listed under the year it was published, 2009.

2. The Center for Cities & Schools was established in 2004 as an interdisciplinary initiative between the university's Graduate School of Education and the College of Environmental Design. They partner exclusively with the Department of City and Regional Planning, and they are housed in the Institute of Urban and Regional Development (URD). The Center conducts research, provides education, and facilitates collaborative policy making between local governments and school districts to help improve urban and metropolitan communities and public education.

CHAPTER 19

Gainesville and the University of Florida Implement Neighborhood Action Plan

Charles E. Young

Students represent a diverse population — undergraduate, graduate or professional; with families or single; international or local; age eighteen or age fifty. The diversity of students attending either the University of Florida or Santa Fe Community College will continue to create diverse city-wide housing demands. For a variety of reasons, some students will continue to live in the residential neighborhoods near the campus. The successful provision of transit service to campus may also make remote neighborhoods more attractive and convenient. Therefore, resolution of neighborhood concerns about student housing must be addressed in a broad context with sensitivity toward the entire community. This report is the result of a combined effort of community and university representatives to identify ways in which the University of Florida can assist in addressing university impacts in single-family neighborhoods.

This plan presents the conclusions and recommendations of the Town/Gown Task Force regarding neighborhood issues. The Town/Gown Task Force dialogue exclusively addressed neighborhood issues, primarily in terms of the physical environment, home ownership and student housing. This plan focuses solely on those actions that involve the University of Florida in a lead or strong support role. In a separate effort, the City of Gainesville has recently involved numerous stakeholders and professionals to develop recommendations related to city ordinances, enforcement practices, zoning and other such issues that are outside the purview of the University of Florida. The University supports the intent of these initiatives, but can provide limited collaborative support to implement those proposed solutions. As a companion effort, this Action Plan presents solutions that involve the University of Florida in a more substantial role.

The University of Florida Town/Gown Task Force was created by President Charles E. Young in the spring of 2002 through an initiative of the Faculty Senate. Members of the Task Force include representatives of the City of Gainesville, Alachua County, UF-Finance and Administration, UF-Graduate Student Council, UF-Student Government, faculty and the neighborhood community. Meeting participants also included representatives from UF-Student Affairs, UF-Public Relations, UF-Research and Graduate Programs, UF-Foundation and the City Commission.

The university's interest in these issues is grounded in the desire to be a good community partner and to preserve a positive environment

Originally published as "Town/Gown Task Force Neighborhood Action Plan," *College Town Topics*, September 18, 2002, by the International Town and Gown Association, Clemson University, Clemson, South Carolina. Reprinted with permission of the publisher.

around the campus that reflects the university's academic excellence. The university benefits in terms of marketing, image and support services when the surrounding neighborhoods are safe, clean, attractive and provide university-oriented housing and commercial activities. Neighborhood deterioration, disinvestment and crime near campus can negatively affect student enrollment and faculty recruitment. Several of the actions described herein may be viewed as outside of the university's academic mission, however, they are justified because a favorable surrounding environment is a competitive advantage for the university.

The Town/Gown Task Force was charged with identifying a university role to address neighborhood concerns about student housing, traffic and related impacts. In recent years, the City of Gainesville has investigated various solutions to these neighborhood issues. In 2001–2002, the City formed four committees to develop recommendations on specific issues including (1) community development, investments and infrastructure; (2) marketing; (3) parking and police enforcement; and (4) regulatory reform (e.g. codes enforcement and landlord licensing). In addition, the City hired a consultant to prepare an analysis and recommendations report regarding student housing and regulatory reform. That report was presented by the consultant to the City Commission in June 2002, and has been reviewed by the Town/Gown Task Force along with reports from the four City committees. The Town/Gown Task Force first met in April 2002 to begin reviewing these prior efforts and identifying issues in which the University of Florida could have a leadership role. The Task Force met regularly for six months to prepare the recommendations contained in this Action Plan.

Issue Identification

The first step for the Task Force was to identify the neighborhood concerns that may relate to the university presence. The initial list of issues was identified as the following:

- Noise
- Parking
- Infrastructure upgrades
- Home ownership
- Neighborhood appearance
- Code enforcement
- Garbage and litter
- Landlord issues
- Traffic
- Nuisance parties
- Property values
- Consistency of rules application & accountability
- Number of occupants in single-family dwellings
- Community values
- Property restoration
- Maintenance incentives
- Change of student culture
- Safety/security issues
- Funding
- Large attendance special events
- Housing demand

Many of these issues have been identified in previous efforts, and the City of Gainesville has taken steps to address some of them. For example, the police Party Patrol, neighborhood parking decal system, neighborhood traffic calming, sidewalk construction, Neighborhood Planning Program, historic district designations, redevelopment district designations, and increased codes enforcement have been implemented to improve conditions in and around the university neighborhoods. Additional recommendations for City action are forthcoming from its current planning analysis.

The Town/Gown Task Force's next step was to identify which issues and solutions have a key role for the University of Florida. Of these, the topics fell into several broad categories: (1) teach students to be good neighbors; (2) strengthen residential neighborhoods; (3) require responsible property management; (4) provide appropriate housing options and information; and (5) manage special events and traffic. These five approaches form the outline of this plan.

The overriding goal of this Neighborhood Action Plan is:

To improve the quality of the physical environment surrounding the University of Florida campus in order to stabilize existing neighborhoods, reduce negative impacts, and provide appropriate development/redevelopment opportunities that serve the needs of the university and community.

Actions

STRATEGY #1: TEACHING STUDENTS TO BE GOOD NEIGHBORS

For many students, particularly younger undergraduates, their college years represent the first opportunity to live as an independent adult in their own household. This experience is new and exciting, but often comes with little preparation for the responsibilities of being a good neighbor. Basic practices and courtesies that are taken for granted by established residents — such as how to put out the garbage, how to maintain a property, and how to be respectful of neighbors' property — are not established habits.

To address this need, a variety of actions have been identified that will provide students with the information they need to be good neighbors and productive citizens of the community. As part of this effort, actions are also identified to instill in students a sense of pride in the neighborhoods where they reside and to provide for positive interaction between students and neighbors.

Action 1.1 Provide Information to Students
Primary Responsibility: UF — Division of Student Affairs and Division of Public Relations
Performance Measure: Number of student contacts and frequency of messages
Public Financial Obligation: Low

Action 1.2 Encourage Student Participation in Neighborhood Clean-Up
Primary Responsibility: UF — Division of Student Affairs
Performance Measure: Number of clean-up events
Public Financial Obligation: Low

Action 1.3 Organize Neighborhood Special Events

Primary Responsibility: City of Gainesville — Cultural Affairs Dept., Neighborhood Associations, and UF — Division of Student Affairs, Division of Public Relations, and Student Government
Performance Measure: Number of events and number of attendees
Public Financial Obligation: Medium

Action 1.4 Provide Community Educators
Primary Responsibility: UF — Division of Student Affairs and Neighborhood Associations
Performance Measure: Number of Community Educators and the effectiveness of their role
Public Financial Obligation: Medium

Action 1.5 Reinforce Penalties for Ordinance Violations
Primary Responsibility: UF — Division of Student Affairs
Performance Measure: Number of complaints made overall and by neighborhood; and the general outcome of these complaints
Public Financial Obligation: Medium

STRATEGY #2: STRENGTHENING RESIDENTIAL NEIGHBORHOODS

There will always be a market for rental homes in the neighborhoods near campus, but the impacts of these rentals can be lessened by reducing their numbers and encouraging occupancy by older student and employee renters. The neighborhoods around the University of Florida can be attractive to university employees as safe, convenient locations to live and to raise families near neighborhood schools. Graduate, post-doctoral and professional students also have housing needs that are often more similar to the established single-family neighborhood residents than to the undergraduate students. Promotion of home ownership and rental occupancy in the university neighborhoods should target these markets. The assets of these neighborhoods should be emphasized through neighborhood associations, real estate marketing and home-ownership programs. Neighborhood ambiance, appearance and amenities can also be enhanced to attract and retain single-family residents. Where multifamily housing is permitted and encouraged adjacent to the university, explore marketing strategies and demand for developments targeted at university staff and faculty.

Action 2.1 Continue to Encourage Neighborhood Organization
Primary Responsibility: City of Gainesville — Community Development Department
Performance Measure: Number of registered neighborhoods and their participation in available programs
Public Financial Obligation: Medium

Action 2.2 Promote Private Initiative and Investment
Primary Responsibility: Neighborhood residents and other private citizens
Performance Measure: Level of private investment and number of privately-sponsored neighborhood activities
Public Financial Obligation: Low

Action 2.3 Enhance Neighborhood Marketing
Primary Responsibility: Neighborhood residents and other private citizens
Performance Measure: Participation of local real estate agents and property managers
Public Financial Obligation: Low

Action 2.4 Engage in Joint Planning for Infrastructure Improvements
Primary Responsibility: City of Gainesville, Alachua County and University of Florida
Performance Measure: Creation of an ongoing coordination forum
Public Financial Obligation: Medium

Action 2.5 Participate in City Code Enforcement Efforts
Primary Responsibility: UF — faculty and/or Division of Student Affairs
Performance Measure: Creation of programs that assist in conducting monitoring inspections of rental properties, and numbers of properties evaluated
Public Financial Obligation: Low

Action 2.6 Increase Monitoring and Enforce Code Compliance
Primary Responsibility: City of Gainesville — Community Development and Police Departments

Performance Measure: Number of citations issued for codes enforcement, parking violations, noise violations, etc.
Public Financial Obligation: High

Action 2.7 Provide Incentive Financing Programs
Primary Responsibility: City of Gainesville — Housing Division
Performance Measure: Provision of new financing programs or expansion of existing programs, and number of program participants
Public Financial Obligation: High

Action 2.8 Investigate University Employee Home-Ownership Programs
Primary Responsibility: UF — Division of Finance and Administration
Performance Measure: Availability of the program and number of participants
Public Financial Obligation: High

Action 2.9 Provide Multi-family Housing for Faculty and Staff
Primary Responsibility: Private citizens with City and County support
Performance Measure: Development of faculty and staff housing in designated locations
Public Financial Obligation: High

Action 2.10 Consider Neighborhood Overlay Districts
Primary Responsibility: City of Gainesville — Community Development District
Performance Measure: Adoption of an overlay ordinance and compliance monitoring
Public Financial Obligation: Low

Action 2.11 Promote Neighborhood Primary/Secondary Schools
Primary Responsibility: UF — Division of Finance and Administration, P. K. Yonge school administrators and Neighborhood Associations
Performance Measure: Establishment of revised admission procedures, and number of students enrolled from adjacent neighborhoods
Public Financial Obligation: None

Action 2.12 Consider Engaging the University in Community Redevelopment
Primary Responsibility: UF — Division of Finance and Administration, and UF Foundation

Performance Measure: Creation of a redevelopment plan with a funding component, and the number of properties renovated by the program

Public Financial Obligation: High

STRATEGY #3: REQUIRING RESPONSIBLE PROPERTY MANAGEMENT

One key to reducing impacts from student rental housing is the willingness of landlords and property managers to perform required maintenance and reinforce tenants' compliance with applicable codes and ordinances. Landlords can play an important role in educating tenants about local requirements, and can hold their tenants accountable by recognizing code violations as a violation of the lease agreement. The City of Gainesville is currently exploring a number of revisions to landlord licensing and rental property regulations, but the following recommendations were identified by the Town/Gown Task Force as holding much promise for success and offering a possible support role for the University of Florida.

Action 3.1 Include Landlords in Education Efforts

Primary Responsibility: City of Gainesville — Community Development Department
Performance Measure: Adoption of required ordinance and compliance monitoring
Public Financial Obligation: Medium

Action 3.2 Implement Performance-Based Landlord Licensing

Primary Responsibility: City of Gainesville — Community Development Dept.
Performance Measure: Adoption of revised licensing requirement and compliance monitoring
Public Financial Obligation: Medium

STRATEGY # 4: PROVIDING APPROPRIATE STUDENT HOUSING OPTIONS

The University of Florida student body is large and diverse with a variety of housing needs. These needs are quite different for undergraduates, graduates, professionals and students with families. The University's housing policy gives priority to housing freshmen on campus with 69 percent of residence hall spaces reserved for first-time enrolled freshmen. In the Fall 2001 semester, 90 percent of first-time enrolled freshmen were housed on campus. Overall, the University housed nearly 22 percent of its Gainesville campus student population in Fall 2001. With recent construction and renovation, that number is expected to rise to 23 percent with an increase of 929 beds for Fall 2002. Ultimately, the University intends to house 25.5 percent of this student body on campus. This percentage is comparable to other major universities and is consistent with market demand for on-campus housing.

Looking ahead, graduate enrollment is expected to increase and result in greater demands for graduate housing. Historically, graduate housing has maintained waiting lists, which have been longer for single graduate students than family graduate students. Because of this trend and the expectation of a growing graduate enrollment, the University is proposing construction of a new 676-bed apartment-style facility for Fall 2007 to house single graduate students. Undergraduate housing has maintained shorter waiting lists for the fall semesters, however, in recent years the demand is nearly equal to the supply and those on the waiting list have been primarily returning upper level students. During the spring semester virtually all housing requests are accommodated as 200–400 beds are relinquished between fall and spring semesters on average. On move-in day of the Fall 2002 semester, there were no waiting lists for single student on-campus housing. This was the first time in 20 years that all housing requests were accommodated due to new construction, renovation and more efficient space utilization. Also in the Fall 2002 semester, 82 percent of all freshmen — not just the first-time enrolled freshmen — were accommodated in on-campus housing. This equals the percentage of freshman that desire to live on campus. In total, an additional 977 freshmen students will be housed on campus in this semester.

The State of Florida requires that university housing operations be financially self-supporting so that vacancies, which do occur at other major universities, would negatively affect the financial stability of the Division of Housing. The national trend in campus housing is toward student preference for off-campus housing which has caused many mid-size schools to close residence halls. The current supply and demand for undergraduate on-campus housing at the University of Florida has reached an equilibrium wherein the majority of students who desire to live on campus are accommodated and the Division does not assume undue risk of vacancies. Projected enrollment trends and availability of off-campus housing do not justify proposals for additional undergraduate campus housing at this time. The Gainesville area student housing market is currently overbuilt with most complexes running at 80 percent occupancy in 2001. Competition for tenants is generating aggressive incentives such as generous amenity packages, reduced rates, security deposit waivers, and free two months rent on annual leases. However, this trend has not significantly slowed off-campus apartment construction.

The end result for the University is that the Division of Housing must aggressively market campus housing and offer a wide variety of programming and other amenities in order to attract students. Currently these offerings include high-speed Ethernet connections, cable television, real-time tutoring via closed circuit television, automated laundry service information, web-based credit card payment, meal plan enhancements, leadership programs, and integrated academic and residential experiences as embodied in the new Honors Residential College at Hume Hall. These services provide a unique on-campus living experience and marketing niche, but also increase construction and operating costs. When compared to peer universities, on-campus housing rates at the University of Florida are slightly below average for single and double accommodations, and slightly above average for suite and apartment-style living. However, the on-campus rates are significantly less expensive than the average for off-campus apartment complexes on a per year per student basis. The Division of Housing anticipates annual rental rate increases will be required for both single and village-style student housing over the next decade to cover increas-

ing operational costs and debt service commitments. In making these rate adjustments, the Division of Housing must continue to be competitive with the off-campus housing market including below cost marketing strategies employed at many apartment complexes.

Action 4.1 Provide Student-Village Off-Campus Housing
Primary Responsibility: Private citizens with City and County support
Performance Measure: Development of student villages in designated locations
Public Financial Obligation: High

Action 4.2 Provide On-Campus Student Housing
Primary Responsibility: UF — Division of Housing
Performance Measure: Percent of the Gainesville campus student population in on-campus residences
Public Financial Obligation: High

STRATEGY # 5: MANAGING SPECIAL EVENTS AND TRAFFIC

Large special events, such as football games, basketball games, and concerts provide benefits to the community in terms of economic activity and entertainment opportunities. The neighborhoods near the Ben Hill Griffith Stadium and the O'Connell Center, have some advantages of proximity to these events, but also bear significant burdens associated with noise, trash, crowds and traffic. In some respects, recurring events such as football games, provide an opportunity to educate people about expected behavior and local ordinances because many people are repeat attendees. Other non-recurring events, such as concerts or high school sport state tournaments, attract new visitors who are unfamiliar with the campus area and local expectations. Major events create the need to address neighborhood parking, waste management and crowd control. Many measures are already in place to provide additional police presence and solid waste collection. However, the neighborhood residents continue to experience unacceptable levels of impacts from seemingly more frequent events.

Action 5.1 Provide Information to Special Event Attendees

Primary Responsibility: UF — Athletic Association, Alumni Affairs, and Division of Public Relations

Performance Measure: Number and type of visitor contacts and frequency of messages

Public Financial Obligation: Medium

Action 5.2 Manage Neighborhood Parking and Traffic

Primary Responsibility: City of Gainesville — Public Works and Police Departments

Performance Measure: Neighborhood satisfaction as measured by the number of complaints received

Public Financial Obligation: High

Action 5.3 Increase Special Event Impact Mitigation

Primary Responsibility: City of Gainesville — Police Department and Solid Waste Division, and UF — Athletic Association and O'Connell Center

Performance Measure: Number of facilities and services provided

Public Financial Obligation: Medium

Action 5.4 Provide Visitor Welcome Information

Primary Responsibility: University of Florida — Division of Finance and Administration

Performance Measure: Provision of campus welcome center, gateway entrances, and visitor information

Public Financial Obligation: High

Implementation and Funding

SET PRIORITIES

One method to begin evaluating recommendations and developing a priority order is to examine the relative cost and benefit of each action. The following matrix demonstrates the degree of anticipated impact for each recommendation along with its relative cost (rated as high, medium or low). Cost considerations for this analysis are based upon public investment required of local governments or the University of Florida

Another method to evaluate priority ac-

tions is to examine the ease with which they can be implemented. In general, initiatives with fewer partners and stakeholders can be implemented most quickly. For example, education efforts from the Division of Student Affairs simply involves a commitment of staff and resources primarily within one organizational unit. By contrast, actively assisting in city code enforcement or engaging students in neighborhood clean-ups involve the coordination of multiple entities. Some of the actions in this document are simply maintenance or expansion of existing programs. Still others are new initiatives, many of which require long start-up times and additional development. Those actions qualified for future "consideration" will obviously require on-going debate and refinement. It is also important in deciding priorities, to share the responsibilities so that no single agency is saddled with the bulk of initiatives in any one time frame.

Overall, the Town/Gown Task Force priorities strive to:

➤ Produce short-term successes;
➤ Disperse responsibilities;
➤ Emphasize high impact, low-to-medium cost actions in the near-term; and
➤ Lay the groundwork for longer-term solutions.

Tier 1 Actions: Continue Current Activities

As a first priority, the Task Force recommends continuation, monitoring and enhancement of the following current activities.

• Encourage Neighborhood Organization
• Provide Information to Special Event Attendees
• Manage Neighborhood Parking and Traffic

Tier 2 Actions: Pursue Short-Term Successes (initiate in 0–6 months)

The following actions can be implemented in the near term and produce satisfactory levels of impact. These actions should be initiated in 0–6 months from the adoption of this report.

• Promote Private Initiatives and Investment
• Enhance Neighborhood Marketing
• Provide Information to Students

- Encourage Student Participation in Neighborhood Clean-Up
- Engage in Joint Planning for Infrastructure Improvements
- Increase Special Event Impact Mitigation
- Organize Neighborhood Special Events
- Include Landlords in Education Efforts

Tier 3 Actions: Pursue Mid-Term Successes and Lay the Foundation for Longer-Term Solutions (initiate in 6–12 months)

The following actions will require a few months of preparation and additional planning before they can be initiated. Some of these actions will start a process toward more long-term solutions. These actions should be initiated in 6–12 months from the adoption of this report.

- Participate in City Code Enforcement Efforts
- Provide Community Educators
- Increase Monitoring and Enforce Code Compliance
- Provide Incentive Financing Programs
- Provide Visitor Welcome Information

Tier 4 Actions: Commit to Long-Term Investment Initiatives

The following actions are long-term solutions that may not be realized for several years, but will require advance financial planning and commitment that should begin in the short-term.

- Investigate University Employee Home-Ownership Programs
- Provide Student Village Off-Campus Housing
- Provide On-Campus Student Housing
- Provide Multi-family Housing for Faculty and Staff

Tier 5 Actions: Continue to Evaluate Complex New Initiatives

The following actions require additional evaluation and input before they are fully developed. This future evaluation could occur within the Town/Gown Task Force structure or be assigned to other appropriate entities. However, this continued debate should follow directly after the adoption of this report so as not to lose momentum.

- Consider Neighborhood Overlay Districts
- Promote Neighborhood Primary/Secondary Schools
- Reinforce Penalties for Ordinance Violations
- Implement Performance-Based Landlord Licensing
- Consider Engaging the University in Community Redevelopment

Link to Academic Programming

Many of the recommendations contained in this report require action in the administrative side of the university, but others relate to expertise and community service available in the academic functions. Linking actions to the academic endeavors, research centers and community service mission of the University will be an important part of implementation. In this approach, the administration must acknowledge faculty work with community benefit as a career enhancing activity that can be measured commensurate with evaluations for traditional teaching and research. In addition, the work should be linked to the academic strategic plan emphasis areas including children and families, ecology and environment, internationalization of the campus and the newly proposed interdisciplinary School of Natural Resources and Environment. Future review of university centers should consider roles that advance the community benefits outlined in this report. Several existing centers such as the Shimberg Center for Affordable Housing, Center for Building Better Communities, Center for Construction and Environment, Center for Real Estate Studies and the GeoPlan Center would seem to be able to contribute toward these goals. Several other centers that focus on issues of social policy, public policy, government, historic preservation and business also have missions that touch on these areas of community need.

Again, other university programs can be examined for ways in which to align Town/Gown goals with the academic mission. The Center for Community and Environmental Development at Pratt University in Brooklyn utilizes a multidisciplinary faculty group to assist local community-based organizations with project development, technical assistance and training, and group facilitation to support neighborhood revitalization and stimulate private investment. The University of Illinois at Chicago utilizes faculty in a Building Sustainable Communities project that provides training for community-based development organizations and supports local affordable housing initiatives with research and graduate intern programs. Faculty at Howard University in Washington, DC, collaborated with the Fannie Mae Foundation to perform streetscape, land use and feasibility studies to revitalize a distressed area around its campus. The University of Arkansas also provides comprehensive planning and design services statewide through its Community Design Service. The University of Michigan combines two existing programs, the Urban and Regional Planning Program and the Legal Assistance for Urban Communities Program (Law School) to assist a local community development and housing coalition for Detroit's Eastside. The University of Pennsylvania's Center for Community Partnerships has worked aggressively with multiple community organizations, including school districts and financial institutions, to improve West Philadelphia neighborhoods. An affordable housing initiative in Birmingham is facilitated by the University of Alabama's Center for Urban Affairs to develop collaborations with financial institutions and other community partners. The University of Alabama's community efforts also incorporate youth education, training, and small business development into their housing initiative.

Expand Funding Sources

The university's involvement in local community development programs can also open doors to expanded funding and grant opportunities. The U.S. Department of Housing and Urban Development's (HUD) Community Outreach Partnership Center Program and the Department of Commerce's University Centers Program are specifically for the use of universities in solving community problems. The University Center Program primarily provides

technical assistance and strategic planning for economic development in partnership with state and local governments, non-profit organizations, and small firms. The U.S. Department of Education's Title XI Program funds university projects focused on critical urban issues including community development, health and housing. Another HUD program, the Joint Community Development Program serves as a catalyst for universities to engage in large-scale building initiatives in distressed neighborhoods. The federal Corporation for National and Community Service provides project grants to institutions of higher education to engage students in service learning to meet community needs including neighborhood clean-up and revitalization. Several other federal agencies including the National Endowment for the Arts and the Environmental Protection Agency offer other applicable grants. Similar grant opportunities exist with State of Florida agencies. Several private foundations, such as the Fannie Mae Foundation, Ford Foundation, Kellogg Foundation, DeWitt Wallace Foundation and the Robert Wood Johnson Foundation (and many others) also fund university-community partnership programs. Research and development funding can also be sought to implement innovative infrastructure solutions that address community issues. Many of these grant opportunities would not be available to the community without the involvement of a university partner.

Maintain Commitment, Momentum and Monitoring

Above all, the recommendations of the Town/Gown Task Force must not sit idle. There is great potential for the University of Florida to serve as a catalyst, resource and partner in contributing to the resolution of university neighborhood issues. The Task Force's implementation plan includes short-term actions that should be quickly pursued. Several other recommendations call for ongoing debate to resolve outstanding issues, address expanded topics or continue coordination on current projects such as infrastructure. The university neighborhood residents are also called upon to directly engage in neighborhood preservation activities and support these city, county and university initiatives.

In order for the University to move forward on any of these recommendations, its administration will need to determine the appropriate forum in which to pursue the actions, assign specific responsibilities, and commit to ongoing progress monitoring as identified for each action item. University administrative divisions with primary responsibility for executing these actions will need to develop more detailed implementation plans complete with specific budgets and target dates. During the process of developing these details, continued coordination with various university constituencies will ensure fairness, collaboration, and effectiveness in implementing these recommendations. With this anticipation, the Town/Gown Task Force respectfully submits these recommendations to the University of Florida President Charles E. Young and the University Faculty Senate.

EDITOR'S NOTES

The original *Neighborhood Action Plan* contains an "Executive Summary," additional information for the "Action" items listed under each of the five "Strategy" topics in the "Actions" section of the report. A list of reference sources is also included at the end of this report. This information may be obtained from the International Town & Gown Association, which is listed in Appendix D.

Also, additional information on this collaborative planning effort between the City of Gainesville, the County of Alachua, and the University of Florida may be obtained from their individual websites, which are listed in Appendix B.

A *Faculty Governance Report*, dated May 2003, provided a follow-up on the actions of this joint Town/Gown Task Force. In this report it was noted that the efforts of the task force were to improve the environment around the university and to reduce the impact of the university upon surrounding neighborhoods. It was noted that members of the committee represented the city, county, and university. It was also noted that many of the recommendations had already been implemented.

CHAPTER 20

Greencastle Benefits from DePauw University's Efforts to Strengthen Community Relations

Luke Beasley

Too often the mere mention of "town-gown" relations is met with sighs, shaking heads or lowered eyes. But the reality is that every DePauw student is a resident of Greencastle, and both groups are neighbors for nine months each year.

"It's tough to have a good relationship when students are so transient ... but everyone has the responsibility," said Residence Life Coordinator Michael Schmeckebier, who lives in a university-owned house situated between student housing and Greencastle homes. He said improvement is needed from both students and Greencastle residents.

Junior Neal Knapp, who grew up on a farm in Putnam County, said that people on both sides of the equation tend to only recognize the "disconnect" rather than try to understand why it exists and challenge its assumptions.

"By deconstructing these negative perceptions of conflict, the community and DePauw can benefit from each other," Knapp said. "It's gotten to the point where people don't even know why there is a divide, but they know it's still there."

Gaps in Economics, Understandings

At $29,798, the median annual household income in Greencastle is considerably lower than the cost of a year's attendance at DePauw — slated at just under $38,000 for the 2007–08 year.

"I know DePauw tries, but the reality is that there is a giant class division between those that go here and work here and the people that live here in the town," said professor Mark Jackson, who has lived in Greencastle for the last year. "That separation causes misperceptions on both sides."

Junior John Sibbitt, a Greencastle native, said that those misconceptions arise from often unfair generalizations and stereotypes.

"It's a misjudgment on both sides," Sibbitt said. "Most Greencastle people view all the students as rich, which is not the case, and most DePauw people view townspeople as hicks, like uneducated hillbillies."

But despite the naïveté of such generalities, Sibbitt thinks they will persist.

"After all, there are always going to be some rich DePauw kids, and there's always going to be the typical townies," Sibbitt said. "Stereotypes don't exist for no reason."

Originally published as "A Look at Town-Gown Relations in Greencastle, Indiana," *The DePauw*, February 12, 2010, by DePauw University, Greencastle, Indiana. Reprinted with permission of the publisher.

Professor Bruce Stinebrickner, with 20 years experience as both a DePauw professor and a Greencastle resident, said that the financial tension between the University and the city is inevitable. While local citizens may appreciate the economic boost provided by the presence of DePauw and its legions of eager consumers, the relationship is often strained.

"There is a kind of built-in jealousy and tension between the biggest institution in town that is, by Putnam County standards, fabulously wealthy and a city that is relatively poor," Stinebrickner said. "Inevitably, those people outside the fence looking in can appreciate the economic impact while having personal resentments of the behavior of its students and faculty. You might call it a love-hate relationship. There is a fundamental, inevitable natural tension."

Though economic divisions can be a source of confrontation, Jackson said it can also provide an opportunity for two separate groups to gain a more accurate understanding of different lifestyles.

"I think Greencastle offers the students at DePauw access to experiences unlike their own," Jackson said. "Most [students] here are urban or suburbanites ... getting to know those people might help them better get to know America as a whole."

Stinebrickner said students aren't the only ones who keep to themselves, pointing to faculty and administrators at DePauw who remain largely uninvolved in civic issues.

"For one thing, those citizens, non-DePauw citizens, think that the DePauw faculty themselves don't get involved in the community," he said. "On average, they're right."

Where Do We Go from Here?

Thomas Fitzpatrick, Greencastle resident and music professor emeritus, said that the University has already come a long way in improving its standing in the community. Fitzpatrick acknowledged the longstanding rift between local youth and DePauw students. But, he said that DePauw students are doing a better job mending that rift by getting out into the community.

"Let's face it, DePauw has contributed so much to the local economy and to the cultural offerings," Fitzpatrick said. "Everything has improved. If DePauw weren't here now, we would have to find another place to live because of the many things DePauw offers and not just with sports and concerts and things like that. But there's so much more, with relationships between students who are offering help to this city and to the citizens and people that need help. It gives it a heart that I don't think would exist if it wasn't here."

Programs like Bonner Scholars and DePauw Community Service are just a few examples of the types of interactions that can continue to strengthen the relationship between Greencastle and DePauw.

"It goes both ways," said Jessica Weasner, DePauw's Coordinator of Community Service and Outreach. "The community can offer a lot to the students that go here. I think the student that goes out and volunteers in the community finds that their time here at DePauw was really enriched by that experience."

Jackson said the University would be well-served by promoting more service-learning projects, where students go out into the community, work with local people on projects and then use those experiences as an educational tool.

"I think that the University could put more students into the community, whether it is at elementary schools or volunteering at one of the many helping organizations here in town," Jackson said. "Then people would get to know the students, instead of imagining someone holed up in their fraternity."

The University has embarked on certain formal initiatives to strengthen community relations and neighborhood rapport. The recent no-event neighborhood housing option, which does not allow registered parties or more than 10 non-residents in the house at a time, has proven to be a successful way to preempt complaints from Greencastle residents who live in close proximity to University housing.

"We've made some changes, and it's a lot more peaceful," Schmeckebier said.

CHAPTER 21

Hamilton and McMaster University Jointly Provide Community Policing Center

Phil Wood

Many McMaster students live in the neighborhood surrounding the university. These students intersect with the local community every single day. It must be very difficult for our neighbors because their schedules are so much different from those of a typical student. I know this first hand because both of my sons live in the neighborhood — one as a student and one (with his wife) as a permanent resident. Indeed both have lived in Westdale and Ainslie Wood for several years at a variety of addresses. When I was looking for a house in 1982 I considered Westdale. The neighborhood had lots of appeal especially because it was so close to work. Ultimately I thought that it would be better for me (and my then very young family) to live a little farther away. Many McMaster faculty and staff members though do live in the immediate neighborhood so I am constantly being up-dated of the goings on. The neighborhood around McMaster University is known as Ainslie Wood/Westdale. It is in the west end of Hamilton and indeed is often referred to as West Hamilton. The village of Westdale is a great place to live. There's a number of shops with great appeal to students and permanent residents alike — things like bars, coffee shops, a theatre, clothing stores, a Pita Pit and even a cup-cake store. It has a number

of fine old homes with relatively affluent inhabitants who live adjacent to the university and have a disproportionate amount of influence with our local city councilor and city hall generally.

On the other hand, the Ainslie Wood area, particularly Ainslie Wood East is known by the students at least as, "the ghetto." It has given over almost entirely to student housing with fewer high-end houses and commensurately less influence with the councilor. That is, the councilor doesn't appear to represent the student interests at all. Students though really seem to enjoy living in this neighborhood as most of their neighbors are also students.

A new development in Ainslie Wood North was the recent building of the West Village Condos. This is a privately owned student residence with beds for 450 students. A previous student union president was hired to market the property and he was successful in filling it by mid summer. The building was not completed on time creating hiccups in early September but construction is continuing and it looks like it will be really nice when it's done. A second private residence is planned for Ainslie Wood West — right across the street from a gigantic grocery store and gigantic (but closed) bar. I went to a neighborhood meeting in the

Originally published as "University-Local Community Relations," *College Town Topics*, September 19, 2007, by the International Town and Gown Association, Clemson University, Clemson, South Carolina. Reprinted with permission of the publisher.

spring where agents for the developer discussed the magnitude of the building and the additional traffic that would be created. The developer already has similar facilities in London, Ontario but the proposal was given a very rough ride by the neighbors who, at the time, were watching the West Village Condos going up and were imaging a potential addition of approximately 1000 students to the neighborhood.

Last night was the 9th Annual General Meeting of the Ainslie Wood/Westdale Community Association (AWWCA)—our local neighborhood association. The highlight of the meeting was to be a presentation by Hamilton mayor Fred Eisenberger "Achieving Town and Gown Balance in Ainslie Wood and Westdale." That's not what he talked about actually. That address was given by the outgoing President of the AWWCA—a theme of previous communications. The mayor talked about how great Hamilton is (using parts of a speech that I heard him give earlier in the day to the Chamber of Commerce). A major feature of the meeting was a Q&A with various stakeholders—for example police, bylaw enforcement, fire inspection, the city councilor and the university's VP responsible for town and gown relations. The councilor seemed extraordinarily proud of a proactive by-law enforcement policy described here. This was also coupled with an increased police presence and applied during the weekend of Welcome Week. The results of the sweep as reported to me were as follows:

Liquor tickets issued: 57

Addresses charged under the Noise By-Law: one residence was issued 4—$120.00 tickets another residence was issued 6—$120.00 tickets

Other residences on: Sterling St., Thornedale Cres., Traymore Ave., Westwood Ave. and Wilmont Ct.

38 other residences were given their first warnings and added to the Proactive Noise list with the charged residences.

The City issued 13 Seven day Orders to Comply for yard conditions.

City also issued 59 Notices to Comply for waste violations.

Police seemed quite "happy" with those numbers whatever that means. Not everybody was impressed with this show of force however. Joey Coleman, a McMaster student who writes a blog for Macleans posted the story he called "Priorities, Priorities".

The Ainslie Wood/Westdale area is *not* a high crime area in Hamilton. Regular crime reports in the Hamilton Spectator document this. Joey resents the proactive enforcement around the university while the real crime hotspots in Hamilton (where he was born and raised) are underpoliced. (Re-read what I said above about undue influence in some neighborhoods Joey).

Certainly the university has grown significantly over the past five years (by more than 50 percent in numbers) and relationships between "town and gown" can get strained. We are constant educating our students on how to be better neighbors between our Off-Campus Resource Centre and the student union run Student Support Network (SCSN). The university and the community have also been proactive in working together towards the betterment of Town and Gown relations. The President's Advisory Committee on Community Relations (PACCR) was created in with the mission to:

Mission

- To evaluate and improve upon the role of McMaster University as a neighborhood partner in the Hamilton community
- To act as an open and visible means for ongoing community liaison in order to maintain and improve relations between the University and its neighboring community
- To identify areas of common interest and concern between major University activities and the neighboring community, and to develop proposals for action to promote co-operation and mutual understanding

The committee is jointly chaired by a university representative and a community representative with representation from the various stakeholders from the community and campus. A complete list of committee members is available on the PACCR website.

Outside of PACCR, McMaster University,

working in partnership with the McMaster Students Union (MSU) has taken several steps to improve the safety and security of McMaster students. It was through an initiative of the MSU that a community policing centre was established in Westdale in partnership with Hamilton Police Services (HPS). McMaster University and the MSU have also partnered with HPS to have paid-duty police officers patrolling the neighborhood on pub nights (Thursday, Friday and Saturday). This sounds like an idea that the City of Saint Catharines and Brock University might like to consider based on a recent report in Standard! Our most recent initiative, and one that Student Affairs is piloting is our "Community Accountability Program" that is described in detail here. CAP is a program to help students, staff, police and local residents deal constructively with minor violations of the law. Instead of ending up with a criminal charge students sanctioned under CAP can be held responsible for their actions and make restitution in cases where relevant.

Building Town and Gown relations is an ongoing job at the university and it has assigned considerable resources to it. It was refreshing to hear from those in the know that the com-munication between the university and the neighborhood is the best in the province and has lead a community member to form the Town and Gown Association of Ontario (TGAO). We are not alone in our efforts to provide a safe, habitable environment for our students while trying to maintain a neighborhood that permanent residents are pleased and proud to live in. In addition to problems in St. Catharines there have been recent reports of problems in London, Kingston and Waterloo. In many ways, we in Hamilton are leading the province in Town and Gown relations.

As for me, as dean of students I get involved in all aspects of student life — particularly in off-campus student life. This is a picture of me in a pasta eating contest at a recent street festival in Westdale. The MSU also brought their final event from Welcome Week (called "Shine-off" a fund raiser for cystic fibrosis) into the community in an attempt to involve the community into their lives. One local group that loves students is the Westdale Business Improvement Area. What merchants wouldn't like to have 20,000 customers plunked into their neighborhood?

CHAPTER 22

Kannapolis and the University of North Carolina Jointly Create a Downtown Research Campus

Mike Legg

This is a success story in the making. Just when you think your back's against the wall, circumstances can change — not by magic but by fresh thinking and smart action. I invite you to consider whether the solutions that are working for Kannapolis will work in your local government as well.

Seven million square feet of textile space stood vacant — the entire downtown of Kannapolis, North Carolina — with no hope of another user. Thousands of jobs were lost. Kannapolis, a city of 42,000, faced this challenge in 2003. Pillowtex — formerly Cannon Mills, then Fieldcrest Cannon — closed its operations and left 280 acres lifeless in downtown Kannapolis.

For more than a year, the mill sat in uncertainty, leaving Kannapolis with no prospects for center city redevelopment or economic recovery. It left 4,500 residents without jobs and with unanswered questions as they pondered life absent the security and familiarity of working in the mill.

The city, located 30 miles northeast of downtown Charlotte, did have the booming Charlotte economy in its favor. Suburban development in several parts of Kannapolis increased as Charlotte's growth rippled outward; however, the silent 280-acre site faced many obstacles. The entire downtown infrastructure — from power to gas to water and sewer — ran through the Pillowtex site, and only a limited number of companies have the financial wherewithal to acquire such a massive property.

The Start of Redevelopment

Then, in late 2004, California-based David Murdock, CEO of Castle & Cooke, purchased the Pillowtex site with only a few general ideas on how to redevelop the largest textile facility in the world. Murdock already owned much of downtown Kannapolis, land he acquired when he purchased Cannon Mills two decades earlier. Murdock sold the mill in the mid 1980s to Fieldcrest Mills, which then became Fieldcrest Cannon. Fieldcrest Cannon later sold the property to Pillowtex.

Murdock, also sole owner of Dole Food Company and a strong advocate for nutrition and healthy lifestyles, hatched a breathtaking plan in partnership with the city of Kannapolis and the University of North Carolina educational system to redevelop downtown Kannapolis. In September 2005, Murdock, the city, and the UNC system announced the North Carolina Research Campus (NCRC).

Originally published as "From Textile to Biotech: One Community's Approach to Economic Diversification," *Public Management*, Vol. 92, No. 1, January/February 2010, by the International City/County Management Association, Washington, DC. Reprinted with permission of the publisher.

NCRC is a $1.5 billion bioscience research campus of massive proportions. In fact, its design and conception are unique in the general industry and biotechnology sectors. Plans for the campus include 10 universities, eventually more than 100 biotech and life science firms, and retail and residential development. Development, beginning with the removal of huge amounts of obsolete textile manufacturing space, encompasses the entire downtown of Kannapolis, making it one of the largest urban redevelopment projects on record in the United States.

The plans are for the project buildout to occur by 2020. Once completed, the campus will contain 3.2 million square feet of office, laboratory, and civic space. The David H. Murdock Core Laboratory alone is 311,000 square feet, costs $170 million, and includes the only 950 MHz nuclear magnetic resonance (NMR) machine the world used for plant genomics and molecular studies.

Universities that will have facilities on the campus include Duke University, UNC–Chapel Hill, NC State University, UNC–Greensboro, UNC–Charlotte, NC A&T University, NC Central, and Appalachian State University. Preliminary discussions with Elon University and Catawba College are occurring to determine the possibility of having their presence at the research campus.

Almost 90 percent of the funds required to build NCRC are coming from the private sector. It also creates a partnership among local, state, and federal government entities.

Replacing a Legacy Industry and Diversifying

Not only does NCRC bring huge change to the traditional economic base of Kannapolis, but other parts of the city are blossoming on account of strategic investments and decisions made in the late 1990s when city officials recognized the slow decline in textile employment and the need to diversity the local economy.

The total for these earlier projects marks the "other billion dollars" in Kannapolis. They range from a city-owned business park that is now built out, advanced manufacturing facilities, and investments in infrastructure, including the extension of utilities along the recently opened four-mile, multi-lane Kannapolis Parkway that has led to high-quality commercial growth.

As the NCRC began to develop, a top priority for the city was to make sure the opportunities presented by the campus were maximized throughout the population of greater Kannapolis. In partnership with the North Carolina Biotechnology Center and Carolinas Medical Center–NorthEast, the city retained a company to conduct a $150,000 analysis of the potential economic impact of the NCRC, as well as its strengths, weaknesses, opportunities, and threats (SWOT). The results were startling.

According to the impact analysis, the campus could generate 37,000 new jobs in the six-county region, including Charlotte, within 25 years of completion of development. Many of these jobs are expected to have an average salary much higher than the traditional textile jobs that once existed in Kannapolis and surrounding communities.

In fact, this report confirmed what city management suspected — that the campus has the potential to become a major economic engine for the region and the state.

The SWOT analysis found, however, that the potential will not be realized unless the city takes well-planned steps to maximize the potential benefits. Market Street completed an in-depth analysis that compared Kannapolis with Cary, North Carolina; Rockville, Maryland; and Rochester, Minnesota. Each of these communities has an economic base strongly influenced over many years of life sciences and other high-tech businesses. After Kannapolis was compared with these places, city management realized that several areas needed to be addressed in order for the economic impact of NCRC to reach its full potential.

Retooling Educational Systems and the Workforce

With the results from the SWOT analysis,

Kannapolis sought community partners to launch a comprehensive workforce and education plan. The Cabarrus Regional Chamber of Commerce, the Centralina Workforce Development Board, and the Cannon Foundation joined together to fund the $135,000 plan. Other partners included all three school systems in Rowan and Cabarrus counties, media representatives, and local private and nonprofit organizations.

The result is a specific action plan finalized in January 2009. The plan focuses on three areas:

• Transform pre–K through 12 education.
• Expand opportunities in higher education.
• Increase continuing-education and lifelong-learning communities.

Works is already under way in these key areas. The Kannapolis City School District has made significant strides in integrating technology into the classroom, including $1.5 million invested in hardware, software, wiring, interactive whiteboards, laptops for teachers, laptop carts, desktop computers, printers, and Web servers.

Students are using social media, including podcasts and wikis, as a part of various units of study. Streaming audio and video are used in the classroom to connect daily lessons and foster collaboration across the district in the same grade level or subject matter.

Rowan-Cabarrus Community College (RCCC) has also been working at full speed to help local residents gain the training and skills they need to transform from textile workers to skilled workers in the biotechnology industry. New courses have been added, and the community college opened a new center in downtown Kannapolis to assist those in need of various retraining services. RCCC also created a new associate degree in biotechnology.

Kannapolis developed a centralized online job board as a resource for NCRC employers to post their positions and for all interested applicants, living anywhere, to view and respond to openings. The site (www.jobsatncrc.com) now has more than 3,000 subscribers to e-mail alerts about new positions opening up.

Building an Entrepreneurial Culture

To help build the entrepreneurial culture necessary to support its economic diversification strategy, Kannapolis once again sought partners. The Cabarrus Economic Development Corporation took the lead in developing a two-county small-business and entrepreneur action plan. The results thus far include the launch of a local entrepreneurial council as well as www.innovatormagnet.com, a website that serves as a resource for small business and entrepreneurs in Cabarrus and Rowan counties.

Other programs that have begun in response to NCRC include IMAF-Charlotte, a member-managed, seed-stage angel capital fund designed to capitalize on the growth in entrepreneurial activity created by the NCRC in the Charlotte region. BioConnect, a networking group for bioscience professionals in the region, formed last year and meets every other month.

Building Public-Private Partnerships

For Kannapolis, one of the major goals of NCRC is to make sure that it stimulates other development throughout the city. To foster this development, the city has partnered with Cabarrus County on a $168.4 million tax increment financing (TIF) package to support NCRC. The bond package will fund the infrastructure needed to support development of NCRC and also provide better access and quality of life to residents in the area.

Redevelopment plans include five parks, one of which will be a seven-acre courtyard in the heart of the campus. The campus will flow seamlessly into the existing downtown. Major intersections and corridors in and around downtown will be improved in preparation for NCRC. Roads will be widened, traffic lights will be upgraded, and many utility lines will be buried underground. There are 24 total projects related to roads, stretching from the core of the campus to the main arteries throughout the city.

One project includes widening one of the main entry roads to the campus, North Carolina 3, to Kannapolis Parkway and Interstate 85. This new corridor will not only become a vital part of NCRC's transportation support system, it will also likely become a major economic support corridor linking NCRC to expanded growth areas annexed to the city.

The city's land use planning initiatives have established the foundation essential to support future private sector investments seeking locations near NCRC that are integrated into the community. These mixed-use and campus development areas will host many of the new jobs, services, and neighborhoods projected to emerge from NCRC in the coming decades.

Building Organizational Capacity

With a change as dramatic as the one facing Kannapolis and the critical nature of transforming the economy to ensure the inclusion of local residents, Kannapolis undertook several changes to the city's staff structure to help facilitate the change.

Primarily, the city manager's office was reorganized. It now includes a community outreach coordinator to facilitate dialogue with local community groups. Because of the rapid change, many residents are uncertain about the future. The person in this new position will bridge the gap between city hall and the average resident. Many residents are former mill workers, and for them the change has been particularly traumatic.

One more additional position was created in the city manager's office: a director of business and community affairs was hired to manage the economic transformation and implement the recommendations from the SWOT analysis. This person's responsibilities include being involved with the city's long-range and strategic-planning efforts.

The city also hired a customer service manager and is in the process of transforming how the city does business with the public. A new customer service center opened in the spring of 2009, and staff members were reorganized to help meet the needs of a changing city.

The city's new focus on customer service included a fresh look at communicating with residents and businesses. It now has a quarterly magazine, two e-newsletters, a new customer-service-driven website, and is developing its social media approach on such sites as Facebook.

Progress Thus Far

Construction of three key buildings at NCRC — the core laboratory, the UNC Nutrition Research Institute, and the NC State Plants for Human Health Institute — are complete, and scientific research is ramping up. Duke University is enrolling local residents in the massive MURDOCK study (MURDOCK is the acronym for Measurement to Understand the Reclassification of Disease of Cabarrus/Kannapolis).

This study (with an initial gift of $35 million from David Murdock) will deepen understanding of major diseases and help identify and delineate subpopulations with certain risk factors that affect the treatment approach.

Construction on a new RCCC biotechnology training building began during the second quarter of 2009, and construction is now complete on a state-of-the-art bio-repository, a partnership between Duke and LabCorp to house the blood and tissue samples for researchers. Several private sector firms are also increasing their operations at NCRC.

So far, the NCRC project has added nearly $400 million to the local property tax rolls and employs some 500 people.

Although NCRC is the main focus of the Kannapolis economic diversification strategy, since earlier in this decade other key initiatives have been occurring in the city to help it move past its focus on textiles.

Several key investments were made to open up the west side of the city for development and create better linkage to I-85. Initiatives included the construction of Kannapolis Parkway, the development of a city-owned business park built in partnership with a private firm, and the annexation of land adjacent to I-85.

New businesses in this western area during the past decade have employed 1,000 while investing $325 million. Several major office parks are in various stages of planning and could easily double the jobs and investment numbers in this area over the next five years.

All told, the key to the Kannapolis transformation — while still a work in progress — comes down to partnerships and a willingness to discard the old model for a new one. Plans include implementing micro-economic development programs, enhancing land use planning for different areas within the city, and continuing to evaluate workforce development needs and concerns.

CHAPTER 23

Kingston and Queen's University Work Together to Improve Neighborhood Security

Michael Fox

Over 150 communities across Canada, both large and small, are home to colleges and universities with an estimated 645,000 full-time university students and an additional 410,000 full-time college students registered in various programs of study.[1] Universities and colleges are certainly a significant asset to their communities, yet they present a unique set of planning and community development considerations, challenges, and an increasing number of threats and negative perceptions about off-campus behavior, especially in those near-campus neighborhoods where students tend to concentrate. With increasing enrolments across the post-secondary sector, universities and colleges have seen higher percentages of their student population living off-campus, where student discipline codes and student activities and behavior are not supervised or regulated. Each September, local residents brace themselves for the various move-ins, orientation activities and homecoming parties that spill-over into the various near-campus neighborhoods.

There Goes the Neighborhood

In recent years, near-campus student housing issues have received national media at-tention during annual fall orientation and homecoming events. The most infamous case was in a neighborhood near Queen's University in Kingston, Ontario. Estimates of 5,000–7,000 revelers took over a two-block student ghetto during Homecoming 2005.[2] National media attention highlighted the drinking, noise, broken glass, an overturned car that was set ablaze, and over 100 police officers ordered into the area with dozens of arrests and hundreds of liquor and by-law violation tickets being issued. "It was a riot. There's no other way of describing it," says Don Rogers, a retired Kingston city councillor.[3]

Yet Kingston is not alone in identifying the growing threat to neighborhood security being felt by residents. Most communities that are home to a university or residentially-oriented college report incidents of what has been defined as "studentification" of near-campus neighborhoods. British geographer Darren Smith coined this concept as an analogy with gentrification, where he reports the social and environmental changes caused by large numbers of students invading particular areas of a town or city, thereby causing a displacement of many of the long-time residents of that area.[4] In Britain, *The Observer*, July 2002 reported that "Students have officially been identified as

Originally published as "Near-Campus Student Housing and the Growth of the Town and Gown Movement in Canada," *College Town Topics*, January 2008, by the International Town and Gown Association, Clemson University, Clemson, South Carolina. Reprinted with permission of the publisher.

the new scourge of Britain's towns and cities in a study blaming studentification for a string of social evils.... They include destroying respectable neighborhoods by driving out families, triggering rat infestations, causing vandalism and forcing closure of corner shops in favor of tatty burger bars and cheap off-licenses." Smith is one of the few researchers investigating this international phenomenon, highlighted in a study he completed for the government and published by the University Vice-Chancellors' organization of the United Kingdom.[5]

Town and Gown Relationships

Within the various communities across Canada, from small towns such as Sackville, Antigonish, Wolfville and Lennoxville, to larger communities such as Kingston, Guelph, Waterloo, Regina, Calgary, Victoria, Halifax and Fredericton, residents have turned to police, university officials and city governments in addressing these on-going threats to their personal security, the value of their properties and the integrity of their neighborhoods. Most of these communities have resorted to enhanced by-law enforcement, policing services, property maintenance standards and rooming house and tenancy policies. Universities have, finally, recognized that they have a role to play in the off-campus lives of their students. Over the past several years, "Town and Gown" committees have been created in a number of university/college communities across Canada. These committees have been created to bring together municipal and postsecondary administrators with neighborhood residents, students and student leaders, landlords and politicians to develop strategies for addressing the conflicts and threats and negative perceptions that exist between the "Town," being the permanent residents and municipal regulations and infrastructure and the "Gown," being the post-secondary students and the administrative representatives of the university or college.

One of the most affected communities in terms of Town and Gown relations has been Waterloo, Ontario. Home to two universities and a college, with over 25 percent of the city's

population being full-time students, the City of Waterloo has hosted Town and Gown Committees since 1989. In 2004, the City and its universities hosted a Town and Gown Symposium on student-community relations where they invited other communities hosting colleges and universities to identify and exchange issues, best-practices, common barriers to improved relations, and possible avenues for improved future relations. The symposium identified a range of coordinated planning efforts, research and best practices in areas such as sustainable housing, student housing demand and supply, community policing and by-law enforcement, and improved communications with provincial ministries and agencies and legal reform to improve housing and community safety.[6] Similar events have now been held in Hamilton and Guelph, Ontario, culminating with a 2005 national forum on Town and Gown Issues at Brock University in St. Catherines.

The growth of the Town and Gown movement is beginning to spread across North America, with international interest from Britain and Australia. The most recent meeting of university, college and community officials took place at the Wilfrid Laurier Brantford Campus, where the Town and Gown Association of Ontario has now been officially incorporated, holding its first Annual Meeting.[7] Already, the Association has close to 100 members, including planners, university and college presidents, deans, community relations and student housing officers, student associations, as well as neighborhood associations, landlords, community development officials, local and regional police and fire officials, property standards and construction associations, and civic leaders.

Adequate Housing and Improved Behavior as the Key to Improved Community Relations

The impact of near-campus student housing cannot be ignored by planners, universities/colleges and civic officials. Numerous studies have highlighted the substantial economic impact that universities and colleges have on the civic economies, housing markets, the arts, and tourism.[8] Smith (2006) argues that, with appropriate planning strategies, studentification need not always be a negative housing phenomenon. It can be a catalyst for urban renewal in communities where downtowns and surrounding neighborhoods are in decline. An excellent Canadian example is occurring in the inner-city of Winnipeg, where the University of Winnipeg has worked with city and provincial governments to convert abandoned housing into student residences. Likewise, the City of Brantford has partnered with Wilfrid Laurier University, Nipissing University and Mohawk College to position post-secondary education as the catalyst for the re-birth of Brantford's decline in the wake of massive industry closures and abandonment of the central business district. The Laurier Brantford Campus is now restoring and converting heritage buildings, abandoned structures, old theatres and churches. This has sparked a multi-million dollar building trend in the downtown, associated with student housing, arts and culture and retail establishments.

While the provision of economic stability and growth, as well as adequate and safe student housing are important aspects of the Town and Gown approach to planning, its more immediate impact has been the development of a shared responsibility for harmonious relations between off-campus students, landlords, local residents and civic officials. More and more communities are taking a pro-active approach to the perceived threat of student housing and an associated lack of civility that may arise in these enclaves. While still a rather under-researched area of study, the early results in communities with Town and Gown Committees is quite impressive. Some of the innovative approaches being taken in these Town and Gown Communities include:

• Student foot patrols that work with police, neighborhood groups and by-law enforcement officers in being visible, pro-active, helpful neighborhood citizens. These often include "safe-walk" programs, as well as litter patrols and noise and unsightly premise reminders.

• Height and density studies, as well as student

rental accommodation review programs. Such programs often include a Code of Standards for landlords and student tenants, housing registries, proactive lot maintenance enforcement, and licensing lodging houses with local governments.

• A September "door knocker" program where university/college officials, student government representatives, neighborhood associations and police go door-to-door in near-campus housing areas to provide both students and non-student households information addressing past issues and perceptions and what it takes to make a good neighborhood work. Such programs allow for a friendly, nonthreatening approach to student occupied dwellings, as well as allowing local residents the opportunity to express their fears and concerns, as well as getting to know the various members of the Town and Gown Committee and their student neighbors.

• Various publications on encouraging neighborhood associations and residents, both student and permanent, to work together in making a safe and livable environment. Access to student newspapers and radio stations for education on housing issues and concerns, as well as local "neighborhood spirit builder" get togethers have been positive approaches to the housing mix found in near-campus neighborhoods.

• Landlord information sessions and landlord inventories have been developed in some communities, with instruction and assistance on such matters as provincial regulations, local by-laws, legal assistance with tenants, planning and zoning information, etc.

• The development of university/college and student government administrative portfolios specifically designed to address the Town and Gown issues that may develop over the year. These are positive, outward signs that universities and colleges are serious about the overall impact of post-secondary educational institutions on the lives and well-being of the community.

Developing a Community Vision

Town and Gown issues highlight the symbiotic relationship between colleges and universities, their students, and the communities that surround them and provide many of the essential services needed in their unique daily coexistence. Postsecondary education has always had a mission to prepare students to be "citizens of the world." Certainly, community concerns regarding a lack of civility on the part of some of these same students needs to be part of the educational experience. As more and more communities raise fears and concerns about noise, parties, late night vandalism and even rioting in the streets, the Town and Gown Committee concept stands as a strategy whose time has come.

The Town and Gown concept is an ideal model for identifying and dealing with community issues associated with spatial concentrations of student housing. The role of post-secondary institutions in dealing with off-campus student behavior, as well as student welfare and the right to safe housing, is the other important part of the equation. Working with student residents, both Town and Gown representatives can move the issues of resident rights and responsibilities, inappropriate behavior, as well as adequate and safe housing, towards an overall community vision and a climate of civility for all.

NOTES

1. CMHC. Student Housing in Canada: Developing a Methodology to Collect Data and Information (Ottawa: CMHC Research Highlight, 2005).

2. J. Pritchett. Students Claim Aberdeen Street as Their Own. *The Kingston Whig-Standard*, October 6, 2005. [Accessed October 6, 2005]. Available at: http://www.thewhig.com/webapp/sitepages/printable.asp?paper=www.thewhig.com&contents.

3. R. Tamburri. Making Nice with the Neighbours. University Affairs 2006 (8–11).

4. Macmillan English Dictionary 2006. [Accessed May 16, 2006]. Available at: http://www.macmillandictionary.com/New-Words/040124-studentification.

5. D.P. Smith. "Studentification": A Guide to Opportunities, Challenges and Practice. London: Universities UK Management Guidelines, January 2006.

6. City of Waterloo Town and Gown Committee. Town and Gown Committee Report (Waterloo: City of Waterloo; 2005).

7. Town and Gown Association of Ontario, 2006. Available at: http://www.tgao.ca/page.php?id=3.

8. Association of Atlantic Universities. Smarter Together: The Economic Impact of Universities in the Atlantic Provinces (Halifax: AAU, March 2006).

CHAPTER 24

Los Angeles and University of Southern California Officials Train Future Public Managers

P. Michael Paules

City and county managers have heard the warning: there aren't enough well-trained local government management professionals ready to take over leadership roles when existing managers retire. Why is this occurring? Some would say it's just a demographic phenomenon as baby boomers retire and are followed by Generations X and Y, whose members place greater value on multitasking, independence, and short-term rewards than their predecessors, whose guiding principles have centered on progressive social change.

But the impending leadership crisis may be more the doing of the retiring generation itself than any particular demographic trend. Budget cutting and organizational streamlining have reduced the number of generalist management positions in many organizations. Important rungs of the career ladder have been removed from organizational charts as generalist positions have been replaced by technical specialists.

Managers reporting to top executives are frequently given extensive line responsibilities, preventing them from developing generalist management skills and an organization-wide perspective. Jobs that once occupied the on-deck-circle for promotions to executive leadership posts have been lost.

Compounding this problem is the relative obscurity in which city and county management professionals work. In today's media-dominated society, little attention is paid to public managers unless things go extremely wrong; then, in assigning blame, citizens find it difficult to distinguish between politicians and administrators, which leads to growing disenchantment.

Today, fewer candidates are prepared to pursue a senior management career track than did so a generation ago.[1] And for those who do enter this track, some of the best and brightest candidates actually feel that the risks and responsibilities of executive management outweigh the rewards.

What Steps Are Needed?

If the soon-to-retire generation of public managers shares some responsibility for the impending leadership void, what steps can they take to help fill the pipeline with capable and energetic individuals ready to take up the challenge of local government management in the 21st century? A unique collaboration between management practitioners and the School of Policy, Planning, and Development (SPPD) at

Originally published as "New and Valuable: University Partnerships," *Public Management*, Vol. 89, No. 10, November 2007, by the International City/County Management Association, Washington, DC. Reprinted with permission of the publisher.

the University of Southern California (USC) offers a model of collaboration and innovation in developing talent in the field of local government leadership.

The public administration program at USC was established in 1929 by a group of suburban city managers and administrators in Los Angeles city and county governments to meet the demands of the growing Los Angeles region,[2] and it has consistently been one of the top-ranked programs in the nation. Now the university and city management community have come full circle by reinventing the partnership that has served both interests so well for the past 60 years.

Last year, Cal-ICMA — California's ICMA affiliate — proposed the creation of a pilot program with USC in which ICMA members and university representatives would work together to provide academic training, professional development, and financial support for graduate students committed to local government management.

Bill Kelly, city manager of Arcadia, California, and members of the Cal-ICMA Next Generation Committee began a series of meetings with SPPD Dean Jack Knott and members of the university's financial aid staff, which led to the establishment of the master of public administration (MPA) City/County Management Fellowship Program (CCMFP).

CCMFP provides each member of a small group of graduate students who are pursuing MPA degrees with an annual $12,000 scholarship funded by the university as well as an extensive array of networking opportunities with local government professionals, including internships, mentoring opportunities, and attendance at ICMA and other local government conferences.

The program structure is established by a memorandum of understanding between the university and Cal-ICMA. An advisory council, consisting of 11 city managers and university representatives, oversees implementation and spearheads initiatives to involve the greater public manager community. Managers who serve on the advisory council solicit funds, recommend criteria used in awarding the fellowships, and facilitate participation by CCMFP

Fellows in local government professional organizations.

In 2007, seven scholarships were provided, and it is anticipated that next year the number of scholarships will grow to 11. Selection is competitive and is based on academic achievements and commitment to the local government management field. The university determines the number and selection of the fellowship recipients with input from the advisory council.

Additional financial support for the CCMFP has been provided by the California City Management Foundation, which contributed $5,000 to professional development activities for participants, including subsidized attendance at ICMA and regional professional conferences. In the coming year, the advisory council plans to contact public management practitioners, particularly SPPD alumni, to invite their involvement through financial support or other activities such as providing internships and offering mentoring to CCMFP fellows.

Spin-offs

A number of spin-off opportunities have resulted from the USC and Cal-ICMA collaboration. Two city managers from the CCMFP advisory council have recently been appointed to the university's MPA advisory board. There are also ongoing discussions with the university about adding practicing city management professionals to SPPD's adjunct faculty roster. The success of the CCMFP pilot program and the interest and involvement of local city and county managers will determine Cal-ICMA's development of future partnerships with other universities.

Mark Alexander, city manager of La Canada Flintridge, California, and vice president of the CCMFP advisory council, recently summarized the program's goals, stating "The USC City/County Management Fellowship Program pioneers a new opportunity for local governments and higher education to work together to develop the next generation of managers."[3]

Support from the university has also been

nothing short of enthusiastic. Dr. Shui Yan Tang, USC's MPA program director, put it this way: "Preparing our students to be leaders in local government has long been a key mission of the MPA program at USC. The new City/County Management Fellowship signifies our continual commitment to this mission. We look forward to working with Cal-ICMA and our alumni in making the fellowship a success."[4]

In these times when shifting politics, job stress, and bad publicity are causing managers to reassess their professional goals, there may be no better way to rekindle the passion for public service than to reach out to the next generation of local government leaders. Sharing time and experience with young professionals through programs like the California City/County Management Fellowship Program pro-

vides managers with an opportunity to give back to the profession and invest in the future of local government.

The retirement clock is ticking, so the time to begin this process is now. The opportunities are limited only by the commitment that ICMA members bring to the task.

NOTES

1. Ralph Blumenthal, "Unfilled City Manager Posts Hint at Future Gap," *New York Times* (January 11, 2007).
2. Frank P. Sherwood, "The Education and Training of Public Managers," in *The Handbook of Organization Management*, ed. William B. Eddy (New York: M. Dekker, 1983), 43.
3. Carl Alameda and John Keisler, "USC to Offer 2007 City/County Management Fellowship Program, Los Angeles Metro Area ASPA Update (Spring 2007): 3, 7.
4. Ibid., 7.

CHAPTER 25

Mentor Citizens Benefit from the Mentor Public School District's Budget

Daniel L. Wilson

The recovery from the most recent recession has been much slower than the historic recovery cycle, taking much longer than most experts predicted. The reality for Ohio's next biennial budget is that K–12 public education funding cannot be sustained at the current levels. The most recent local property tax passage rates resulted in approximately 36 percent of new money requests passing and 8 percent of no tax increase renewals failing. Clearly, local taxpayers are not able or willing to replace reduced state funding, so local school districts must focus on actively managing expenses.

In fact, the current economic climate may provide once-in-a-lifetime opportunities to fundamentally restructure the budgets for K–12 public education. This is suggested in the emerging discussions about revisions to Ohio's collective bargaining laws, an increasing number of local districts delaying or freezing salary schedule step increases, increasing discussions of consolidation of the smallest school districts, increasing sharing of administrative and operational expenses, and a growing body of research on the rationality and effectiveness of the current teacher salary schedule structure.

Making the Most of Limited Options

Local school districts are bound by the Ohio Constitutional provisions requiring balanced budgets and prohibiting local growth in property tax revenue. The only local school district options to a reduction of state revenue are to reduce expenses, raise new local revenue, or a combination of both.

The most effective and most difficult option is to reduce expenses. Many local efforts are focused on non-personnel expenses which represent only 15 percent or so of the operating budget. Reducing the use of photocopier paper or office supplies might lower spending, but the impact on the total operating budget is negligible. The management strategies that produce the most budgetary impact are those that focus on the largest expenses: salaries, employee benefits, special education expenses, and the number of classrooms in operation. A fundamental business principle is that you can manage only what you measure. An effective management strategy is to break down these four major expense categories into individual subcategories, as shown below, allowing individual and specific expense reductions to be developed and implemented.

Originally published as "Managing Public School District Budgets," *Government Finance Review*, Vol. 27, No. 4, August 2011, by the Government Finance Officers Association, Chicago, Illinois. Reprinted with permission of the publisher.

SALARIES

Require the development of five-year staffing budgets as a part of the current five-year forecasts. The staffing budget should also support and be connected to the local school district's strategic plan.

- The number of staff members should be connected to the projected number of students, as well as class size limits, if any, imposed by the local school district.
- The types of pay (i.e. regular, substitute, supplemental, and overtime) should be budgeted separately.
- The salary schedule structure, including cost of step increases, cost of longevity, and cost of additional educational training, should be budgeted separately.
- The type of employee should include unit costs to provide budget information on the impact of adding or reducing staff (e.g., an instructional aide versus a teacher versus a teaching assistant).

BENEFITS

Benefits are often directly linked to salaries; however, local school districts still have budget management opportunities.

- Determine the types of employee benefits to offer, such as health, dental, vision, or life insurance. For example, providing term life insurance is much less expensive than offering a whole life insurance program.
- Districts that do not participate in a group purchasing program for health, dental, or vision insurance need to explore the potential cost benefits of self-funding the insurance programs.
- Require direct employee participation in health management, including financial contributions for all employee insurance programs. This engages employees more fully in strategies to reduce future costs of insurances, as well as providing budget reductions.

SPECIAL EDUCATION PROGRAMS

There are many complex legal requirements regarding programming for identified disabled students. Notwithstanding the legal restrictions, there are budget management possibilities.

- Ensure a standardized individualized education plan that includes central office involvement and budget impact discussions.
- Analyze the budget impact of out-of-district placement versus in-district placement of students with disabilities.
- Develop direct parent reimbursement for certain transportation needs in lieu of district-provided or contract-provided special needs transportation.

NUMBER OF CLASSROOMS IN OPERATION

The number of classrooms needed should be a function of how many students are enrolled and the grade configuration.

- The number of classrooms should be connected to the number of current and projected students enrolled as well as any local class size limits. Building utilization should be analyzed on a periodic basis.
- Grade configuration decisions should include the budget impact of various configuration options.

Conclusions

The current economic climate creates a need for considering structural changes to the local school district's operating budgets. Evaluating all instructional programs and extracurricular programs as well as operational aspects of the school district, based on each community's unique values, can identify opportunities for structural changes within the four major expense categories. An effective evaluation and budget restructuring will require participation of the board of education, superintendent, chief financial officer and/or treasurer, administrative team, collective bargaining units, and representatives of the community.

CHAPTER 26

Meredith Works with Plymouth State University to Provide Housing for Internship Program

Rob Baker *and* Carol Granfield

Helping Prepare the Next Generation

In 1993, this author (Rob Baker) had a brainstorm while trying to work out a local government summer internship for one of my students in her hometown of Muscatine, Iowa. Having a background in small-town administration, I am aware of the fact that local governments have projects that need attention but a lack of resources prevents their completion.

Undergraduate students are clamoring for meaningful internship experiences that will enhance their understanding of the real world of local government management and at the same time, help them make important decisions about their futures. These two facts, in addition to my preference for experiential learning options, helped me in developing an integrated internship program for students interested in management.

My experiences taught me that positive internships had to meet the needs of three key stakeholders: (1) the local government host, (2) the student intern, and (3) the academic institution.

GENESIS OF THE PROGRAM

To meet these specific needs I devised a program that consists of an internship combined with an academic seminar that is portable and conducted under the auspices of any local government jurisdiction. Students would be placed as interns in local government departments for a period of nine weeks and given one or more projects to complete by the end of the program.

They also would take a class twice a week and attend selected local government meetings. Aside from teaching the seminar, my role would be one of daily mentor and administrator at the work site for students to consult on their projects, to troubleshoot any issues regarding supervision, and to help facilitate the independent work that would be required for the students to complete their projects.

Since the internships would be unpaid and students would be paying tuition, it seemed the only way this would be financially feasible was if the host local government provided the housing and utilities. Given these basic parameters, I proposed the idea to a colleague who at the time was city administrator of Grand Island, Nebraska.

He was enthusiastic, and we began plan-

Originally published as "Two Perspectives on Local Government Management Internship Programs," *Public Management*, Vol. 88, No. 1, January/February 2006, by the International City/County Management Association, Washington, DC. Reprinted with permission of the publisher.

ning how to pilot the program the following summer. In 1994, 13 students participated in the initial program, which proved to be a great success. It was followed by two more iterations — Fernandina Beach, Florida, in 1997, and Grand Island, in 2000 — and numerous projects were completed for the host local governments. A list of projects can be found on the Web site at www.localintern.org.

In an effort to expand the program to new localities, I worked to get commitments from potential hosts that had expressed an interest in it, only to have them drop out during the planning stages for various reasons. I was frustrated because I knew the value of the tremendous work students were accomplishing for the communities that had initially agreed to participate.

The students were uniformly energized, and the host governments were able to obtain — essentially for free — the full-time services of eager college students who were supervised by university staff with extensive local government experience. The only cost to the government was housing, and they were at liberty to be creative to work out agreeable arrangements.

It was at this point that I thought the International City/County Management Association (ICMA) could be a clearinghouse for highlighting the benefits of the program, and it seemed that ICMA might view this as a way to promote the local government management profession to undergraduates.

As it turns out, the Association had been focusing intently on what it viewed as a "quiet crisis" of a graying profession. It was launching new initiatives to try to offset trends that seemed to suggest a potentially serious lack of new managers coming into the profession to fill pending retirements. Much of ICMA's effort, however, was focused on graduate students.

Since my program was for undergraduates, it could fill another niche in ICMA's Next Generation strategic plan. In the winter of 2003-2004, I proposed to the ICMA staff that we partner resources to pilot a process where potential local government hosts could submit proposals to ICMA, and ICMA would provide a clearinghouse and publicity function for the program.

This effort was agreeable with all parties, and the first go-round was the fall of 2004 for a summer 2005 inauguration of the new partnership. Initially, some seven potential hosts demonstrated interest and Meredith, New Hampshire, was chosen as the first local government participant.

PILOT PROGRAM

Meredith was an ideal site for the pilot program for several reasons. First, Town Manager Carol Granfield was enthusiastic and extremely supportive of the need to help educate young people about careers in local government management.

Second, as a smaller town but located in a popular summer tourist area, Meredith had been experiencing significant growing pains, which its small-sized staff was struggling to deal with. Several projects had to be left unattended as staff members worked diligently to wrestle with providing quality services in the midst of tremendous growth pressures.

Third, as a New England town, the style of government presented a unique learning opportunity for the students. Given these advantages, Carol and I, along with program co-director, Dr. Jeff Ankrom, began planning for our arrival in Meredith on May 29. Carol's experiences in this regard, as well as her assessment of the program, follow.

Planning and Implementing the LGMI Program

As a local government manager for more than 32 years, I (Carol Granfield) must say that one of the primary challenges of managing a small community is having sufficient staff and expertise to handle the varied tasks and projects that the community and elected officials expect to be addressed effectively and efficiently.

Meredith, New Hampshire, has a permanent population of just over 6,700. As a quaint tourist community on Lake Winnipesaukee, however, the population triples during the summer and fall foliage seasons. With fewer than 100 employees, department heads and the manager must wear several hats and juggle many activities. Consequently, I am always seeking grant opportunities, volunteer work, and other innovations to accomplish progressive, beneficial, and cost-effective community projects.

After reading about a joint venture between the ICMA and Wittenberg University seeking a community to host a Local Government Management Internship Program (LGMIP), I thought, "What a great idea." Given Meredith's small size and corresponding resources, it seemed like the kind of opportunity that would help provide assistance to accomplish various projects our departments need to be working on but often don't have the time or resources to begin or complete. So I decided to pursue the possibility of Meredith hosting the program.

While the program's advantages were evident, several hurdles needed to be crossed. The first was to gain support from Meredith's elected officials and management team. The board offered support if there was no cost to the town, although they were somewhat apprehensive. The management team also understandably had mixed reactions and some concerns about the need to "train" the interns and supervise them adequately. I indicated that the purpose of the program was to be beneficial, not detrimental, and would seek more information to help all of us make the final decision.

Program with Advantages

Two aspects of the program were particularly attractive. One was the opportunity to have several interns working for the town at no cost, providing the chance to mentor students interested in a public sector career. The benefits and challenges of public sector careers are often not known by college students, and I applaud Bob O'Neill and ICMA for promoting the venture to introduce these opportunities, especially given the concern about the baby boomer generation (me included) retiring in large numbers over the next several years, taking vast experience with them.

The other unique aspect of LGMIP was the involvement of on-site professors who could answer various questions from the interns and point them in the right direction for research

or contacts. These aspects were helpful to me in gaining support from my community.

A key step was developing the projects that interns would work on. I wanted to have a wide range of projects. Some were initially developed based on projects I had asked departments to do that just didn't get done due to a lack of time, personnel, or funding for consultants. Others came from staff suggestions.

My goal was to have the projects as fully detailed as possible before the interns arrived. I also planned a first-day orientation with the management team, a bus tour of the town, and a dinner the first evening that included an invitation to the sponsors.

A challenge was arranging housing for the nine-week program at no cost to the town, particularly since it was during our prime tourist season and typical hotel space was limited. Host families were an option but not preferred, as the intent was to keep the interns together and make them fairly self-sufficient.

Through business associates connected with Plymouth State University, 20 miles away, I was able to find a relatively inexpensive rental-housing unit in Plymouth. To fund the cost, I sent letters to various businesses, civic organizations, governmental groups, and spoke to the local Rotary Club. I outlined the projects that would be completed and as a result, was able to receive funding for housing the professor and interns for the entire period of time.

We found that local governments can be quite creative with housing options. Aside from Meredith's use of sponsors to pay for lodging at a rooming house, examples from the previous programs included turning offices in an old city hall into bedrooms and the break room into a kitchen; renting a multi-bedroom house for the students and putting the professor up in an inexpensive motel suite; and renting apartments from a local business college.

Making It Interesting

I attempted to provide the interns with broad exposure to many facets of local government. They attended board of selectmen meetings, as well as the state manager's conference; participated in a meeting and tour of the state municipal association; and attended an ICMA

Web cast. Individual department heads also involved interns in their department and professional meetings.

The turnaround from apprehension and skepticism to total acceptance and support happened the very first week at a selectmen's meeting that was televised on cable TV. The selectmen not only welcomed the interns but publicly commented that they were mistaken in their original apprehension as they already had seen the positive benefits.

Initial skepticism of some department heads also quickly abated. In the first week, for example, I had a department head tell me that he had to talk to me about a problem. The professor and I met with him and learned that he thought his department was going to be assigned one of the interns but that the intern was also working on another department's project. This concern was addressed by designating the intern solely to his department for several projects. Now, instead of not wanting the interns, departments were vying for them.

Interns accomplished a significant number of positive projects, including a citizen perception survey with an estimated value of several thousand dollars if completed by a consultant, which provided Meredith with a report card on services, a town-wide sign inventory, a multi-year playground equipment replacement program, and a comprehensive parking-space study.

The projects will not only assist Meredith but can be models for other communities as project information will be provided to state municipal associations as a resource. Meredith also realized some intangible benefits by hosting the program. Most significantly, the interns' positive energy rekindled employee enthusiasm for more program innovations and involvement.

CONSIDER HOSTING

My advice to local government managers is to seriously consider hosting the internship program. Key aspects to begin working on are sponsorships to assist with housing if that is a concern. Options to seek for housing include hotels, colleges, and other group-type facilities.

A primary focus can also be to identify several projects that can be started immediately upon the interns' arrival. This can be done by simply thinking of all the items you have on the to-do list that have not yet been accomplished. Also, review what projects you have requested departments to work on that have not yet been completed for various reasons.

Preplanning and organization are important. I encourage anyone who is interested in pursuing this program to contact me. I'd be happy to share experiences and offer suggestions.

CHAPTER 27

Middletown Works with Wesleyan University to Develop Long-Term Neighborhood Plan

Laura Brown

Joan Liljedahl has lived in her home at 48 Brainerd Ave. for the past 35 years. From her seat on the porch (where she spends most of her time), she can tell you which houses have had drug deal busts, point out the floor that Professor of Music Tony Braxton lives on, and introduce you to every single student walking by.

One of those students is Lauren Sonnabend G'09 who got stopped by Liljedahl coming out of her house across the street.

"All the students love her," Sonnabend said. "She's so sweet, and she's been here for decades. You can't fool her."

Liljedahl has seen the neighborhood and the University go through significant changes over the years: the adjustments after women were admitted to the University in 1970; the rapid increase in enrollment that created a housing crunch; and the University's decision to begin buying up homes in the neighborhood to accommodate the higher number of students. Indeed, by the 1980s, the area's demographics had tipped toward student residents.

Frustration with student noise and lack of respect led to residents founding the Association of Wesleyan Area Residents (AWARE) in 1999. The group has a goal of changing student behavior and developing a long-term plan for the neighborhood.

Wendy Berlind is the wife of Professor Emeritus of Biology and AWARE member Allan Berlind. The couple has lived at their dark brown home on Miles Ave. since 1972, and their experience with students echoed many AWARE members' complaints.

"They [students] come out at 11, 12 at night, and we go to bed at 10:30; just speaking in the street is enough," Berlind said. "There'll be groups on Fountain, Pine … screeching and bellowing is common. After 10 or 11, that's really hard on people."

AWARE meetings with the Wesleyan Student Association, Public Safety, and members of the administration have helped influence policies like the selling of the InTown student housing units in 2005, and making Home, Brainerd, and Lawn Avenues into quiet streets in 2004.

According to Liljedahl, the change to quiet status on all three streets made a huge difference.

"This used to be a nightmare all night on Friday nights," she explained, pointing towards the former student houses near the corner of Brainerd and Lawn Avenues.

According to the WSA guidelines, living in a quiet house requires that all noise generated must not be audible outside the house. Unlike

Originally published as "Residents React with Ambivalence," *The Wesleyan Argus*, September 30, 2011, by Wesleyan University, Middletown, Connecticut. Reprinted with permission of the publisher.

117

houses on other streets, where first noise violations receive warnings, a noise violation by a quiet house will automatically be referred to the Student Judicial Board (SJB).

According to Rob and Peggy Johnston, however, who have lived at their home on the corner of Brainerd and Lawn Avenues for the past six years, the administration's punishment system for noise violations is not enforced.

"We called three times on one house in the same night," Peggy said. "They just don't follow through with what they say ... they don't want to discipline."

The Johnstons, who have met several times with University administrators such as former Vice President and Secretary of the University (and current Professor of Earth and Environmental Sciences) Peter Patton and Vice President of Student Affairs Mike Whaley, complained about things such as noisy students routinely walking by late at night (on their way to and from parties, according to Peggy), vandalism of their fence, and even student urination on their lawn.

"You can talk until you're blue," Rob said. "Patton, Whaley, they're worthless. They're song and dance people. They'll tell you what you want to hear, but then there's never anything done."

Peggy admitted the University did replace their torn-down wire fence with a new wooden one, but added that the very next weekend they spotted a student climbing over it. She said she didn't realize what living next to students would be like.

"We knew it'd be different, but I didn't expect the students to be this disrespectful," she said. "There's no respect from students for private homes."

Rob, however, said the University administrators were also to blame.

"I don't want to totally blame the students; it's partly a management problem," he said. "If they [the administration] doesn't do anything, why would students do anything?"

As far as the role that Public Safety plays in disciplining students, Professor Emeritus of German Studies and Wesleyan Chimemaster Peter Frenzel, who has lived with his wife Laurie at their home on Miles Ave. for the past

25 years, said Public Safety was usually successful in getting noise and disruptions under control.

"Oh, we've got their number; we used to call them when there were noise problems," Frenzel said. "They've done a good job for us."

Rob agreed, saying that when Public Safety stood out on the street near their home, the noise was not a problem.

"They do what they are there for — I give them high credits," he said. "They do a good job."

While seemingly all residents in the area have heard or read about the arrests occurring in the spring of this year on Fountain Ave., they generally have widely varying accounts and opinions of the incident. The Frenzels both said that they hadn't heard the noise that night, which was very unusual for a student gathering of that size.

Liljedahl said she had only read about it later on, but thought the police action was excessive.

"That's too much force; they're not bad kids," she said. "Maybe a little noisy, but not bad."

Liljedahl continued, saying she thought that while the quiet streets had helped the noise problems, the students in recent years also seemed more respectful and friendly than in the past.

"They're delightful," she said. "I think the element has changed — they're more selective with their kids. I think the students that come here appreciate the opportunity to be here."

Peter Frenzel, who still has an office in Fisk Hall, agreed that the students he knew were wonderful, and living so near to campus gives him extra opportunities to spend time with them.

"It was great when I was teaching," he said. "If the class was small enough, we always had them over for dinner."

According to Laurie Frenzel, her husband also agreed with the sentiment that students had been getting better in recent years.

"[Peter] told me that this year's Wesleyan students are the best he's ever had," she said. "I'm hoping it's true."

When asked why they had stayed in their

home even when noise was a problem, Laurie said the benefits of the area had been enough to keep them there.

"We love it here," she said. "We have sidewalks! We can get to all the concerts, all the plays; we can walk over and watch a football game if we want. We're right in the center, and we love Middletown."

Liljedahl agreed.

"I love living here," she said. "I love to watch students: their spirit, their movements, to see what they're wearing! I'm so blessed to be here and enjoy this."

CHAPTER 28

New York City Benefits by Columbia University Working with Local Neighborhoods

Michael Porter *and* Paul Grogan

To better understand the role of leadership and a comprehensive implementation of the strategic framework, ICIC and CEOs for Cities conducted two in-depth case studies, one of Columbia University in New York City and the other of Virginia Commonwealth University in Richmond.

Both of these institutions offer highly instructive examples of an urban-based university playing an active role in the revitalization of its surrounding communities. The case studies show the mechanisms and rationales for the universities' role in local job and business growth. They offer examples of strong leadership, effective institutional setup, and meaningful community engagement. Moreover, both cases illustrate that a methodical, patient approach to integrating the community into university growth strategies holds the promise of sustained economic impact.

Columbia University, specifically, shows how an urban-based university can align its interests with those of its surrounding community, creating a strong "win-win" relationship. VCU, moreover, shows how such an institution can take not only local but also regional leadership in anchoring economic growth.

In-Depth Case: Columbia University in New York City

Located in the Morningside Heights neighborhood of Upper Manhattan, Columbia University employs more than 13,000 people and has an annual operating budget of nearly $2 billion. In fiscal year 2000–2001, Columbia directed $60 million in purchasing to local vendors,[1] paid $18 million to local construction contractors, developed 19 master contracts with local vendors and suppliers, and established or expanded business relationships with 208 local vendors.

For decades, talk of expansion and fear of gentrification resulting from inadequate policies of the university pitted many in the Upper Manhattan communities of Harlem, Morningside Heights, Washington Heights, and Inwood against Columbia. An often-cited culmination of these conflicts was the 1968 protest over Columbia's attempted construction in Morningside Park. Protests over a proposed gymnasium brought the university's plans to an eight-day standstill and resulted in the arrests of 700 protestors. These conflicts and their consequent public relations problems further eroded Columbia's political support and even its endow-

Originally published as "Vision and Strategy in Action: In-Depth Case Studies," *Leveraging Colleges and Universities for Urban Economic Revitalization: An Action Agenda*, March 2002, by the Initiative for a Competitive Inner City and CEOs for Cities, Boston, Massachusetts. Reprinted with permission of the publisher.

ment fund. "From the late '60s to the '80s, Columbia may have lost as much as a billion dollars in contributions," says George Rupp, President of Columbia University.

As a response, the university sought to improve its relationship with the community. President Michael Sovern, in office from 1980 to 1993, created Columbia's Office of Government Relations and Community Affairs to change the university's image and take concrete steps to improve relations. More fundamental changes, however, were to follow.

Columbia's trustees came to recognize that strong relationships with neighboring communities were an integral part of the institution's mission. They went so far as to create a Community Relations Subcommittee to encourage and monitor efforts to build stronger ties with the community. In searching for a new president in the early 1990s, they took special care to select someone who had a proven track record and strong commitment to community engagement. George Rupp's success as President of Rice University and his teachings at Harvard Divinity School on pluralism and commitment to community made him a strong choice.

Upon becoming President in 1993, Rupp made engagement in the community a top priority for Columbia. This translated into initiating a strategic-planning process, internal reorganization, ramping up internal and external communications — especially with media, securing partnerships with community groups, and being present at community events.

One of his first moves was to recruit additional senior public affairs staff members who were sensitive to the city's complexity and committed to strengthening the university's role in the local community and its commitment to economic development. Similarly, he brought senior administrators to his team who had experience working with local communities. Rupp provided his new team with the resources necessary to enhance Columbia's involvement in the surrounding neighborhoods, giving them the time and the staff necessary to actively engage in the communities.

With faculty, staff, and students, Rupp emphasized the importance of community involvement to Columbia, ensuring awareness of his administration's commitment to these initiatives. Rupp's major priorities were summarized as increasing the amount of local spending, increasing purchasing from local vendors, and employing more people from surrounding communities.

REAL ESTATE DEVELOPER

With 20,000 students and more than 13,000 employees crowded into 36 acres — a small-sized city crammed into five square city blocks — Columbia is constantly searching for additional space. In the extremely tight real estate market of Manhattan, this is no easy task. It is also a task made very complicated by Columbia's previous lack of sensitivity to Upper Manhattan residents. Over the past decade or so, Columbia has taken steps to improve its battered relationship with the surrounding communities, and there seem to be solid gains.

Its first conciliatory step dates back to the early 1980s. The newly created Office of Government Relations and Community Affairs opened Columbia's campus to the surrounding community, encouraging both elected officials and local community groups to use the campus for meetings and events. Some community members, however, still felt unwelcome and distrusted the university's outreach efforts. Local officials feared that no one would attend a town hall meeting that was held at Columbia, while community groups viewed coming to campus as "selling out."

Columbia continued to reach out, despite initial resistance. The outreach has focused on more open and active communication between the university and the community, including cosponsoring events with groups such as the National Urban League, the Greater Harlem Chamber of Commerce, and the Harlem Business Alliance. As a part of this open communication, Columbia regularly presents capital project plans for community feedback at local community board meetings, as well as offers of assistance to local civic associations. For instance, planning a mixed-use faculty housing and elementary school in the Morningside area, the university attended more than 40 community board meetings, presenting project plans and modifying them to reflect community feed-

back. The university not only incorporated design suggestions but also allotted half of the
space in the elementary school to local children.
In response, the community board — the local
arm of city government — endorsed this project, an occurrence unimaginable a mere six
years ago.

President Rupp and his committed team
of administrators have proven to be the deciding factor in Columbia's success in recent years.
"The main decision makers show up at community meetings," says Maritta Dunn, former
chairperson of Community Board 9. "When
Emily Lloyd [Executive Vice President of Administration at Columbia] comes to a meeting,
people know that if she says 'yes,' it will get
done. They can trust her." She continues, "Also,
important ground work is done by Larry Dais
[Columbia's director of community affairs],
who has close relationships with community
members. The community knows that both of
them have strong support from President
Rupp." Though tensions arise over specific proposed projects, conflicts are resolved — and are
resolved much faster. Dunn explains, "Six or
seven years is too short to turn around 30 or
40 years of bad blood, but the current administration has made major strides toward accomplishing that goal."

Aligning university interests with those of
the community has enabled Columbia to begin
turning around anti–Columbia sentiments.
Local purchasing and hiring (discussed below)
are part of Columbia's reconciliation strategy;
however, active communication with the community on the front end of capital projects,
involvement of senior administration in key
community meetings, and incorporation of
community interests have proved to be the win-
ning combination in the short term.

Opportunities exist for Columbia to use
its development efforts to anchor economic development in Upper Manhattan. Currently, the
university is considering future development
sites, including midtown locations, as well as
underutilized sites that it owns in West Harlem
near the waterfront. Although the university
believes that the Harlem alternative has strong
merits, both for the institution and the broader
community, Columbia is approaching it very

cautiously. "We will not be going into Harlem
unless we're invited," said Alan Stone, Columbia's Vice President for Public Affairs.

INCUBATOR

As New York City worked to bring the
multi-billion-dollar biotechnology industry
closer to home, it partnered with Columbia
University. In 1995, the city and state of New
York worked with Columbia to develop the
Audubon Business and Technology Park. The
park serves as a vehicle to spark university collaboration with industry and commercialize academic research, providing New York City and
Columbia with an opportunity to capture the
economic value of a rapidly growing industry.

Over $25 million in joint funding from
Columbia, the Empire State Development Corporation, and the New York City Economic
Development Corporation led to the development of the first building in the 700,000-
square-foot park, located next to Columbia's
Health Sciences Campus in Upper Manhattan's Washington Heights neighborhood. This
six-story facility, the Mary Woodward Lasker
Biomedical Research Building, encompasses
105,000 total gross square feet, including
60,000 square feet of lab space, 10,000 square
feet of retail space, and the city's only biotechnology business incubator.

A key piece of the Park's business development role is 5,000 square feet of finished lab
space that is designed in 500-square-foot modules for small companies. To date, 35 biotechnology startups have benefited from the affordable rent and business development support
provided by the incubator. Eighteen companies
have graduated, 16 of which are still in business.

Columbia is currently assessing the incubator's economic impact on New York City.
While commercializing research generates economic value, to capture substantial local
benefits requires that graduating companies remain in the city.

PURCHASER

In fiscal year 2000-2001, Columbia directed $60 million to local purchasing. Com-
pelled by President Rupp's call, Columbia's ad-

ministrative departments on the Morningside Campus focused on increasing this spending. Their efforts are showing initial signs of success. In fiscal year 2000–2001, local purchasing by these departments amounted to $19 million, with some offices increasing spending by 40 percent in one year. Columbia's local contracting also shows sizable growth: increasing 55 percent over the past four years to a total of $18 million.

A number of earlier efforts laid the foundation for Columbia's current focus on local purchasing. In the late 1990s, Columbia held on-campus vendor fairs. At these events, purchasing personnel held detailed discussions with several businesses, the UMEZ, and other local organizations concerning ways in which the university might increase its local spending. Through these earlier initiatives, the university began to understand the local business community and forge relationships with vendors.

These initial efforts, however, were insufficient to make substantial inroads in linking Columbia to local vendors. They suggested the need for a more comprehensive, systematic approach. Under a directive from Emily Lloyd, Executive Vice President of Administration, Columbia launched such an initiative in October 2000. This new approach included an in-depth analysis of the local vendor base — an analysis that was built on the decentralized nature of purchasing at the university, that emphasized relationship building, and that is making Columbia's purchasing more small-business friendly.

To start, each administrative department that reports to Ms. Lloyd — including Administrative Information Systems, Facilities Management, Human Resources, Institutional Real Estate, Purchasing/Support Services, and Student Services — was asked to identify areas with potential for increased local purchasing. In order to perform this analysis, each department compared its spending patterns by industry with a database of approximately 6,000 businesses in the targeted communities, compiled in conjunction with the Upper Manhattan Empowerment Zone (UMEZ).

In the Administrative Information Services Department (AIS), for example, the "Look Local First" action plan laid out strategies for identifying local vendors and integrating these vendors into the department's procurement process. New local vendors were targeted in the areas of hardware, car services, temporary employment agencies, florists, food services, and office supplies. In 2000, Columbia's central administrative departments focused on the primary goal of the initiative's first phase: fostering new local business relationships. Collectively, they established — and in some cases reestablished — relationships with 200 local vendors, a 54 percent increase over the prior year.

There have been challenges in transitioning to local vendors. For instance, some departments were initially resistant to working with local vendors, citing concerns about unproven track records with the university and potentially higher costs. To address this concern, senior administrators allowed for moderate increases in cost to ensure product and service quality. Columbia views these slight cost differences as an investment in the local business community.

Another concern among purchasing personnel was the limited capacity of some smaller local vendors. Faced with this concern, some departments have progressively increased the vendors' contracts. For example, the Facilities Management Department has agreed to contract with a local extermination company for services on a single-building basis. By contracting for one building at a time, the department is able to monitor the quality of performance by the vendor, provide feedback to the vendor, and progressively increase the size of the contract.

Another solution has been tapping into internal university expertise to provide project oversight. For instance, when the Human Resources Department wanted to print documents for wide distribution, the University Printing Services recommended a local vendor and agreed to oversee the production process.

A fourth solution has been to build local-vendor capacity through business partnerships between larger and smaller firms. For instance, several local cab service firms were identified as potential vendors to the university. However, most of these enterprises were unable to meet the university's insurance requirements. To overcome this limitation, the purchasing department identified a car dispatch company that met the university's contracting requirements and used a network of small car services. As a condition for awarding a master agreement to this dispatcher, the contract required that the large dispatcher use several of the local cab companies within its network.

The university has also developed an effective system to transfer knowledge internally on vendor performance and lessons learned. There are regular interdepartmental meetings — which include senior management — where new local vendor performance is discussed. Moreover, a group of departmental administrators meets twice a month to share positive and negative experiences with new local vendors. Often, these meetings enable administrators to recommend vendors for future purchasing to other colleagues.

The university continues to experiment with ways to make Columbia purchasing small-business friendly. For example, the newly inaugurated procurement card allows small businesses with shorter cash-flow cycles to become suppliers to the university. With these cards, university departments can pay vendors in just three days, as opposed to up to a few months under the former payment system.

Columbia derives several key benefits from local purchasing. Most important, working with the community to enhance economic stability and growth improves Columbia's relationship with local businesses, residents, and their elected officials. This, in turn, garners greater support from the community for real estate development, expansion, and other strategic initiatives that are fundamental to pursuing its educational mission. Local purchasing also improves the economic conditions of the surrounding community, enhancing the stability and livability of the community. This makes Columbia a more accessible and attractive place for both current and potential students and faculty, as well as for local residents.

In addition, university purchasing managers have found that many local vendors provide two key competitive advantages over larger, national firms. First, because of their proximity, local vendors provide efficient delivery and immediate access to goods and services for many student, faculty, and administrative needs. Second, they provide more personalized services. Many of the smaller local vendors are often willing to adapt the delivery of goods and services to guarantee a steady flow of business with the university. As Bob Lewis, owner of Minority Data Forms, claimed, "Our delivery is much better than Columbia has ever experienced. Order today. Product tomorrow. And they [Columbia purchasing personnel] have noticed. Our business with them is climbing every week."

EMPLOYER

Columbia University is a major employer in the New York metropolitan area. As of October 2000, Columbia employed 13,700 permanent, full-, and part-time employees. Of those, 70 percent live in New York City, and 37 percent live in the immediate Upper Manhattan area.

In 1999, Columbia partnered with the Morningside Area Alliance (MAA or the Alliance) to hire more local residents and develop stronger economic ties with the surrounding community. MAA is a nonprofit organization that includes 19 of the large institutions located in the Morningside Heights neighborhood between 110th and 125th Streets. Columbia worked with the MAA to create the Job Connections Program — a program that identifies, screens, and refers potential candidates to Columbia and the other large local institutions in the Morningside area.

Job Connections has yielded some promising results. Since 1999, Columbia has hired 71 Job Connections applicants for the 600 positions open, filling 21 permanent and 50 temporary positions. This service is funded by the annual membership fees that Columbia and other Morningside institutions pay MAA, as well as private grants and contributions. Columbia pays no additional fees for the Job Connections Program.

More recently, Columbia has started to work with other local groups, such as Dominican Sunday, a grassroots organization affiliated with a local Manhattan Valley church, to explore ways to increase local hiring in their communities. In 2001, the university worked with Dominican Sunday to fill 30 of the university's open positions. Of the 66 people referred by Dominican Sunday, Columbia hired 20, filling two-thirds of the 30 targeted positions. Though the majority of these hires were for temporary positions, Columbia is tracking these and similar hires in order to move those who perform well into permanent positions as they become available.

The university is also working with the MAA on a second phase of the local hiring initiative, tied to a $1 million grant from the Department of Labor for establishment of a wage subsidy program that includes a significant employment-training component. Under the program, the Alliance will provide the university and other local employers with a six-month wage subsidy when they hire applicants referred by MAA. The employer commits to hiring these workers permanently at the end of the subsidized period. During the subsidy period, MAA provides employees training that reinforces critical skills and works with hiring managers to monitor performance. Once hired permanently, employees referred through the program are eligible for all educational and other benefits associated with their job level at Columbia.

Essential to the success of these programs are local organizations, such as MAA and Dominican Sunday, that leverage their trusted name among community residents to generate interest and offer support in a process that may be unfamiliar to some. Also essential are the university hiring managers, supported by senior administration, who can facilitate relationships between Columbia and these local community organizations. These personal relationships give hiring managers an opportunity to talk about exactly what they need in a candidate and give the job counselors an opportunity to search their pool of applicants for the right person.

ADVISOR/NETWORK BUILDER

Another way in which Columbia contributes to business and job development in its surrounding community is as an advisor to local businesses and business groups. Various departments in the university offer advisory programs that channel their knowledge and expertise to the surrounding communities. Key among these are (1) the Urban Technical Assistance Program (UTAP) in the Graduate School of Architecture, Planning, and Preservation and (2) the Small Business Consulting Program (SBCP), housed in the Columbia Business School. UTAP's work impacts primarily the business environment, making the inner city more conducive to business and community development, while SBCP offers expertise for improving the performance of companies.

UTAP, started in 1995, provides infrastructure development and commercial development assistance to economically distressed urban communities, primarily in New York City. UTAP's immediate focus is on assisting community organizations in the various neighborhoods of Harlem on their revitalization and community development efforts. Since its inception, UTAP has completed 34 projects — six of which have been repeat engagements — and worked with more than 40 organizations, including community development organizations, government agencies, and foundations. The estimated investment in the inner city as a result of these projects is over $100 million.

Critical to the success of UTAP has been the input of Columbia students and faculty. With one program director and one administrative staff, UTAP has been able to bring, since its inception, 60 student interns and numerous faculty members to participate in its projects. UTAP is funded on a project-to-project basis by community organizations and foundations, and it receives annual administrative funding from the university. Going beyond the typical course-level consulting project, UTAP represents a sustained, continuous mechanism for Columbia's impact in the community.

Another advisory program, Columbia's Small Business Consulting Program (SBCP), which started in 1998, is a student-run program that partners teams of MBA students with local businesses and nonprofit organizations, providing pro bono management-consulting advice on strategic challenges. Although not specifically focused on the inner city, it is estimated that about 30 percent of the businesses involved in the SBCP each year are from the surrounding inner-city community. The SCBP has a four-fold mission: (1) help small businesses and non-profits benefit from the knowledge existing within the Columbia University community, (2) provide MBA students with tools and hands-on experience that will make them more effective managers and consultants, (3) improve Columbia Business School's impact on the community, and (4) leverage the energies of MBA students in philanthropic activities.

Columbia's SBCP is a step in the right direction toward improving conditions for the local business community. Local community groups and businesses highlight these advisory services as a valuable source of expertise and an area in which Columbia should continue to increase the breadth and depth of its activities. The SBCP could focus more on the local communities. The law and engineering schools could get involved in assisting local businesses. The students, faculty, and expertise of Columbia's many schools represent potent, yet under-utilized, resources for local business growth.

CONCLUSION

Columbia's success thus far hinges on several key factors:

Support of Columbia's Leadership

The roots of much of the success of Columbia's outreach have been the support received from Columbia's leaders: the Board of Trustees, Columbia's president, and senior administration. Together, these individuals are building the internal framework, developing the strategies, and seeing to the implementation of these economic development activities.

High Value of Activities for Columbia

By aligning its interests with that of the surrounding communities, Columbia has been able to develop a new leadership position in Upper Manhattan, reinforce its brand as a truly

urban institution, create goodwill in the community, and expedite the construction of capital improvements and new facilities critical to its mission.

Integration of the Community into the Central Functions of the University

Integrating community interests into the central functions of the university — such as purchasing and employment — is the key to sustained economic impact.

Focus on Long-Term Impact Strategies

All too often, an unsustained flow of funding and other short-term resources define university outreach to the local community. Columbia's methodical, patient approach to integrating the community holds the promise of long-term capacity building and impact.

Partnerships with Key Players in the Community

Columbia has already developed good working relationships with many key organizations and individuals in the Upper Manhattan community. Two key examples are its partnerships with the Harlem Business Alliance and the local community boards. Columbia has also developed strong working relationships with many of the region's elected officials and economic development organizations. Buy-in from these influential sources is indispensable.

NOTE

1. "Local vendors" are defined as those located in the Upper Manhattan Empowerment Zone (UMEZ).

EDITOR'S NOTES

1. The "In-Depth Case Studies" section of this report contains two case studies, which are both presented in the "Best Practices" section of this volume.

2. Various charts, tables, and other graphics are contained in this report. To see the entire report, please refer to the Initiative for a Competitive Inner City and CEOs for Cities websites, both of which are contained in Appendix C.

CHAPTER 29

Newark and Its Public School District Improve Their Environment and Economy

Todd Wilkinson

Monique Freeman does not know what the word "environmentalist" means. The smart, 13-year-old middle-school student has grown up in the gritty Central Ward of Newark, New Jersey, without the word in her vocabulary. At the moment she sits, a quizzical look on her young face, in a shabby classroom at Eighteenth Avenue School, built in the 19th century and today encircled by barbed wire. Not a single blade of grass grows on the school grounds.

"But you are an environmentalist, Monique, whether you realize it or not," Donna Kirkland tells her. Kirkland is an outreach co-ordinator for The Trust for Public Land who lives in the same tough neighborhood. She reminds Monique about how she was a leader in the school's recycling program and helped pick up 64 bags of trash on Earth Day. "You're doing something you can be proud of your whole life," Kirkland says, watching the girl's eyes light up. "Not many kids can say they made their city a better, more beautiful place."

Freeman and a group of her friends also helped plan the much-anticipated Nat Turner Park, which now is rising from a blighted vacant lot next door to the school. The nine-acre park is a budding symbol of hope in a city that has been ridiculed nationally as a poster child for urban despair.

Newark may seem like an unusual place for an environmental movement, says Carl Haefner, director of TPL's Parks for People-Newark initiative, which is spearheading the Nat Turner Park effort. But across this city of 280,000 people, a new investment in urban parks, playgrounds, and green spaces is having a profoundly positive effect on the lives of people like Freeman and Kirkland, while modeling a new kind of urban environmentalism.

For more than a decade, neighborhood leaders, with the help of TPL and its foundation partners — but without much support from City Hall — have been building parks and playgrounds in some of the city's toughest neighborhoods. The election of 38-year-old Cory A. Booker as mayor in 2006 has injected a new sense of optimism into this conservation work. City Hall has signaled its support for parks and open space, not only to improve life in the neighborhoods but as a key component of its aggressive strategy for Newark's renaissance.

Since Booker's election, the city has cast its support to neighborhood park efforts and has moved aggressively to create the new Joseph G. Minish Passaic River Waterfront Park, named for a former congressman. The new park will cover 2.2 miles and link Newark's bustling downtown to the densely and diversely popu-

Originally published as "Newark Goes for the Green," *Land & People*, Vol. 19, No. 2, Fall 2011, by The Trust for Public Land, San Francisco, California. Reprinted with permission of the publisher. Sign up for a complimentary issue of *Land & People* by visiting "tpl.org/freemag."

lated Ironbound neighborhood. At the Booker administration's request, TPL is expanding its partnership with the city to include developing this new park and refurbishing Newark's two largest existing city parks, while continuing to focus on playground construction and expansion. The goal for TPL and the City is to provide more than 80 percent of Newark's residents with easy access to recreational space.

"We are grateful that so many organizations are working on parks in a focused partnership, and chief among them is TPL," says Deputy Mayor Stefan Pryor. "Parks can and should be regarded as oases for people who live in densely populated environments. We know they are a pivotal component of our social infrastructure."

Parks for People

Settled on the banks of the Passaic River in 1665, Newark is one of the nation's oldest cities. The city is flanked by the river on the east and anchored on the north and south by Branch Brook Park and Weequahic Park, both designed by the legendary landscape architect Frederick Law Olmsted and owned and managed by Essex County. In between these natural landmarks, however, lies one of the most densely populated and park-poor urban cores in the country. According to *Newark, New Jersey: An Open Space Analysis*, a report published by TPL in 2004, Newark offers only 2.9 acres of parks per 1,000 residents: two and a half times below the average for comparable cities. In practical terms, that means that more than half of Newark's kids do not have any significant green space within a quarter-mile of their homes.

As far back as the early 1970s, TPL began partnering with local foundations and neighborhood groups to address this dearth of green space, and in recent years has spearheaded the creation of seven new neighborhood parks and playgrounds. TPL is nearly halfway into its $16.8 million Parks for People-Newark campaign, with major contributions from the Victoria Foundation and The Prudential Foundation. "TPL's commitment to this community

has taken decades to evolve, and we as an organization will be here long into the future," Haefner says. "We are not here to get in quickly and then get out." As further evidence, TPL will open a satellite office in Newark this fall.

"By hiring from the community and having a physical presence in the city, TPL wants to send a message that we believe in Newark's future and long-term success," says Terrence Nolan, TPL's New Jersey state director.

All of TPL's projects in Newark have been founded on community energy. One dramatic park effort began in 1998, when neighbors around 3.3-acre Mildred Helms Park, in the city's South Ward, organized the Mildred Helms Park Resurrection Committee. The park, named after an elderly community activist, had fallen into such disrepair that families stayed away out of fear for their safety.

"You wouldn't believe what it looked like," says Fannie Mae Harris, a 77-year-old great-grandmother and founding member of the resurrection committee. "It was all overgrown in weeds and covered in trash. There was gang graffiti spray-painted on the asphalt, and you'd often find crack vials and needles from addicts who came here to shoot up at night." Working with the committee, TPL helped raise $2 million from public and foundation sources, including a federal grant from the National Park Service, to transform the park from a menace into a major asset within easy walking distance of 6,300 residents.

Today the park offers a walking path, swings and basketball court, wild berry bushes, nesting songbirds, a gazebo, a picnic area — and a map of the United States set into the asphalt. More than 300 people showed up for the rededication ceremony in 2005, and over the last few years the park's restoration has served as an impetus for neighbors to fix up their properties. "With so many people coming into the park, the neighbors didn't want the public to see their places run down," Harris says. "The park has lifted up the people along with many of the properties surrounding it."

Creating parks in poor inner-city neighborhoods is not as simple as planting grass seed and trees on a dilapidated lot, giving it to a neighborhood, bidding good luck at a ribbon-cutting ceremony, and walking away, says Carl Haefner, who has worked on TPL's Newark program since 2004. The long-term success of any park, he says, is linked inextricably to its social environment. "You have to confront the barriers that prevent people from having a sense of being civic stakeholders in a park." In Newark these include chronic poverty and unemployment, a shortage of affordable housing, and poor health care.

Key to creating parks under such conditions is a participatory design process whose goal is to build parks that meet neighborhood needs and that communities will support over the long haul. Monique Freeman and other students at Eighteenth Avenue School helped design the new Nat Turner Park, working with TPL and landscape architects. In addition to proposing amenities such as an outdoor amphitheater and running track, Monique innocently asked where the high metal fences, metal detectors, and armed police officers would be positioned. "The kids just assumed, based upon their experience, that parks couldn't exist without those things," explains Colleen Graves, TPL's Parks for People program manager in Newark. "If you ask the kids and their parents what their priorities are, safety concerns rank at the top of the list."

Serving Students

Faith Blasi, a fifth-grade teacher at Eighteenth Avenue School, looks forward to the opening of Nat Turner Park. On paper, the nine-acre, rubble-strewn lot has been Newark's largest city-owned park since the city acquired the land in the 1970s. Three decades later it is about to become a showplace park within easy reach of Eighteenth Avenue School, Cleveland Elementary School, and the new Central High School slated to open in 2008. TPL has already raised the $7 million needed to build the park.

Getting outdoors more often will allow students to release pent-up aggression and learn to negotiate interpersonal disputes better, Blasi says. She looks forward to using the park as an outdoor classroom. "What will success look like?" she asks. "It will be a park that is used,

that is taken care of, and that the kids realize belongs to them."

Creating parks and playgrounds near schools is particularly important in a place like Newark, says Newark native Dr. Raymond Lindgren, executive assistant to Newark Public Schools Superintendent Marion A. Bolden. The average age of Newark schools is 85 years, and many playgrounds have been converted into faculty parking lots, often rimmed with barbed wire for extra security. Lindgren recalls the damage done by rioting that swept some areas of Newark in 1967. "After the riots, some neighborhoods in the Central Ward looked like bomb zones for the better part of three decades," he says. "But you can't keep the problems of the world out simply by building a larger wall around your personal space; nor do barbed wire fences encircling our schools make the kids feel any safer."

Many students live in single-parent households anchored by mothers who may work a couple of jobs but can't afford to send their kids to private day care. Latchkey kids in particular need parks and playgrounds after school and are the most vulnerable to bad influences that can destroy a young person's future, says Bertha Martin, who oversees the after-school program at Quitman Street Community School in the heart of the Central Ward.

In 2000, TPL refurbished that school's two-acre concrete schoolyard as the Quitman Street Community Playground. Like TPL's other parks and playgrounds, this one was designed not only with community input but also with the promise of continuing community stewardship to keep it open and supervised, even when school is not in session. To this end, the Community Agencies Corporation maintains a community center on the Quitman site. The playground offers a mini-track where meets are held; a basketball court and assorted playground equipment; karate classes; theater, dance, and band activities; a drill team; and paid adult chaperones. Almost 250 kids are enrolled in the after-school program, and there's a long waiting list.

Having the playground available after school has made a huge difference in the lives of latchkey kids and other students, Martin says. "The school used to do little beautification projects to make things look nice, but that wasn't enough. These kids needed supervision," she notes. "Our kids are so smart. They know what's good for them. It gives them comfort to know that when school ends tomorrow, they'll be able to be back here in a safe haven."

Passaic River Revival

Nothing has so advanced the cause of green space in Newark as the election of Cory A. Booker as mayor in 2006. "Cory Booker represents the next generation of young urban leaders, who possess both impressive academic pedigrees and larger imaginations for thinking about what great cities are supposed to be," says Dr. Clement Alexander Price, distinguished professor of history and director of the Rutgers University Institute on Ethnicity, Culture, and the Modern Experience. "These new leaders are well aware that environmental issues and public health concerns are the new frontiers of the civil rights movement."

Through all its troubles, Newark has remained a key economic center for industries such as transportation, telecommunications, wholesale and retail trade, and insurance. And increasingly the city is attracting residents in search of affordable urban living convenient to Manhattan. By working with TPL and other partners, the Booker administration is determined to support neighborhood greening as a way to advance redevelopment and economic revitalization throughout the city. "We believe that parks, playgrounds, and new public open spaces can play a vital role in sustaining livable neighborhoods and building the city's economic future," Mayor Booker says.

The new Joseph G. Minish Passaic River Waterfront Park is a vital component of this work. Under the park plan, two miles of riverfront will have walking trails, public plazas, mini-parks, and athletic fields woven into a mosaic of commercial and residential areas to attract new businesses and residents. In addition, the plan would create areas for active recreation near the Ironbound neighborhood, a vibrant, multiethnic, working-class enclave

nestled in a bend in the river. Today the 45,000 residents of the historically Portuguese neighborhood include more than 50 other ethnic groups. The $80 million riverfront plan has gotten a boost from Congress, which has approved $5.5 million through the leadership of the New Jersey congressional delegation, with an additional $3 million appropriation pending next year.

Greening the neighborhood's riverfront is a social justice issue, says Joe Della Fave, director of the Ironbound Community Corporation. The Passaic River once powered the factories on which much of Newark's wealth was based, and defunct chemical and industrial plants left the river and its embankments deeply contaminated. Promoted by the Ironbound Community Corporation and endorsed by TPL, the restoration effort represents an opportunity to clean up polluted sites, revive the waterfront for the benefit of a neighborhood that bore the brunt of Newark's industrial past, and spur economic growth. TPL will develop a comprehensive plan for the waterfront parkland, pursue public and private funds for the project, acquire the remaining parcels and easements necessary to complete park development, and initiate a design for improvements.

Whether seen in action along the Passaic River or in the Central Ward, environmentalism in Newark is more than restoring green space, creating trails, and putting grass and trees on the ground. It is about changing the way people feel about their city, their stake in it, and their ability to affect their own lives. Along with TPL, Monique Freeman, Fannie Mae Harris, Bertha Martin, Joe Della Fave, and others working on the greening of Newark are forging a new kind of urban environmentalism.

"TPL is opening an intergenerational, interracial discourse on environmental issues and bringing Newark into a movement that has largely ignored poor people in cities," says Professor Clement Price. "In my view, TPL is leading the rediscovery of urban New Jersey as a place for grassroots conservation."

EDITOR'S NOTES

1. The guiding principles of The Trust for Public Land's Newark Playground Projects include: Participatory design

by students and community members, green space included in playground features, playgrounds open to community members after school hours, and a partner organization to guarantee long-term community stewardship.

2. TPL's Parks for People initiative works in cities and suburbs across America to ensure that everyone — in particular, every child — enjoys access to a nearby park, playground, or natural area.

Parks are essential to the health of individuals and communities. They offer recreation and renewal, promote exercise, reduce crime, revitalize neighborhoods, protect the environment, and bring communities together. Children without access to parks suffer from higher levels of obesity, diabetes, asthma, anxiety, and depression.

In some of our nation's cities, as many as two in three residents have no access to a nearby park, playground, or open space. TPL's initiative seeks to address this critical need by creating parks where they are needed most, shaping the future of American cities — and American lives — for generations to come.

For more information on TPL's Parks for People initiative, go to www.tpl.org/pforp.

CHAPTER 30

Orange and Chapman University Jointly Plan for the Future

John W. Sibley

The benefits of colleges and universities to a community are many. Colleges and universities enhance a community's cultural offerings; they bring a more diverse ethnic mix to a community that reflects our nation as a whole; they provide access to knowledge and resources on campus; and they can bring about economic benefits and revitalization to a community. Local residents in a "college town" can reap a wealthy of enrichment, both culturally and financially, from these institutions.

However, there are also some universal concerns that arise when a town shares its community with a college, particularly in the areas of housing and parking. Whether the residence halls on campus are full or not, every college town has a certain amount of off-campus housing as rental property that certain students desire. Habits and hours of college students are often different from the neighborhood in which they reside, and this can become a concern for neighborhood residents. In addition, there is hardly a college campus in the country that does not have parking problems. In a small community, these problems overflow into the neighborhoods near campus. The high number of student-owned vehicles can overtax the community's municipal lots, and create parking problems within a community's central business district.

For these reasons, positive and proactive town and gown relationships should be the goal of all colleges and universities and the communities where they are located. The first step to finding solutions is, quite simply, enhanced communication between the community's business and political leaders and the university's administrative staff. With superior communication and joint planning efforts, problems can be dealt with before they become too expensive or too difficult to manage.

Strategies for Success

The Santa Fe Depot Specific Plan area is adjacent to, and even surrounds some Chapman University facilities, including the Partridge Dance Center and newly built Dodge Film and Media School. With the update of the Santa Fe Depot Specific Plan, the City has the opportunity to act upon the opportunities that the presence of Chapman facilities bring to the community by creating a vibrant and cultural mixed-use district.

Mixed-use areas adjacent to college campuses should contain a variety of uses that are desirable to both local residents and students, including retail, entertainment, services, parking, and housing. A mixed-use district can support and attract students and faculty to the area, and many of the university's program needs can

Originally published as "Santa Fe Depot Specific Plan Update," *Fact Sheet: Town and Gown Relations*, 2006, by the City of Orange, California.

also contribute to the success of a mixed-use district. There are several strategies that communities are using to create a safe and healthy environment for education and socialization:

- Strongly encouraging private developers to provide a variety of housing types that target both current and future needs of the overall community and campus.
- Recruiting retailers that provide campus and community serving businesses and uses and targeting a percentage of retail jobs for students.
- Sharing academic programs and resources with the community by locating them within the district, proximate to community users. Such programs can include continuing education classes, adult education, child development and daycare, health outreach programs, performance and art venues, housing and caring for the elderly, etc.
- Providing sensitive land transitions and landscaped buffers where residential neighborhoods might experience noise or light from campus activities.
- Encouraging a "permeable" edge with the community where interaction is desirable, especially in areas where a high proportion of students live in proximity to the campus.
- Providing strong connections within and around the campus and its edges to promote walking, bicycling and transit use, rather than vehicular traffic.
- Locating public-oriented uses, such as performance facilities, galleries and major sports venues, where they can be easily accessed and where they can contribute to the vitality and economic health of businesses in the area.

Public Review and Update Process

Welcome to the City of Orange Santa Fe Depot Specific Plan Update report. The City of Orange is going through an exciting process of refreshing its vision for the historic Santa Fe Depot and its environs. You are cordially invited to participate in this exciting planning process by attending public meetings and offering your viewpoints on the future of the Santa Fe Depot area.

The Santa Fe Depot Specific Plan was originally adopted in December 1993 with policies and standards for new development in the area immediately surrounding the City of Orange's Santa Fe Depot train station and Orange County Transit Authority (OCTA) bus transfer station. The Specific Plan was originally conceived to address the development of a commuter rail station, as well as aesthetic and physical improvements to existing infrastructure, preservation of historic buildings, and the concentrated integration of specialty retail uses and housing around the Depot. While the Metrolink Station has been phenomenally successful, the Specific Plan area has struggled economically and has yet to live up to its full potential of becoming a viable and cohesive mixed-use district that links the Depot to the Plaza business district.

Many changes have occurred within the Specific Plan since 1993. The City has seen the ongoing revitalization of Old Towne and its designation as both a local and National Register Historic District; Metrolink service has been established, with the Orange station experiencing the highest level of use among stations on the Orange County line; OCTA has announced its intent to spend $28 million on parking improvements at the Metrolink Station; the Orange Barrio Historical Society has organized to represent a historic Latino neighborhood adjacent to the Specific Plan area; and Chapman University has recently completed the construction of the Lawrence and Kristina Dodge College of Film and Media Arts directly north of the planning area. In response to these important developments and the dynamics they introduce to the area, the City of Orange would like to update the Specific Plan with innovative and up-to-date policies, development standards and implementation tools. The ultimate goal is to further the original objectives of the 1993 Specific Plan, and transform the Depot into a vibrant transit-oriented district while strengthening its connections to adjacent residential neighborhoods and the Old Towne Historic District.

The Future

Since the Santa Fe Depot Specific Plan was originally adopted in 2006, a number of reports and meetings have been held to implement and revise this plan. The following listing represents municipal actions taken from April 2006 to the Spring of 2012 with regards to implementation and updating of this plan. The major dates and the various meeting and planning steps involved in this process are highlighted below.

- April 2006:   *Project Kick-off Meeting with City Staff*
- Spring-Summer 2006:   *Background Data Research, Study and Analysis*
- Summer 2006:   *Public Workshop #1: Visioning, Opportunities & Constraints*
- Summer 2006:   *Public Workshop #2: Visioning, Opportunities & Constraints II*
- Late Summer 2006:   *Preparation of Land Use Alternatives*
- Early Fall 2006:   *Public Workshop #3: Land Use Alternatives Design Charrette*
- Fall 2006:   *Preparation of Preferred Land Use Alternative*
- Winter 2007:   *Public Workshop #4: Walking Tour*
- Winter 2007–Spring 2009:   *Refinement of Preferred Land Use Alternate*
- Summer 2009–Fall 2011:   *Preparation of Public Review Draft Specific Plan*
- Summer 2009–Fall 2011:   *Preparation of Environmental Impact Report*
- December 2011:   *Release of Specific Plan & Draft EIR for Review*
- Spring 2012:   *Planning Commission and City Council Hearings*
- Spring 2012:   *Preparation of Final Specific Plan*

The update report also notes that the Santa Fe Depot area is an important component of campus and community interaction with the Partridge Dance Center and the new Dodge Film and Media School in the heart of the neighborhood. Functions and events at these facilities, the report states, can help enliven and revitalize this area.

The updated report also notes that universities are enormous assets to their communities, but that the presence of all the students can have a disruptive influence on a neighborhood. Both town and gown are starting to recognize the need to work together to ensure that we can all get along.

EDITOR'S NOTE

1. The City of Orange's website continually updates its information on the process relating to the implementation and revisions of the Santa Fe Depot Specific Plan. Fact sheets are also available in this regard. The names and telephone numbers of staff representatives are indicated to contact for additional information, along with their e-mail addresses. The City of Orange is listed in Appendix B.

CHAPTER 31

Phoenix and Arizona State University Receive Voter Approval for New Downtown Campus

Debra Friedman

Significance of the Outreach/ Engagement Partnership

This application for the 2008 C. Peter Magrath Engagement Award recognizes an extraordinary partnership at a significant scale between Arizona State University and the City of Phoenix that resulted in the establishment of the ASU Downtown Phoenix campus in 2006, now serving 3000+ undergraduate and graduate students and expected to grow to 15,000 by 2020. Only rarely are cities able to reinvent themselves, and universities infrequently do so. On March 14, 2006, the voters of the City of Phoenix approved propositions securing $223M in funding for the development of the Downtown Phoenix campus of Arizona State University. This proved to be a defining moment for both the city and the university, and a vital step towards building both.

The New American University now emerging at ASU is characterized by excellence, impact, and inclusion. The new Downtown Phoenix campus allows ASU to advance the broad educational interests of business, government, and nonprofit organizations. The Downtown Phoenix campus of ASU lends critical mass to other educational and cultural institutions located downtown. The colleges and schools on the Downtown campus have a common focus on the public mission of ASU and a commitment to the social and economic advancement of the many diverse communities of the metropolitan region. On March 8, 2006, President Michael Crow noted, "The evolution of the Downtown campus is an important statement ... and an opportunity to leave to our children and our children's children a prosperous and vibrant urban environment in which to live." The significance of this partnership is measured in its importance to the future both of the city and the university. One writer for a local magazine captured it in this way: "As ASU and Phoenix battle, build and spend their way toward their respective desired destinies — a New American University and a vibrant urban center — the downtown campus is the symbiotic overlap of both pursuits. It is a time of becoming for both city and university."[1]

Relationship and Reciprocity Between the University and Community

Why did ASU and Phoenix come together in this far-reaching partnership? The motivation was powerful: the future of both the city

Originally published as *An Extraordinary Partnership Between Arizona State University and the City of Phoenix*, 2009, by Arizona State University, Phoenix. Reprinted with permission of the publisher.

and the university depended on it, and it became more urgent as the growth rate for both reached exceptional levels.

No lasting partnership springs fully formed from whole cloth, however, so how did this one begin? There are a number of ways to tell the story. One might start in 1985 when Downtown Phoenix business leaders urged then ASU President Russell Nelson to create a university presence in central Phoenix, culminating in the opening of an ASU Downtown Center. Or one might choose 1990 as the date of conception, when the Arizona Board of Regents approved the establishment of the College of Extended Education/ASU Downtown Center and it moved to a central location. But the proximate history of the ASU — City of Phoenix partnership begins with a breakfast meeting five years ago between two visionary and ambitious leaders, ASU President Michael Crow and City of Phoenix Mayor Phil Gordon. At that breakfast, they sketched the outlines of what is now the ASU Downtown Phoenix campus ... on a napkin.

Long-time City of Phoenix Manager Frank Fairbanks writes about this city-university engagement, "To be successful, [they] not only had to build a trusting partnership, but all parties had to embrace the need to reinvent the visions and plans of their institutions. We knew we couldn't be successful without strong, progressive support from state government, the state Board of Regents, and the private and nonprofit sectors."[2]

Each party had a great deal of work to do to get from vision to reality. The City of Phoenix assembled and acquired 18 acres of land in the downtown core; developed public support; provided capital funding; and worked with the community at large and downtown neighborhoods to ensure support. The mayor and city council developed a $863M bond issue, of which $223M in general obligation bonds was to build the first phase of the new ASU Downtown Phoenix campus. ASU leadership developed support among the Arizona Board of Regents, the ASU faculty academic senate, and worked intensively with the colleges slated to move in the first phase. Together they rallied to encourage passage of the bond in a spring 2006 election. On March 8, 2006, the bond passed with overwhelming support from the voters, and the partnership took a huge leap forward. On August 16, 2006, classes opened at the Downtown Phoenix campus in the Colleges of Public Programs, Nursing and Healthcare Innovation, and University College — colleges previously housed at the ASU Tempe campus — in 300,000 square feet of renovated space for academics and academic support, welcoming a student body of 2500+ undergraduate, masters, and doctoral students, and providing on-campus housing for 250 students. From that time on, and to this day, the Deputy City Manager convenes a partnership meeting every other week with decision-makers from both the City and ASU to review the list of issues, make decisions, and to ensure that the common project moves forward. In a partnership of this breadth and depth, the commitment of time and focus to this meeting — complementary, of course, to a multitude of other meetings from the highest levels to those with specific focus — ensures that the relationship continues to deepen and increase in productivity and impact.

What did each party expect to gain? The list of expected benefits is long. The public, private and nonprofit leaders saw the potential to build the future of the city on a foundation dedicated to cutting-edge knowledge, use-inspired research, and significant educational opportunity. They also understood the potential economic impact of the ASU Downtown Phoenix campus, as outlined in a commissioned economic impact study[3]: an average of 1,300 jobs created annually with an economic output of $166.8 million; $5.2 million annually in taxes and fees to the state of Arizona, $1.5 million annually to Maricopa County, and $1.7 million to the City of Phoenix during the construction phase; and at build-out, an annual operational impact of $569.5 million with revenues for the state of $18.7 million annually, with another $8 million to the county and $7.3 million to the city. R. Neil Irwin, Chair of the Downtown Phoenix Partnership notes that "In a two block radius immediately surrounding the new campus there has been and will be in the next 6 months $996 million dollars invested, not including the cost of the campus itself ... or the new light rail line which will open at the end of this year."

For ASU it was an opportunity to continue to meet the educational demands of post-secondary student enrollment growth, so critical to its core mission of access. It was also a chance to bring a host of programs dedicated to public service close to their community partners to increase the density of engagement and therefore impact.

Impact

Examples of impact do not fall conveniently into those benefiting the community and those benefiting the university; this division does not capture the intrinsically reciprocal nature of these partnerships. Each benefit for a community partner is accompanied by a corresponding benefit for the university partners, and vice versa. When students, faculty or staff engage with the community on a problem of genuine importance and contribute to the solution to that problem, they themselves gain in education and experience. When an academic unit improves in quality or attracts new investments, their community partners are sure to benefit, as well. Each of the examples below captures that interplay.

EXAMPLE ONE

It would be hard to do better than Mayor Phil Gordon has done in enumerating the many ways in which the ASU Downtown Phoenix campus has had impact in the community: collaboration on research projects outlining policy options, drawing on scientific research for carrying out public mandates, the exchange of ideas in classrooms and the exchange of ideas in public forums. Below are five examples of significant and pressing community needs that the faculty and students of the ASU Downtown Phoenix campus have been instrumental in addressing.

- How best to provide health care to the underserved, a critical community need? Here is one example: The College of Nursing and Healthcare Innovation collaborates

with Grace Lutheran Church in an initiative called Breaking the Cycle Community Health Care to provide family planning and health care services, 0.3 miles from the College site. They serve individuals in their childbearing years. More than 90 percent of the clients are Hispanic, live below the federal poverty guideline and do not have health insurance. This collaboration has been supported by Title X contract funds, as well as funding from the Arizona Department of Health Services, other grants and private donations.

- Issues in science and math education are prevalent, and like other school districts throughout the country, Phoenix is seeking to improve the opportunities available to students. The Phoenix Union High School District has benefited from collaboration with the School of Letters and Sciences (University College) to provide students with hands-on experiences that promote scientific investigation and understanding, serve predominantly underrepresented students, and extend science and math resources to students and teachers in charge of accelerated programs.

- How will changes in the public sector affect the private sector? The Phoenix Urban Research Laboratory, located on the Downtown Phoenix campus as an arm of the College of Design in Tempe, conducted a study with the City of Phoenix, METRO light rail, citizens and business owners of the Camelback Corridor to study the impact of the incoming METRO light rail on the character of the neighborhood and community. One of the principal partners, a planner from the City of Phoenix, notes, "I was skeptical because I was unsure whether students could handle both the political and professional expectations of the community and the city ... [but] the student presentations were well-received by the workshop participants and the final report is professional quality."

- What are the best practices in local government, and how might these be applied to the rapidly growing demands on the public sector in Greater Phoenix? The School of

Public Affairs (College of Public Programs),
working with the Arizona City Management Association, the American Society of
Public Administration, and the National
Forum of Black Public Administrators, attracted the Alliance for Innovation to
Phoenix, an organization of 400+ cities
around the country interested in innovative
practices in local government. Moving its
headquarters from Tampa, it is now located adjacent to the School of Public Affairs in the University Center on the Downtown Phoenix campus, providing economic
benefit to Phoenix, and the opportunity
for local governments in the area to benefit
from cutting-edge developments in governmental practice.

• Can parents who have not graduated from
high school and do not speak English pro-
ficiently — as describes so many of the immigrant parents in this community — be
effective in helping their children to succeed in school? Partnering with 12 school
districts and 41 schools in the Phoenix area
since October 2006, the American Dream
Academy of the ASU Center for Community Development and Civil Rights (College of Public Programs) has provided in-
depth intensive parent education and
advocacy training designed to empower
parents to help their children become successful students and ultimately graduate
from high school, even when they themselves often have not done so. Parents of
2,599 students have been served thus far.
The American Dream Academy has been
supported by corporate and foundation
gifts, the school districts, and ASU investments.

EXAMPLE TWO

Students are the primary beneficiaries of
the transformation that has occurred as a result
of the establishment of the ASU Downtown
Phoenix campus. Anxious to be good partners
from the first, what usually takes years at universities to accomplish was accomplished in
record time. New academic programs, expanded internship opportunities, exposure to
expert practitioners on a daily basis, and a sense

of being a part of an academic enterprise de-
voted to social responsibility all are at the core
of the student experience on the ASU Downtown Phoenix campus. Thus, while it would
have been easy to move from the Tempe campus to the Downtown Phoenix campus without
making any significant changes, academic units
have seized the opportunity to transform their
academic offerings as well as their identities and
missions. A few examples follow:

• For the first time in its history, the School of
Public Affairs took on an undergraduate
major, Urban and Metropolitan Studies,
and went through a strategic planning
process prior to the move, changing their
mission from one that was inwardly focused to one that better served, advancing
urban governance in a global context.

• In recognition of the needs of the proximate
community, a number of new academic
programs have been started since August
2006, including:
  –A master's degree in Nonprofit Studies.
  –A doctoral degree in Nursing.
  –A new School of Letters and Sciences,
  designed to serve the general education
  needs of the Downtown campus students, and to house high-demand majors
  from other campuses at ASU.

• In response to the needs of the local and regional economy, a number of centers and
offices have been established since August
2006:
  –The Megapolitan Tourism Research
  Center (College of Public Programs), in
  recognition of the economic and social
  centrality of tourism in this area, which
  studies tourism security, sustainability
  and social impact globally while bringing
  results to communities locally.
  –The Office of Latino Projects (School of
  Social Work), in recognition of the
  growing importance and needs of the
  Latino community in Phoenix.
  –The Center for Policy Informatics (College of Public Programs), in recognition
  of the complex public policy issues for
  which sophisticated tools for decision
  making are required.

–The Center for Healthcare Innovation and Clinical Trials (College of Nursing and Healthcare Innovation), in recognition of the need for more effective evidence-based practice in community nursing.

–The Hartford Center for Geriatric Nursing, in recognition of the elder population in this region.

• Other centers have been transformed. The most dramatic example is The Center for Nonprofit Leadership and Management (College of Public Programs) which attracted a $5 million investment from a local partner, the Lodestar Foundation, in recognition of its centrality and importance in the Phoenix community of nonprofits. The Center provides direct training and education to local area nonprofits through its Nonprofit Management Institute, mentors the next generation of diverse leaders in a partnership program, Public Allies (supported by a national grant), and is known locally and internationally for its research on community impact of nonprofits. In March 2008 the Center will be renamed the Lodestar Center for Philanthropy and Nonprofit Innovation.

Example Three

There is growing appreciation for the role that universities can play in the revitalization of cities. James Carr noted that "By partnering with community-based organizations, local governments, school districts, and public housing authorities, universities are helping to improve economic, social and physical conditions of their neighboring communities while providing opportunities for students and faculty to apply academic knowledge to real-world conditions."[4]

The Downtown Phoenix campus of Arizona State University is a grand-scale exemplar of just this kind of partnership. Its demonstrated impacts are economic, social, and education, transforming both the University and City in which it is housed. The magnitude of the investment of the citizens of a city in a state university — $223 million — is unparalleled in American higher education. In 2006, the Colleges of Public Programs (including the Schools of Social Work, Public Affairs, and Community Resources and Development), Nursing and Health Care Innovation, and University College moved from ASU Tempe to become the foundational colleges of this new campus, located strategically to advance the three cornerstones of the ASU mission — access, excellence, and impact — as well as to become the finest examples of two of the design principles of the New American University, use-inspired research and social embeddedness. The campus and its more than 40 major and degree programs presently serve over 3,000 students, will serve 4,000 by fall of 2008, and is expected to grow to 15,000 by 2020. Since 2006, the colleges of the ASU Downtown Phoenix campus have attracted more than $10 million in private support and an equal amount of external grant funding, much of it in support of research with, and in service of, community partners. Public, private and nonprofit sector partners within a two mile radius of the campus attest to its importance in advancing their effectiveness and shaping their futures. From the experience thus far, there are numerous lessons about the factors that contribute to its success: the importance of proximity in reducing the costs of engagement, the optimal conditions for collaboration and capacity building, and the design of institutional forms that are more likely to advance sustained engagement. Both the development of the campus and its impact provide a powerful case study for engagement on a grand scale that has implications for other cities and their universities.

Lessons Learned and Best Practices

What has made for the exceptional success of Arizona State University's Downtown Phoenix campus in partnership with the public, private, and nonprofit sectors of this community? To begin, the mission of Arizona State University itself — the design principles of the New American University — set the stage for meaningful partnership. It was never a matter of torquing the University's mission to accommodate engagement, as at so many other research universities. Instead, it was a matter of figuring out how to act upon those principles; in short, how to turn the design principles to action principles.

Reflecting on this work, there are three action principles that contribute toward the explanation of its success:

Action Principle #1

Location, location, location: Proximity diminishes opportunity costs for on-going collaboration. For the many adults who work within 1½ miles in the public, private, and non-profit sectors, the location of the ASU Downtown Phoenix campus reduces their opportunity costs in pursuing additional education and advanced degrees. One student pursuing a master's degree in public administration in the School of Public Affairs immediately switched from Tempe to Downtown as soon as the program started, noting that the program "Is close to my job, it is new so it is a nice facility, and the classrooms facilitate discussion." She appreciates the night classes since she works for U.S. Senator John McCain's office as a staff assistant. Another student, Sam Feldman, in the Urban and Metropolitan Studies program has an internship in the youth development program in the City Manager's Office. "Here we experience what we learn," he says.[5]

Action Principle #2

Relationships, relationships, relationships: Relationships are the foundation upon which the capacity for collaboration expands. In order to be successful, collaborations have to be able to develop, change and grow with new circumstances and changing conditions. These depend upon personal relationships of a particular kind: an academic expert with a practitioner expert. This relationship is built upon mutual respect and self-interest. Both benefit from the other's contribution. To be maximally effective, these relationships become central nodes in a social network, and serve as a portal to the rest of the University. There must be numerous such dyads, and the range of these core relationships must come fairly close to matching the key needs of the community. Dr. Robert Denhardt, a member of the National Academy of Public

Administration and director of the School of Public Affairs observes, "I've often noted that what strikes me as most dramatic is that every time I go out for lunch, I run into someone from local or state government that I know. Previously, that meeting would have taken a month to schedule, thirty to forty-five minutes for me to drive downtown and park. We would then have the meeting and I would take the same thirty to forty-five minutes to get back to my office. Now these meetings just happen naturally."

Action Principle #3

Certain institutional forms in the academy are better suited to advancing partnerships than others. In particular, centers and institutes have considerable advantages over schools or departments in advancing embeddedness. There are several reasons that this is so: (1) relative to schools and departments, centers and institutes typically have a far more circumscribed mission; (2) centers and institutes are often designed explicitly to be outward-looking; (3) centers and institutes often have action-oriented research agendas with specific practical applications; (4) they frequently provide direct service and non-credit education to community partners; and (5) schools and departments must always make the education of students their primary mission, and so partnerships, while important, will always be secondary.

There are challenges, to be sure. One of them is an overabundance of opportunity. These close collaborations breed ideas and more ideas. Choosing among opportunities and focusing our partnerships efforts are important in continuing to deliver. Another challenge is that faculty, students, and staff, as well as their community partners, are operating in a context of exceptional growth and change. All partners have to adjust continuously to different contextual conditions … at a rapid pace.

The benefits of the partnerships of the ASU Downtown Phoenix campus have been described throughout these pages: unparalleled education for students; ready access to academic expertise for partners; growing up together as both a New American University and, simultaneously, a New American city; an increased level of educational attainment for the community as a whole; and a myriad of economic and social benefits.

The Future

Outreach and engagement are in the very fabric of the logic and operation of the ASU Downtown Phoenix campus and its city partners. For all of the reasons noted above, the partnerships will grow and expand and the roots of this engagement will grow ever deeper into the foundations of the City and the University. The addition of the Walter Cronkite School of Journalism and Mass Communications will bring an additional 1,500 students to the campus in August 2008 in a brand new building presently under construction. That building will also house ASU's television station, KAET. The major newspaper in the region, The Arizona Republic, has its headquarters two blocks away, and other key newspapers — the Arizona Business Journal and The Capitol Times — are within a mile. This will produce a whole new set of examples mirroring those above. Also in August 2008, new dormitory facilities are scheduled to open with spaces for 750 students.

PROGRAM AWARDS

$6000 Regional Award

We would use the money to work with our key partners to develop a case of this partnership for dissemination to academic institutions in urban settings and communities seeking to develop deeper understandings of best practices and challenges in developing partnerships. It will be prepared consistent with the standards of the case study method so that faculty may use it for teaching, if they so desire.

$20,000 National Award

This money would be used to develop a template for a long-term research study on the partnership between the ASU Downtown Phoenix campus and its public, private, and nonprofit partners. There is a lot of interest in the question of the impact of such partnerships but no longitudinal research projects upon which to draw. The template would build in routine data collection mechanisms so that, over time, our knowledge about what works and what doesn't could be informed by empirical research. While there would be results each and every year, the true benefit would come in being able to demonstrate impact and change over time in a way that was complementary to existing narratives.

Arizona State University's Downtown Phoenix Campus also received letters of support from the following individuals and organizations:

- President, Arizona State University, Phoenix, Arizona
- Mayor, City of Phoenix, Arizona
- Chairman, Board of Supervisors, Maricopa County, Phoenix, Arizona
- Executive Director, Childhelp, Scottsdale, Arizona
- Regional President, Wachovia Bank, Phoenix, Arizona
- Chairman, Phoenix Community Alliance, Phoenix, Arizona
- President, St. Joseph's Hospital and Medical Center, Phoenix, Arizona
- President, Professional Medical Transport, Tempe, Arizona
- Chairman, Downtown Phoenix Partnership, Phoenix, Arizona

NOTES

1. Gregory Collins, "If You Build It..." *Kontakt Magazine*, Issue 11, p. 74, December 2007/January 2008 (Issue 11).

2. Frank Fairbanks, "Overcoming Rivalries to Bring Higher Ed Downtown." GOVERNING.com, January 23, 2008. Published in collaboration with the Government Innovators Network at Harvard's Kennedy School of Government.

3. "Economic and Fiscal Impact of the Proposed Arizona State University Capital Center Campus," prepared by Elliott D. Pollack and Company, Scottsdale Arizona, May 2004. (Note that the original name proposed for the Downtown Phoenix campus was the Capital Center Campus which speaks to its close proximity to the state Capitol.)

4. James H. Carr, "It's Not Just Academic: University-Community Partnerships are Rebuilding Neighborhoods," Housing Facts and Findings, Vol. 1, No. 1, Spring 1999.

5. Reported in "Learning by Osmosis" in the *Arizona Capitol Times*, January 25, 2008.

CHAPTER 32

Pittsburgh, the University of Pittsburgh and Other Cities and Schools Learn to Include Citizens in Their Planning Process

Yesim Sungu-Eryilmaz

Although city officials, neighborhood residents, and local businesses generally see universities and colleges as positive economic and cultural assets, clashes between town and gown are commonplace, especially in land use and development processes. Institutions of higher education often find themselves at odds with residents whose goals are to maintain the stability and character of their neighborhoods. Concerns about university expansions generally relate to social equity due to displacement of residents and businesses; spillover effects that erode quality of life; lack of community involvement in the planning process; and loss of property tax revenues.

Social Equity

As colleges and universities have become important drivers of urban revitalization and as they expand to meet their academic missions, their actions (and inactions) have raised social equity concerns among neighborhood residents, businesses, and nonprofit agencies. These stakeholders have argued that educational institutions largely ignore neighborhood social issues and problems to such an extent that they have created a climate of distrust. In some cases,

policies aimed at neighborhood redevelopment have had little regard for social impacts related to displacement of long-time residents and businesses, and sometimes the destruction of historic sites.

These kinds of concerns often arise even when other economic impacts may be considered positive for the city or community. For example, as cited in the previous chapter, Indiana University–Purdue University helped to anchor urban redevelopment in Indianapolis, but it changed the class and racial composition of the downtown and displaced an historic section of the city's African American community (Cummings et al. 2005).

In the late 1980s, the University of Washington announced that a new branch would be developed in Tacoma near the central business district in a largely abandoned former warehouse district. Although the new campus has spurred investment in an economically depressed area, protected some historic buildings, and received strong support from some sectors, residents of a nearby low-income neighborhood complained that the university was ignoring their needs and concerns, and was providing only upper-end jobs (Coffey and Dierwechter 2005).

Columbia University's development plans

Originally published as "City and Neighborhood Interests in University Land Development," *Town-Gown Collaboration in Land Use and Development*, Policy Focus Report, 2009, by the Lincoln Institute of Land Policy, Cambridge, Massachusetts. Reprinted with permission of the publisher.

led to similar conflicts. The school is one of the largest landowners in New York City, after the Catholic Church and the city government (Marcuse and Potter 2005). Its planned expansion into an area of West Harlem/Manhattanville raised major objections from the neighborhood, primarily related to the potential displacement of long-time residents and businesses through gentrification.

Spillover Effects

Universities and colleges primarily acquire land and structures that support their core mission or immediate growth demands. It is not uncommon, however, for surrounding communities to criticize universities for their unresponsive development policies or lack of a plan to mitigate negative spillover effects. For neighborhood residents, some of the major concerns relate to quality of life issues, such as conversion of houses and other buildings to student occupancy; upward pressure on rents; adaptation of shops and facilities to student markets; and increases in traffic, noise, and parking problems (Harasta 2008).

The presence of students is typically the greatest concern to residents, and both on- and off-campus student housing have locational impacts. Residents often try to block attempts to expand student housing out of fear that development of new dormitories will alter the character of their neighborhoods. In addition, many students seek private housing in nearby neighborhoods that may be unprepared or unwilling to receive them.

In Boston, for example, 42 percent of the nearly 62,000 students attending local colleges and universities lived off campus in 2006. While students have moved into all 20 Boston neighborhoods, slightly more than half are concentrated in just four of them (Kowalcky and Perkins 2006).

Land banking is another issue for neighborhoods and municipalities. As major landowners, colleges and universities hold some parcels until they have a specific need for development. During the current economic downturn, declines in financial resources such as en-

dowment funds or state monies may lead institutions to slow their expansion plans and leave land parcels vacant. If town-gown relations are strained when universities feel flush with cash, they clearly will be tested in times of financial distress.

Harvard University, for example, planned to construct a $1 billion science complex on part of the 250 acres that it owns in the Allston neighborhood of Boston. After a sharp drop in its endowment fund in 2009, Harvard put the project on hold. Both neighborhood residents and the City of Boston raised concerns about the delay — primarily relating to the university's lack of a plan for using the parcels and for improving the neighborhood in the meantime (Jan 2009).

Involvement in the Planning Process

Universities see their faculty, students, alumni, and donors as their primary constituencies, and their development priorities are designed to meet the requirements of these groups (Webber 2005). But because their land and building policies are embedded in the larger urban fabric, colleges and universities in fact have a broader constituency that can result in complex and conflict-ridden interactions.

Residents who share space with colleges and universities often want to be active participants in determining future land uses and development in their neighborhoods. As one community member said when discussing Boston College's expansion plans in the Brighton section of Boston, "You have a neighbor who is acting without concern for the other neighbors — they have to discuss with the community uses for the property that will be beneficial to both the residents and the institution. It's not a novel approach. I guarantee that they are teaching their students courses on social responsibility — why don't they practice it a little bit in their own backyard?" (Axelbank 2007).

When the University of Pittsburgh decided to expand into the adjacent Oakland district in the 1970s, it took the approach of finalizing a master plan internally and then sharing it only with the Oakland Chamber of Commerce and the City of Pittsburgh's planning department — neither of which offered major objections. But Oakland residents were upset by both the plan and their exclusion from the planning process (Deitrick and Soska 2005).

Loss of Property Tax Revenue

Local governments generally see colleges and universities as positive local economic and cultural assets. In some cases, municipalities make trade-offs when colleges and universities want to expand, because they want to improve their public image, create potentially positive impacts on the local economy, and attract a young population and qualified labor force to the area.

That was the case for the University of South Florida, St. Petersburg, and the City of St. Petersburg when the campus expanded in the 1990s. The city played an important role through the purchase of 142 parcels at a cost of nearly $13 million, with the assistance of the City Council, the St. Petersburg Chamber of Commerce, the State Legislature, and the Board of Regents. Most of the property was transferred from city ownership to the university system and was removed from the tax rolls (Tobin 1989).

However, in an environment of rising costs to maintain and improve public services and infrastructure, most local governments constantly look for new opportunities to expand their revenue sources. Although colleges and universities contribute greatly to urban economic and community development, their tax-exempt status is a growing concern for some governments, especially when institutional expansion represents a loss of potential property tax revenue.

Recent cutbacks in state and federal aid have prompted some cities to mobilize to prevent academic institutions from expanding their campuses or to seek tax dollars from campus properties that generate revenue for the institutions. Some of these cases have caused long-running disputes between the city and the university. For example, the town-gown dispute between the City of Berkeley and the University of California resulted in a referendum calling for the university to adhere to planning laws and to pay $1.2 million in fees to the university (Harasta 2008).

In another example, the City of Pittsburgh challenged the tax-exempt status of a $22 million apartment building owned by Duquesne University, which had bought and converted the building into housing for 750 students as part of a multiyear plan to increase enrollment. Although the purchase meant more student housing for the university, it also meant the loss of tax revenue for the City of Pittsburgh (Associated Press 2004).

REFERENCES

Associated Press. 2004. Cities increasingly challenge tax status of universities. *USA Today,* March 16.

Axelbank, Rachel L. 2007. Community concern grows as BC expansion continues. *Jewish Advocate.*

Coffey, Brian, and Yonn Dierwechter. 2005. The urban university as a vehicle for inner-city renewal: The University of Washington, Tacoma. In Perry and Wiewel 2005, 80–97.

Cummings, Scott, Mark Rosentraub, Mary Domahidy, and Sarah Coffin. 2005. University involvement in downtown revitalization: Managing political and financial risks. In Perry and Wiewel 2005, 147–174.

Deitrick, Sabina, and Tracy Soska. 2005. The University of Pittsburgh and the Oakland neighborhood: From conflict to cooperation, or how the 800-pound gorilla learned to sit with — and not on — its neighbors. In Perry and Wiewel 2005, 25–44.

Harasta, Joe. 2008. Town-gown relations: University and neighborhood leaders' perceptions of college and community relations. Ph.D. Thesis. Wilmington University, New Castle, DE, July.

Kowalcky, Linda, and Gregory Perkins. 2006. *America's college town.* Boston, MA: Boston Redevelopment Authority Research Department.

Marcuse, Peter, and Cuz Potter. 2005. Columbia University's heights: An ivory tower and its communities. In Perry and Wiewel 2005, 45–64.

Tobin, Thomas. 1989. Slowed USF plans keeping land idle. *St. Petersburg Times,* January 22:1.

Webber, Henry S. 2005. The University of Chicago and its neighbors: A case study in community development. In Perry and Wiewel 2005, 65–79.

CHAPTER 33

Plano and Collin College Provide Student Internships, and Everyone Benefits

Robin Popik

Internships have been around for more than a decade, and numerous local governments have toyed with the idea of offering them but not as part of the community's volunteer program. Could it be that some volunteer managers just aren't sure how to sell the idea to local leaders, or maybe staff just aren't buying the concept?

Who Is the Intern?

The typical college student who scurries to find an internship opportunity has initiative, goals, and high expectations for the future. This student not only wants to build a resume but also wants to see if college goals are a good match for them. The student sees an internship as a stepping-stone to bringing a career to life. That enthusiasm has a tendency to be contagious for those who work with the student.

Interns can be paid or nonpaid; and the individual could be working on a bachelor's degree or a master's degree, or could already be finished with these degrees. The basic premise of an internship is to take the organization or field of work out for a test drive. Depending on the level of the intern, the organization can also test drive the person for compatibility as a future employee.

How Do You Sell the Idea?

Government organizations that need temporary staff for special projects are a great place to use internships. Challenge the intern to bring out the value of the project. Don't shortchange the intern or your organization by providing only menial tasks to supplement the secretarial pool; if you do, you'll both be disappointed.

Interns want to learn and apply program theory and management to work flow. In local government, internships directly related to the student's area of study can be in numerous departments, including building inspections, environmental services, park planning, engineering, local government manager's office, and fire.

Practicum and cooperative education provide workplace settings in which students gain practical experience in a particular discipline, enhance skills, and integrate such knowledge as libraries, finance, or police.

Internships offer the opportunity of better-trained employees while developing new talent in an employer's organization. Not only does an intern bring enthusiasm to the workplace, the person also brings up-to-date theories and business practices that relate to a specific field. Not to mention that internships are just point blank great recruitment and retention tools for any organization.

If the best public relations tool is an em-

Originally published as "Volunteer Internships Benefit Local Governments and Students," *Public Management*, Vol. 91, No. 1, January/February 2009, by the International City/County Management Association, Washington, DC. Reprinted with permission of the publisher.

ployee, then the second best is an intern. That individual is a great resource to educate the community about what happens within the local government organization.

Local governments can champion this concept by using interns to teach about the governmental process and politics in a way most textbooks miss. The partnership between the educational institution and a government organization can also foster other community or training opportunities.

As the workforce continues to age, governments like all other organizations are looking for educated individuals to fill needed positions. These internships bring to the forefront students who may otherwise not have come via the local government service route. Where better to teach students how their government runs or introduce them to politics?

Local governments have diversity in departments, from police to park planning and libraries to environmental services, where students can use their talents and explore a career in this public sector.

How Do You Start an Internship Program?

Start with what you know by reviewing your organization's existing job descriptions to determine the ones applicable to college interns. Next, talk to departments in the organization and collect their ideas for projects that an intern can do.

Write a job description for the internship and advertise it on your organization's Web site, on www.volunteermatch.com, or through an area volunteer center or local college. It's best to start with just one or two places. Another place to list your internships is on co-op and service learning Web sites.

You can also opt to post a generic job description that reads something like this: "College interns can volunteer throughout the year using their skills while they learn more about leadership. Our office would be happy to work with your college to find places for students in different departments. For more information, contact xyz."

Plano, Texas, advertises for college interns throughout the year and matches them as they contact the city. In the past year, interns were used in building inspections, engineering, park planning, environmental services, police, health department, Plano's television network, and parks and recreation. It's a surprise to see the projects that departments can organize once the staff knows a student is available and interested in their area.

Requests will usually be sent by e-mail. When students approach your program, review their interests to see if their skills and academic major fit one of your departments. You can request more information before actually meeting with a student and can suggest the individual visit your organization's Web site to find the department that best complements the student's field of study.

This past summer, Plano had 12 interns. Three interns worked for the police department, where they use interns all year long. The job descriptions were ready, and assignments were easy to make. The libraries are always willing to accept a student in a library science field of study, which they did this past summer.

In June, the health department made a special request for a student with a science or biology major to assist with a special research project. The other students were matched up by reviewing the answers to questions that were sent by e-mail, through a phone conversation with the volunteer manager and volunteer supervisor, and with an outline of requirements from their schools.

At first you might decide to stay with safe choices, such as office assistant, database development, Web site design, data entry and scanning, research projects, newsletter writing, or environmental specialists, but actually the possibilities are endless.

The length of the internship depends on the school and the number of credits the student requires. Service-learning requirements can start with as few as 15 hours, while credit internships can extend as long as 360 hours. This information should be discussed up front with the student and the department director, so they both know what's expected and can plan ahead.

The school or student should share the course description, course focus, and course competencies with the volunteer supervisor. Here's an example:

Course Description

Career-related activities encountered in the student's area of specialization offered through an individualized agreement among the college, employer, and student. Under the supervision of the college and the employer, the student combines classroom learning with work experience.

Course Focus

Work experience should:

A. Add a unique dimension to classroom instruction through on-the-job experience and training.

B. Test career aptitude and interest against practical job requirements before graduation.

C. Develop self-confidence, maturity, professional skills, and an understanding of human relations.

D. Help gain a professional contacts that may be used as a reference for after-graduation employment.

Course Competencies

A. Improve interpersonal skills in class and on the job.

B. Work as a team member to accomplish the employer's goals.

C. Meet with members of your work group to identify problems that need to be addressed.

The final grade will be determined by criteria established by the student's college. However, here is an example of possible criteria:

Course Work Percentage

Contact information:	5%
Daily log:	10%
Supervisor evaluation:	15%
Book review:	30%
Quizzes:	15%
Discussions:	25%
Total percentage:	100%

The volunteer manager completes the course agreement form, establishes learning objectives with the student and the instructor with the student and the instructor or coordinator, evaluates the learning objectives to decide whether they are completed in a satisfactory manner, and completes an evaluation form.

The student is under the direct or close supervision of a qualified college faculty member who will provide the local government with the necessary paperwork. Steps to supervise an intern are similar to supervising an employee or volunteer: orientation, training, guidance, and review of the student's activities.

The additional supervision might include sending e-mails to the college faculty to understand what is expected of the student and completing mid-session and end-of-session evaluation.

College academics are just one part of preparing for a future career. New graduates' resumes need to offer something extra to prospective employers, and that's where an internship is helpful. An internship also helps students gain hands-on experience and show employers they have taken extra steps to learn more about their career choices.

Best of all, internships introduce supervisors to their next generation of employees.

Editor's Note

It should be noted that students that live in the city of Plano go to school all over the United States, and that the Volunteer Resource Group works to find internship placements in a department of special interest to each student if they are seeking such an internship opportunity. The program's annual evaluation at the end of each summer shows how much these students like their experience with the city of Plano. The city's website is listed in Appendix B.

CHAPTER 34

Portland Works with Portland State University to Create a University District Plan

Yesim Sungu-Eryilmaz

Positive Practices for Town–Gown Relations

Despite frequent town-gown tensions, many colleges and universities have engaged successfully with their host cities and neighborhoods. A variety of practices have shifted the relationship from being adversarial to collaborative by joining stakeholders in partnerships to achieve common goals, facilitating buy-in from the community, and achieving long-lasting change.

INCORPORATING SOCIAL AND ECONOMIC PROGRAMS

Effective land development policy requires coordination of social and economic programs (Fainstein 1994). Some colleges and universities have succeeded in addressing these issues in the process of revitalizing the neighborhood or expanding to meet their academic goals. Positive practices may include providing affordable housing to prevent displacement of residents, along with promoting local business development.

Northeastern University in Boston, Massachusetts, provides a good example of this approach. The university's Davenport Commons project consists of 125 units of housing for stu-

dents and staff, 60 affordable owner-occupied townhouses, and 2,100 square feet of retail space. Community members were concerned about a range of issues related to the project's physical design and the threat of neighborhood gentrification.

The development process was complex, involving many stakeholders and negotiations (Calder, Grant, and Muson 2005). The university partnered on the project with Madison Park Development Corporation (MPDC), a local community development corporation, as well as with two local developers. Along with negotiating a community benefits package of affordable housing, MPDC helped homeowners set up a condominium association and provided both technical assistance and education for first-time homebuyers.

In other cases, institutions have actively promoted local business development by giving neighborhood vendors priority (Strom 2005). For example, the University of Pennsylvania has a local contracting program that generated more than $65 million in business for West Philadelphia firms in 2002. Nearly 90 percent of that spending was directed to women- and minority-owned businesses operating in the neighborhood.

Originally published as "Positive Practices for Town-Gown Relations" and "Moving Toward Successful Town-Gown Collaborations," *Town-Gown Collaboration in Land Use and Development*, Policy Focus Report, 2009, by the Lincoln Institute of Land Policy, Cambridge, Massachusetts. Reprinted with permission of the publisher.

MANAGING SPILLOVER EFFECTS THROUGH PLANNING

Cities and communities have put both regulatory and nonregulatory mechanisms in place to manage the impact of university-led land use and development through balancing the interests of the university, neighboring residents, and the city as a whole (Taylor 2007). Regulatory mechanisms include district plans, land use regulations, and design standards to guide development and encourage community participation in project planning.

In Portland, Oregon, for example, the planning processes of the city and its universities are largely intertwined. The goal is to give institutions the support they need while also providing the surrounding communities greater certainty about how the area will be developed. When Portland State University (PSU) sought to expand in 1988, Portland's Central City plan called for creation of a new plan that would allow for this growth and provide some direction for development of the neighborhood.

The Portland Bureau of Planning created the University District plan in collaboration with the university and the Downtown Community Association, integrating the public vision for the downtown with the needs of the university. The plan required mixed uses and provided guidelines for transit, retail, student and market-rate housing, amenities, and academic facilities. The plan also provided the regulatory framework needed for the desired uses (Taylor 2007).

Nonregulatory mechanisms such as Memorandums of Understanding (MOUs) are used to manage interactions on specific projects and to define the roles and responsibilities of each party. MOUs can address a range of issues such as boundary determination for campus development, guidelines for mitigating impacts on adjacent neighborhoods, and standards for physical development, including site planning, storm water management, and roadway improvements. While there is no legal recourse if a party fails to honor the MOU, these agreements help to eliminate ambiguity about the roles of the city and the university, while also providing a mechanism to track progress and monitor accountability (Taylor 2007).

San Jose State University, for example, signed an MOU with the city in 2006 to embark on a joint planning effort — known as the South Campus District Plan — for the community surrounding the university (City of San Jose 2009). The partnership envisioned the district as providing expanded recreational amenities for residents along with a regional facility for sports events and tournaments. The plan also focused on improved parking and pedestrian accessibility throughout the area. Having recognized the need to involve a full range of community stakeholders, the city and university dedicated a significant part of the planning process to community outreach and resident participation efforts.

INTEGRATING UNIVERSITY BUILDINGS THROUGH DESIGN

The development requirements of the modern urban campus are no longer served by the separation of the university from its surroundings. Two new principles that guide physical design include communicating institutional values through the built environment and finding points of intersection with the local community (Blaik 2008).

These design principles have shaped many mixed-use development projects and helped to improve the integration of university buildings into a community. At the University of Illinois at Chicago, South Campus, for example, university buildings are "city buildings," with city services and retail stores that are mixed with academic facilities and student residences (Perry, Wiewel, and Menendez 2009).

A citywide initiative at Syracuse University (SU) provides another good example of efforts to integrate campus and city. The Connective Corridor is a 1.5-mile, L-shaped connector that ensures that students and faculty can get to the downtown, and that the downtown can benefit from the university and more than 25 arts and cultural venues in the area. The goal is to stitch these locations together with new urban landscapes, bike paths, imaginative lighting, public and interactive art, and signage systems. The SU Office of Engagement is leading the initiative, with support from the city, the state, the regional transportation authority, local utility companies, and the arts community (The Connective Corridor 2009).

The College of San Mateo in California has received several awards for its College Vista rental housing development for faculty and staff. The 44-unit complex is located on a former parking lot behind the Administration Building of the San Mateo County Community College District.

Because of the vocal opposition of several neighborhood groups to development at this location, the principals of Education Housing Partners initiated an extensive outreach campaign to understand community concerns (College Vista 2009). The primary issues for residents related to the introduction of affordable housing "in their backyard," and the development's visual and economic impacts. Through a series of meetings, the college addressed these concerns to the neighbors' satisfaction by making design modifications and creating operating guidelines to ensure the long-term maintenance and upkeep of the property.

FORMALIZING STAKEHOLDER PARTICIPATION AND LEADERSHIP

Academic institutions, city governments, and communities used to rely on quick fixes to problems that were episodic and project-based or task-oriented (Perry and Wiewel 2005). These ad hoc approaches only solved problems temporarily and did nothing to improve overall university relations with the city and neighborhood.

In developing more formal relationships, highly visible leadership and ongoing communication from all sides are essential. The City of Boston, for example, has created a position in the Mayor's Office to serve as liaison with institutions of higher education. Many universities have established an Office of Community Affairs or Office of Community Engagement. The leader of that office is typically someone from the community rather than from the academic ranks. The office — preferably an adjunct to the President's Office — serves as both the portal to the university and its liaison to the community.

Several colleges and universities have also developed formal and ongoing relationships with their neighbors. Clark University in Worcester established a partnership with local residents, businesses, and churches to revitalize its neighborhood in the early 1980s. This partnership with the Main South Community Development Corporation (MSCDC) was formalized in 1995, and Clark University holds a seat on the board of directors.

Now known as the University Park Partnership (UPP), its scope includes a broad-based strategy emphasizing the development of neighborhood amenities and the expansion of economic opportunities for neighborhood residents and businesses. The partnership has received funding from a variety of federal and private sources. In 2004 it was awarded the inaugural Carter Partnership Award, the nation's most prestigious recognition for collaborations between universities and their communities (Brown and Geoghegan 2009).

A Partnership for Change is a project initiated by the University of Wisconsin–Milwaukee and the City of Milwaukee to advance the UWM campus and surrounding neighborhoods. This project originated from concerns about maintaining and enhancing the area's quality of life, improving the physical and social town-gown relationship, and finding appropriate strategies to resolve campus-neighborhood conflicts.

The planning process for the neighborhood engaged stakeholders to set priorities, develop strategies, and identify actions on key issues. Several groups contributed to the development of the plan, including neighborhood associations, special interest groups, two business improvement districts, the City of Milwaukee, Milwaukee County, and the university. The key principle of this initiative was a coordinated long-term strategy for addressing neighborhood issues and to create an ongoing university-neighborhood collaboration (City of Milwaukee 2003).

OFFSETTING TAX-EXEMPT STATUS

With local governments under increasing fiscal pressure, some cities and colleges have negotiated arrangements to make payments in lieu of taxes (PILOTs) and other fees, in some cases through a participatory and inclusive policy process. A range of practices, policies, and programs related to PILOTs has emerged at both the state and municipal levels to compensate for the tax-exempt status of nonprofit institutions.

In 1929 Harvard University became the first recorded case of an academic institution paying PILOTs to a local government. Today, Harvard pays more than $2 million annually to Cambridge, where its core campus is located. It also pays $3.8 million a year until 2054 to the Town of Watertown, where it recently purchased land, and in 2008 the university paid $1.9 million to the City of Boston, where it owns several medical schools and research centers and where it expects to build new facilities on land it owns in other parts of the city.

The State of Connecticut instituted a program in 1978 based on the recognition that colleges and universities benefit everyone residing in the state, not only those who happen to live in the particular city in which an institution is located. To distribute the tax burden more equitably within this framework, the state makes payments to local governments that have colleges, universities, and hospitals in their jurisdictions to compensate for the revenue foregone from these tax-exempt institutions. Although the state is unable to reimburse the full cost of the property tax payments, funding levels were close to 64 percent of the assessed taxes in 2004 (Leland 2006).

Leland (2006) has also identified several city-level examples of PILOT programs. For example, four colleges in Providence, Rhode Island, agreed in 2003 to pay $50 million to the city over the next 20 years. In West Long Branch, New Jersey, Monmouth University is the township's largest employer and voluntarily contributes $190,000 a year to municipal coffers.

Moving Toward Successful Town-Gown Collaborations

Colleges and universities decide on a variety of property-related actions. Some of them do not require input from their surrounding neighborhoods and host cities, such as routine renovations of existing buildings and the maintenance of grounds. Other types of development activities may call for bilateral decision making, such as joint research centers between the university and private industry. New or changing land use and development decisions, however, tend to be much more complex and contain the seeds of future conflicts if the concerns of all stakeholders are not addressed and resolved satisfactorily. This complexity puts land development projects in the category of decisions that require more dedicated collaborative processes.

It is clearly difficult to devise a formula for land use and development that functions efficiently and effectively while also honoring many stakeholders' perspectives. Moreover, there is no single template for how such a partnership should be framed since each situation is different. Several considerations provide general guidelines for designing successful town-gown collaborations.

BALANCING UNIVERSITY AND COMMUNITY INTERESTS

The fundamental goals and interests of universities, municipal governments, and neighborhood residents obviously have some common elements and others that are divergent and potentially conflicting. However, these anchor institutions, municipalities and neighborhoods must recognize that they are part of a large, complex system and that their fates are intertwined.

Universities play an important role by contributing to the economy, civic life, and built environment of cities by attracting human capital and technological innovation and boosting the skills of the workforce. The city and neighborhood in turn support the university's ability to function well by offering the public services and social and cultural amenities that help to keep people and jobs in the area.

WORKING TOGETHER TOWARD COMMON GOALS

Universities and colleges are major landowners and powerful players with relatively steady revenue streams. In contrast, community members — whether residents or community organizations — often have unstable revenue sources at best, and are often perceived as impediments to development. Any effort to develop a trusting relationship must be mindful of this power imbalance and strive to minimize the differences. According to Judith Rodin, former president of University of Pennsylvania, "Universities have a lot of great potential to be partners within cities, but too often are more like the 4,000-pound gorilla, exercising their interests in a way that isn't always neighborhood-friendly" (Chan 2007).

Working together to develop collaborative projects helps to identify common interests and problems. True town-gown collaboration thus means that the university, city, and neighborhood must work toward specific goals and objectives by sharing responsibility, authority, and accountability for achieving results.

CREATING LASTING CHANGE

Successful collaboration requires a sufficient investment of time and resources from each stakeholder to create lasting change founded on ongoing communication and long-term relationships. These efforts can generate good will in the community and support in the public sector, as well as a sense of cohesion and cooperation within the university itself. By acknowledging each other's concerns and constraints, and the costs and benefits inherent in any long-term working relationship, all parties can look to the future as a win-win opportunity for positive growth and change.

Today, many universities and other anchor institutions understand their unique role in urban economic and community development by becoming engaged with their cities and neighborhoods. However, "Colleges and universities are the most successful institutions of urban development to the extent that they operate as 'fully vested' urban institutions, i.e., fully engaged in producing the collective capacity of a range of city leaders to achieve the multiple interests of cities and communities, as well as universities, in ways that are mutually agreeable" (Perry, Wiewel, and Menendez 2009, 4).

REFERENCES

Blaik, Omar. 2008. Urban anchors: Creating places, remaking cities. Paper presented at University as Civic Partner Conference, February 14–16, 2008, Phoenix, AZ.

Brown, John, and Jacqueline Geoghegan. 2009. Bringing the campus to the community: An examination of the Clark University park partnership after ten years. In *The Impact of Large Landowners on Land Markets*, ed. Raphael W. Bostic. Cambridge, MA: Lincoln Institute of Land Policy.

Calder, Allegra, Gabriel Grant, and Holly Hart Muson. 2005. No such thing as vacant land: Northeastern University and Davenport Commons. In Perry and Wiewel 2005, 253–267.

Chan, Sewell. 2007. When the gown devours the town. *The New York Times*, November 16.

City of Milwaukee. 2003. *A strategy and vision for the UWM neighborhood*. Milwaukee: Department of City Development.

City of San Jose. South campus district plan 2009. http://www.sanjoseca.gov/planning/district_plan/.

College Vista. 2009. http://smccd.edu/accounts/smccd/collegevista/.

The Connective Corridor. 2009. Overview. http://connectivecorridor.syr.edu/.

Fainstein, Susan S. 1994. *The City Builders: Property, Politics, and Planning in London and New York*. Cambridge, MA: Blackwell.

Leland, Pamela. 2006. Robbing Peter to pay Paul: Concerns and contradictions in payments-in-lieu-of-taxes (pilots) as a source of municipal revenue. Working paper. Cambridge, MA: Lincoln Institute of Land Policy.

Perry, David C. 2008. Changing the research paradigm: From applied to engaged. Paper presented at University as Civic Partner Conference, February 14–16, 2008, Phoenix, AZ.

_____, and Wim Wiewel. 2005. *The University as Urban Developer*. Armonk, NY: M.E. Sharpe and the Lincoln Institute of Land Policy.

_____, Wim Wiewel, and Carrie Menendez. 2009. The city, communities, and universities: 360 degrees of planning and development. Working paper. Cambridge, MA: Lincoln Institute of Land Policy.

Strom, Elizabeth. 2005. The political strategies behind university-based development. In Perry and Wiewel 2005, 116–130.

Taylor, Jill S. 2007. *Mechanisms for Cities to Manage: Institutionally Led Real Estate Development*. Working paper. Cambridge, MA: Lincoln Institute of Land Policy.

CHAPTER 35

Richmond and Other Cities Work with Their School District to Make Students Better Citizens

Deborah L. McKoy, David Stern
and Ariel H. Bierbaum

Work-based learning (WBL), an important part of the 1990s "School to Work" movement,[1] is a core component of the Linked Learning strategy which is now shaping efforts to improve secondary education in California[2] and around the nation in cities such as Detroit, New York and Philadelphia. WBL can include not only classic internships and "co-op" placements but also school-based enterprises and other activities in which students produce goods or provide services for other people.[3] The National Academy Foundation, in collaboration with other organizations involved with Linked Learning, has described a continuum of WBL experiences, including a "career practicum" that complements academic and technical coursework to prepare a student for both college and careers.

However, discussions to date have not fully recognized the particular importance of the civic sector as a site for WBL. The civic sector, including public agencies and nonprofit organizations, is vital to both a strong economy and a healthy democracy. The aim of this chapter is to explain the idea of WBL in the civic sector and offer an in-depth look at a model of civic WBL — the Y-PLAN — in action.

The Case for Civic Work-Based Learning

The civic sector is large; it offers unique opportunities for all students to acquire concepts and skills for civic engagement; and WBL in the civic sector can directly empower students from low-income communities of color that tend to be less involved in civic affairs. Because of its size and diversity of job offerings, the civic sector also offers possible future employment for many students. In 2007, nonprofit organizations employed approximately 9 million people.[4] In 2011, government agencies employed 22 million, of whom 14 million worked for local governments.[5] Together, government and nonprofits thus account for about 24 percent of all 131 million non-farm jobs in the United States. Clearly this sector is too big to ignore. Whether or not a student is interested in future employment in this sector, WBL in public and nonprofit agencies provides opportunities for all students to develop career-readiness skills such as critical analysis of complex problems, collaborative teamwork, and communication. Unlike work experience in other sectors, WBL in the civic sector can increase students' awareness of the institutions and

Originally published as "Work-Based Learning through Civic Engagement," *Y-Plan Report*, July 2011, by the Center for Cities & Schools, University of California, Berkeley. Reprinted with permission of the publisher.

processes of government and collective action. Education for citizenship has long been considered one of the principal purposes of compulsory public education in this country. Jefferson famously wrote in 1786, "…our liberty can never be safe but in the hands of the people themselves, and that, too, of the people with a certain degree of instruction. This is the business of the state to effect…." The U.S. Supreme Court affirmed in the 1954 *Brown* decision and again in its 2003 *Grutter* ruling that "education … is the very foundation of good citizenship." A 2000 Gallup poll showed that these statements are in accord with public opinion: the most frequently affirmed goal for public schools is "to prepare people to become responsible citizens." Yet the 2010 NAEP assessment of students' knowledge of civics found only 24 percent of 12th graders scored proficient or advanced — down from 26 percent in 1998 and 27 percent in 2006 (U.S. Department of Education, 2011). One of the five areas of knowledge tested by the NAEP assessment is "What are civic life, politics, and government?" Another is "What are the roles of citizens in American democracy?" Students finishing high school evidently have not mastered ideas necessary for responsible and competent participation in civic matters.

Engaging in civic WBL has been found to improve students' knowledge in these areas. Accumulating evidence shows that service learning, which mainly takes place in the civic sector, can develop students' skills, knowledge, and commitment to participate in addressing collective problems in the community and society (Billig, Root, & Jesse 2005; Kahne & Sporte 2008; David 2009; Levinson 2009). Leaders in the field of civic education have endorsed this kind of engagement as one of several ways schools can help to develop competent and responsible citizens (Gibson & Levine 2003). Levinson (2009, p. 35) emphasizes the importance of the experiential component: "Civic education at its heart must be about active participation, not passive observation." At the same time, Kahne and Westheimer (2003, p. 36) caution that effective education for democracy must be "more than good deeds." It also must include knowledge of governmental institutions and opportunities to analyze and debate collective issues. Kahne and Sporte's study of high school students in Chicago found that gains in students' civic commitment was strongly associated both with classroom discussion of civic issues and with participation in active service learning projects.

In particular, civic WBL can engage students with the basic concept of a shared or collective good.[6] This concept is fundamental to understanding the role of government and nonprofit enterprise in relation to the private sector and for-profit business. Conventional economic theory says that private goods can be efficiently provided through market exchange, but ordinary markets are not efficient in providing or protecting common goods such as clean air. Some kind of collective action, usually through government, is required to produce efficient allocation of shared or public goods. (We use the terms "shared," "public," and "collective" goods interchangeably.)

Despite the prominence of this idea in standard economics and political science,[7] high school students seldom learn it. According to a study by Walstad and Rebeck (2001), market failure and the role of government were the least well understood microeconomic concepts assessed by the Test of Economic Literacy. Public debates on these issues are often complex, contentious, confusing, and driven by ideology rather than informed discussion. Because many political issues have to do with how best to provide collective goods and the proper role of government relative to the private sector, a clear understanding of what is and what is not a shared good is essential.

Finally, civic WBL can address persistent racial and socioeconomic differences in civic participation. Voting, volunteering and other kinds of civic participation are less frequent among low-income minority groups. As in 1998 and 2006, the 2010 NAEP civics test found African American and Hispanic students scored lower than White and Asian students in grades 4, 8, and 12 (U.S. Department of Education, 2011). Students whose parents had completed less schooling also scored lower on the NAEP civics test. Differences in attitudes and participation show similar patterns as differences in civic knowledge. Levinson (2009) reports that, among young people age 15–25, Latinos and African Americans are less likely than whites to agree that "I can make a difference in solving the problems of my community." Hispanic young adults (ages 18–24) in particular have much lower rates of voter registration and community involvement than their white and black peers.

Instead of narrowing these gaps, the prevailing pattern of educational opportunity tends to widen them. Kahne and Middaugh (2008) conducted a survey of 2,366 California high school seniors, and found that African American students had fewer civic-oriented government classes, current event discussions, and experiences in an open classroom climate than white students. Latino students reported fewer opportunities to participate in community service, simulations, and open classroom climates than white students. Kahne and Middaugh also summarized results from the IEA Civic Education Study of civic learning opportunities, which surveyed a nationally representative set of classrooms from 124 different schools throughout the country. The IEA found students in classes with higher average SES levels were: 2.03 times more likely than students in classrooms with average SES scores to report studying how laws are made; 1.89 times more likely to report participating in service activities; and 1.42 times more likely to report having experiences with debates or panel discussions in their social studies classes. Differences in current civic learning opportunities evidently mirror the racial and socioeconomic differences in the larger society. Providing civic WBL as part of Linked Learning would begin to offset this perverse pattern of civic educational opportunity.

Y-Plan: A Model of Civic WBL for California and the Nation

Y-PLAN TURNS SCHOOLS INSIDE OUT; COMMUNITIES BECOME A TEXT FOR LEARNING AND STUDENTS BECOME AGENTS OF SOCIAL CHANGE

Over the past decade, the award-winning Y-PLAN (Youth-Plan, Learn, Act, Now) initiative has been implemented in the Bay Area and across the nation. Y-PLAN engages young people as agents of change in authentic planning and community development projects linked to their school work. Y-PLAN centers on shared places as a public good—this is central to the field of city planning and community development. Questions from civic leaders focus on efforts that enhance the physical and social spaces in communities, such as creating safe and inviting community parks and recreations centers. Though this process, Y-PLAN bridges the worlds of city planning and public health with civic engagement and academic development to foster on-the-ground change that promotes health and well-being for all residents. Y-PLAN provides a vehicle for civic leaders to ask young people for feedback on pressing community challenges, for educators to use these questions to engage students in civic projects, and for young people to develop innovative solutions that address a public good.

Y-PLAN operates as both an in-class and out-of-school time educational model and has traditionally worked with low-income communities of color, groups that are typically left out of conversations about the physical and social transformation of their communities. Participants in Y-PLAN are supported by a range of professional advisors—faculty from local universities, civic and business leaders, professional practitioners—representing many professional disciplines and working together to solve real world problems.

To date Y-PLAN has engaged over 1,000 young people as agents of change and over 100 educational and civic leaders as adult allies and client partners in efforts that revitalize local neighborhoods and build community connections in diverse places. Y-PLAN has facilitated and supported these communities of practice as they plan for real changes in their schools, neighborhoods, and cities. Y-PLAN projects have ranged from the revitalization of neighborhood parks to overcoming tense intergenerational neighborhood relationships to master planning for housing redevelopment to creating youth-friendly walking tours of hidden neighborhoods. Today, Y-PLAN is recognized as exhibiting all of the characteristics of high quality

WBL programs as defined by the Linked Learning movement.[8]

Characteristics of High-Quality WBL Programs

- Meaningful engagement in the workplace.
- Connection between workplace experience and classroom learning.
- Structured opportunities for critical reflection and exploration.
- Careful assessment of learning to validate benefits and ensure ongoing innovation.

Meaningful Engagement in the Workplace

Y-PLAN participants engage directly in the field of community development as young urban planners; they tackle many of the issues and utilize diverse tools that go into professional planning and "placemaking"—the process of "looking at, listening to, and asking questions of the people who live, work and play in a particular space ... to create a common vision for that place." Y-PLAN action projects and proposals capture both short term implementation ideas and long term strategies that ultimately "bring benefits to public spaces and the people who use them."[9] Students engage with their community to address local challenges and policy questions and develop innovative solutions as engaged civic actors. Authentic community problems engage diverse stakeholders including local elected officials, government agencies, planners, neighborhood residents, teachers, and young people. Often, Y-PLAN leads to deeper volunteer or employment opportunities, such as serving on citywide youth councils or working as interns in the public agency or a non-profit organization that served as their client partner during the Y-PLAN process.

Connection between Workplace Experience and Classroom Learning

Educators' role in Y-PLAN is to connect planning projects and processes to classroom teaching—across a range of curriculum—working with real-life civic projects and leaders in public and non-profit agencies. Developed from years of collaborative work and partnerships with leading teachers, administrators, and policy makers, the Center for Cities & Schools (CC&S) has developed a pedagogical framework and a set of tools that guide school districts and communities through a 5-module inquiry process that yields simultaneous academic development and community change. Y-PLAN has proven to be a very flexible tool adaptable to a wide range of academic curriculum from social studies and economics to career academy and pathway elective courses in technology, hospitality and tourism, and finance. The Y-PLAN 5-module inquiry process aligns with rigorous, scientific method and basic research practices:

- *Module 1: Start Up:* Learn about each other, the Y-PLAN framework, individual and team strengths and "client" project questions and milestones and create a roadmap for work ahead
- *Module 2: Making Sense of the City:* Conduct community mapping activities to identify assets and challenges in the community and consider relationships between people and places; work together to understand project questions through additional research and data collection; and create final posters "telling the story of the community"
- *Module 3: Into Action:* Get inspired by learning about other models and projects; identify and understand a variety of stakeholder perspectives; create a vision and plan of action for the project; and create a plan of action for the future
- *Module 4: Going Public:* Create a public, multi-media proposal presentation; present ideas publicly to a panel of project stakeholders and policy makers; receive feedback for future action
- *Module 5: Looking Forward, Looking Back:* Evaluate personal participation and prepare reflective essays; follow up with "clients" on utilization plans for proposals; and outline next steps for sustained engagement

The Y-PLAN tools serve as an agreed-upon learning plan where all educators and civic partners identify how different aspects of the curriculum will support both academic development and the production of meaningful projects and urban planning proposals.

Structured Opportunities for Critical Reflection and Exploration

Critical reflection is a key component of the Y-PLAN process enabling students to make direct connections between their engagement on civic challenges and their academic work. With Y-PLAN, learning is no longer a function of knowledge-acquisition, but rather of knowledge-production by both young people and adults (McKoy and Vincent 2007). This reciprocal and iterative process—*learning to plan, planning to learn*—takes the form of the 5-module inquiry process that guides participants through their projects and ensure that students understand what they have done and how it relates to both their education and the community at large. Following each module, young people engage in individual and collective reflection through writing and discussion. Critical analysis focuses on both project questions and the Y-PLAN process, allowing for real-time adjustments if needed. Ultimately, young people stand out as innovators and critical thinkers able to directly inform the process by which they engage in improving the communities where they live, play, and learn.

Careful Assessment of Learning to Validate Benefits and Ensure Ongoing Innovation

Authentic assessment is a key aspect of Y-PLAN. One of the most powerful components of Y-PLAN is the culminating event at the end of each planning process where students present their final proposals to their client partners and a panel of civic and educational leaders. Using an agreed upon assessment rubric, civic leaders provide teams of Y-PLAN students with feedback on a range of core competences including expression of team work, creativity, connection to core curriculum, critical analysis of data, and understanding of community context.

Y-PLAN rests on the foundational principle that all participants work together in a community of practice; adults share decision making with young people, valuing their input and giving them a noticeable role in outcomes sharing expertise and deep knowledge—likewise, young people share their insights and knowledge of the places they live, work and learn. Y-PLAN assessment also focuses on the role and learning of educators and client partners to ensure that the process meets key classroom learning goals of teachers and supports the placemaking work of client partners.

Civic WBL in Action: 3 Cases of Y-PLAN in the San Francisco Bay Area

In 2011, six cities across the country are utilizing Y-PLAN with the support of organizations such as the University of California's Office of the President, W.K. Kellogg Foundation, and National Academy Foundation. These yearlong initiatives in Richmond, Oakland, San Francisco, Dallas, New York City, and Detroit represent a diversity of partnerships and demonstrate the power of Y-PLAN as an adaptable pedagogy for implementing civic WBL.

Following are detailed descriptions and analyses of three recent Y-PLAN projects. Each illustrates innovative civic WBL practices designed to reinforce classroom learning, connect students to postsecondary institutions, engage teachers, and other community leaders, and develop positive change for the public good.

NYSTROM UNITED REVITALIZATION EFFORT (NURVE), RICHMOND, CA

Project Background and Community Challenges

Nestled in Richmond, CA, is a small, historically underserved community called Nystrom that today is undergoing significant transformation under the banner of NURVE, the Nystrom United ReVitalization Effort. NURVE aims "to create a safe, diverse and thriving place, where kids walk to quality schools, people of all ages use the parks and community facilities, and a variety of housing options meet the needs of local residents." Launched in 2001, NURVE emerged from the conviction that changes in the built environment are key to a community's revitalization and transformation. NURVE partners are aligning the planning and implementation of four large capital development projects:

- Modernization of the Nystrom Elementary School by the West Contra Costa Unified School District
- Renovation of the Martin Luther King, Jr. (MLK) Park by the City of Richmond
- Rehabilitation of the Nystrom Village housing development by the Richmond Housing Authority
- Historic preservation of the Maritime Center, part of the Rosie the Riveter World War II Home Front National Historical Park by the National Parks Service and in partnership with a local non-profit, the Richmond Community Foundation

While each of these projects poses distinct development challenges, civic leaders recognize that they all required a high level of public participation to ensure they met the needs of local residents. Because of high rates of youth violence and lack of opportunities for youth in Richmond, adults in the community are particularly interested in creating a vibrant neighborhood that would provide activities, enrichment, and support for youth. Leaders also believe that engaging the public in the planning and design of these places would foster a sense of pride, ownership, and stewardship among residents, young and old, once the projects are built.

Since 2008, Y-PLAN has served as a vehicle for civic leaders to structure an inclusive process, and for teachers at Kennedy High School to engage students in civic WBL. Working with school site leadership and as part of the Architecture, Construction, Engineering Technology (ACET) career academy, Y-PLAN has supported over 150 11th and 12th grade students build core college and career skills, connect with civic leaders, and cultivate an identity as engaged civic actors contributing to the broader community.

The Y-PLAN client partners include the leadership from the range of civic sector agencies involved in NURVE: City of Richmond City Manager and Mayor, West Contra Costa Unified School District Superintendent and Facilities Manager, Executive Director of the Richmond Housing Authority, and key staff from the Richmond Community Foundation.

Together, these adult leaders sought to pose very real and pressing questions to the young people. For example, in 2008, the focus of inquiry was on the MLK Park, and specific questions included:

1. What recreational needs do youth have?

2. What amenities would encourage youth to spend more time at MLK Park?

3. What strategies do youth have for ensuring that MLK Park is safe and free from vandalism?

4. What design and programming elements will support multigenerational use of MLK Park?

Students' Visions for a Vibrant MLK Park

In February of 2008, over 30 11th grade Kennedy High School students embarked on a 12-week Y-PLAN process. After meeting their clients and digesting the specific questions, Y-PLAN students engaged in community-based research, mapping the assets, challenges, and opportunities near the MLK Park and in the Nystrom neighborhood. Working with their U.S. History teacher, students connected their personal experiences and investigation with their classroom learning — bearing witness to the legacy of Richmond's significant World War II contributions. Students examined demographic data and discovered that while Richmond has a rich African American history, the city was rapidly changing, and now home to many Latino and other new immigrant families. This research reflected the students' class demographics back to them, and allowed for their teacher to draw important connections between their individual experiences and broader societal changes and city dynamics.

The students' final proposals/urban plans integrated their personal experience, classroom learning, and community-based research into innovative, original ideas that addressed the client questions. Students worked in small teams, and debated their design proposal priorities, coming to consensus, and crafting PowerPoint presentations and three-dimensional models. Students also wrote essays.

In a final presentation to over 40 civic leaders, parents, and community stakeholders, students called for greater amenities and services for themselves and their families. Students articulated the connections between the built environment and the social amenities they need to support their personal and collective aspirations. These young planners proposed new ideas for safe pathways and recreational fields with a network of "blue light" telephones for quick access to police services. They asked for adult English language classes and job training for their families and bilingual tutoring assistance for their peers. They suggested historical markers that honored the legacy of their neighborhood as home to "Rosie the Riveter" and brought beauty into their lives today. They identified spaces that could meet the needs of young children, such as a tot lot, adjacent to benches and tables for the elders that watch the children during the day.

The Public Good Realized

Immediately following the final presentations, participating adult allies — including the Mayor, City Council members, City Manager, and others — adapted their understanding and the vision of the NURVE project priorities and needs accordingly. Residents and families feel more confident in the neighborhood planning process, which has been ongoing for nearly a decade. As the Executive Director of the Richmond Children's Foundation noted, "It is largely the visible role of young people that has kept all parties coming back to the table and accountable to each other." As a result, residents and stakeholder group leaders are motivated to move forward because they agree that the future of the community depends in large measure on supporting the next generation of residents.

Through Y-PLAN, young people learn that "change takes time." Understanding the balance between short- and long-term change, a core group of Y-PLAN students formed the MLK Youth Advisory Council, to provide some immediate activities for youth to get involved with and to stay involved in the NURVE processes. The Youth Council found a home at the Richmond Community Foundation, where many of the members received stipends and additional professional development training. The Youth Council members served as facilitators

at a number of public meetings concerning the design and development of the park, and their innovative design ideas were incorporated for discussion among the broader community. As of 2011, the original members are still engaged, while attending community college and working nearby.

On May 6, 2011, the fourth Y-PLAN cohort from Kennedy High School presented their vision for a new linear park, the Richmond Greenway to the City Manager, Mayor, and Superintendent of schools. City Manager Bill Lindsay, inspired by these new designs, reassured the group that he and his staff were and are listening closely. The next day, on May 7, 2011, civic and community leaders, residents, and youth participated in a ribbon-cutting ceremony at MLK Park, which included a number of the design elements envisioned by that first Y-PLAN cohort in 2008.

THE CENTER OF COMMUNITY LIFE, EMERYVILLE, CA

Project Background and Community Challenges

For the past decade, the City of Emeryville and the Emery Unified School District (EUSD) in California have come together on a number of initiatives out of a shared commitment to provide comprehensive services to young people in the city. The development of the city's Youth Services Master Plan in 2002 launched a joint city and school district visioning process, laying the foundation for the ongoing planning processes and attendant strategic plans. These efforts culminated in the vision for Emeryville Center of Community Life (ECCL), an innovative multi-purpose, joint use facility that will house Emeryville's K–12 public schools along with a childcare facility, a recreation center offering both indoor and outdoor activities, an arts center for visual and performing arts, and a forum that will provide community services focused on wellness, health, and other areas. According to project publications, the ECCL "creates a new framework for a 21st-century urban place where we will play, learn, grow, and come together as a community. By offering a variety of educational, recreational, cultural, and social opportunities, as well as services and programs that support lifelong learning and healthy lifestyles, the Center will transform the quality of life of all Emeryville citizens."

From 2006 through 2009, Y-PLAN served as a vehicle for civic leaders to structure an inclusive planning process, and for teachers at Emery Secondary School to engage students in civic WBL. Working with key teachers and district staff, Y-PLAN has supported over 75 10th, 11th, and 12th grade students build core college and career skills, connect with civic leaders, and cultivate an identity as engaged civic actors contributing to the broader community.

The Y-PLAN client partners included the EUSD Superintendent and architect, City Manager, and City parks and recreation staff. Together, these adult leaders sought to pose very real and pressing questions to the young people, as the vision for the ECCL was first evolving. Specific questions included:

1. What recreational, health, and social service needs do youth have?

2. What kinds of places would youth spend time after school?

3. What indoor and outdoor design and programming elements will support multi-generational use of the Emeryville Center of Community Life?

Student Visions for the Emeryville Center for Community Life

In January 2006, the first Y-PLAN cohort at Emery Secondary School began their inquiry process into the conceptualization of the ECCL. These 10th grade students conducted community-based research, talking to peers and investigating their surroundings. They gathered demographic data on Emeryville and their school community and identified diverse needs. Their history teacher successfully connected broad concepts of World History to the local dynamics; for example, she tied issues of capitalism to Emeryville's history as an industrial center of the Bay Area.

Y-PLAN students identified top priorities as safe "hang out" spaces, nursing and counseling services, healthier cafeteria food, and more sports facilities. Students highlighted the alien-

ation they often felt from local businesses and suggested specific ways that the ECCL could foster a welcoming environment, including specific signage, public art, and youth-run businesses. Students also focused on outdoor spaces, identifying areas for community gardens, outdoor classrooms, sports facilities, and public art. In addition to providing input on the design of and programming for the ECCL, students advocated for a long term and sustained voice in the planning and development process.

The Public Good Realized

The intensive youth participation in the planning and visioning of the ECCL has served to open up city government to a broader cross-section of the community. The Mayor and City Council members recognized that the first Y-PLAN presentation in City Council chambers in 2006 marked a turning point: for the first time the council chambers room was filled with families of color. Y-PLAN served an important role in opening up formal policy-making processes to an underrepresented constituency of residents and stakeholders.

In the short term, EUSD responded to the student's ideas around additional nursing and counseling services by partnering with local universities that placed students in nursing and social work on campus. EUSD also incorporated comments about healthy and tasty foods in their food service planning. Further, in response to student interest, the City and EUSD have restructured several working committees to include youth representation. This transformation mirrors the work City and District leaders have undertaken on joint decision-making and governance in general. The City-Schools Committee, made up of all school board and city council members, meets monthly and is an operating committee fielding all partnership and joint decision making issues. A student representative now sits on the City-Schools Committee, selected through an application process jointly managed and mentored by school and city staff.

Finally, the planning process for the ECCL continues. Now, five years after that initial Y-PLAN cohort put pen to paper on designs, the City and EUSD have had two conceptual plans developed and in 2010, a bond measure passed allocating funding to the actual construction of the ECCL. The 2006 and subsequent Y-PLAN cohorts engaged in planning meetings, presented their ideas to consultant teams and civic leaders, and crafted recommendation memos to ensure that their youth perspective persisted in the designs.

GALILEO HIGH SCHOOL, ACADEMY OF HOSPITALITY AND TOURISM, SAN FRANCISCO, CA

Project Background and Community Challenges

Tourism is one of San Francisco's major economic engines. The global recession hit the otherwise resilient Bay Area, however, January 2009, visitors to the city and local hotel revenue were at an all time low. While many think of big hotel chains and airlines as taking a hit, local independently owned neighborhood businesses also suffer when tourism is down, impacting San Francisco residents and the vibrancy of those neighborhoods. San Francisco Travel (formerly the San Francisco Convention and Visitors Bureau) is the non-profit organization responsible for ensuring that visitors to San Francisco have information about key activities, restaurants, and other destinations of interest. San Francisco Travel works closely with city agencies to ensure that the city is clean, safe, and welcoming for the over fifteen million worldwide visitors each year.

From 2004 through 2009, the San Francisco Unified School District utilized the Y-PLAN methodology across ten career academies in five high schools. In 2008, the Y-PLAN client, San Francisco Travel, asked Galileo High School's Hospitality and Tourism Academy to identify innovative hotspots for tourists. These adult leaders sought innovations from young people that would directly impact the economy and vibrancy of neighborhoods and San Francisco as a whole. Specific questions included:

1. What neighborhoods have opportunities for tourist traffic?

2. What places and activities would appeal to young people visiting San Francisco?

3. How can San Francisco Travel make getting around diverse neighborhoods interesting and easy for tourists, particularly focused on attracting families and young people?

Student Visions for a Dynamic City of Neighborhoods

In the fall of 2008, the cohort at Galileo High School began their inquiry process into the options for tourists in the neighborhood. The 11th grade students conducted community-based research, talking to peers, current tourists, local business owners, and investigating their surroundings. They gathered demographic data on visitors to the city and on the local neighborhoods, and conducted surveys of nearby businesses and tourists. They reviewed industry data and other pre-existing tours provided from their client. Their math teacher connected their survey analysis to core curriculum and analyzed local statistical patterns of visitors to the targeted neighborhoods, and they worked with a technology teacher to realize their final project by creating a series of powerful multimedia presentations and more.

Y-PLAN students determined that something that San Francisco lacked was an easy, free way for tourists to experience various "niches" of San Francisco life. Students also wanted to showcase things that would attract youth and families. They decided to create "niche tour" podcasts. Working in teams, they each identified a specific topic area, and then conducted additional topic-specific research. They crafted a script, honed their mapping skills, and recorded a walking tour of dynamic and often unseen elements of San Francisco.

The Public Good Realized

Students' niche tours included: the *Hidden Gem* (Hayes Valley neighborhood), *Golden Gate Park Scenery Tour, Family Fun,* and *Live Like a True San Franciscan.* The podcasts each have an accompany map with walking tour, and students created exit surveys to get critical feedback from users. The tours highlight local businesses and youth- and family-accessible locations. In January of 2009, students presented their tours to leaders at San Francisco Travel and other city and school district leaders. The podcasts and maps are available for free download at Galileo High School[10] and have been enjoyed by many and students also garnered the attention of local media.[11] The Y-PLAN project was considered a great success and win-win for everyone involved. As one client partner said, "They're looking at San Francisco through eyes that are much younger than mine, and a mind that is much more open and that's a really beautiful thing to really share a young person's perspective about San Francisco; it's going to be different than other people."

Conclusion and Call to Action

Civic WBL as part of Linked Learning initiatives is a win-win proposition: civic organizations can pursue their missions by offering high quality WBL experiences; educators can connect civic engagement to core academics and their students' communities; and young people have meaningful access to a vital part of the economy and a functioning democracy.

In this chapter, we have developed this proposition by

- Showing how civic WBL can be used to address the growing civic education gap — creating and reinforcing critical relationships between students, families, and entire communities to public and non-profit leaders and institutions
- Offering the Y-PLAN as a proven example of what works in civic WBL, thereby addressing the important nuts-and-bolts concerns of implementing civic WBL experiences
- Documenting where a growing number of students and communities, who would otherwise be left on the margins of our educational, civic, and workforce sectors are drawn to Y-PLAN initiatives that empower them to make a tangible difference in their communities

Today, the Linked Learning approach is itself a unique opportunity for California and states across the nation to effectively support students as they establish a solid foundation for success in college and careers. With the renewed focus on civic WBL advocated here, Linked Learning will be better positioned to realize its full potential of preparing students to succeed in school, work, and civic life.

NOTES

1. For example, see D. Stern, M. McMillion, C. Hopkins, and J. R. Stone III, "Work Experience for Students in High School and College" (*Youth and Society*, 21[3]: 355–389, March 1990).

2. California Department of Education, *Multiple Pathways to Student Success: Envisioning the New California High School* (Sacramento, 2010). Available at http://www.schoolsmovingup.net/mpstudy/downloads/Multiple_Pathways_Report_2010.pdf

3. S. Darche, N. Nayar, and K. Bracco, Work-Based Learning in California: Opportunities and Models for Expansion. San Francisco: The James Irvine Foundation, 2009. http://www.irvine.org/images/stories/pdf/grantmaking/work-basedlearning.pdf

4. A. Butler, "Wages in the Nonprofit Sector" (U.S. Department of Labor, Bureau of Labor Statistics: *Compensation and Working Conditions* April 15, 2009).

5. U.S. Department of Labor, Bureau of Labor Statistics, *The Employment Situation—April 2011*.

6. What defines shared or collective goods is that benefits received by one person do not diminish benefits for other people, and excluding anyone from these benefits would not be feasible. Categories of collective goods include:
- Environment — protection or improvement of air, oceans, climate, natural landscapes, and other aspects of the environment.
- Infrastructure — roads, bridges, parks, sanitation systems, national defense, law courts and other such physical and institutional infrastructures are all collective goods when they are not congested.
- Public health measures — prevention of communicable diseases or promotion of practices that preserve health.
- Culture — preservation and advancement of science, art, and other cultural achievements.

7. The prevailing definition of collective goods in economics was first formulated by Paul Samuelson (1954); for a more recent exposition, see Joseph Stiglitz (2000). Samuelson was the first American to win a Nobel Prize in economics, Stiglitz shared the Nobel in 2001. The 2009 prize was awarded to political scientist Elinor Ostrom in large part for her research on efficient allocation of shared resources (for example, see Ostrom, 1990).

8. http://irvine.org/grantmaking/our-programs/youth/linked-learning; CDE. *Multiple Pathways to Student Success, Envisioning the New California High School 2010*.

9. Project for Public Spaces, *What Is Placemaking?* http://www.pps.org/articles/what_is_placemaking/.

10. http://galileoweb.org/aoht/audio-tours-of-san-francisco/

11. http://abclocal.go.com/kgo/story?section=news/local/san_francisco&id=6632375&rss=rsskgo-article-6632375.

REFERENCES

Billig, S., S. Root, and D. Jesse. (2005). *The impact of participation in service-learning on high school students' civic engagement*. Denver, CO: RMC Research.

David, J.L. (2009). Service learning and civic participation. *Educational Leadership*, May, pp. 83–84.

Gibson, C., and P. Levine. (2003). *The Civic Mission of Schools*. New York: Carnegie Corporation of New York, and The Center for Information and Research on Civic Learning and Engagement.

Kahne, J., and E. Middaugh. (2008). Democracy for Some: The Civic Opportunity.

Gap in High School. Working Paper #59. Washington, DC: Center for Information and Research on Civic Learning (CIRCLE).

Kahne, J.E., and S.E. Sporte. (2008). Developing citizens: The impact of civic learning opportunities on students' commitment to civic participation. *American Educational Research Journal*, 45(3): 738–766.

Kahne, J., and J. Westheimer. (2003). Teaching democracy: What schools need to do. *Phi Delta Kappan, 85*(1): 34–40, 57–66.

Kemple, J.J. (2008). *Career Academies: Long-term Impacts on Labor Market Outcomes, Educational Attainment, and Transitions to Adulthood*. New York: MDRC.

Levinson, M. (2009). Taking action: What we can do to address the civic achievement gap. *Social Studies Review* 48(1): 33–36.

McKoy, D.L., and J.M. Vincent. (2005). Engaging Schools in Urban Revitalization: The Y-PLAN (Youth — Plan, Learn, Act, Now!). *Journal of Planning Education and Research*, 26: 389–403.

McKoy, D.L., J.M. Vincent, and A.H. Bierbaum. (2010). Trajectories of Opportunity for Young Men and Boys of Color: Built Environments and Placemaking Strategies for Creating Equitable, Healthy, and Sustainable Communities. In C. Edley and J. Ruiz de Velasco (eds.), *Changing Places: How Communities Will Improve the Health of Boys of Color*. Berkeley: University of California Press.

McKoy, D.L., A.H. Bierbaum, and J.M. Vincent. (2009). *The Mechanics of City-School Initiatives: Transforming Neighborhoods of Distress & Despair into Neighborhoods of Choice & Promise*. Berkeley: Center for Cities & Schools, University of California.

Ostrom, E. (1990). *Governing the Commons: The Evolution of Institutions for Collective Action*. New York: Cambridge University Press, 1990.

Samuelson, P. (1954). The pure theory of public expenditure. *Review of Economics and Statistics* 36: 386–389.

Stern, D., M. Raby, and C. Dayton. (1992). *Career Academies: Partnerships for Reconstructing American High Schools*. San Francisco/New York: Jossey-Bass/John Wiley.

Stiglitz, J. (2000). *Economics of the Public Sector*. New York: W.W. Norton.

U.S. Department of Education (2011): *The Nation's Report Card: Civics 2010. NCES 2011-466*. Washington, DC: National Center for Education Statistics.

Walstad, W.B., and K. Rebeck. (2001). Assessing the economic understanding of U.S. high school students. *American Economic Review* 91(2):452–457.

CHAPTER 36

Richmond Citizens Benefit from Virginia Commonwealth University's Investments

Michael Porter *and* Paul Grogan

To better understand the role of leadership and a comprehensive implementation of the strategic framework, ICIC and CEOs for Cities conducted two in-depth case studies, one of Columbia University in New York City and the other of Virginia Commonwealth University in Richmond.

Both of these institutions offer highly instructive examples of an urban-based university playing an active role in the revitalization of its surrounding communities. The case studies show the mechanisms and rationales for the universities' role in local job and business growth. They offer examples of strong leadership, effective institutional setup, and meaningful community engagement. Moreover, both cases illustrate that a methodical, patient approach to integrating the community into university growth strategies holds the promise of sustained economic impact.

Columbia University, specifically, shows how an urban-based university can align its interests with those of its surrounding community, creating a strong "win-win" relationship. VCU, moreover, shows how such an institution can take not only local but also regional leadership in anchoring economic growth.

In-Depth Case: Virginia Commonwealth University in Richmond

In the past decade, the Virginia Commonwealth University (VCU), a state-owned university, has been a critical partner in the economic development of the Greater Richmond area. Through strong leadership, more than $580 million in real estate investments, and willingness to leverage partner resources, VCU has anchored both local and regional economic growth.

Locally, VCU's investments in its surrounding areas have turned a once distressed, crime-ridden area into a rapidly revitalizing neighborhood. VCU's investments along Broad Street — a major traffic artery cutting along the northern boundary of VCU's academic campus — have spurred significant private-sector development. Lowe's Home Improvement Warehouse has built a signature complex on Broad Street, Kroger is building a supermarket just off Broad, and 455 private housing units are being built in the immediate surroundings. Lowe's is the first-ever hardware and home-renovation store in Richmond's central city, while Kroger's new outlet is the first major supermarket to come to Richmond in over a decade.

Originally published as "Vision and Strategy in Action: In-Depth Case Studies," *Leveraging Colleges and Universities for Urban Economic Revitalization: An Action Agenda*, March 2002, by the Initiative for a Competitive Inner City and CEO's for Cities, Boston, Massachusetts. Reprinted with permission of the publisher.

Regionally, VCU has leveraged its highly regarded Medical College of Virginia (MCV) campus and the VCU Health System to propel Richmond as a center of biotechnology, a field that many local leaders see as the next emerging economic growth engine. "Many of us see biotechnology doing for Richmond what information technology did for Northern Virginia," said Robert Grey, an attorney and former chair of the Greater Richmond Chamber of Commerce (GRCC). VCU turned this regional vision into concrete action by spearheading the development of a 34-acre biotechnology park, a bioscience incubator that nurtures 15–20 companies at any given time, and an entirely new life-sciences initiative and microelectronics department for the university. These departments will conduct research in nanotechnology and other cutting-edge technologies.

To account for VCU's success in accomplishing so much in just a few years, almost all fingers point to one person: VCU President Dr. Eugene Trani. Trani—who was variously described as a "visionary," a "risk-taker," a "deal maker," "domineering," a "Fortune-500-like CEO," and a "benevolent dictator"—has been at the helm of VCU's role in Richmond's economy. Upon becoming president of VCU in 1990, he set out to court local leaders. Jim Dunn, President of GRCC, recalls that in their first meeting, Trani clearly indicated that he "wanted the university to become an active, viable partner in the economic growth and development of the region."

In 1991, the GRCC sponsored a "visioning" process that brought together government, business, and community leaders from both the city of Richmond and its surrounding counties. During this process, local leaders determined the top priorities for the region in the 1990s. Trani committed to taking on two of the major economic development priorities: the establishment of a biotechnology park and the creation of a school of engineering. VCU accomplished both tasks and, in the process, delivered on even more.

These accomplishments catapulted VCU into a regional economic leadership position. During his decade-long tenure at VCU, Trani has taken over the chairmanship of two key

business development organizations: the Greater Richmond Chamber of Commerce (1997–1998) and the Richmond Renaissance (2001), a downtown redevelopment organization created to facilitate cooperation between white and African American business and government leaders.

Several factors account for Trani's ability to bring VCU into this leadership position. First is his brash, go-getter approach, an approach that works particularly well in Richmond—a city with a weak mayoral form of government, which often results in a citywide leadership vacuum. When word got around that he was about to take over the chairmanship of Richmond Renaissance, a politically sensitive and complex responsibility, "I got calls from friends saying, 'Don't do it, Gene,'" Trani recalled. "But someone has to do it. Someone has to step up to the plate."

Second, Trani's vision is the vision of local and regional leaders. In this respect, he is not fighting an uphill battle. In fact, because of this, he has focused not on "selling" deals, but on making deals, an ability for which he has gained a solid reputation. "He thinks like those CEOs he is trying to get into deals with. He has a very clear, well-researched ask," one local business leader said.

Third, Trani has a strong understanding of the nexus between the university and the business community. He has been extremely proactive in addressing the concerns of the business community. When the Martin Agency, a national advertising firm headquartered in Richmond, expressed the need for a higher quality workforce, VCU created its nationally ranked AdCenter. This graduate program works with agencies around the world to ensure that the students are being trained to meet the needs of this specialized industry, with a specific focus on copy writing, art direction, and planning.

Fourth, he also has a clear sense of VCU's capabilities and the unique value that it adds. "I'm not going to reinvent the wheel," explained Trani in an interview for this study. "I'm always looking for partners with whom I can combine my resources to create something greater than each of us can do separately." For example, he has promoted partnerships with cultural organizations, such as Theater Virginia, when hiring faculty; joint-funded faculty is a "win win" for both partners. In the realm of business partnerships, VCU and the Center for Innovative Technology, a state-chartered nonprofit corporation, jointly funded the Central Virginia Entrepreneurship Center (CVEC). Housed at VCU's Business School, CVEC helps start-up and small technology companies, drawing heavily from the VCU information systems faculty and students.

Fifth is his long-term commitment. He has created lasting institutions for university involvement. Since he took over, there is a Division of University Outreach and an Office of Community Programs that facilitate interaction and engagement with the surrounding communities. He has established Community Advisory Boards that meet quarterly to garner input from surrounding neighborhoods. A strong partnership has been formed with the Carver community that allows the community to tap into university expertise and resources. He has also created interdisciplinary units such as the Center for Public Policy, which provides survey research, program evaluation, and economic impact analysis for community projects.

Finally, Trani has been able to assemble a team of highly capable and connected people that effectively execute the vision and the programs. For instance, he brought in Robert Skunda, a former Virginia Secretary of Commerce and Trade, to run the Virginia Bio-Technology Research Park. For finance and administration, he brought in Paul Timmreck, who headed powerful finance positions in state government: the Director of the Virginia Department of Planning and Budget and the State Secretary of Finance.

The story of VCU and Eugene Trani, though unique in some respects, offers valuable lessons in leadership, partnerships, commitment, and execution. In 1990, the VCU Board of Visitors selected Trani as president after a search process that focused on identifying a leader who could position VCU more successfully with its external communities. During the search process, Trani emphasized the preeminent role that urban universities could assume

in the 21st century. Over the past decade, Trani has set out to implement this vision, which has enabled VCU to have significant impact on the economic prospects of inner-city Richmond, the city of Richmond, and the Richmond metropolitan area.

The strategic framework summarizes all VCU activities relating to regional and local job and business growth. The subsequent sections describe in great detail VCU initiatives in real state development, business incubation, and business advising. These are initiatives that are particularly instructive.

REAL ESTATE DEVELOPER

VCU is the second largest real estate holder in Richmond, after government, with more than 126 acres in the central city, in addition to 431 acres in the surrounding counties. In the past decade, VCU has invested $589 million in real estate development in Richmond. VCU's real estate projects are often deemed the catalysts to getting the city moving again. Specifically, two projects warrant mention:

• The Virginia Bio-Technology Research Park, which is positioning Richmond as a regional technology center
• Broad Street Redevelopment, which anchored revitalization of an economically distressed area

Richmond's 1991 visioning process determined that the region must strive to become a national center for biotechnology. "Richmond missed the information technology wave that started in the late '70s and '80s, but it couldn't miss the next big thing," explained a local business leader. The visioning process further determined that a biotechnology park was critical to positioning Richmond as such a national center.

A biotech park would allow companies to benefit from aggregation in one location, facilitating rapid transfer of learning. It would also enable the companies to tap into research being conducted at VCU's MCV Hospital, a reputable medical research center with a hospital that has been ranked among the best in the country. Moreover, estimates suggest that it would bring up to 3,000 jobs to the city of Richmond. The idea of such a park had surfaced years before with downtown development groups, but it did not become reality until VCU committed to taking the lead on the project.

There was common consensus that a park like this had to be located in the urban core, preferably adjacent to the MCV Campus of VCU and close to the life-sciences research activity. There was regional recognition that the region's economic health was directly related to the health of the core. In the middle of a rapidly growing region, Richmond's center had, for the most part, remained abandoned. Eugene Trani seized this opportunity. The Park would play a critical role in building up VCU's life-sciences focus. It would offer faculty research commercialization opportunities, and it would offer students hands-on industry experience. The city of Richmond was attracted to the development because of the newly created companies and jobs, which in turn would create a new tax base in an underutilized area of downtown.

Trani committed VCU to spearhead the development of the Bio-Technology Park and set out to assemble the large number of partners that could make a project like this a reality. "He hit everyone he thought had a stake in this," recalled Jack Berry, head of Richmond Renaissance and former Hanover County Administrator. Though he was working on a central-city downtown development, Trani did not spare county officials. "He came to me," continued Berry, "and said, 'We're going to have companies that will outgrow this Park and will be looking to move to your county. You have to help us make this happen.'" The three surrounding counties helped to finance the Park's feasibility studies. Since then, the Park has established more extensive relationships with surrounding counties. For instance, it now has "satellite" locations in Chesterfield County, where 325 acres have been set aside at the Meadowville Technology Park. Similar arrangements have been made with Henrico County at the White Oak Technology Park.

VCU and the city identified the 34 acres of land for the Park in downtown Richmond. On the south, the site bordered the Medical College of Virginia campus and hospitals, and on the west, Jackson Ward — a historically significant African American community that is working to revitalize itself. It included 7 acres of university land and 15 acres of city land, with the remainder privately held. These parcels were primarily used as gravel parking lots.

The Virginia Bio-Technology Research Park began as a joint venture between VCU and the city of Richmond. The Commonwealth of Virginia joined the partnership in 1993, with the creation of the Virginia Bio-Technology Research Park Authority, a political subdivision of the Commonwealth, with broad powers to own, develop, finance, and manage the facilities in the Park. The mission of the Authority is to create new jobs and businesses in the biotechnology industry for Virginia and position the state to compete in this industry.

Development in the Park has principally been financed through lease revenue bonds issued by the Authority. However, the Park has also relied heavily on VCU for a variety of support and direct contributions. In addition to providing staff support in financial and real estate services, the university has also donated land, provided annual operating subsidies to the Park, and backed the revenue bonds for Biotech One, the first multitenant building, with a master lease. The VCU Real Estate Foundation and Health Systems Foundation have also assisted with loans and by acquiring properties to reserve them for future acquisition by the Park.

Land acquisition remains the top challenge facing the Park. Approximately 15 acres of the land within the 34-acre master-planned boundaries are held in private ownership or by the Foundations, the city, and other entities. In 1999, the state appropriated $1 million, which was given to the Park in the form of a grant from the Virginia Economic Development Partnership. Last year, the city expanded its redevelopment boundaries to include the Park, thereby allowing the Richmond Redevelopment and Housing Authority to use eminent domain, if necessary, to acquire lands on the Park's behalf. Even though the tools are in place, the resources needed to acquire the remaining lands are estimated at $20 million, a number which is escalating as the Park's own success and other new activity make downtown sites even more valuable.

The Park currently houses 34 companies, 3 university institutes, and 2 state agencies. It encompasses five buildings — with two more under construction — and almost 320,000 square feet in leaseable space. The Park will eventually grow to 1.9 million square feet and represent more than $500 million in investment in a previously deteriorated area of the city.

As of June 2000, companies and institutes in the Bio-Tech Park employed 829 people. According to plans, the Park will eventually employ 3,000 people. While some of these will not be new jobs for Richmond (e.g., Biotech 6 will house the Virginia Division of Consolidated Lab Services, which is relocating from other buildings in the city), most will be newly created or attracted to the city.

Critics have voiced concerns that some of the current tenants, such as the state agencies, are not consistent with the purpose of the Bio-Tech Park. They are not start-up companies, they do not commercialize research, and they do not develop new products in biotechnology. Moreover, they are not new job creators. Even some of the tenants slated to move into the Park, such as the organ donor database, as significant as they may be, are not consistent with the mission of the Park, according to some critics.

Defenders, however, are quick to respond: "VCU, in fact, showed great flexibility and political astuteness to start filling the space up in a slow economy. Otherwise, they would have a white elephant in their hands," says Robert Grey. Moreover, by bringing in state agencies that have a medical sciences focus — forensics and consolidated labs — the Park is approaching that critical mass necessary to draw in more companies.

While the Bio-Tech Park has anchored the redevelopment around the VCU medical campus located in downtown Richmond, VCU's developments along Broad Street are anchoring the redevelopment of the area around the academic campus, which is located less than three miles from the downtown medical campus. In response to VCU's investments along Broad Street, the private sector is reentering an area that it has overlooked for more than 40 years.

The private sector is building 455 housing units in the surrounding area, Lowe's hardware retailer has built a signature complex on Broad Street, and Kroger (a regional supermarket) is building a store just off Broad Street. According to John Woodward, Richmond's Director of Economic Development, "Broad [Street] was an utterly abandoned corridor. VCU single-handedly turned it around."

The academic campus is nestled between the Fan, Carver, and Oregon Hill neighborhoods. The Fan is an affluent, high-density residential district. Carver and Oregon Hill are among the poorest neighborhoods in the region. Carver is a primarily African American residential neighborhood with some industrial properties, while Oregon Hill is a primarily white residential neighborhood.

A growing student population in the 1990s, which is expected to grow even further with the inauguration of new academic programs, forced the university to seek student housing and services close to campus. After severe opposition from the Oregon Hill community (south of the academic campus), VCU turned its focus to the north — to Broad Street and the Carver neighborhood.

VCU began its expansion on Broad Street by building a recreation center, a parking structure, a large bookstore, a 396-bed student dorm, and an art school complex. All these facilities were built on empty or abandoned properties; hence, no area residents or businesses were relocated.

From the onset of VCU's northward expansion, however, the Carver community voiced concerns about preservation of affordable housing for current residents and preservation of the architectural integrity of the neighborhood. Shortly after Trani's inauguration as president in 1990, VCU set up two Community Advisory Boards (one for the academic and another for the medical campus), which met quarterly to address community concerns. These Advisory Boards were created in response to a firestorm of opposition from the Oregon Hill community on a master plan for campus expansion, developed prior to Trani's arrival, without consultation with local residents. Upon prompting from the community, VCU also set out to create the Carver-VCU Partnership, which addresses long-term community concerns in education, health, land use, and economic development.

Through these Boards, VCU has involved the neighborhoods in the campus expansion planning process, at times modifying projects to accommodate neighborhood concerns. For example, during the Community Advisory Board meetings related to the athletic facility, the community expressed concern over the original plan, which had a blank brick wall along a street marking the boundary of Carver. To many local residents, this felt like the university had turned its back on the community, not to mention the deadening impact that the wall had on a space frequently used by local residents. The façade was softened with windows and other details to meet these concerns.

The student-housing complex offers another example of successful cooperation. The new dormitory was initially designed as a four-story building; however, based on community input, the Carver side of the building was redesigned to have three stories. VCU also included community space in this dormitory. This space includes meeting and office space, as well as a 14-terminal computer lab exclusively for the use of the community. The Partnership hopes that this space will be used by the Carver residents for job and computer-skills training.

By all accounts, the VCU-Carver relationship has been a success. The university has expanded its real estate without alienating the neighborhood most affected by the expansion. Moreover, through the Community Advisory Boards and the Carver-VCU Partnership, there are mechanisms in place to deal with problems and future projects.

A test of the resilience and sustainability of these mechanisms, however, is in the making. In a recent interview, Barbara Abernathy, head of the Carver Civic Improvement League, stated that "the community will not support the building of another [student] housing facility [in or next to Carver].... We feel that a new dorm will have a grave impact on the marketability of our community for single-family housing," a use outlined in a recently developed master plan for the community. The Carver Civic League is concerned that an overwhelming number of students at the community border would deter families from buying houses in the neighborhood and that property values will decrease because of negative perceptions about possible high-noise and high-traffic student activities. The university, on the other hand, believes that the situation will ultimately be beneficial not only to the university but also to the community. This is an emerging discussion between the community and VCU, and solutions will be found in an ongoing, meaningful dialogue between the two. Such a dialogue is far more plausible because of the existing mechanisms, but ultimate success will depend on commitment to aligning interests.

ADVISOR

VCU has a great number of student and faculty advisory programs directed at businesses and improving the business environment. The business school, for instance, has several programs that provide advice and research to businesses in Richmond. The most innovative advisory service at the university, however, is the Community Service Associates Program (CSAP), started in 1991.

CSAP provides funding for 10 faculty members each semester to work on a community development-related project with a local nonprofit, civic, neighborhood, or government group. This offers invaluable faculty expertise to local organizations without additional cost to them. To date, faculty service associates have completed 230 projects, involving 164 clients and faculty from 44 different university units.

In general, the faculty members involved are relieved of one teaching requirement so that they can dedicate themselves to the project. The program was designed to help break down barriers between VCU and the community, as well as build valuable relationships between faculty and local organizations that do work in line with the faculty member's research agenda. This program is considered highly successful. Even after the projects are completed, many participating faculty members have continued to stay involved with the organizations they served — serving on boards; providing consultation; or keeping informal, ongoing relations.

The program, however, has its challenges. Some departments do not have resources to allow the faculty members to be relieved of their teaching responsibilities. Consequently, a faculty member may take on a project on top of an already full schedule of teaching and research commitments.

While the focus of the program currently is on the nonprofit and government sectors, it could be expanded to offer services to small businesses from the local community in order to enhance the business development impact of the program.

CONCLUSION

VCU's successful economic development engagement has been contingent on several key components, almost all of which are replicable:

Strong and proactive leadership

Dr. Eugene Trani has seized opportunities to propel the university into an economic leadership position in the region. He has taken active interest in regional economic strategy, made himself available to head the regional chamber, responded quickly to business and public-sector mandates, has sought highly leveraged partnerships, and has surrounded himself with highly competent administrators who have established networks with the business, governmental, and academic communities.

A commitment to working with, rather than acting upon, the community

In the past 10 years, VCU has come a long way in establishing strong relationships with the community. Previously seen as an "ivory tower" institution that was unconcerned with, and uninvolved in, the community, VCU now has formal structures in place to connect the community with the university. Community Advisory Boards that meet quarterly are one of the effective mechanisms for connecting VCU to its neighboring communities.

A focus on the economic development strategies of the greater region

VCU, along with the other major players

in economic development in the greater Richmond area, has realized that regional cooperation is essential to a strong central city. Hence, VCU has connected the growth of the university to the growth strategy of the greater region. In the process, it has made itself far more competitive as a place for biotechnological research, attracting high-quality faculty and students.

A capacity for timely response to community and regional priorities

Universities are not well known for their rapid-response capabilities. VCU has the leadership and the infrastructure that enables it to respond in a timely manner to requests that are initiated by community organizations.

A clear understanding of the strengths and limitations of the university

VCU, particularly through the leadership of Trani, has a clear understanding of the strengths of the university. At the same time, VCU understands that other organizations and individuals bring resources to the mix as well; therefore, it does not try to do everything itself.

Development and support of university and key faculty who conduct applied research with community organizations

VCU has recognized that the technical assistance it provides to the community and the region is often absolutely essential in conceptualizing and developing major initiatives.

EDITOR'S NOTES

1. *U.S. News and World Report*, 1999 and 2000 Hospital Ratings.

2. In the first half of the 20th century, the ward was referred to as "the Harlem of the South" for the cultural and entertainment venues it offered.

3. The "In-Depth Case Studies" section of this report contains two case studies, which are both presented in the "Best Practices" section of this volume.

4. Various charts, tables, and other graphics, are contained in this report. To see the entire report, please refer to the Initiative for a Competitive Inner City and CEOs for Cities websites, both of which are contained in Appendix C.

CHAPTER 37

Roanoke's Eat for Education Program Helps Fund Its Public School System

Ann H. Shawver

In March 2010, the Roanoke City Council took a bold step to support K–12 education, unanimously voting to increase the local meals tax by 40 percent at a time when anti-tax fervor was sweeping the Commonwealth of Virginia. Then the city worked with community and private organizations, using the tax increase to rally the public, encouraging them to eat at local restaurants in support of K–12 education. The program succeeded, in large part because of the clear and timely financial information provided to local media and the community.

Deciding to Focus on Schools

About a year before the recession struck, the city, the city council, and the school board started down a path to improve the performance of the city's public schools. The school board increased its level of commitment to improving school performance. New school administration was hired, and the city council increased its support.

The performance of Roanoke city schools was poor. The graduation rate was less than 50 percent, and almost 70 percent of students received free and reduced-rate lunches. Numerous schools were unaccredited, and some failed to achieve federal Adequate Yearly Progress standards. People who lived and worked in the Roanoke Valley often hesitated to send their children to Roanoke's public schools because of these performance issues, as well as social and behavioral woes within the schools.

Faced with deep cuts in funding from the commonwealth, coupled with a reduction in funding from the City of Roanoke under a local tax-sharing formula, Roanoke City Public Schools was expecting budget reductions of up to 10 percent from fiscal 2010 to 2011— in the range of $10 million to $14 million. Though the city council had provided funding above and beyond the tax-sharing ratio the year before, in an effort to maintain school funding, the cuts expected for fiscal 2011 appeared to be damaging to recent efforts to resurrect the schools.

Roanoke City Council members knew that for Roanoke's success in the arenas of economic development and quality of life, school performance had to improve. City council members feared that such progress would be impossible without adequate funding and that if funding to the schools was reduced, it could have permanent devastating effects.

Two Cents for Two Years

During the early part of the fiscal 2011 budget cycle, one of the city council members came up with an idea to address the problem:

Originally published as "Eat for Education: Roanoke, Virginia, Provides Fiscal First Aid for K–12 Education," *Government Finance Review*, Vol. 26, No. 4, December 2010, by the Government Finance Officers Association, Chicago, IL. Reprinted with permission of the publisher.

a meals tax increase that would be dedicated to the city's public schools. After looking at the revenue that would be generated and the tax rates of surrounding jurisdictions and other Virginia localities, he made his case. He proposed increasing the existing meals tax by two percentage points, to 7 percent from 5 percent, effective from July 1, 2010, until June 30, 2012, at which time the rate would revert to 5 percent.

This idea immediately won praise from K–12 supporters, and it drew little criticism. Other alternatives were examined, but none provided as sizeable an impact on revenue — approximately $2.2 million per percentage point of tax increase. Other attractive features were that this plan taxed those who had the ability to pay for restaurant meals, and the tax was funded in part by non-resident visitors to Roanoke. As a city, Roanoke had the authority to increase its local tax without approval by the commonwealth and without holding a voter referendum. Roanoke leaders did not believe that this revenue initiative would have a major affect on people's dining habits, but some parties were concerned that this could be a risky move at a time of economic challenges because it would make Roanoke's meals tax rate the highest of any city in Virginia.

Alternatives

During Roanoke's budget season, city officials considered a number of alternatives to provide additional funding to the schools. One of these was an increase in the real estate tax, which would generate approximately $750,000 for each penny of increase. This option was not popular among elected officials, however, for several reasons. First, assessment increases throughout the past decade had left citizens skeptical about the fairness of how their homes were taxed. Roanoke's tax of $1.19 per $100 assessed value was already one of the highest rates in the immediate area, comparable with many urban communities in the commonwealth. Increasing the real estate tax was also unpopular as a source of school funding because it would place an additional burden on elderly and others on fixed incomes.

Some elected officials and citizens inquired about the possibility of raising the local sales tax. While this was a logical suggestion, the city lacked local authority to increase this tax rate without approval by the general assembly — and language introduced in the 2010 session to give local governments such authority was soundly defeated.

As discussions progressed, some officials suggested considering the lodging tax for an increase, along with the prepared food tax. There were drawbacks to this idea, though, that led some Roanoke officials and community leaders to decide this tax would be a poor fit for support of the school division. First, increasing that tax by one percentage point would provide only $360,000 in revenue. Also, that revenue had historically gone to the local convention and visitors bureau.

Another idea was increasing the prepared food and beverage tax by two percentage points for two years or so, and then permanently increasing the tax by a lesser amount such as 1.5 percent. While the latter might have been a more sound solution from a budgetary standpoint, the "two percent for two year" proposal had already caught on by that point, and supporters of the concept were quick to condition their support on the requirement that it sunset in two years.

As required for all tax rate increases, a public hearing was held to allow citizen input. At the public hearing, numerous educators and school supporters voiced support for the increased tax, and the general citizenry voiced no opposition. The restaurant community, however, felt it had been singled out as an industry, and numerous restaurant owners took to the podium to object, although many felt that this tax increase was probably a done deal.

Forecasting the Impact

The city council unanimously approved the "two percent for two year" plan. The city had to consider any potential negative impact on the performance of the meal tax, given that it would be considerably higher than other communities in the valley — in fact, 7 percent would be the highest in the state. In preparing the fiscal 2011 forecast, the finance office determined an appropriate revenue estimate at the 5 percent level. Next, it determined the revenue equivalent of each percentage point of increase. In computing the expected revenue at an increased 7 percent tax rate, the incremental revenue for a two-percentage point increase was discounted by five percent. Thus far in fiscal 2011, this appears to have been a relatively conservative forecasting method, given the dynamics in place.

The Roanoke School Board was to receive nearly $4.4 million in funding from the tax rate increase. The money was dedicated to:

- Restoring K-8 staffing above the standards of quality minimums
- Restoring key high school positions
- Funding the Drug Abuse Resistance Education program
- Funding school resource officers
- Teaching elementary Spanish in grades 4–6
- Providing key central office staff
- Restoring athletics, chess club, and maintenance spending

In the end, the additional revenue meant restoring a majority of the positions that were to be cut when the fiscal year 2010-2011 budget was adopted, many of them teaching positions.

The Eat for Education Campaign

In the truest spirit of seeking ways for the community to work together in support of common goals, Roanoke's city manager quickly realized that an increased tax in the middle of an economic recession could only be viewed as a win-win situation if the city found a way to work with the restaurant community and generate support for dining in public restaurants as a means of supporting public education. Thus, the Eat for Education campaign was born. Fittingly, the city enlisted assistance from the same public relations firm that represented the restaurant industry when it resisted the rate increase.

There are five partners in the Eat for Ed-

ucation Campaign: the City of Roanoke, the Roanoke Valley Convention and Visitors Bureau, the Roanoke Regional Chamber of Commerce, the Roanoke Valley Hospitality Association, and Downtown Roanoke, Inc. (a not-for-profit downtown development organization). The campaign is also supported by the student chapter of the Public Relations Society of America at Radford University. This group is working with the public relations firm and the City of Roanoke's office of communications to promote the campaign and assist with details such as restaurant contacts, community outreach, and coordination with local organizations that can help promote the program.

The Eat for Education campaign was launched with a press conference on June 30, 2010. A Web site was created to promote the program (www.eatforeducationroanoke.com), and a letter campaign invited 130 locally owned restaurants — those with patrons most likely to be attracted by the project — to participate. The city's partners in the campaign also reached out to local restaurants. The Convention and Visitors Bureau provided free membership to all restaurants, along with dining out promotions on its Web site. The Chamber of Commerce tailored its Small Business Assistance Program specifically to address the special needs of restaurants. In addition, a video segment explaining the Eat for Education Campaign was aired on the local government access channel's "Inside Roanoke" program, explaining to citizens how the increase in the meals tax was entirely dedicated to public schools.

The city's Web site page contains a link to campaign information: the video segment, a link to the Eat for Education Web site, and graphic presentation explaining the allocation of the tax. The existing meals tax was already subject to a funding formula, so the graphic presentation was developed to show how the revised tax would be allocated. This was done to maintain full disclosure and to help the public understand how the full tax would be distributed.

Development of the Eat for Education campaign was timed so that the campaign would be in place by the start of the school year. Letters explaining the campaign and encouraging families to participate were distributed throughout the schools to take home to parents.

Ongoing Reporting

An important element of the Eat for Education program is transparency about the performance of the tax and how revenue compares to both the budget and the prior year. Roanoke's finance department has developed a tracking tool that models the typical ebb and flow of the meals tax throughout the course of the fiscal year, and this tool is applied to the fiscal 2011 revenue estimate to gauge the amount of revenue anticipated each month. At the end of each month, city accounting staff can review results and share the information with others. The local media have shown significant interest in the Eat for Education program and revenue results. Finance staff work to help media personnel understand how the growth or decline in the tax is measured, as adjusted for the change in tax rate to measure true economic performance.

As of September 2010, three months into fiscal 2011, meals tax results were relatively stable at a 0.5 percent increase from the previous year, when adjusted to eliminate the impact of the tax rate change. Actual meals tax results for the same period exceed budget by 3.3 percent.

In a further effort to keep citizens, business owners, educators, and the broader community informed, a Facebook page was also created for the program: Eat for Education Roanoke. This page shares public relations initiatives and is a good way to announce winners of the monthly drawings for restaurant gift certificates.

The tax has also been helpful in making city and school leaders and staff more aware of the value of dining at restaurants within city limits. People keep this in mind when entertaining guests or planning events for groups, and they think about supporting Roanoke venues and the Eat for Education campaign. This awareness also helps support other retail in Roanoke.

The Questions

When the tax increase was put into place, citizens and the media immediately began asking questions about how it worked. There was a misconception that it was a state tax and that funds flowed first to the commonwealth and then back to Roanoke. It became apparent that teaching the public about the steps in the tax collection process would be helpful, so the city include a segment in the "Inside Roanoke" video to explain the process — the tax on restaurant patrons is collected at the point of sale, and restaurants are required to remit their prepared food and beverage taxes to the City of Roanoke by the 20th of the following month. The city's office of billings and collections processes these taxes and initiates collection efforts against entities that do not remit the money.

An interesting point to study will be whether the Eat for Education program helps Roanoke reduce its delinquency rate on prepared food and beverage tax. It is too soon to tell whether there will be an impact to this rate, which averages approximately 4 percent.

Another interesting element of the tax increase is the potential for debate about whether the tax increase is helping or hurting the restaurant business. Finance professionals must be careful not to get overly caught up in this debate, but they must be responsible for publishing information that is accurate, up to date, and easy to understand. Ironically, there are questions and debate about the stagnant or slightly declining performance of the tax, but naysayers seem to be forgetting that the reason a tax increase was needed was because the stagnant (and declining) economy had led to severe revenue reductions to the schools.

Conclusions

The two-cent meals tax increase is an example of fiscal first aid. It also provides an interesting story about how government and private sector can work together, in this case through a public outreach program that supports the restaurant industry while publicizing the Eat for Education effort to raise funds for

Roanoke Public Schools. Fiscal resiliency will mean finding ways to permanently reduce school system expenditures so the reduction in revenue can be absorbed when the tax increase sunsets in June 2012.

The city does not yet have enough data to assess whether this campaign is accomplishing its objectives. The only measure Roanoke officials have currently is the revenue collected for the meals tax, and so far that is exceeding expectations. However, city leaders believe the true success of the campaign will be measured not so much by how much revenue is collected or how many restaurants participate, but by the campaign's ability to affect public perception of the city as wanting to help the community. The hope is that, in addition to providing financial support to schools and helping to promote city restaurants in general, the campaign will create an atmosphere of good will toward Roanoke City Public Schools and our community for turning a negative (the meals tax increase) into a positive (supporting the school system) during difficult economic times.

Elements of the Eat for Education Campaign

The elements of the City of Roanoke's successful "Eat for Education" program includes the following characteristics:

Restaurant Enrollment. Restaurants that enroll in the Eat for Education campaign benefit from its marketing. Letters were sent to restaurants during the summer to invite them, and enrollment is optional and free of charge. The Eat for Education Web site publishes the list of member restaurants, including links to their Web sites. Restaurants that enroll receive a window cling they can display to announce their involvement.

Monthly Drawing. When patrons of participating restaurants declare they are "eating for education," they are invited to complete an entry form (supplied to participating restaurants) for a drawing held each month. Participating restaurants each draw one form and send that name to Eat for Education headquarters. All names are placed in a hat and Downtown Roanoke draws names for $50 gift certificates that can be used at any of the participating restaurants.

School Lunch Day. Weekly, on a day to be selected, professionals will be invited to join the Eat for Education program by leaving their brown bags at home and dining out in support of education. Restaurants are encouraged to offer school-themed specials on this day.

Educator's Day. One day a month will be Educator's Day, and showing their city school employee IDs allows Roanoke City School employees to take advantage of specials for breakfast, lunch, or dinner.

Family Night Out. This promotion, which will be rolled out soon, will encourage restaurants to offer family specials each Tuesday for a family night out.

CHAPTER 38

Rockland Students and Others Benefit from Public School's Use of Business Model

Irving H. Buchen

Many people in the United States are unhappy with public education. Teachers complain about being battered and intimidated, educational administrators find themselves and their contributions unappreciated, school boards are increasingly criticized for micromanaging, parents are beset by a whole new set of alternative schooling choices, and students are being tested to death.

In spite of stresses and strains on the educational system, there is more to celebrate than to lament, especially over the long term. In short, education has a future — indeed, a significant and interesting one. If we could leap ahead 25 years to view the current educational scene, we would see four factors driving educational change: decentralization and educational options; performance evaluation and success measurement; changes in leadership and leadership roles; and reconfigurations in learning spaces, places, and times.

School Choices

Although competition arrived late in the history of education, it rapidly changed virtually everything. By offering a wide range of possibilities rather than a single focus, competition has given education a new lease on life.

Traditionally, education offered three choices: public, private, and parochial schooling. Public education dominated, and for good reason: It educated the poor and middle classes, prepared them for work or college, acculturated wave after wave of new immigrants, and provided significant employment for many professionals. Private and parochial schools continue to appeal to middle- and upper-middle-class families disenchanted with public education; homogeneous and traditional, their future is rooted in the attitudes of the past.

The variety of educational choices has dramatically increased. Home schools, for instance, enrolled an estimated 850,000 students in the United States in 1999, according to the National Center for Education Statistics, and support for this method of instruction continues to increase. Charter schools enrolled nearly 580,000 students, according to Center for Education Reform 2001 statistics. Run by different private groups in a variety of ways, charter schools receive public financial support from their home district.

Because high schools with large numbers of students can be unmanageable, school district administrators have restructured many into a series of schools within a school, each with a core of teachers serving between 100 and 150

Originally published as "Education in America: The Next 25 Years," *The Futurist*, Vol. 37, No. 1, January/February 2003, by the World Future Society, Bethesda, Maryland. Reprinted with permission of the publisher.

students. Students and teachers in each smaller school know and relate to each other. Although restructuring does not alter class size, it reduces student-teacher ratio.

Private educational management companies have intensified the competitive environment of education. Often invited to take over failing schools, many of these companies are publicly owned, have stockholders, and are committed to making a profit. Although evidence for their success is mixed, they are a permanent fixture on the educational scene and add significantly to the range of available choices.

Private companies such as William Bennett's "K12" education program offer online curricula through electronic schools, so students can complete and graduate from a basic high-school program online. Electronic offerings also provide advanced placement, language, and special studies courses that normally attract few students. They are a boon to small rural districts and serve as a key underpinning for home schooling.

In short, education in 2025 will be totally decentralized, offering parents, students, adult learners, and citizens in general a dazzling menu of choices. Many people will opt for an amalgam of different educational sources that may be altered as desired. Whatever the selection, students and their parents — not schools — will drive educational choice.

Measuring Success

Major shifts will occur in the ways educational success is measured; some of these shifts are discernible now. Teachers were once evaluated on how they organized lesson plans, gained student interest, and involved the entire class in discussion. Now the focus is student achievement, usually measured by class performance on high-stakes mandated tests. Data now dominates the current educational scene, and its importance will intensify in the future.

Because allocating funds is increasingly tied to student performance, school district comptrollers often divert substantial appropriations to designing, administering, and evaluating tests, compromising instruction as a result. Many teachers, therefore, are "teaching to the test"—which would not be bad if, as one superintendent wryly observed, there was a really good test to teach to. School officials assign teams of extra teachers, tutors, and specialists to schools with low scores or failing grades, sometimes stripping the curriculum down to only tested subjects. Some schools in competitive environments advertise their test scores to attract students, further accelerating the process of constant testing. Parents have been known to request test scores of schools within a district to decide where they should send their kids.

In Florida and other states, students in schools that fail basic skills tests twice consecutively are offered financial vouchers to use in whatever school they wish. Preliminary research shows that voucher programs help drive improved student performance. Vouchers also drive choice and decentralization and significantly drain enrollment from "mainstream" schools.

A number of state governments have taken over failing schools, placing them under receivership or turning them over to private management companies. Philadelphia's school district was turned over to a private management company, Edison Schools Inc., because of poor student performance. In New York City, private management companies operate some 30 schools. Perhaps the most embarrassing consequence of this is a cynical reversal of graduation requirements in many states and schools that tie graduation to test scores. Many schools have postponed implementing requirements, lowered minimum scores, or revised graduation tests for students failing to achieve minimum scores but who were already scheduled to graduate, accepted to college, or had jobs.

The Principal's Changing Role

According to the U.S. Department of Labor, the school administration profession faces a shortage of 40,000 principals by 2005. That has been intensified by the reduction of school superintendents' terms of office to an all-time low of two to three years. Part of the difficulty of attracting administrators is that a principal's salary is not much higher than the highest paid teachers in a district; and when longer hours and more days of work are taken into account, the difference is often minuscule. As an indication of education increasingly becoming subject to business market forces, there is the trend toward hiring MBAs rather than education MAs, and even changing the title of superintendent to CEO. In fact, New York City split the top job into academic and business components. Los Angeles followed suit with an additional twist: Signaling the extent to which superintendency is increasingly political, the head of the Los Angeles school district hired a former governor of Colorado (Roy Romer) as school superintendent. But like the decentralization of schools, leadership is no longer solely of one type. The variety of leaders mirrors school choice.

Recently, the National Association of Elementary School Principals (NAESP) published a 96-page document calling for principals to be instructional leaders and to lead the charge on behalf of student achievement. To many outside the field, that might seem an odd request. Haven't principals always done that? Actually, they seldom did because of bureaucratic, financial, and security tasks heaped on their plates.

NAESP called for appointing assistant principals to provide relief and free principals to become instructional leaders. Whether school boards with tight or reduced budgets are willing or able to increase administrative staff at a time when teaching staff is stretched has yet to be determined. But if they do, a whole new corps of principals will emerge who are far more visionary, aggressive, and knowledgeable about school reform and improvement. They will resemble their business counterparts more than principals of the past do.

Do We Really Need Principals?

Although clearly there are principals who are effective leaders no matter how burdened they are, a significant new form of management is appearing. At Chicago's McCosh School, for example, the principal and her team of teacher-managers run the school. The principal still reports to the superintendent and the board, but once she has her marching orders and budget, she and her team take it from there. How effective has that arrangement been? McCosh has the best test scores in the district, and the morale of teachers, students, and parents is high.

This arrangement has an advantage over even the most exemplary performance of a number of assertive principals: There are no subject matter or competency gaps between administration and instruction. The typical principal struggles with the handicap of being outside the classroom, perhaps for many years, and leading teachers in all subjects without possessing the credibility of pedagogical competence. But a management team of certified teachers already possesses subject matter competence. Harvard University education professor Richard Elmore calls this *distributed leadership* and sees it as the future of site-based management. It creates a democratized structure in which the traditional vertical management structure has been leveled to horizontal collective action.

Perhaps the most dramatic and radical version of distributed leadership is where the responsibility for running the school is in the hands of teacher-leaders and learning teams consisting of teachers, tutors, technical advisers, counselors, parents, and students. There are no principals at all. The teacher-leader oversees the team following the principle of author Robert K. Greenleaf: *primus inter pares*—first among equals. Being first is not fixed but rotates based on situation needs.

But perhaps the most futuristic aspect of this new development, setting it apart from other developments and standing perhaps the best chance of becoming a significant part of education in 2025, is its attention to both *external and internal integration*. Externally, distributed leadership unites school, parents, students, and the community. Internally, through its basic collaborative governance structure, distributed leadership aligns and combines administration, instruction, and evaluation.

Parents' New Roles

Parents are taking on more assertive roles, moving well beyond the stereotype of running bake sales. For example, parents in South Pasadena, California, serve as teacher aides and tutors. Their major task, however, is to raise substantial amounts of money annually to supplement the budget. They have successfully built and stocked a computer lab, turned the library into a state-of-the-art electronic information and resource center, and created an extensive budget for teacher professional development.

In this and other ways, parents have become leaders involved in significant and often unique school reform. One of the most promising examples is a proposal by the Parents Center for Education Reform for students to lead teacher and parent conferences. Under this arrangement, students would set the agenda and facilitate discussion about their own performance. The fact that this initiative arose from a parents' group rather than from the public education mainstream dramatizes the extent to which parents have assumed a greater leadership role. The U.S. Department of Education officially recognizes and facilitates parental leadership through its Partnership for Family Involvement in Education.

The National Network of Partnership Schools based at Johns Hopkins University focuses on a comprehensive and aggressive plan of parent-teacher-student involvement and interaction. It features a program for teachers to generate homework assignments that require family participation. Teachers and parents use holidays and summer vacations to develop skills, anticipate academic problems, and develop solutions. All these and other efforts improve communication not only between schools and families, but also within families.

Linking Business to Education

Driven by a desire for a well-trained and motivated workforce as well as a sense of social responsibility, many CEOs have forged partnerships with schools. For example, Florida-based Paradigm Learning, which develops corporate board games, developed a high-school game called "Strive to Drive." The game takes students through all the steps of choosing, buying, financing, maintaining, and paying for a car; the game significantly and rapidly improved reading, math, and planning skills in the process. Tutor Inc., an online tutoring service, developed a partnership with the Boys Choir of Harlem, buying laptop computers for choir members to stay on top of assignments while traveling and providing access to the company's computer tutors to keep them current and on target.

The most important leadership contribution of business executives is that they are forming direct relationships with educational administrators, including sharing and exchanging different ways of effective management. Thus, the Public Education and Business Coalition received a grant to train some 100 principals in the Denver area. What business leaders discovered is that educators read and hearken only to other educators writing about education—they know little or nothing about the business world, the effect of increasing competition, the difficulty of balancing quality control with productivity—in short, precisely what education is newly encountering.

The Pearl River School in Rockland, New York, uses a continuous improvement business model to set incremental goals for students, raising achievement every year since 1989. The number of students graduating from Pearl River with the academically rigorous state regents' diploma has jumped from 32 percent to 86 percent.

A few business CEOs are sharing libraries, research resources, and attendance at executive conferences with education CEOs. There is a strong likelihood that such business CEOs may become school superintendents in the future. If so, then education may increasingly be defined or perceived as a business.

Business leaders have created a number of organizations to support school reform, such as the Business Coalition for Educational Reform, the National Association for Partners in Education, the National Employer Leadership Council, and the School-to-Work Learning

Center. Looking only to education for education leadership impoverishes the resources and sources of change.

New Learning Spaces

Seldom, if ever, do parents or citizens who already have raised and schooled their kids revisit schools. If they did, they would find many things have remained the same but some things have changed dramatically. Technological changes would top the list, but these are perhaps predictable compared with the reconfiguration of learning places, spaces, and times.

The size, holdings, and sheer physical variety of a fairly new high school are overwhelming. Built to accommodate a small town of thousands of students, a new school is surrounded by many practice and playing fields — perhaps even a football stadium — as well as extensive parking spaces for daily student use as well as for athletic events. Inside is a modern gymnasium equipped with seats for 2,000 students and a huge auditorium with seats for 3,000 and state-of-the-art theater equipment. The library, equally enormous but generally underused, is completely computerized with relatively few real books in sight.

When demographics (especially in the suburbs) indicate a significant increase in the school-age population, municipal planners quickly draw up plans to build new school-cities. Of course, expenses for building a new school are higher than they were for building the last school, not only because of increased costs of construction and materials, but also because some communities try to outdo others by constructing bigger and more splendid high schools. Yet research studies suggest that schools can be too big and impersonal.

Extending the School Day

Once again, economics rears its ugly head when discussion of extending the school day, lengthening the school year, or reducing class size begins. In the face of severe budget cuts, many communities are naturally unwilling to extend the school calendar or reduce class size. The obvious solution is technology.

Technology can reduce class size to one student. School days can be extended easily and laptop computers mean education can continue during vacations and trips. A total tested electronic curriculum already exists. It has been used by high schools that do not have enough students to take certain advanced or specialized courses, foreign languages, or advanced placement courses. Electronic instruction has bailed out many rural schools with too few students to permit face-to-face teaching at acceptable costs. Electronics already has helped many high schools reconfigure themselves into smaller schools — within schools — by providing them with their own electronic curriculum, including specialization in arts, sciences, business, and communications. Moreover, the availability of such electronic courses has spread as a number of states bind together in electronic consortia, making their curricula available virtually without cost. Accepting technology as a legitimate and equal teaching partner will make this happen.

Student-Led Learning and Schools

Every school district placing an ad for administrators or teachers claims to have student-centered schools. Usually that means allowing students to express their views at great length, but ultimately ignoring them. Student-led schools are something else. Allowing students to conduct teacher-parent conferences is an example of a genuine learning and mastering experience for all involved, especially for the student. But many student-led schools go far beyond that.

In large part, what drives student learning is just that — student learning. The learning focus is not on different subjects but on comprehensive projects, including community-based ones. Because that requires knowledge of many subjects, an academic progression develops not unlike the system of apprenticeship. Using dialogue, mentors steer students to an initial plan to test the project. The process is subject to an incredible number of revisions. Gradually, the dominant mentor moves to the periphery as the student moves toward the center. The gradual exchange of positions signals the beginning of mastery. Only then does student leadership appear, earned through sweat equity and the accumulation of a knowledge and research base. Initially, the mentor talks and the student listens; eventually, the student talks and the mentor listens.

Such arrangements do not occur only at the high-school level or only with exceptional students. At Rover Elementary School in Tempe, Arizona, former principal Sandra McClelland explored the future of education with various organizational theorists, not just by reading materials about education. The result is not just a student-centered but a student-driven school. Student leadership teams have replaced the student council to make basic structural and political decisions. A collaborative group of teachers, students, and administrators implements the school's vision and goals. Team learning is the dominant mode; older students mentor younger ones. There is a concerted search for financial supplements and greater independence from state funds; toward that end, teachers are given, are in control of, and are accountable for their classroom budget. Finally, a formal pedagogical partnership has been formed with Southwest Airlines: The school shares its effective and collaborative teaching strategies, Southwest its team management training. Clearly, Rover is a futures lab.

What to Expect from Education in 2025

Here are some of the most likely essential features of education by 2025.

- Education will be intensely decentralized, offering a significant number of choices to teachers, parents, and students.
- Increasingly, school and learning will be related to time rather than to place, available everywhere that there is connectivity 24 hours a day all year.
- Space and place for learning will exist for the community and no longer be reserved for the young.
- Increasingly, learners will become autonomous, almost totally free agents; nevertheless, they must earn their independence through mastery of prescribed knowledge bases.
- Cost controls and supplemental financing will steadily take hold as municipalities divert federal, state, and local funds away from education to other social crises such as health care and the aged. Education has at most only another 10 or 15 years as the favored focus of funding and attention.
- Increasingly, teachers will be at the center of administration, instruction, and evaluation; in some programs, they may replace principals.
- Horizontal collaboration among teachers, students, and parents — rather than vertical hierarchies — will characterize school governance. A commonality of vision and purpose will be arrived at and implemented collectively.
- Parents will become indispensable to effective learning. Very busy parents may hire parent surrogates as substitutes.
- Initially, business practices will only benefit education; eventually, educational innovations will provide models for business.
- Increasingly, minorities will take over educating minorities, mostly through charter schools. They will accomplish more through chosen rather than *de facto* segregation, and, in the process, save a whole generation of urban kids.

Machine Teaches and the Future

Machines — computers and/or other technology — can and probably will replace teachers in the future because they can provide solid and competent instruction. However, three major obstacles continue to keep technology out of the classroom for the immediate future:

- **Economics**
  Education's insulation from economic and market forces has done it an enormous disserv-

ice. Economic incentives have yielded powerful, sophisticated, and flexible teaching and learning technologies, changing how we learn and acquire knowledge. Education should be at the center of these innovations, but its isolation has kept it from benefiting from technology to the fullest possible extent.

- **Teacher Fears**

Technology is ubiquitous, invasive, and substitutive, and most teachers know it. So they ignore technology. Nothing matches the variety and subtlety of human activity, they say; no one enlivens and inspires students better than a teacher. Teachers' objections and fears of technology are profound, the number of converts few, and the prospects for new perspectives dim.

- **Critiquing Technophiles**

Education cannot reaffirm its traditional position or stake its future role without asking substantive questions (What problem does this technology solve? What new problems does it create?) that challenge the technology community and incorporating these questions into teaching. Challenging and critiquing technophiles will result in the best of both worlds, where education asks the questions and technology performs the tasks. If this partnership falters or fails, there is little doubt that technology will fill the vacuum and appear as both educator and performer.

Creating technologically savvy teachers as well as machines to serve as teachers depends on examining these obstacles. Whether the change will be gradual, accelerated, or radical depends on how fast we overcome them.

CHAPTER 39

Sacramento and Its Public School Districts Have Model for Joint Infrastructure Planning

Deborah McKoy, Jeffrey M. Vincent *and* Carrie Makarewicz

California's Golden Opportunity

California sits at an historic moment. The state's policymakers and voters have aggressively ramped up their investment in public school buildings, providing more than $35 billion in state funds in the form of general obligation bonds to modernize existing schools and build new ones since 1998. Additionally, the *California Strategic Growth Plan* won voter approval and in 2006 state leaders began the first phase of a comprehensive twenty-year plan to upgrade critical infrastructure. The plan calls for spending $211 billion through 2016 — with $42 billion in bonds already approved — on transportation, water systems, public safety, housing, the judiciary, and education facilities. By including public schools as one of six key pieces of critical infrastructure, state officials and voters recognized the importance of school facilities in shaping California's growth and prosperity. Ongoing school construction investment, coupled with the new, broader infrastructure investment, creates a strategic opportunity for California to improve the way it plans, funds, constructs, modernizes, and operates its schools, and to make school planning an integral part of community and regional development, rather than an isolated endeavor.

California's public schools educate the largest and most diverse student population in the nation. Nearly 6.3million students attend the state's 10,000 K–12 schools. By 2030, the number of school age children will increase dramatically, making up twenty percent of California's estimated fifty million residents. That's four million more students than today. Successfully accommodating this nearly two-thirds increase in enrollment needs to go beyond simply providing enough seats in classrooms. Planning public school infrastructure takes place within California's increasingly complex landscape. The all-too-common reality of "siloed" planning results in tremendous missed opportunities to make better land use and service decisions to better support students, families, and communities. New school planning must be inclusive, comprehensive, and integrated with community and regional planning. School planning must be coordinated with the housing, transportation, and work needs of the families and teachers of students as well as the communities that surround and support the schools.

Originally published as "Integrating Infrastructure Planning: The Role of Schools," *Policy Brief Report*, Fall 2008, by the Center for Cities and Schools, University of California, Berkeley. Reprinted with permission of the publisher.

The Importance of Public School Infrastructure in Shaping Urban Growth

It's well understood that the quality of California's schools has a significant influence on student achievement, and in turn on California's future economic competitiveness. But schools are also public infrastructure, and their location, design, and physical condition may well be one of the most important determinants of neighborhood quality, regional growth and change, and quality of life. As physical infrastructure, schools have significant impacts on transportation patterns and roadway service demands, residential choices, housing development and prices, as well as water and utility demands. The planning of school infrastructure thus needs to be integrated with the planning of other infrastructure and development at local, regional, and state levels. The costs of continuing to *not* do so are too great.

Currently, however, there is no formal policy apparatus at local or state levels that requires or offers incentives for school districts and local governments to work together to plan school infrastructure as part of the larger urban development plan. Indeed, in California, as in most other states, school districts have a unique autonomy from other local government agencies, including the real estate and land use decisions school districts make. For example, when a California school district is looking for a location for a new school, it is not required to check with the local government planning agency to choose a site. Being exempt from local zoning laws, school districts can put a new school on a site the local agency planned to use for something else. Many school siting choices do not align with local land use and transportation plans, and some have caused a problem of "school sprawl," where school districts have been accused of choosing sites far from existing housing, which helps promote more rapid, and often low-density, development of land. Remote school sites lead to increased vehicle miles traveled, because students must travel farther to reach these schools. If school bus services are not available, as is increasingly the case in California, then families may have to drive their children to school, which can greatly increase total vehicle miles traveled in the region and state. Parents getting to and from schools to drop off and pick up their children can also create traffic congestion during rush hours.

Indeed, because they are accessed by so many people each day, schools can be major contributors to traffic and emissions problems; some have estimated that school traffic accounts for as much as five to ten percent of morning peak travel. Despite that, and despite their significant use of energy and water, schools are currently exempt from AB32, the statewide initiative to reduce greenhouse gas emissions.

Separation of Schools from Urban Planning Processes

School district autonomy exists historically for many good reasons; it was intended to disentangle our schools from the strains of local politics, and to leave school planning to educational experts to ensure that educational needs drive decision making. However, decision autonomy has not insulated California school districts from severe financial pressures, and because schools are funded in part by property taxes and development exactions, they are never truly separate from urban development decisions. Instead, they both affect urban development and are affected by it. Formally, however, California school infrastructure planning is disconnected from other planning — governance, finance, and policymaking — in three important ways.

First, school district geographic boundaries rarely match the boundaries of other local planning entities. A school district might lie within several cities, for example, or encompass both incorporated and unincorporated areas. The Sacramento region shows the kind of disconnected, overlapping boundaries that make it difficult to coordinate school plans with city or county plans. In the Sacramento area, there are five counties, fifteen unified school districts, nine secondary and twenty elementary school districts, 29 cities/towns, and 446 schools. Statewide, while there are only 58 counties and 478 incorporated cities, there are 1,052 school districts.

Second, the exigencies of school finance often result in school location and design decisions that are aligned with neither educational needs nor urban development needs, but instead are driven by land costs or developer exactions. Schools ultimately must base many facility design and location decisions on funding availability, and in many areas, the district must look outside of developed areas to find affordable land. In other cases, developers, not districts, choose new school sites. Developers' donations of land, which may be required as part of the development approval process, save schools the costs of securing new sites themselves, but these parcels may or may not be the most optimal for the school, the district, or the region, and may not support broader transportation, land use, or environmental goals, such as those outlined in AB32.

The third disconnect, noted earlier, is the lack of a state policy framework for school districts and local, regional, and/or state agencies to work together to integrate infrastructure decisions. In rare cases, local agencies have built relationships to plan together. Some progress at the state level has been made in connecting school planning and local planning. For example, the Office of Public School Construction (OPSC) has a program to fund the construction of joint-use school facilities through local agency partnerships. Nevertheless, most school infrastructure planning is still done largely in isolation, missing opportunities for efficiencies and coordinated investments. Most municipalities and school districts develop their general or operating plans separately from one another. Local conflicts often arise over how much traffic mitigation the school districts are responsible for when they site and build a new school. Even their time horizons are different: school districts usually create five- to ten-year capital plans, while cities' general plans tend to cover twenty years into the future.

How Schools Affect Urban Development and Transportation

Excellence in public schools is one of the most important factors contributing to metropolitan vitality. Many stakeholders, recognizing these links, seek to define what makes a "good school" and a "quality education." The State of California, for example, measures and ranks every school based on test scores. Other educational organizations focus on different measures. What is often left out of nearly all definitions of a high quality school, however, is the condition of school facilities — despite increasing evidence of its importance to teaching and learning, as well as the vitality of the community. Natural light, indoor air quality, temperature, cleanliness, acoustics, and classroom size can positively or negatively affect learning and productivity. Poor ventilation, dust, and mold in ceilings and walls — all factors found in many older urban school buildings and portables — can lead to respiratory infections, headaches, sleepiness, and absenteeism. Several studies have found that students attending school in newer facilities outperform similar pupils in ageing schools, even when controlling for socioeconomic differences. Studies are beginning to find that the *size* of schools also matters. Smaller schools (less than 500 students) and small learning communities within larger schools have been associated with better student performance, less absenteeism, and increased student engagement. Research shows that teacher retention is higher when school facilities are in better shape.

School quality also affects housing demand and housing affordability, as parents of school age children bid up housing prices in communities with high public school rankings. In turn, this affects public finances. Higher housing prices mean more tax dollars, but financing their share of schools also may push local governments to compete for more commercial and retail development to increase the tax base, in part to support the schools.

School locations affect how children and staff get to school, which affects local traffic, congestion, and pollution. At least one fifth of the state's current population travels to and from a K–12 public or private school each weekday, nine months a year, so it matters how and when they travel. And school design can shape the types of educational programs the school can offer, and the opportunities for shared uses with the community or other government entities. In other words, location, land use, and community activities can all be greatly influenced by school siting and design.

New Funding, New Opportunities?

Until the late 1990s, there was a dearth in capital spending on schools in California. For the two decades prior, California school conditions deteriorated, and by 1995, a federal government study found them to be among the worst in the nation. Our recent research finds that in the decade following this finding California school districts spent much less per student on school construction and modernization than the national average, even though California leads the country in terms of total amount invested. Given the great need and the fact that construction work tends to be more expensive in California, this is a troubling statistic. As a result, many schools are severely overcrowded and have to rely on portable classrooms (more than 85,000 statewide). Because there has been little money for school infrastructure, there was little pressure to coordinate school investment and planning with other infrastructure plans, and the issue did not often arise outside of new growth areas. Two fairly common exceptions have been shared playing fields and the use of public transportation and transit passes for school access, but even on these issues planning and coordination remain spotty.

California's surge in school infrastructure funding since 1998 and the much-talked about next statewide school construction bond likely in 2010 open up new opportunities for integrating school and metropolitan infrastructure planning to address schools' land use and transportation effects. Better coordination could

help meet regional transportation planning goals and reduce the impact schools have on the environment.

The transportation opportunities are mutual: both schools and communities could greatly benefit from better coordination of transport services. California is one of three states that does not require school-funded transport, yet ninety percent of its districts report transport expenditures. The state's fastest-growing school enrollments are in the lowest-density areas where public transit options are sparse and where families live too far from schools for walking or bicycling — and absent a change in direction, this trend will continue. Could smaller schools located closer to homes reduce the need for school busing and parental driving, allowing more students to walk or bike to school? Similarly, could higher density neighborhoods planned with schools also decrease busing and driving to school? Could infill projects, urban revitalization, and school upgrades bring more of the student population back to communities that have lost students, further reducing school transport needs and opening up public transport options for older students? These are the sorts of questions that could be explored with new funding and new incentives for integrating planning.

Conclusion and Policy Recommendation

Three key recommendations could help align infrastructure planning and investment. These proposals stem from five years of work at the UC Berkeley Center for Cities and Schools in partnerships with local, regional, and statewide educational and civic leaders.

Create a statewide vision for California's ongoing major public investment in school facilities that is connected to broader goals of educational outcomes, community development, environmental protection, regional growth, and other infrastructure investments. Without vision, the current finance-driven model for school facility decisions is greatly influenced by projections of demographic shifts based on current housing markets, local housing restrictions, land cost and availability, and characteristics of proposed sites (e.g., the need for environmental cleanup, topography, or acreage per student), rather than goals for smarter growth, creating schools as centers of community, or reducing greenhouse gas emissions. As a result, too many new schools are often simply "adequate," lacking the innovative siting and design ideas that could enhance teaching, learning, and community life.

Offer incentives to coordinate local and regional infrastructure planning. California will need legislative and policy changes to better inform, encourage, and provide guidance for the largely local practice of planning and siting new school facilities. Perhaps most important is the need for policy where none exists, such as ways to motivate interagency collaboration.

State policies should do more than just *encourage* local governments to include school facilities in their short- and long-range comprehensive plans, and school districts to incorporate local and regional plans into their master facility and capital improvement plans. State policies should establish incentives for these entities to strategically align their planning documents. The cost to build new schools in California has skyrocketed, and state and local education agencies are competing with the private market for land, labor, and materials. If local governments and schools coordinate their plans, opportunities arise for both to reduce costs by locating schools near existing infrastructure, by creating joint uses, by involving the community early and throughout the process, and by identifying opportunities to reinvest in urban assets. Including schools in plans for urban redevelopment, congestion reduction, and open space preservation offers new opportunities for meeting regional environmental goals.

Planned in collaboration with roads, housing, water, and other public infrastructure, schools can be made more accessible, allowing school users to walk and bike and thereby increasing physical activity and lessening road congestion. Schools also generate and attract economic activity for surrounding communities, and should be part of community and economic development plans. Joint use of school facilities creates opportunities for reduced operations costs and allows residents and students to pool resources. Coordination and community partnering is not only good for the environment and the community but may also contribute to school reform and should be common in school planning, not the exception.

Conduct research and provide education to guide integrated infrastructure planning. Research and training can address institutional inertia, state and federal legal requirements, fear of litigation, lack of knowledge of other agencies' processes, and other barriers that currently make working together across agencies a challenging process. Researchers need to analyze and measure the benefits and potential costs of more integrated infrastructure planning systems, of operating joint-use schools, and of the range of policies identified in this article. Longitudinal analysis of new schools built with innovative siting and design strategies would demonstrate the benefits and drawbacks of these strategies for schools and communities.

California will continue to grow, and the state will continue to make important major investments in new public school facilities. Now is the time to craft a vision and strategic supporting policies to ensure educational, community, and regional growth and prosperity for generations to come.

EDITOR'S NOTES

1. Resources to prepare this report were also obtained from and provided by the Transportation Center, University of California, Berkeley.

2. Various pictures, charts, and tables, as well as a list of further readings, are available in this report. To access this information, please check out the website of the Center for Cities and Schools, University of California, Berkeley, which is listed in Appendix C.

CHAPTER 40

St. Paul Public Agencies Benefit from University of Minnesota's Technologies and Software

Carissa Schively Slotterback

Numerous technologies are now emerging with the intent of making participatory planning processes more efficient, informative, and inclusive. These technologies include, on the high tech end, web-based mapping systems, real time scenario evaluation tools, virtual reality, and computer generated flythrough. More accessible technology applications such as project websites, computer edited images, and keypad voting are also becoming more widely used. While previous research suggests that many planners are using at least basic technologies,* there are still a number of constraints that may be limiting broader deployment.

A recent study conducted at the University of Minnesota related to planners' perspectives on the use of technology provides insights into some of the reasons why the use of technology may not be growing as quickly as some might expect. The study gathered feedback from planners about opportunities to integrate technology into typical participation processes through a series of five focus groups. In addition, a survey of over 100 Minnesota planners was conducted to gather additional insights related to the feasibility of integrating a range of different technologies into participation processes.

One of the key constraints that emerged

from the study was access to the technology itself. A number of planners raised concerns about access to technology in their organization, including both the hardware and software needed. Relative to GIS-based technologies, concerns were also raised related to the availability of data. While many of these technologies allow for the creation of sophisticated maps, 3-D models, and build out scenarios, they are unable to function without underlying data depicting land use, transportation, and nature features. For the respondents in Minnesota, these concerns were lower in the Twin Cities metro area as compared to those working in smaller communities and rural areas in the state. A similar issue emerged related to Internet access. There were concerns raised about the speed of access available to practitioners working in more rural areas and broader concerns about access to online technologies such as project websites and discussion forums intended for public use.

Another constraint is related to resources available to purchase and use technologies in participatory processes. Concerns were raised related to staff capacity to use technology, particularly in small communities or organizations with limited resources. Costs for the technology and training to use it were also cited as roadblocks limiting broader use.

Originally published as *Minnesota Planners' Use of Technology*, Spring 2009, by the Urban and Regional Planning Program, Humphrey School of Public Affairs, University of Minnesota, Minneapolis. Reprinted with permission of the publisher.

Finally, an additional set of constraints surround the issue of value added by using technology in participatory processes. Planners noted that technologies may not be able to deliver better outcomes than more traditional participation methods, nor would they attract greater numbers of more diverse participants. There were also concerns that participants may distrust the technology or data being used, allowing the technology to "steal the show" or distract from the issues and interaction that might otherwise take place.

Based on this very brief summary of concerns that planners have and some of the constraints associated with using technology in participatory processes, it is possible to identify some potential solutions to concerns about access to technology, availability of resources, and creating value through technology use.

Providing Access to Technology. The costs of specialized hardware and software can be important limiting factors for communities desiring to use technology. Providing shared access through universities or regional planning agencies might be an option to spread costs among a number of organizations. Concerns about access to data emphasize the importance of centralized and publicly available data sets such as the Minnesota Department of Natural Resources Data Deli and the publicly-funded Minnesota Land Cover Classification System, which has been completed for approximately ⅓ of counties in the state.

Making Resources Available. Focusing on universities or regional planning agencies as technology providers also helps ensure the availability of knowledgeable users that may be able to assist planners working in communities with fewer staff and financial resources to fund training. Establishing technology outreach programs, such as University Extension, may be one option for offering technical assistance for those organizations lacking capacity internally.

Enhancing the Value Added. A key opportunity here is to emphasize that technological enhancements in participatory processes are only part of the picture. In many cases, they function best as add-ons to existing participation efforts. Using technology to provide enhanced spatial or real-time information can contribute to the education function of public meetings. Online discussion forums can help gather feedback from those unable to attend meetings or who may be uncomfortable speaking in public. Project websites may help organize information about a planning process for those already involved and those who may be interested in engaging.

Much of the research on using technology in participatory processes has focused on the technologies themselves, exploring how effective they are in certain contexts. As more communities begin to use these technologies, it is just as important to gather insights about how planners make decisions about using technology and how they implement them in the real world.

Other participatory and collaborative planning processes, using state-of-the-art technologies and software, and even student interns from the University of Minnesota, including the following successful and popular programs in the St. Paul-Minneapolis, or the Twin Cities, area.

U-PLAN Community Planning Studio

U-PLAN is a community planning studio located on University Avenue in St. Paul. U-PLAN "provides high quality technical services to support the grassroots planning efforts" that are occurring because of a new light rail line. Over one billion dollars are expected to be invested in this new transportation infrastructure, and the surrounding area expects significant redevelopment as a result.

U-PLAN is a studio that provides free assistance for those that will be affected, including small business owners and community organizations. U-PLAN provides mapping and visualization assistance, including impact analysis and Sketch-Up™ visualizations of various options.

In partnership with the American Institute of Architects, U-PLAN held a series of block by block workshops to address the challenges and opportunities of the proposed light rail. The summaries of the workshops are at the

U-PLAN storefront and will be included in station area planning.

Their website provides basemaps, 3D visualizations of what specific station areas might look like, and an opportunity for users to create Mashups, with relevant information, using Google My-Maps™.

In a world-flattening move, U-PLAN is also making use of the Web 2.0 concept of "crowd-sourcing." The U-RESEARCH segment of the website allows citizens to ask questions of residents of other cities that have put in light rail. Questions are distributed via websites, online information exchanges, and education institutions. They include things like "How was station placement determined?" Answers have come in from San Diego, Portland, Sacramento, Denver, and other parts of Minneapolis.

The U-PLAN studio is providing a transitioning community with valuable technology and having significant impact on the ground.

Twin Cities Metro Council's Use of GIS

The Twin Cities are recognized in the planning community as having some of the best regional planning resources and authority in the U.S. Part of the success of the regional authority here, the Metropolitan Council, rests on its extensive GIS database and application of spatial data for planning.

MetroGIS, the program of the Metropolitan Council that collects and distributes GIS, has over 221 datasets that cover all seven counties in the region. Their DataFinder web portal allows users to search the database for available data by topics such as Business and Economic Data or Biology and Ecology.

Another reason for the Twin Cities' success at regional thinking is the frequent and extensive collaboration between multiples entities and jurisdictions to analyze and address regional problems using GIS data.

University Collaboration

For example, the Twin Cities have the University of Minnesota, and in particular the Center for Urban and Regional Affairs (CURA), as a frequent partner and resource. CURA is leading the way in terms of applying new technologies to planning, and is a resource for data, tools, and expertise in applying them.

The links between the University, the City, and the Metropolitan Council are strong and effective. For example, CURA, the City of Minneapolis, and neighborhood organizations are working together to use and maintain the Minneapolis Neighborhood Information System. The MNIS receives nightly updates of parcel level data from the city assessor, planning, and inspection department databases. Neighborhood organizations sit on the steering committee of the system and, in exchange, receive project assistance and GIS expertise. Over half of the City's neighborhoods have participated. The system is now being updated to help track and prevent foreclosures.

The University and the Twin Cities have used their extensive GIS databases to help resolve town-gown conflict. GIS data has helped to determine where student housing is affecting neighborhoods. The University can then implement strategies to help stabilize these neighborhoods like encouraging faculty and staff to live close to the University. Through exploring the effects of the University on the surrounding neighborhoods, the City and the University recommended that a University Community Partnership District be created, and the Governor allocated funds to do so in 2007.

Collaboration on Foreclosures

Regional GIS data has also helped to track and prevent foreclosures in the Twin Cities area. Representatives from each city, and nonprofit housing, development, and funding organizations created the Minnesota Foreclosure Partners Council. This group collected housing and foreclosure data for the seven county region. From this data, patterns of foreclosure were discovered, and strategies were developed to prevent foreclosure in higher risk neighborhoods. This effort is now statewide.

EDITOR'S NOTES

1. The author's research has focused on participation in environmental and land use decision-making, environmental impact analysis, and planning processes and implementation.

2. For more information about the programs and research provided by the Urban and Regional Planning Program, the Humphrey School of Public Affairs, University of Minnesota, check out its website (http://www.hhh.umn.edu/).

3. For more information about the programs and services provided by the U-Plan Community Planning Studio and the Twin cities Metro Council's approach to GIS, check out their websites (http://www.u-plan.org and http://www.metro council.org/).

CHAPTER 41

San Francisco Area Benefits from Center's Studies Linking Transit Development, Families and Schools

Ariel H. Bierbaum, Jeffrey M. Vincent
and Deborah McKoy

Central to a vision of sustainable and equitable development is the goal of creating "complete communities," whereby all residents, regardless of race or class, have equal access to jobs, services, and community amenities. Many policy leaders and planners see infill development, generally, and transit-oriented development (TOD), specifically, as key strategies to realize this goal. TOD is real estate development adjacent to transit hubs, with the primary goals of increasing transit use, decreasing private auto use, and increasing transit revenues. TOD generally takes a mixed-use approach that includes combining housing and retail/businesses close together in relatively high densities.

TOD projects have grown in number across the country in the last decade, but most TOD has produced higher-end housing, often targeted at empty nesters and/or young, primarily childless professionals, as opposed to families.[1] Despite this trend, the goals of developing "complete communities" and many of the principles of TOD do align with the goals of community development practitioners — aiming to improve the quality of life and economic opportunity for low-income communities and communities of color. Accordingly,

advocates and policy leaders are beginning to push more aspirational strategies of infill development and TOD that focus on a mix of jobs, shops, community services, and homes affordable to families across a mix of incomes.[2] By incorporating broad goals about serving families and mixed-income residents through TOD, these leaders aim for a different TOD model than has typically been seen across the country.

Bringing to fruition new, ambitious models of TOD that provide opportunities for families of varying incomes will require new thinking by local agencies and developers. Implementing conventional TOD remains challenging; realizing more equity-oriented TOD will be even more so. When it comes to TOD that serves the needs of families, equity and access around educational opportunities for children should be top priorities. The interconnections between how and why families choose where to live and how that relates to their perception of access to high quality schools is a complex reality that is highly dependent on local contexts.[3] Targeting families into mixed income TOD requires a deeper understanding of these interconnections to ensure that TOD becomes a tool in equitable development and

Originally published as "Linking Transit-Oriented Development, Families and Schools," *Community Investments*, Vol. 22, No. 2, Summer 2010, by the Community Development Department, Federal Reserve Bank, San Francisco, California. Reprinted with permission of the publisher.

not a cause of exacerbated segregation. And, it will require a broader network of individual and institutional stakeholders to join TOD planning stages, most notably, families and local schools/school districts.

The Center for Cities & Schools (CC&S) at the University of California, Berkeley is currently exploring ways of making more equitable, "family-friendly" TOD a reality across the country. In the San Francisco Bay Area, our efforts include case study research that examines the relationships between TOD, families, and schools—with special consideration of the increasing educational opportunities available for children (e.g., magnet schools, small autonomous schools, charter schools, inter-district transfers, in order to realize the aspirational goals of TOD among area leaders.

Ten Core Connections between TOD, Families, and Schools

Through our action research with community stakeholders, city and school leaders, and young people, we have developed a list of Ten Core Connections between TOD and Education, which identify key considerations for fostering successful mixed-income, family-oriented TOD. The list provides guidance for policymakers, developers, community development practitioners and other stakeholders interested in promoting equitable TOD that serves the needs of families. Central to these connections is how transportation infrastructure can leverage additional benefits, notably supporting families and students and enhancing local schools.

1. School quality plays a major role in families' housing choices. Access to quality schools plays a pivotal role in the housing choices families make. Thus, TOD that attracts families with school-aged children must include access to high-quality schools and other educational opportunities.[4]

2. A wide housing unit mix is needed to attract families. Unit mixes that include 3- and 4-bedroom apartments and townhomes offer family-friendly options. However, to make

TOD more easily "pencil out," developers have primarily built studios and 1-, and 2- bedroom apartments. While some of these units may attract younger couples, larger families and households with older children require more bedroom space.

3. Housing unit mix, school enrollment, and school funding are intricately related. The majority of public schools are funded on the basis of their student enrollment numbers; new housing will likely affect enrollments at nearby schools, which by extension impacts school operations and school district funding. Enrollment and school capacity situations will differ from school to school, but in general, unexpected changes in enrollment— increases or decreases—are difficult for districts to manage and can be cause for tension.

4. Children often use transit to get to and from school and afterschool activities. Access to safe, reliable, and affordable transit facilitates students' on-time and consistent arrival at school (reducing problems of truancy and tardiness) and to afterschool activities that enhance their educational experience. For many students, access to transit often means the difference between participating in or being excluded from these kinds of productive, engaging, and academically enriching opportunities.

5. Multi-modal transit alternatives support access to the increasing landscape of school options. The educational landscape across the country is continually changing, and students and families now have an increasing number of school options. Children do not always attend their closest neighborhood school; rather they may enroll in a charter or theme-based magnet school, a private school, or a school with specialized programs. Additionally, school districts may have an assignment policy that disperses students throughout the district to relieve overcrowding or integrate schools. Access to safe, affordable transportation options plays an important role in determining whether families have the opportunity to choose the most appropriate schools for their children from among multiple options.

6. Mixed-income TOD provides opportunities for educational workforce housing. The combination of modest teacher salaries and high housing costs often creates a challenge for school districts to retain high quality teachers. Mixed-income TOD could be an attractive incentive for area public school teachers and their families.

7. **TOD design principles support walkability and safety for children and families.** Across the country, researchers have seen drastic declines in the number of children walking and/or bicycling to school.[5] TOD design principles inherently address concerns of distances between home and school, traffic, and "stranger danger." First, TOD emphasizes pedestrian infrastructure, including sidewalks and crosswalks. Second, mixed-use TOD aims to create active, vibrant street life that increases safety through more "eyes on the street." Finally, TOD's outcome of increased ridership enhances safety and reliability, increasing the demand and desirability of transit for families.

8. **TOD brings amenities and services that can serve families closer to residential areas.** The mixed-use nature of TOD provides opportunities for amenities and services that can attract and support children and families. For example, childcare centers and preschools located within or adjacent to TOD place these daily destinations within walking distance of transit, which may increase the likelihood that working parents utilize transit while balancing the logistics of getting to daycare and work each day.

9. **When schools are integrated with TOD planning, opportunities emerge for the shared use of public space.** In many infill locations, open space is lacking. If an existing school is located adjacent to or near the TOD, there are opportunities to use the school site as open space through shared use arrangements. Access to school site spaces for public use becomes an attractive amenity to families considering moving to a TOD, a way to build broader public support among childless residents for schools as community assets, and a strategic tool for developers to meet open space requirements for their new developments.

10. **TOD offers opportunities for renovating and building new schools in developments, which draws families.** Partnering with school districts can leverage additional capital resources to improve existing school buildings and/or to create small, charter, magnet, or other specially-focused schools. While most people tend to think of schools as stand-alone buildings, this does not necessarily have to be the case; in Portland, Oregon, for example, the public school district is leasing storefront space in a new, mixed use, affordable housing building.[6]

Overcoming Challenges and Leveraging Opportunities

While these Ten Core Connections may seem common sense, using these insights to leverage mixed-income, family-friendly TOD means swimming against a strong tide. Building mutually-beneficial and sustainable collaborative policies and practices between local governments and public school districts is tempered by a tenuous foundation of entirely separate governance structures, vastly different project and policy timeframes, and often competing state and/or local regulations. Most often, civic and educational leaders rarely work in tandem to leverage opportunities for integrated and mutually-beneficial outcomes.[7] However, increasingly, school districts and cities recognize that they ultimately are serving the same constituents and families and are striving for many of the same goals—providing high quality education, housing, quality of life, and opportunity to all residents.

Thus, uncovering and understanding these interconnections should not provoke more finger-pointing, but rather generate a discussion on how these issues are related and how to design complimentary efforts for realistic "win-wins" making cities more attractive and livable. From our Ten Core Connections described above, we have identified four key areas of future work and research:

Collaborative, cross-sector partnerships can leverage opportunities linking TOD, families, and schools. Aligning the opportunities and mitigating the potential impacts TOD may have on schools will require collaborative, cross-sector partnership. In particular, local public school districts need to be active participants in the TOD planning processes. The Ten Core Connections presented in this paper provide the rationale for including school districts as key stakeholders in TOD planning, and begin to illuminate the incentives for schools to participate. Planning for population and school enrollment changes linked to a TOD appears to be a natural converging point of interest; the potential for the joint use of public spaces or inclusion of small specialty schools in a TOD is another, and can only happen through partnerships across agencies.

The "story" of TOD can more explicitly include families and schools. The overall "story" of TOD can better support the goal of mixed-income, family-oriented housing. Given that TOD is largely aimed at young professionals and empty nesters, neither of whom is expected to have children, considering schools in relation to TOD may seem unnecessary. However, market demand among young professionals can change over time.[8] When couples without children living in a TOD have children, they are more-or-less forced to relocate to accommodate their growing family, often giving up their multi-modal lifestyle. TOD focused at least in part on accommodating families can both attract new populations to TOD living and help retain current residents in TOD areas. The case for creating mixed-income TOD will provide the opportunity for families that would not otherwise have access to such transit-accessible housing to cut down on both their housing and commuting costs. Given the realities of implementing TOD, including affordable, family-oriented housing is no easy task; developers and cities will need additional policy mechanisms and financial subsidy to do so.

Capacity-building is needed to support cross-sector partnerships. Effective cross-sector partnerships are built upon trust, communication, and procedural tools. Stakeholders may be engaging in such partnerships for the first time and could benefit from capacity-building that prepares them to be more effective partners. Our research has revealed diverse stakeholders — including elected leadership, city and school district staff, and private (for- and non-profit) developers — who each play

critical roles in planning and implementing TOD and need capacity building support to engage in collaborative TOD planning. We identify four key capacity-building areas:

1. Communications infrastructure. Formal and informal avenues of communication are critical to sustained collaboration and trust building; "2 × 2" committees (where the district superintendent and school board chair meet with the mayor and city manager), quarterly joint city council-school board meetings, or other consistent modes of communication are all good options.

2. Data- and information-sharing. Data is of critical importance in conversations about schools and development. However, there is no single, easily accessible source of data on both cities and schools. For example, the question of how many students a new housing development will generate requires a system and set of resources where planners and districts can agree on demographic projections.

3. Incremental successes. Trust and collaboration can be built on diverse projects and initiatives. Often, districts and cities collaborate at a smaller scale, for example sharing school resource officers or after school programming, which can lay the foundation for partnerships in bigger infrastructure and development projects. While a crossing guard program may seem small compared to a large infrastructure development initiative, this incremental success serves as a foundation for relationship building, and its success can be leveraged for larger projects in the future.

4. Points of effective partnership/engagement. To determine the best time, place, and reason for schools' engagement, all stakeholders must understand TOD and school-related planning and implementation processes, what specific action occurs in those phases, and how any impacts are most directly relevant to the work of cities and school districts. For example, while planning processes set the stage for land allotment, it may not be until the implementation phase that the unit mix of a TOD is set, thus determining actual student generation rates. Likewise, different phases of the process provide opportunities to leverage city and school constituencies. For example, students may participate in a TOD planning process as part of a service-learning class, and subsequently bring their parents into planning activities, thus providing developers and planners with access to a broader constituency. Further, schools may use public meetings during an implementation phase to reach other city residents who may have an interest in supporting schools and/or joint use of school facilities.

Performance measures and outcome indicators are needed to assess successful TOD outcomes supporting families and schools. To effectively align and assess TOD outcomes that simultaneously support equitable development, families and schools, districts, cities, and developers need established performance measures and outcome indicators. While conventional TOD success metrics focus on revenue for transit agencies and increased transit ridership, the idea of "TOD 3.0" has been proposed, in which "Livability Benefits" become the driver of the technical processes of transit and land use planning for TOD.[9] Education-related components are narrowly defined around early childhood education, out of school time, charter schools, and magnet schools[10]—not considering the bevy of other traditional public school district and school site initiatives and opportunities that interrelate with TOD efforts. However, even when benchmarks are set for these types of quality of life issues,[11] there is limited focus on operationalizing what this means in practice for families — especially where schools and the inclusion of school site and district stakeholders are concerned. Further research and case study development should be utilized to construct tangible performance measures and outcome indicators for successful TOD planning processes and outcomes that support families and local schools.

Conclusion

Improving cities and improving schools go hand in hand; one will likely only be successful in tandem with the other. Opportunities exist to use TOD to increase transit ridership,

create great communities, realize equitable development, support families, and provide high quality educational options for all children. While transit agencies and private developers have driven the TOD concept, community development practitioners are increasingly seeing the power of building community connections and enhancing quality of life for all residents through this emerging development tool.

Think Tank

The Center for Cities & Schools (CC&S) is an action-oriented think tank and interdisciplinary initiative between the University of California, Berkeley's Graduate School of Education and the College of Environmental Design. CC&S works to position high quality education as an essential component of urban and metropolitan vitality to create equitable, healthy, and sustainable cities and schools for all.

NOTES

1. Transit Cooperative Research Program (2004). Report 102 Transit-Oriented Development in the United States: Experiences, Challenges, and Prospects, the Transportation Research Board, p. 7. Available at: http://onlinepubs.trb.org/Onlinepubs/tcrp/tcrp_rpt_102.pdf.

2. Transit Oriented for All: The Case for Mixed-Income Transit-Oriented Development in the Bay Area. A Great Communities Collaborative Framing Paper. June 2007. Available at: http://communityinnovation.berkeley.edu/publications/GCCFramingPaper_FINAL.pdf.

3. See McKoy, Deborah L., and Jeffrey M. Vincent. 2008. Housing and Education: The Inextricable Link. In *Segregation: The Rising Costs for America*. Edited by James H. Carr and Nandinee K. Kutty. New York: Routledge.

4. See Rusk, David. 2003. Housing Policy Is School Policy: Remarks to the 44th Annual Meeting of Baltimore Neighborhoods, Inc. May 6. Available at: http://www.gamaliel.org/DavidRusk/DavidRuskLibrary.htm; McKoy, Deborah L., and Jeffrey M. Vincent. 2008. Housing and Education: The Inextricable Link. In *Segregation: The Rising Costs for America*. Edited by James H. Carr and Nandinee K. Kutty. New York: Routledge; American Planning Association & American Institute of Certified Planners. 2000. The Millennium Survey: A National Poll of American Voters' View on Land Use. Washington, DC: APA/AICP.

5. McDonald, Noreen C. 2007. Active Transportation to School Trends Among U.S. Schoolchildren, 1969–2001. *American Journal of Preventive Medicine* 32(6): 509–516.

6. Carinci, Justin. "School district tests a creative strategy." *Daily Journal of Commerce Oregon*, December 1, 2009. Available at: http://djcoregon.com/news/2009/12/01/school-district-tests-a-creative-strategy/.

7. For more information on our research-based, systemic-oriented efforts to reverse this trend, see the Center for Cities & Schools' PLUS Leadership Initiative http://citiesand schools.berkeley.edu/leadership.html.

8. Understanding the Choice to Reside in a Transit-Oriented Development (2009). Prepared for the Metropolitan Transportation Commission by Cambridge Systematics.

9. Fostering Equitable and Sustainable Transit-Oriented Development: Briefing Papers for a Convening on Transit-Oriented Development. Convening held by the Center for Transit Oriented Development, Living Cities, and Boston College's Institute for Responsible Investment at the Ford Foundation. February 24–25, 2009. p. 31. Available at: http://www.livingcities.org/leadership/trends/transit/.

10. Ibid. p 33.

11. The Center for Transit Oriented Development (CTOD), for example, includes a performance measure that TODs "create a sense of place" http://www.reconnecting america.org/public/tod.

CHAPTER 42

San Jose and San Jose State University Build Joint Public Library

Lorraine Oback

In the mid–1990s, the city of San Jose and San Jose State University (SJSU) faced a similar dilemma: They both needed to build new libraries to replace their old ones, which were too small and technologically outdated, and both entities had limited financial resources.

Extensive Planning for Building and Operation

Implementing the project involved years of planning and community input. Teams of staff from both libraries were established to review building specifications for functional design and create operational plans for the transition and management of the joint library. Consultants were hired to assist with technology planning and customer satisfaction benchmarking. The two libraries had very different organizational cultures, so determining how to merge their operations was challenging; from choosing what type of library automation to purchase to how to share coverage of reference and circulation desks. Multiple change management tools were employed to inform and encourage integration of staff. Planning for the move of 1.5 million items was time intensive and complex, yet the phased move-in took a mere 2.5 months.

Architectural Excellence

At 475,000 square feet, the joint library is the largest all-new library west of the Mississippi.

The architects were challenged to create a large building that would be appealing on a human scale — distinctive but compatible with campus and downtown revitalization. Their design centers around an eight-story atrium, through which natural light pours in. A ground floor promenade links the public and campus lobbies. The most popular and widely used materials are located on the first four floors. Special collections are on the fifth floor, and the university's academic research collections fill the top three floors. A large reading room on the eighth floor offers a spectacular view of San Jose.

The goal of making the Dr. Martin Luther King Jr. Library a center for intellectual and creative thought extended to the process of creating 33 pieces of public art for installation throughout the library. Internationally renowned artist Mel Chin engaged the community in lively discussions about how art should be used to reflect the diversity of the community.

Originally published as "San Jose Builds Joint Library to Serve Both City and University." © 2005 League of California Cities. All rights reserved. Reprinted with permission from *Western City* magazine (www.westerncity.com), the monthly publication of the League of California Cities.

Funding and Cost Savings

The King Library is a large-scale example of resource sharing among public entities. The project cost of $170 million drew on public and private sources: $70 million from the city, $86 million from the State of California fund for California State University capital projects, $5 from SJSU and $9 million from private funds.

Savings for the City of San Jose and State of California taxpayers have been significant. Eliminating the need for two stand-alone library buildings (155,000–180,000 square feet each) saved approximately $24 million on construction and reduced annual building maintenance costs by an estimated $1.5 million.

According to PG&E, the energy efficient design of the library is saving 1.5 million kilowatt-hours (kWh) per year, well above California's Title 24 Energy Code requirements. High quality glazing and new technology in lighting design and control systems have reduced the cooling requirements of the building by 44 percent and the heating requirements by 31 percent.

Improving Service Delivery

Residents now have easier access to the university's intellectual resources while the campus community has convenient access to the public library's collections of popular books and media. Additional benefits include:

- A landmark downtown building whose distinctive architecture and size transform a quiet campus corner into a bustling center of activity;
- Expanded hours of operation plus 24/7 online access to extensive electronic resources and research databases;
- Multilingual collections of San Jose's highly diverse ethnic populations plus separate resource center space for Africa, Asian American and Chicano collections;
- Equal access for all, from an undocumented day laborer with limited English language skills to an internationally renowned professor with multiple academic degrees; and

- An intellectual and cultural center for the city, reflecting the unique creativity and energy of Silicon Valley.

Effect on Community

The vision of the Dr. Martin Luther King Jr. Library is being realized: a world class library serving the lifelong learning needs of both the city and the university.

Whether they have attended SJSU, some other college or no college at all, residents feel comfortable in the King Library and experience it as a welcoming place where they can read, learn, research, think, create, relax and enjoy new ideas and information.

Most public agencies are caught between the need and/or desire to improve the delivery of service to constituents and limited financial resources. The King Library is an excellent example of how public agencies can pool their resources to develop community assets that are mutually beneficial. It is also a unique collaborative model for library design that could be replicated in many regions of California and throughout the United States.

EDITOR'S NOTES

1. In February of 1997, San Jose Mayor Susan Hammer and San Jose State University President Robert L. Caret announced their intention to build a new library that would serve both as the SJSU Library and as the City's Main Library. This new library would be (and still is) the first joint use library in the United States shared by a major university as its only library and a large city as its main library.

2. In December of 1999, the California State University Board of Trustees and the San Jose City Council and Redevelopment Agency Board approved two documents: The Development Agreement to design and build the library, and the Joint Library Operating Agreement on how the library would be governed, operated, funding for utilities and operating expenses, as well as the co-management of the library facility.

3. In May of 2000, the city and university agreed to name the new library after Dr. Martin Luther King, Jr. The grant opening celebration of this library facility brought the city's leaders and residents together with the university community.

4. Today the King Library houses over 1.5 million volumes, seats more than 3,500 people, and receives over 2 million visitors each year. It provides 40 group study rooms and 300 public access computers as well as computer classrooms for librarians to teach information literacy to both SDSU students as well as the general public. Wifi is available throughout this library facility.

CHAPTER 43

San Pablo and Its School District Partner to Revitalize a Neighborhood

Ariel H. Bierbaum, Jeffrey M. Vincent *and* Erika Tate

As the landscapes of our cities evolve, school buildings remain a constant. Desperately in need of repair, modernization, and beautification, especially in the urban areas, schools are frequently called upon to provide essential support services for the families and communities of the children they serve. To meet the new dual demands of education and social service programming, urban school districts are beginning to invest in neighborhood revitalization and modernizing school facilities.

School facility capital spending is a form of place-based community investment, so it's not surprising to see school investment goals coalesce with city redevelopment and planning goals. Stakeholders in school facilities and program planning now include city officials, social service providers, and community residents, in addition to the parents, teachers, administrators, and students. These coalitions are formalized in some places and work in tandem without any institutionalized commitment, in others.

Such collaborations between public institutions are notable, as historically, school districts and city governments have often had antagonistic relationships. Furthermore, the process of participatory visioning and planning used in these projects represents a transformative moment in governance for both institutions. The result has been a nationwide emergence of a move towards "community-centered schools" that are more intimately connected to their physical surroundings and local communities.

Building Schools for the Whole Community

School districts, often perceived as isolated and bureaucratic entities, are forging partnerships, policies, and processes to revitalize or plan new school buildings that are more open, participatory, and often characterized by non-traditional school designs, such as joint use recreation and community service facilities, adaptive re-use of non-school buildings, and schools built on urban infill sites. The planning and construction of public school facilities is moving away from the 1950s industrial model towards one that integrates community services with educational programming.

Joint use schools, which first emerged in the 1990s, are schools that share one or more of their spaces with another public entity or community-based organization. Sometimes called "full service schools," the advantages they offer their communities include:

- Services, such as on-site health clinics, counseling offices, recreation opportunities, and financial literacy information.

Originally published as "Building Schools and Community," *Race, Poverty, and the Environment*, Vol. 15, No. 1, Spring 2008, by Urban Habitat, Oakland, California. Reprinted with permission of the publisher.

- Amenities, such as swimming pools, libraries, and computer labs.
- Savings on costs of construction and maintenance.

By bringing the benefits of recreational and health services to the broader community of residents, these multifaceted facilities expand the definition of "school stakeholder" beyond students and their caregivers. In other words, joint use developments can increase parental participation, raise general community support of schools, and provide new or improved infrastructure in the urban landscape, contributing to the beautification, safety, and vibrancy of our cities.

Community Integrated School Buildings

The new Helms Middle School building currently under construction in the City of San Pablo in the Bay Area, has evolved out of more than 10 years of work grounded in comprehensive programming and service provision. In 1994, the West Contra Costa Unified School District (WCCUSD) administration, as well as several elementary and middle school principals applied for a Healthy Start grant from the California State Department of Education. Among the schools selected to receive startup money to build a small learning center that included community services was Helms Middle School in San Pablo. Out of this funding emerged the Helms Community Project (HCP)—a school-community collaborative comprised of district and school staff, community-based mental health service providers, parents, and community members—and a partnership aimed at supporting the academic successes of the schoolchildren and their families.

Since its initial funding, the project has expanded to offer a growing list of programs that are a working example of how seemingly separate services can be integrated when housed in the same physical space. A student referred for counseling may receive a weekly appointment with an on-site therapist and/or be connected with a mentor or healthcare provider,

recommended to participate in an after-school program, have his/her parents called in for an academic/behavioral appointment, and/or receive a home visit by an HCP parental outreach staff. Most importantly, having all of these resources housed in the Helms Middle School has made them easily accessible to the students and their families.

Although students are the core constituency of this school-community collaborative, they are not the only beneficiaries of HCP's extensive programming. LaZena Jones, director of HCP, says that the project often functions as the eyes of the community. The staff has worked to familiarize faculty with the lifestyles of their students, the challenges they face in their communities, and the impacts on their academic experience. One recent example of such an effort was a school-wide community-mapping project for which the Helms faculty, staff, administration, and community members walked around the school neighborhoods, identifying challenges and assets. Such interventions enable teachers, parents, and community to develop the empathy needed to support students from a variety of perspectives and represent the school's holistic approach to education.

City Council Member Genoveva Calloway calls Helms Middle School a mini-replica of San Pablo for the wide-ranging and integrative services offered by HCP. Recently, the City of San Pablo has begun to formalize its collaborative efforts with HCP. Vice Mayor Leonard McNeil is also one of HCP's consistent champions. In recent years, the city has done everything from co-writing grants with the School District, to matching grant monies, to earmarking city funds for after-school academic enrichment programs, demonstrating that education is not just the bailiwick of school districts, but rather, a community's shared responsibility.

With the new partnerships and processes at hand, the city now excitedly awaits the construction of the new Helms Middle School facility (funded by a bond secured by the WCCUSD in 2002), which will include San Pablo's Community Center building—funded, in turn, by the city and situated on land granted by the school district. Now referred to as San Pablo's Center of Community, the center is the product of a 10-year program needs assessment conducted among school service providers and stakeholders under the direction of former Principal Harriet McLean and with the collaboration of the city and the Helms Project. The resulting facility is designed to enable small learning communities to function within the larger school and also to include space for community service providers to work.

Currently, the City of San Pablo, HCP, and the WCCUSD participate in the PLUS (Planning and Learning United for Systems change) Leadership Initiative of the Center for Cities and Schools at the University of California, Berkeley. Since last summer, the PLUS team has worked to institutionalize HCP partnerships that have been established over the years. Ultimately, the PLUS team hopes, the physical presence and ongoing utilization of the Center of Community will serve as a beacon of their vision of a transformative collaboration between school and community, in addition to being a landmark in the urban fabric of San Pablo.

Centers of Community Life, Emeryville

A few miles south of San Pablo, down San Pablo Avenue, the Emery Unified School District (EUSD) and the City of Emeryville have been cultivating their own vision for connecting community and educational programming. In this 1.2 square mile city, the school district, the city government, community members, and local businesses have been working together for seven years to craft a redevelopment plan that puts education for everyone at the center of community life in Emeryville. This vision of supportive services and high quality education is coupled with the creation of public spaces and buildings built to foster and enhance a collective learning environment. As school board member Josh Simon puts it, "We don't want to just build the Center of Community Life. We want to be the center of community life and then build a building around what we are."

In 2001, following poor student performance and an impending fiscal crisis, EUSD was

taken over by a state administrator, setting in motion a series of changes, which included the election of an entirely new school board whose members were keen on re-thinking the school-community connection. A broad coalition of stakeholders — made up of city officials and staff, school district representatives, teachers, residents, and other community members — came together under the Emery Youth Services Advisory Committee (EYSAC) to craft a vision for turning the schools around. In 2002, it was recommended that the city and district work together to redevelop the schools and other city parcels into a vibrant, mixed-use community center to serve all the people of Emeryville and the idea for Emeryville's Center of Community Life was born.

The Center was originally envisioned as a multi-acre site, consisting of new "green" school facilities, community health and service support centers, joint use recreation facilities, business and retail facilities, a fire or police station, and some mixed-income housing — to create a place that is diverse, vibrant, and a "center of community." Also in 2002, influential business leaders and the Chamber of Commerce publicly supported a successful parcel tax vote to raise desperately needed money for the school district. Then again, in November 2007, Measure A — another parcel tax increase — passed with an overwhelming majority, thanks to a concerted "get out the vote" effort by city officials, business leaders, community members, and students.

At this moment, Emeryville's many stakeholders are in discussion to plan and create not one, but many smaller Centers of Community Life. The district is currently engaged in renovating the elementary school and is working on plans for a Family and Community Wellness Center located at the Emery Secondary School campus. The design and development of the Center will include input not only from school district and city staff, but also from young people and their families. The Y-PLAN, an initiative of the Center for Cities and Schools at the University of California, Berkeley, which partners university student mentors with high school students to work on local community planning projects, will work with Emery Secondary students this year on the Family and Community Wellness Center, slated to open in September 2008. As Roy Miller, the architect working for EUSD, says, "The Wellness Center is not the final piece. It's another learning increment — we are taking on a piece that we are able to tackle and accomplish. It's simply another step in the evolution of this process. And that's the truth of change — there is no final end point. Rather, we are just taking steps, putting them in place, learning, and then doing it all again."

In other words, the ultimate hope of the city of Emeryville is that the physical infrastructure, along with the services and activities it offers, will serve as a catalyst for productive and supportive cross-cultural, inter-racial, and intergenerational interactions.

An Endless Loop of Possibilities

The two innovative joint use school projects featured here, in many ways, embody the potential of new and rehabilitated school buildings to manifest the collaborative work of two important public institutions — school districts and city governments. Beyond that, they represent the shared vision cultivated by parents, students, teachers, and other community members. Schools no longer need to be built as traditional stand-alone facilities that are open only during school hours; rather, they can be designed and built to be community centers that offer services and amenities to local neighborhoods. As San Pablo and Emeryville show us, joint use facilities are not merely an end point of a long collaborative, but also a part of structuring the process of building mutually beneficial partnerships across public agencies, community-based organizations, parents, students, teachers, residents, and other community members.

CHAPTER 44

State College Officials Seek Student Liaison from Pennsylvania State University

Adam Smeltz

State College Borough Council encouraged Monday the concept of a Penn State student liaison, but did not endorse a proposal for a non-voting student seat on the council.

"I think there's a lot of merit in" appointing a liaison to represent student interests and share borough information with the University Park Undergraduate Association, said Ron Filippelli, the council president.

At a council work session, he told Christian Ragland, the UPUA president, that "I don't think we're that far apart."

Ragland has proposed the eventual inclusion of a non-voting student seat on the Borough Council, a measure that he said has already taken shape in four Big Ten host towns: East Lansing, Mich.; Lincoln, Neb.; Iowa City, Iowa; and Bloomington, Ind. Ragland said a non-voting seat would help enhance students' role as stakeholders in the community, strengthen communication between town and gown, and help foster a better sense of local community among undergraduates.

Under Ragland's proposal, the UPUA would move in three phases. First, it would appoint an official contact for communications with council; that person would attend all council meetings.

Next, the UPUA would make a concerted effort to encourage students to apply for the volunteer, appointed positions on the borough's authorities, boards and commissions. Members of those groups generally serve at the pleasure of council and often advise council members on key issues. The borough has struggled in the past to gain student recruits for those positions, though a relative handful have served in recent years.

Finally, under the Ragland proposal, if council were comfortable with the idea, elected members could appoint a non-voting student member to the council. The non-voting member would attend all meetings and work sessions and be particularly visible in the community, Ragland said.

He suggested the council could choose the non-voting member with input and recommendations from the UPUA.

While council member Peter Morris said he supports Ragland's pitch, others were more reserved. They said that they encourage students to take a more proactive role in applying for authority, board and commission seats, and that they would welcome a student liaison from the UPUA.

But from a legal and philosophical standpoint, they aired reservations about a non-voting council seat. Filippelli said he opposes the

Originally published as "State College Council Encourages Student Involvement, State College, Pennsylvania," *Town & Gown Network*, August 10, 2010, by Colorado State University, Fort Collins. Reprinted with permission of the publisher.

concept, explaining that "I don't think it's appropriate. Borough Council members are elected and represent all the citizens."

Council member Tom Daubert said he thinks anyone who's appointed to represent student interests ought "to be someone who cares about the Borough of State College, not someone who wants to push an agenda from the HUB." Any appointment should avoid purely political climbers, Daubert said.

Morris, meanwhile, said that "I just can't oppose this (non-voting-seat proposal) as a matter of principle. Speaking democratically, it seems to be a natural thing to do."

Ragland thanked the council for hearing the pitch. He said he will look more at operations in Big Ten towns with non-voting student representatives and return to Borough Council for more discussion. He also said he will look to focus specifically on student involvement in the borough's authorities, boards and commissions.

In other business Monday night, the council voiced reluctance over a request from the borough Human Relations Commission. The commission, formed in 2007, has sought a broadening of its role so that it can hold occasional public meetings and invite "people to discuss issues of diversity," commission Chairman Charles Dumas said.

Dumas said the meetings could yield advisory memorandums for council's consideration.

But council members voiced concern that such diversity meetings could turn the commission into an advocacy body — a role that may compromise its primary role as an adjudicator, council members said.

The commission was established to hear complaints filed under the borough Anti-Dis-

crimination Ordinance, established in 2007; however, the commission has yet to hear any complaints, according to the borough.

The local ordinance bans discriminatory behavior in employment practices, particularly with regard to gender identity and sexual orientation. Those characteristics are not covered under state and federal anti-discrimination legislation.

Council member Don Hahn was among those who voiced concern about the legal implications of altering the Human Relations Commission's charge. Still, he also commended Dumas for stepping forward.

"It's certainly been my experience in this community that a lot of discrimination does occur," Hahn said. "Unfortunately, there's been little more than lip service done."

He said the State College Area School District's anti-discrimination policy "has been violated so many times with very little consequences."

The council agreed to seek input from the borough solicitor, Terry Williams, concerning the Human Relations Commission matter. In the meantime, borough Manager Tom Fountaine said, the borough can facilitate a meeting among the Human Relations Commission, the Community Diversity Group and the Centre County Advisory Committee to the state Human Relations Commission.

Fountaine said the borough staff has recommended more collaboration among the groups. The state Human Relations Commission documented 23 employment-related discrimination complaints from Centre County in the 2007-2008 reporting period, according to an annual report. It's not immediately clear which of those are from State College borough.

CHAPTER 45

Sugar Land and University of Houston Work Together on New Campus for Educational and Economic Reasons

Allen Bogard

The Need

BACKGROUND

About 10 years ago, there was a vision of our residents attending college here in their own community, rather than trekking 22 miles to Houston. Sugar Land had a small satellite campus of Wharton County Junior College, but the courses were limited and the facility was in a 35-year old strip mall. Sugar Land experienced dramatic growth (150 percent) in the decade of the 90s and the current decade — the fastest growing city in Texas for several years. (In January 2009, the city's population was 79,732 and another 35,000 in the extraterritorial jurisdiction which will be annexed in seven or eight years.) Sugar Land was fast becoming an employment hub and recreational/cultural destination for this area south and southwest of Houston.

The City of Sugar Land, the State of Texas, the University of Houston System, and the community partnered in a highly unique and innovative manner to facilitate an accelerated development of higher education opportunities for Fort Bend County in order to promote quality of life and economic development. Under planning and construction for nearly five years, the University of Houston at Sugar Land campus opened in 2002 as a facility to address the community's educational needs. In a time of economic pressure on higher education, the City utilized its resources to expedite higher education opportunities and, additionally, community recreational needs faster than could have been otherwise accomplished.

Program Implementation and Cost

THE FIRST PART

Former Sugar Land Mayor Dean Hrbacek recalls: "I worked with the former Texas Lieutenant Governor, Bill Hobby, who was named Chancellor of the University of Houston System after he left office in Austin. He was one of the most respected Texans ever, and his view was that the university should provide service to its customers, wherever they were living, and we both felt — and a lot of people felt the same and supported us — that Sugar Land was a prime market for the University of Houston. We looked to find an area of land for the university. We were very fortunate that the State of Texas owned a substantial amount of land within our ETJ [extraterritorial jurisdiction] at that time. Bill Hobby approached the state leg-

Originally published as "Extraordinary Partnership Brings College Campus to Sugar Land," *Community Partnership Award Application*, office of the city manager, city of Sugar Land, Texas.

islature with his vision of bringing education to this community; we spent a good amount of time in Austin and Bill Hobby testified, cashed in a lot of chips, and we ended up with 248 acres for the university and another 428 adjoining acres of park land for the city of Sugar Land. Governor Bush signed the legislation. It was the very first time that the State of Texas had donated this large a parcel to a municipality."

Another very positive aspect of this land grant was the opportunity for the City to establish a one-of-a-kind park incorporating both recreation and conservation along nine miles of Brazos River within its city limits.

"Here we are with UH Sugar Land today, and it's a tremendous asset not only to the city but to the surrounding area as a whole by being able to provide a quality university in our backyard," says Hrbacek.

Sugar Land committed $3.5 million towards the construction of the $11 million, 57,000 square foot building. The City joined with UH in an aggressive campaign to find private donations and foundation grants to help fund the building. The UH campus building has general classrooms, a multi-media center, library resource center and four interactive television rooms. A community education room is available for public use. This collaborative effort was remarkable for two reasons: It was the first time in Texas history that the state legislature actually gave away — donated — land to another jurisdiction. The university received 248 acres and the City of Sugar Land received 428 adjoining acres. Additionally, this was an effort involving a municipality helping to fund a state project — another first — demonstrating the City's commitment to education and work force development. The City of Sugar Land's ability to participate in the building project was made possible through the Sugar Land 4B Corporation, an economic development corporation which is financed through one-quarter of one cent of the City's share of sales tax. (The Texas Development Corporation Act of 1979 enables cities to allot tax monies for economic development.)

THE SECOND PART

The University of Houston at Sugar Land offered junior and senior level courses and graduate courses. Soon after the opening of the Albert and Mamie George Building, the City and UH in 2005 extended their partnership with the plans of a second building which would offer space to Wharton County Junior College, thus creating a full undergraduate curriculum. In January 2006, plans for a second building of 145,000 square feet were announced. The City committed another $3.5 million for the "Building Futures Together" campaign, and construction of the second building. In turn, UH leased to the City an adjacent 52-acre tract of land that the City will maintain as parkland and looks to develop such amenities as a park and recreation center. These amenities can be enjoyed by those attending college and the general public.

The new Wharton County Junior College (WCJC) building — Brazos Hall — has 44 classrooms, a performance hall, five computer labs, nine science laboratories and a nursing skills laboratory. A School of Nursing is shared by both facilities. The new facility also features a two-level, 150-seat auditorium and large multipurpose room. Construction was paid for, in part, with a $4 million gift from the George Foundation and a $3.5 million contribution from the City of Sugar Land's 4B Corporation as a long term lease agreement for nearby UHSSL property.

In January 2009, students registered in 25 courses and began the Spring semester at WCJC. It was now possible to earn a baccalaureate degree right here in Sugar Land.

Tangible Results or Measurable Outcomes of the Program

The UH Sugar Land campus was immediately full with 2,300 students when it opened in the summer of 2002 offering 34 graduate and undergraduate programs. UH anticipates a 5 percent enrollment growth annually. WCJC had 2,100 enrollees in its Spring 2009 semester.

"This collaborative vision demonstrates our continued support of this very important educational institution," says Sugar Land City Manager Allen Bogard. "The partnership provides greater opportunity for our residents to access higher education and recreational facilities."

Lessons Learned During Planning, Implementation and Analysis of the Program

PARTNERING INCREASES LIKELIHOOD OF SUCCESS

This was an extraordinary partnership involving a city, state, state-supported university and a county-supported junior college. The generosity of citizens and foundations also contributed to the success of the campus.

Under the leadership of the late Lieutenant Governor Bill Hobby, the Texas Legislature took action that made the property (formerly owned by the Texas Department of Transportation) available to the City of Sugar Land and the University of Houston System; it is the first of its kind land donation in Texas. To further ensure the success of this venture, Sugar Land pledged a total of $7 million toward construction of the two buildings; to our knowledge, a municipality pledging this amount of funding to a state entity is exceedingly rare — if it has ever occurred at all.

The University of Houston System had broad experience in creating branch campuses. The UH System has satellite campuses at Victoria, Texas; in downtown Houston, six miles from the main campus; Cinco Ranch in Katy, Texas; Clear Lake, Texas; and the University of Houston Distance Education program.

Wharton County Junior College, founded in 1946, is also experienced with satellite campuses, the Sugar Land campus becoming the school's fourth.

The citizens of Sugar Land embraced the partnership — and no wonder: 59 percent of Sugar Land adults hold a bachelor's degree or higher, the highest education attainment in the region.

The benefits of the UH System campus in Sugar Land are varied. The educational opportunities add immeasurably to the quality of life. The positive effects the campus will have on the work force is expected to be dramatic. The UH Computing Services alone offers Sugar Land residents instruction in laptop, mobile computer, multimedia lab computing; the Computer Science/Information System Instructional Computer Lab is utilized by all disciplines. The campus is intended to be a high-tech hub connected to workplaces, schools, homes and the other UH campuses.

Affordable learning is more accessible than ever in Sugar Land, Texas. Conveniently located together with the University of Houston System at Sugar Land, the new junior college makes it easy to take the first two years of courses at WCJC and pocket substantial savings before transferring credits to a four-year college. This unique transfer-driven new campus offers more than 25 different courses and an opportunity for students to take part in the WCJC/University of Houston System Partnership 2 + 2 Joint Admissions Agreement. This agreement facilitates the admission of WCJC students to the University of Houston System (UH, UH–Clear Lake, UH–Downtown, UH–Victoria) so that they may continue their studies in four-year programs, including those at the University of Houston System at Sugar Land.

CHAPTER 46

Tampa Benefits from University of Florida Bringing More Students Downtown

Yesim Sungu-Eryilmaz

Colleges and universities have emerged as some of the largest landowners and developers in their cities, exerting a powerful influence on the built environment (Perry and Wiewel 2005). At the end of fiscal year 1996, urban institutions held almost $100 billion in land and buildings (book value), including $8 billion in purchases from only the prior year (ICIC and CEOs for Cities 2002). They have several motivations for undertaking land development activities: ensuring their capacity to meet growing demands for student housing and other facilities; fulfilling their educational and research agenda; enhancing the quality and security of their surroundings; and maintaining or improving their reputation and standing.

Student Housing and Recreational Needs

Colleges and universities often invest in land and new buildings to meet growing demands for on-campus housing and recreational facilities. Some of this pressure reflects a more than 50 percent increase in U.S. college enrollment between 1970 and 2005, with continuing growth projected.

In addition to the traditional practice of providing housing to freshmen and sometimes all students, many colleges and universities are making the transition from being primarily commuter schools to more traditional residential campuses by adding student dormitories and expanding sports facilities. Some of the schools that have recently made this shift are the University of South Florida in Tampa; Northeastern University in Boston, Massachusetts; the University of Nebraska at Omaha; Wayne State University in Detroit, Michigan; La Salle University in Philadelphia, Pennsylvania; and San Jose State University in California.

In some cases, universities lack land for housing or recreational projects, and must look for alternatives on the edge of campus. That was the case for Georgia State University in Atlanta when it made the transition to a traditional campus-style university in 1993. Georgia State invested in building both undergraduate and graduate student housing as a way to create a viable community (Kelley and Patton 2005).

Three housing development projects are notable. Georgia State Village includes housing converted from Atlanta's Olympic Village, located one-and-a-half miles from the campus on the edge of downtown. The university purchased the Olympic Village after the games and opened the facility in 1996 as housing for 2,000 undergraduates.

The second project, University Lofts, offers housing for graduate and international

Originally published as "University Motivations for Land Use and Development Projects," *Town-Gown Collaboration in Land Use*, Policy Focus Report, 2008, by the Lincoln Institute of Land Policy, Cambridge, Massachusetts. Reprinted with permission of the publisher.

students on the edge of the campus. The Lofts opened in 2002 and contains 231 apartments for 460 residents, parking, and street-level retail space. It was built on land owned by a local hospital and used as a surface parking lot. The hospital agreed to a 40-year lease of the land for the expansion of student housing.

In 2007, the university developed a third project of 2,000 units of undergraduate housing north of campus on a six-acre site bought from a former auto dealership. This $168 million project was funded by the largest bond issue in the United States for the purpose of housing students.

Research Facilities and Related Needs

Many colleges and universities took on an expanded role in basic scientific research and in research and development (R&D) after World War II. Between 1970 and 2006, academia's share of all R&D in the United States rose from about 10 percent to about 14 percent. In 2006, these institutions conducted more than 30 percent of the nation's basic research and were second only to the business sector in performing R&D.

One direct implication of this new focus is the addition of research facilities to campus activities. Indeed, institutions that conduct research built more space for that work on their campuses from 2001 to 2005 than in any other five-year period since at least 1988. They added some 185 million net assignable square feet for research between fiscal 2003 and fiscal 2005 alone.

In 2005, 64 percent of newly built research space and 67 percent of construction funds were dedicated to the biological and medical sciences (National Science Foundation 2008).

In some cases, universities have struggled to accommodate their growing research needs on campus. Smith College in Northampton, Massachusetts, for example, became the nation's first women's college to have an engineering school in 2000. While the new academic major quickly became one of the most popular on

campus, development of the engineering program was limited by the college's aging science buildings and the lack of space to build new facilities.

To accommodate its growing role in women's science and engineering education, Smith had to demolish a number of college owned properties that had provided housing and retail space (Smith College 2009). The college offered tenants relocation information and financial assistance, and has worked with developers to provide affordable housing nearby.

Revitalization of Adjacent Neighborhoods and Downtowns

For some colleges and universities, the primary driver of land development is their desire to enhance the surrounding neighborhood and promote urban revitalization. Unlike corporations that might choose to leave a distressed area, most universities are place-bound. In the past, institutions responded to a decline in their communities simply by putting up walls and expanding police or security services.

More recently, however, urban colleges and universities have tried to spur economic and community development beyond their borders. Indeed, universities now sponsor activities or create entities that will have a significant local economic impact or serve as the centerpiece of a downtown revival program. These activities may include developing retail stores and housing, enhancing historic landmarks or parks, improving local schools, and even providing sanitation and security services for the area.

Howard University in Washington, DC, had been buying and holding blighted property near its campus for decades, and in 1997 launched a massive revitalization initiative in LeDroit Park. The initial plan was to rehabilitate 28 vacant houses and build new housing on 17 additional vacant lots.

Since then, Howard has expanded its plans to include rehabilitation of a former bread factory into university offices and a community association center; renovation of a neighborhood hospital; opening of a neighborhood security office; completion of street and alley resurfacing, sidewalk bricking, tree planting, and traffic-calming measures; redevelopment of open space; a major telecommunications infrastructure project; and a home-ownership program for Howard employees and local residents.

In September 2008, Howard received a $700,000 Office of University Partnership grant from HUD to begin restoration of the historic Howard Theatre, expand local business development programs, and address accessibility issues at the community association center (Pyatt 1998).

In another example, the City of Indianapolis attempted to revitalize its declining downtown throughout the 1980s and 1990s. By directly engaging Indiana University–Purdue University at Indianapolis (IUPUI) as an important player in the city's larger urban development agenda, the city targeted the arts, entertainment, tourism, and sports facilities as central strategies. IUPUI and the associated Indiana University Medical School and hospital acquired many acres of land to permit expansion. Local corporations, business leaders, the Lilly Foundation, and state government strongly supported the university's land acquisition policies and programs.

From 1974 through 1999, more than 50 major development projects were initiated in the downtown area, and the university's investment in the Indianapolis campus totaled more than $230 million. Several of the projects were related to sports activities. Seven national sports organizations moved their governing offices to Indianapolis in 1989, and the National Collegiate Athletic Association followed in 1999. Development of the IUPUI campus has been identified as one of the principal economic development engines for downtown Indianapolis (Cummings et al. 2005).

control development at the campus periphery. Many universities construct mixed use buildings or purchase commercial and industrial properties that will be leased to generate revenue rather than redeveloped into traditional campus buildings.

Victoria University at the University of Toronto has created a large portfolio of properties acquired over decades. While its original goals were to accommodate possible future needs and control development at the campus edge, the university eventually created mixed-use developments and then leased the properties (Kurtz 2005). Today, the university has a stable real estate income stream with almost half of its endowment based in real estate while the other half is invested in securities.

REFERENCES

Cummings, Scott, Mark Rosentraub, Mary Domahidy, and Sarah Coffin. 2005. University involvement in downtown revitalization: Managing political and financial risks. In Perry and Wiewel 2005, 147–174.

ICIC (Initiative for a Competitive Inner City) and CEOs for Cities. 2002. *Leveraging colleges and universities for urban economic revitalization: An action agenda.* Chicago, IL: CEOs for Cities.

Kelley, Lawrence R., and Carl V. Patton. 2005. The university as an engine for downtown renewal in Atlanta. In Perry and Wiewel 2005, 131–146.

Kurtz, Larry R. 2005. Leasing for profit and control: The case of Victoria University at the University of Toronto. In Perry and Wiewel 2005, 222–238.

National Science Foundation. 2008. *Science and engineering indicators.* Washington DC: National Science Board.

Perry, David C. 2008. Changing the research paradigm: From applied to engaged. Paper presented at University as Civic Partner Conference, February 14–16, 2008, Phoenix, AZ.

_____, and Wim Wiewel. 2005. *The university as urban developer.* Armonk, NY: M.E. Sharpe and the Lincoln Institute of Land Policy.

Pyatt, Rudolph A. 1998. In LeDroit Park, Howard is teaching by example. *The Washington Post,* December 28.

Smith College. 2009. Ford Hall: Construction Information. www.smith.edu/fordhall/construction/background.php.

Land Banking for Future Use and Income

Colleges and universities acquire and develop land to diversify their portfolios and to

Warrensburg Benefits from Central Missouri State University's Economic Contributions

Bob Adebayo

The purpose of this study is to provide an estimation of the short-term economic impact of Central Missouri State University on the local economy and the region as a whole. The results certainly depict that CMSU is a major economic contributor to the local community in which it is located. The study reports expenditures and impacts by the university, its students, faculty, staff and visitors in FY 2004–2005.

- The university contributes to the local and state economy through local expenditures associated with its operating expenses. In FY 2005, the university spent approximately 22 million for operating expenses (contractual services, utilities, supplies and materials).
- Students' expenditures had the greatest local economic impact, $134 million.
- The $69,021,860 expended during the 2004-2005 fiscal year by CMSU students ripples through the regional economy to generate a $138,043,720 impact.
- The university itself had about $48 million impact on the local economy in FY 2005.
- The estimated 467,000 visitors who came to the CMSU campus for various activities in FY 2005 expended an estimated $8,433,400.

- Actual economic impact of CMSU on the local economy in fiscal year 2005 amounted to $277,357,778.
- Total economic impact of CMSU on the regional economy in FY 2005 was estimated at $304,091,416.

Central Missouri State University is an integral part of the socio-economic environments in which it is located. As a major comprehensive higher education institution with more than 10,600 students, CMSU has provided the Warrensburg community a stable source of jobs and income.

The purpose of this study is to explore the short-term economic impact of Central Missouri State University on the local and regional economies in fiscal year 2004–2005. Short-term economic impact is measured by examining the magnitude of the direct and indirect contributions, allocable to the university, that are being made to cash flow through a local economy. These measurable contributions come from four major sources: the institution (expenditures for operating and maintenance), its employees (faculty and staff spending), its students (student spending), and visitors (spending by out-of- area visitors to the CMSU campus).

Originally published as "A Study of the Economic Impact of Central Missouri State University on the Local/State Economies," *College Town Topics*, April 2006, by the International Town and Gown Association, Clemson University, Clemson, South Carolina. Reprinted with permission of the publisher.

The 2002 IMPLAN I/O Model, which is widely used in economic impact studies, was used for this study.[1] This model provides reasonable, conservative estimates of economic impact. This framework yields direct, indirect and induced expenditures for each category of university related expenditure.

The figures used for estimating the economic impact of CMSU are derived from the financial statement data provided by the Office of Finance administration. Enrollment data and other information are provided by the Office of Institutional Research. The study uses a multiplier[2] of 2.0 after a review of recent economic impact studies from across the country.[3] Economic impact studies conducted in New York, Georgia and Missouri have applied multipliers ranging from 1.9 to 3.0. The Commission on independent Colleges and universities recommends a multiplier of 2.5.

Components of Economic Impact Model

1. University Expenditures. The university contributes to the local/regional economies through local expenditures associated with its operating expenses, which includes all of the expenditures the institution made to businesses and other contractors within the service area for such items as the purchase of office supplies, utilities, projects, repair services, insurance and other various items, excluding taxes and payment made to employees. In FY 2004-2005, Central Missouri State University spent approximately $28 million for operating expenses.

2. Employee Expenditures. The University is one of the area's largest employers. As of October 2005, CMSU employed a total of 1,731 individuals (full time and part time). This component of the economic impact model is based on the disposable income of employees. Employees of the university purchase goods and services in the local economy. In FY 2004-2005, a total of $51,166,879 in wages (less taxes and deductions) was paid to CMSU employees.

3. Student Expenditures. Student data for this analysis were based on fall 2005 enrollment. Student spending was estimated for only those activities pertinent to their attendance at CMSU excluding payment made for tuition and fees. Students contribute to the local economy by spending on goods and services, including books, education related materials, transportation, and room and board.

Students were estimated to spend a total of $7,600 each per nine-month school year. Student expenditures do not include students who remain in the Warrensburg area during the summer months and attend the university year round, thus impacting the regional economy. Total student expenditures are considered "new money" (purchases by students from outside the region), including international, and out-of-state students. Student expenditures vary depending on the enrollment status (part-time and full time and their place of origin). Adjustments were made for enrollment status and location.

4. Visitors' Spending. In addition to economic impacts resulting from CMSU's operational expenditures, faculty and staff spending and student spending, the university attracts out-of-town visitors. Visitor expenditures attracted by university held events are a significant source of revenue for the community and probably would not have occurred if not for the presence of the university.

Visitor expenditures include spending on lodging, meals, and other incidentals by visitors from outside the community who visited the campus for various reasons, such as meetings, orientation, conferences, seminars, commencement, continuing education programs, high school summer programs, sporting events, festivals, music or arts presentations, Homecoming and reunions. In fiscal year 2004–2005, an estimated 467,000 visitors came to the CMSU campus for various university-related activities. It is estimated that on average, each visitor expended about $100 per visit (both one-day and overnight visitors).[4]

Economic Impact of CMSU on the Local Economy

Source	Total Value
Expenditures for operations & maintenance Discounted by 15% for "leakages"*	$47,838,186
Expenditures by the employees Discounted by 15% for "leakages"*	$86,983,684
Expenditures by students Adjusted for students enrollment status and place of origin	$134,102,608
Expenditures by visitors at local businesses	$ 8,433,400
Total University Economic Impact	$277,375,778

*A leakage identifies the proportion of direct expenditures that leave an impact area and have no further effect within the area.

Regional Economic Impact of CMSU

Source	Total Value
Expenditures for operations & maintenance	$56,280,218
Expenditures by the employees	$102,333,758
Expenditures by students	$138,043,720
Expenditures by visitors at local businesses	$ 8,433,400
Total University Economic Impact	$304,091,416

Conclusions

This study provides a reasonable, conservative estimate of the short-term economic impacts of CMSU on the local/regional economies. It is evident that CMSU has a major impact on the local economy and on the state as a whole. Through its expenditures, Central Missouri State University has substantial impacts on the local and regional economies. This is expected to increase as enrollment increases.

While this economic impact analysis focuses only on the measurable economic benefits to the local community, the university provides other intangible effects on the local/regional economy. By educating tens of thousands of Missouri residents, the university has increased the earning power of its graduates by many millions of dollars. CMSU also serves a hub for social and cultural experiences in the community.

The preceding analyses of the spending impact of the university and the tax increments that will accrue from CMSU graduates provide justification for public financial support.

A full economic impact study will provide a better picture of the university's economic impact on the state/region.

NOTES

1. John Caffray and Herbert H. Isaacs, 1971. *Estimating the impact of a college or university on the local economy,* Washington, D.C.: American Council on Education.

2. The multiplier captures the "ripple effect" that CMSU's expenditures have on the local/ regional economies as dollars spent are re-spent or reinvested by local businesses.

3. The City University of New York, 1995, Return to New York: The CUNY Investment, A Report on the Economic Impact of the City University of New York; Lange, J.E., *The economic impact of Jefferson College on the community and the state,* Office of Institutional Research, Jefferson College, February 1994; Seybert, Jeffrey, *The economic impact of higher education on the Kansas City metropolitan area 1988–89,* A report prepared for the Kansas City Regional Council for Higher Education, April 1991.

4. Visitor daily spending is based on estimates used in recent studies.

CHAPTER 48

Washington, DC, and Georgetown University Try to Relieve Town-Gown Tensions

Kara Brandeisky *and* Jake Sticka

The Office of Planning's recent recommendation to require Georgetown University to house 100 percent of undergraduates on campus would both severely damage Georgetown student life and fail to achieve the campus plan opponents' objectives. A better approach would be to make campus a more desirable place to be.

If Georgetown improved student gathering spaces, brought back Healy Pub, reduced restrictions for on-campus parties, added more housing and helped students avoid problematic landlords, many students would voluntarily move on campus and spend more social time there.

OP's report followed more than two years of negotiations over Georgetown's 2010 campus plan and changed the debate considerably. Recognizing that there is likely no room to build enough dormitories to house 100 percent of undergrads on Georgetown's campus, the OP report would mandate that the University reduce enrollment to equal the available housing.

In the Zoning Commission hearings, OP representatives also hinted that they would look favorably upon satellite housing and forced triples, like there are at American University. But satellite housing would only further fragment campus life.

Freshmen should not be forced to live in 170-square-feet triples while paying for some of the most expensive University housing in the country. Reducing enrollment by nearly 25 percent would represent a huge blow to the University's already constrained financial resources. These losses could lead to layoffs at the District's largest private employer.

Additionally, requiring all students to live on-campus would reduce the vibrancy and diversity of the already fairly staid surrounding community. Students live off-campus so that they can assert their independence and learn what it is like to live on their own. This arrangement, which furthers student ties to their community, should be encouraged, especially by a city hoping to expand its tax base.

Fortunately, the OP seems to recognize that their recommendations are not the only way forward. At the May 12 Zoning Commission hearing, OP representative Jennifer Steingasser repeatedly said that she was open to other solutions, so long as they brought students back on-campus and mitigated objectionable impacts in the community.

These solutions are possible. Today, Georgetown students spend time off-campus because they are frustrated by a lack of on-campus space that meets their needs. There's no real

Originally published as "Improve Campus Life to Fix Georgetown Town-Gown Relations," *Town & Gown Network*, June 2, 2011, by Colorado State University, Fort Collins, Colorado. Reprinted with permission of the publisher.

reason to live close to the center of student life, because there isn't one.

As long that is true, students will continue to socialize in the community and frequent bars on M Street, even if they are barred from living off-campus. A more holistic plan to remedying the objectionable impacts that OP sees is needed. Such a plan, which both recognizes the need to draw students back on-campus and their right to live off-campus, is laid out below.

Increase Student Space

For years, students have been advocating for more student space on campus. In 1999, a group of student leaders compiled the Report on Student Life, which recommended that the University reorganize Leavey Center and invest in a real student union. Plans for a New South Student Center were included in the 2000 Campus Plan but never came to fruition, and the proposal is again part of the 2010 Campus Plan.

Last year, the Student Space Working Group released a report that found that the same problems still exist a decade later. When surveyed, 64 percent of students said they desired more study space, 56 percent desired more social space, 49 percent desired more space for eating, 41 percent desired more meeting space, and 32 percent desired more student club space. The longer the students had been at Georgetown, and the more involved they were in extracurricular activities, the more frustrated they were with the space available.

What's more, when asked to identify the center of student life on campus, a plurality of students (33 percent) said it was Lauinger Library. This perception demonstrates a core problem. The spaces available do not meet the full variety of student needs, which means students need to use space in a way that conflicts with its intended purpose — for example, we socialize in an area where other people are trying to study — which renders the space ineffective.

As a result, a full 17 percent of those surveyed answered that there was no center of student life at all.

The closest thing we have to a student union — Sellinger Lounge in the Leavey Center — has not become the student-centered space it was envisioned as because of the presence of hotel guests and Georgetown Hospital staff.

If the campus were the real center of student life, more students would choose to live on-campus. The University can and should create spaces and opportunities for a healthy social scene to thrive.

Bring Back Healy Pub

Many alumni still wistfully remember Healy Pub, the bar located in the basement of Georgetown's signature building. In 1987, responding to the higher drinking age, the University ordered the pub to shut down. Town-gown struggles began in full-force in the early 1990s, as student social life began to shift to private parties in Burleith and West Georgetown.

Now, a group of students are trying to bring the pub back. Since 2001, the student body has been paying into a Georgetown University Student Association Endowment Fund. The interest from the fund was supposed to finance student activities once the fund reached $10 million by 2011, but the University reneged on its promised $3 million contribution, so the fund has only reached $3.4 million. The student association leaders now consider the endowment a failure and plan to re-appropriate the money. We have $3.4 million to spend, and the Endowment Commission, identifying the same lack of student space we have, voted last month to put $3.23 million towards the pub.

The proposal is to model the pub after Queen's Head Pub at Harvard. On weekend nights, the area would function as a bar. Those under 21 would be allowed to enter, but they would not be allowed to drink. The rest of the time, the space would function as a lounge, where students could meet, socialize, work, eat snacks and reserve private rooms for meetings.

There are obvious obstacles. Once running, the pub will need an alcohol license, which obviously requires support from the Georgetown Advisory Neighborhood Commission.

Also, the Financial Aid Office and other administrators currently occupy Healy basement, so students need the University's assistance — and blessing — in relocating the people already there to space that will be opened up with the completion of the new science center.

Although the New South Student Center is a necessity and a part of the plan that students welcome, it is not enough. A student-designed, student-run, student-financed space in the heart of Georgetown's historic campus would go a very long way to creating a stronger sense of on-campus community and toward bringing socialization back on-campus.

Reduce On-Campus Party Restrictions

During finals week in 2007, Vice President of Student Affairs Todd Olson surprised students with the announcement of a new alcohol policy. Administrators had decided to institute a one-keg limit, require host training for parties, require students to register parties by Thursday morning, limit the number of students, and increase sanctions for violations, with a third violation leading to suspension. At the time, the *Georgetown Voice* termed the changes "draconian."

The following September, the student association president led administrators on a tour through campus on a Saturday night. To their surprise, "There were about eight people standing around [on the rooftops] ... and when they moved on to Henle, they could hear crickets in the courtyards." Before, it had been one of the biggest party weekends of the year.

Neighbors complained that they noticed an increase in off-campus parties and student noise. Students expressed fear of throwing parties on-campus, citing the new increased sanctions and party registration requirements.

Now, the dynamic has shifted somewhat. Many students express similar fears of 61-Ds for noise violations or Office of Off-Campus Student Life sanctions for off-campus parties.

Students know that despite their best efforts, parties often take on a life of their own, especially at the beginning of the year when

groups of freshmen search high and low for a party to crash. Therefore, students decide to throw their parties on- or off- campus depending on where they perceive they'll attract the least trouble.

If we want students to socialize on-campus, we should consider this constant calculus. To an extent, we can shift the party culture by simply shifting the incentives. As we have seen in the last few years, it's not enough to increase the punishments for out-of-control off-campus parties. We need to also loosen the restrictions on on-campus parties.

Meet all undergrad demand for on-campus housing, starting with hotel and 1789 Block.

The University maintains that it has provided housing for all undergraduates who have requested it. However, should the above measures be implemented, more upperclassmen will want to live on-campus so that they can be closer to the center to student activity. This is especially true if the expansion locations are well-integrated with existing student patterns.

Considering the existing campus, the two sites for additional housing that seem most sensible are the Leavey Center hotel and the block bounded by Prospect, N, 36th, and 37th, known informally as the "1789 block."

Although the Leavey Center has many flaws as a student center and should ultimately be replaced, it has recently become more student-friendly with the opening of the Hariri Business Building, which connects to Leavey. This trend will continue when the new science center opens in fall 2012 (plans call for the science center to connect to Leavey via open lounge spaces). The addition of student housing to Leavey will help ensure that foot traffic in the building returns to being predominantly student-driven, as opposed to hotel guest- or hospital staff-driven.

The "1789 block" which was once a part of the 2010 Campus Plan, would add up to 250 beds and 8,500 square feet of neighborhood servicing retail in the middle of a university-owned block right outside the university's gates. This project would be within a block of three other university dormitories and two university academic buildings. The "1789 block" would be closer to the front gates than the preexisting Nevils apartment complex and LXR dorm. This space is already a center of student activity, and additional commercial areas so close to campus would entice more students to the area.

The University estimates that these two projects could house approximately 500 undergraduates. This would bring the total number housed on-campus to 5,553, which represents about 92 percent of Georgetown's traditional undergraduate enrollment. This figure compares favorably to every university in Washington and is in line with schools like Harvard, Princeton and MIT, which OP praises in their report as models.

Rate My Landlord

Even if these measures are successful, approximately 8 percent of undergraduates will still have the ability to live off-campus.

However, those students who choose to move out of University housing often pay high rents for low-quality neighborhood housing. Slum landlords regularly fail to maintain their property or respect tenant rights. Students are blamed for the unsightly rental houses, when it is the landlord's responsibility to pay for upkeep.

Theoretically, the Georgetown Office of Off-Campus Life is there to "address the needs and concerns of off campus students." In practice, the office spends at least as much time serving its secondary function: acting "as a liaison between the university and our neighbors, encouraging dialogue about issues of mutual concern."

Lost in the shuffle are the students, who need a stronger advocate in their negotiations with landlords.

One service that would make a big impact would be a "rate my landlord"-type website, where students and other subletters could share information about rental rates, housing quality, upkeep and landlord responsiveness.

Students don't want to live under poor conditions. With more transparent information, students can demand better treatment and drive the slumlords out of business.

The Takeaway

In the long run, holistic solutions that aim to improve campus and community life will be far more effective than draconian mandates, which will mire us in legal battles for years to come. We ask that the Zoning Commission, University, and community rethink their approach. The only solutions that can truly address persistent town-gown tensions will be the ones that also take student interests into account.

CHAPTER 49

Williamsburg and the College of William and Mary Form Joint Neighborhood Relations Committee

Brian Whitson

The time is ripe to make serious progress on neighborhood issues near campus, William & Mary President Taylor Reveley told a packed room of city residents, students and local officials Monday night.

To make that happen, five groups — city officials, homeowners, students, university administrators, and landlords — need to work together, Reveley said. While that hasn't always been the case, a recently formed Neighborhood Relations Committee (NRC) includes representatives from each group and is charged with working with residents and students to address town-and-gown issues.

"There are five players in this game," said Reveley, who joined Williamsburg Mayor Clyde Haulmann in providing welcoming remarks during the committee's first public forum Monday night. "All five of us have to pull our oars if we are going to make progress."

Reveley added that the 2010-11 school year is a prime opportunity. Town and gown relations in general are very good, he said. And following last year's changes by City Council to the so-called three person rule and May's election of recent graduate Scott Foster '10, the students are more receptive than ever to working with city residents on issues related to student housing around campus.

"I believe this academic year can be a time of real progress ... on neighborhood issues," Reveley said to those in attendance at the Williamsburg Community Building. "That's one of my goals for the year."

During the two-hour meeting, residents asked questions of committee members, watched a video from a Vermont town on improving neighborhood relationships, and heard from the mayor and president.

Haulman discussed ongoing activities to improve relations, including recent Williamsburg signs welcoming students, a welcome during move-in day, Thursday's jointly sponsored performance by the Virginia Symphony and an upcoming ice cream social on Sept. 26 for local residents and students.

"We are on the right track, and both the city and College are committed to this in the future," said Haulman, who is also an economics professor at William & Mary.

The Neighborhood Relations Committee was formed last year following a progress report by city and College officials on town-gown relations. The committee is designed to build on the ongoing community conversation as part of the city's focus group on rental housing. The committee, which began meeting in the spring, includes Al Albert (landlord representative), Bill

Originally published as "Neighborhood Relations Committee a New Tool for Students, Residents," *William & Mary News*, July 6, 2011, by the College of William and Mary, Williamsburg, Virginia. Reprinted with permission of the publisher.

Talley (neighborhood representative), Assistant to the President Chon Glover (William & Mary representative), Emily Gottschalk-Marconi '12 (student representative) and Deputy Planning Director Carolyn Murphy (city representative).

Reveley said the College is committed to bringing more student housing on campus or close to campus. Next fall, Tribe Square will open on Richmond Road next to the Wawa and bring 56 new beds for upperclassmen in a mixed-use development of retail and apartments. The College is also committed to finding space on campus to build at least one more dorm of 200 additional beds, he said.

"William & Mary is a residential campus. That is part of who we are," Reveley said. "Right now, 75 percent of undergraduates live on campus. I would like to see that be more than 80 percent."

A major issue, everyone agreed, is the impact of absentee landlords who don't take care of their property, take advantage of student renters, and treat their rental units as simply a money-making business. One idea floated to the committee was developing a website where students could evaluate landlords and report problems with specific rental units.

Reveley agreed a website to evaluate students' experience with rental properties was a good idea. He also said neighbors must continue to work with city officials to deal with houses that are eyesores and operated in ways that degrade the neighborhood, often houses owned by absentee landlords.

"The Neighborhood Relations Committee can be powerful means of helping on all fronts," said Reveley. "We need to breathe life into it."

The following information was provided by a joint news release by the City of Williamsburg and the College of William and Mary, dated December 11, 2009, that explains both the City's and the College's recommendations relative to their respective reasons for forming this joint neighborhood committee. The roles of the various stakeholders are shown, as well as the final town-gown recommendation.

Mayor Jeanne Zeidler speaking for the City, and President Taylor Reveley speaking for the College have jointly summarized the actions and responsibilities of their institution. They have also recommended responsibilities of others, specifically, owner occupants, student renters, and landlords. The goal is to improve relationships and goodwill among all the parties, and to improve the quality of life for all in city neighborhoods.

Recommendations

WILLIAM AND MARY

- WM will be an active participant in seeking solutions.
- President will continue meeting with Mayor and City Manager on a monthly basis.
- Senior administrators will continue meeting on a regular basis with the Morton Hall Group — citizens representing the Neighborhood Council of Williamsburg.
- Long term housing solutions will be addressed. WM undergraduates want to live on a residential campus. This is not the norm at most other state-owned VA colleges. WM will begin planning for additional bed spaces on campus — later this year — that will include 200 beds. WM will also continue planning for mixed use retail/residential building (56 beds) near the WaWa on Richmond Road. Presently, WM houses 74 percent of our undergraduates on campus. These additional beds will raise WM's percentage close to 80 percent, and the cost of these two projects will total more than $30M.
- Among public colleges only VMI (100 percent) and Longwood (75 percent) house more. Other examples — UVA houses 40 percent; JMU houses 34 percent and Virginia Tech 38 percent. WM will continue working with City and County on more student retail and entertainment options — New Town, High Street.
- Office of Student Affairs and Dean of Students Office will address off campus behavior issues by:
  - Distributing "How to Be a Good Neighbor" to students at the beginning of each semester that includes guide-

lines for students living in neighborhoods and tips for living off campus.

○ Establishing a website (www.wmoffcampus.com) to provide additional information about off-campus living and available housing, the City of Williamsburg Guide for Students, etc.

○ Playing a role in resolving complaints of persistent problems; such a complaint process must also involve neighbors, landlords and City Police. If a resident is unable to remedy a problem involving students after reaching out to them, the resident can call the Student Affairs Office during normal business hours at 221-1244. (Note: see Neighbors section for night time process). As necessary, the student(s) will be asked to meet with an administrator.

○ Working with the Athletic Department to assist any players creating problems off campus.

• College will review current alcohol policies as part of its review of the Student Handbook.

• Campus Police will join City Police in responding to overnight complaints involving students and will provide a report to the Dean of Students Office the following morning.

CITY

• City of Williamsburg will continue to take an active and aggressive role to promote successful, healthy neighborhoods near campus, and to promote the interests of both owner occupants and renters.

• Mayor and City Manager will continue to meet with WM President and Chief of Staff monthly.

• Senior City officials will meet with student representatives (Student Assembly and others) on a frequent basis.

• City will join the College in establishing a "Williamsburg Neighborhood Relations Committee," (as recommended by the Focus Group on Housing Near Campus) composed of city, college, student, homeowner and landlord representatives.

• City will administer its "Rental Inspection Program" to upgrade the condition and safety of rental housing.

• City will administer the "Property Maintenance Program" to improve care of houses and yards in neighborhoods near campus.

• City will enforce Noise and Nuisance Ordinances working closely with Campus Police, both with directed patrols and response to complaints.

• City will enforce the "Unrelated Person" Zoning Ordinance, and implement the recently adopted modifications to the Zoning Ordinance to allow four unrelated persons for qualified properties.

• City will educate landlords, renters, and owner occupants by:

○ Conducting annual door to door information sharing in vulnerable neighborhoods.

○ Hosting two annual "block parties."

○ Informing landlords in writing of any code violations involving their renters.

○ Distributing city produced literature such as the "Resident Guide-Student Edition" via multimedia annually.

• City will encourage and work for more student-oriented retail near campus.

• City will promote through land use designation, additional opportunities for student-oriented housing off campus but accessible to campus by walking, cycling and/or transit.

NEIGHBORS

• When students move in, neighbors will welcome and introduce themselves, discuss neighborhood needs and issues with noise, trash, etc.

• Work with City to inform absentee landlords about condition of rental properties and the behavior of tenants in those properties.

• Call the City if violations are observed of any City Ordinance.

• If issues with student renters persist after reasonable efforts to resolve, call the Student Affairs Office at 221-1244 to explain situation or ask questions.

• Encourage absentee landlords to assist renters and/or to sell to owner occupied.

STUDENTS

- Receive and review information on "How to Be a Good Neighbor" and learn responsibilities of off-campus living.
- Respond to neighbors' welcome and reasonable requests.
- Understand the College will now be more engaged through the Division of Student Affairs and the President's Office and aggressively seek remedies to any off campus problems.
- Support Student Assembly's plan to create an "Off Campus Housing Association" to further provide training for off campus responsibilities (student to student) and work cooperatively with the College, City, citizens and landlords to promote understanding.

LANDLORDS

- Provide information to tenants at beginning of rental that will assist with how to be a good neighbor.
- Take actions against tenants for violations of leases.
- Maintain proper condition of the property — cut grass, paint, repairs, other improvements appropriate to neighborhood to ensure code and safety regulations are met.

Final Recommendation

In order to better hold the parties accountable for living up to their responsibilities, and to create an ongoing forum for dialogue and new recommendations, the City and College support the creation of a "Williamsburg Neighborhood Relations Committee." This is to be accomplished before the start of the 2010 spring semester and include one representative from the College (selected by the President), Neighborhoods (selected by the Neighborhood Council), City (selected by the Mayor), students (selected by the Student Assembly President) and landlords (selected by the Mayor) to assess progress and make recommendations to improve relationships. The Committee would organize itself and meet on a monthly basis.

EDITOR'S NOTES

1. The Neighborhood Relations Committee was formed in 2009 by the City of Williamsburg and the College of William and Mary, as a result of the joint recommendation prepared by the city (mayor) and the college (president). Its mission is to monitor and encourage the contributions by various parties — the city, college, students, neighbors, and landlords — to improve the quality of life in the neighborhoods, and to build and maintain effective working relationships across the board. This group meets once a month.

2. Additional information on the Neighborhood Relations Committee can be obtained from the City's and College's websites, which are listed in Appendix B.

PART III. THE FUTURE

CHAPTER 50

Urban Renewal

Michael Porter and Paul Grogan

As America transitions to a knowledge-based economy, institutions of higher education have become engines of economic growth. While academic institutions have always been important in educating, their role has broadened and become more important. Urban academic institutions are increasingly recognized as centers of science and technology, incubators of companies, major employers, creators of housing, and purchasers of goods and services. Emerging partnerships across business, government, and academia have helped to fuel business growth and innovation in fields as diverse as computing, telecommunications, and health care. In many respects, the bell towers of academic institutions have replaced smokestacks as the drivers of the American urban economy.

While the broader influence of universities on the regional economy is becoming better understood, the role of universities in urban areas and economically distressed inner cities remains relatively unexplored. Many of the country's colleges and universities are located in or near poor urban areas. They have much to offer to the economic revitalization of these areas. Many of their operating and academic activities can materially impact the economic vitality of surrounding communities. With more economically vibrant surroundings, these institutions can more readily attract high-quality students and faculty. Greater economic vibrancy and more successful academic institutions will in

turn contribute to the competitiveness of the broader urban and regional economy. Unlike mobile corporations, colleges and universities are largely guaranteed to stay in their present locations. They are enduring components of urban economies and can become leaders in enhancing urban vitality.

Though there are initial efforts, much more can be done to redirect colleges and universities to strengthening our cities. To showcase some of these initiatives and to expand on them, the Initiative for a Competitive Inner City (ICIC) and CEOs for Cities have joined forces to understand and advance the role of colleges and universities in urban and inner-city economic development. This study identifies opportunities and develops a framework for action.

The study was based on an extensive literature review, expert interviews, a survey of 20 colleges and universities, and two in-depth case studies of Columbia University in New York City and Virginia Commonwealth University (VCU) in Richmond. The 20 institutions were selected based on the findings in the literature review and interviews with experts in the field who cited pioneering efforts of these institutions. For the 20 that we focused on, we also tried to balance geographic and institutional diversity, ensuring that we have institutions from the South, the West Coast, the East Coast, and the Midwest, as well as community, state,

Originally published as "The Opportunity," *Leveraging Colleges and Universities for Urban Economic Revitalization: An Action Agenda*, March 2002, by the Initiative for a Competitive Inner City and CEO's for Cities, Boston, Massachusetts. Reprinted with permission of the publisher.

and private institutions. The two in-depth case study universities were selected for their instructive value. Columbia University, specifically, shows how an urban-based university can align its interests with those of its surrounding community, creating a strong "win-win" relationship. VCU, moreover, shows how such an institution can take not only local but also regional leadership in anchoring economic growth.

This initiative confirmed previously held (but loosely based) beliefs and revealed some surprising insights, including these findings:

- Leveraging academic assets in urban economic growth strategies remains one of the greatest untapped urban revitalization opportunities in the country.
- Academic, public, private, and community leaders are joining together in new, innovative, and bold partnerships to promote urban and inner-city economic development as never before.
- More can be done to accelerate the formation of these partnerships to rebuild our urban communities.
- Economic development opportunities arising from these partnerships do not require massive funding or heroic changes in day-to-day operations of colleges and universities, governments, or community groups.

The Untapped Economic Resource

Despite their considerable size, colleges and universities are often an overlooked component of urban economies. Their impact on these economies can be enormous. More than half of all the colleges and universities in the nation are located in the urban core: central cities and their immediate surroundings. They have significant purchasing power, attract substantial revenues for their surrounding communities, invest heavily in local real estate and infrastructure, are major employers, and help to train workforces and nurture new businesses.[1]

Colleges and universities are key players in nurturing or incubating new businesses, especially ones that are on the cutting edge of today's economy. In fact, universities in urban areas are helping to place cities at the frontier of economic growth and competitiveness. Close to 19,000 licenses of innovations made at academic institutions were active in 1999. In the same year, with only 25 percent of these licenses generating revenue, they contributed to over $40 billion in economic activity and supported 270,000 jobs. Business activity associated with the sales of these products is estimated to have generated $5 billion in tax revenues at the federal, state, and local levels.[2]

The more than 1,900 colleges and universities in the urban core spent a total of $136 billion on salaries and goods and services in 1996 — nine times greater than all federal spending on urban job and business development in the same year.[3] Many of these institutions generate considerable inflows of resources to the local area. For example, for every nine dollars that Brown University spends in Rhode Island, only a dollar comes from sources inside the state.[4] In 1999, Harvard University spent a billion dollars more in the Boston metropolitan area economy than it raised in tuition and fees locally.[5]

Urban colleges and universities directly impact economic growth in their surrounding areas. They hold vast amounts of real estate. In 1996, the original purchase price of land and buildings held by urban-core colleges and universities was $100 billion (current market value is several times greater), a net increase of $8 billion from the prior year.[6] Almost all of the 20 colleges and universities interviewed for this study had major capital improvement projects in progress, with estimated cost of over $800 million for the largest project.

Colleges and universities are also major employers. They offer a large number of stable, well-paying jobs. Nationally, colleges and universities employ nearly 3 million workers, with 65 percent working in urban areas. In the greater Boston area, the 65 colleges and universities employ more than 94,000 people — 5 percent of regional employment. Significantly, colleges and universities are among the fastest-growing employers in the country. Analysis of nationwide industry clusters shows that Education and Knowledge Creation is the second fastest growing cluster in the country. Colleges and Universities are by far the fastest-growing industry within that cluster, adding 300,000 jobs between 1990 and 1999.[7]

Aside from direct employment and purchasing, these institutions can be indirectly responsible for significant economic impact. For instance, 25 years ago, before the creation of the Medical School at Brown University in Providence, the vast majority of Rhode Island residents traveled outside of the state to receive tertiary medical care. Now the trade balance has completely reversed. People come from all over the region to receive expert care — making Health Care a major export industry for Providence and the state's leading sector.

New Civic Collaborations

While business, government, and universities have always coexisted in our nation's cities, proximity alone has infrequently led to concentrated efforts to boost business and job growth. Institutions across sectors have not always perceived nor pursued common interests and have, at times, adopted adversarial positions on issues related to economic development. Chronic disputes over issues ranging from land use to academic institutions' tax-exempt status have too often led to deep skepticism by communities about the benefits of colleges and universities to the local economy. Colleges and universities, for their part, have seen cities and communities do little to enhance — and much to impede — the growth and competitiveness of their institutions.

Yet in recent years, the growing importance of technology, combined with new thinking about economic development, has in the best cases led to significantly closer ties between the sectors. Metropolitan areas with robust cross-sector alignment such as Austin, San Jose, and the Research Triangle in North Carolina demonstrate the extent to which economic growth can be realized when these sectors engage in collaborative and collective growth strategies. In order to better compete, institutions across sectors and across the country are

coming together to resolve issues of contention and to form new partnerships. Key among these issues of overlapping interests is the revitalization of our urban economies.

Colleges and universities play an invaluable role in promoting many elements of a healthy inner-city economy. They have, for many years, worked to improve urban schools, offered health and legal services to the urban poor, and have more recently become active in urban housing. These types of public and community service have been core to the operating and learning agenda of colleges and universities.

As they begin to recognize the value of local engagement and collaboration, colleges and universities are stretching beyond traditional faculty and student community service. Several universities are now taking an active interest in the economic development of their local communities through business and job growth. These institutions are following a new path of "enlightened self-interest," recognizing that the economic competitiveness of their communities directly correlates to the health of their institutions and vice versa.

Colleges and universities have much to gain by partnering with local leaders to improve the economic well-being of their communities. Indeed, this report suggests that the destinies of city and university are closely intertwined. Just as colleges and universities are in increased competition with one another to attract and recruit high-caliber students and faculty, so their cities are in increased competition with urban areas around the world to grow and retain businesses. Just as colleges and universities seek to build and maintain healthy endowments and research funding, so their cities seek to nurture and develop a financial and intellectual capital base to sustain and accelerate economic development.

Business, government, academia, and community groups frequently partner on a variety of economic and social issues. However, these partnerships have largely been missing from inner-city economic revitalization. This has been caused in part by a lack of a useful framework to guide action. This report offers a roadmap by which colleges and universities might join forces more closely with business and government in pursuit of their increasingly common destiny.

A Call for Action

ICIC and CEOs for Cities hope to encourage urban colleges and universities to accept our call for a new urban agenda. We are optimistic that many institutions will be inspired by the examples in this report to further advance economic opportunities for all citizens. While this is an ambitious agenda, we offer the following bite-size action steps:

College and University Leaders Can:

1. Create an explicit urban economic development strategy focused on the surrounding community. The strategy should mobilize the multiple ways in which colleges and universities can create economic impact and ultimately advance their own interests.

In many successful instances of university engagement, the college or university president, with board-of-trustees support, has advanced an economic development strategy to integrate university interests with those of the surrounding community. President Rupp of Columbia University initiated an economic development strategy to channel more university purchasing and contracting to businesses in Upper Manhattan. Through dialogue with the community and including its interests, Columbia University has achieved results unimaginable just a few years ago.

2. Include meaningful community participation and dialogue in formulating this strategy.

As many examples illustrate, meaningfully incorporating community input, particularly in university expansion plans, enhances the operational efficiency of the university. Plans get approved faster, avoiding costly political battles with the community.

3. Charge specific departments and offices with explicit economic development goals.

The University of Pennsylvania and Columbia University, for instance, incorporated explicit economic development goals for purchasing departments. At Penn, purchasing staff performance evaluation is in part based on meeting local purchasing goals. Meeting these goals often involves embracing a change in practice, such as making purchasing protocol small-business friendly.

4. Create a high-level coordinator to oversee and advance the effort.

To ensure continuity and political support, a college or university president should create a coordinator to implement the institution's economic development strategy. This person should be directly accountable to the president. For example, at the University of Illinois at Chicago, its Great Cities community engagement program was initiated and grew rapidly because there was a special assistant to the chancellor in charge of coordinating the entire program.

5. Deploy college and university leadership to serve on the boards of business associations, community organizations, and public-sector bodies.

College and university leaders should seek to serve at the highest levels of local and regional leadership bodies. Virginia Commonwealth University President Eugene Trani served as the chair of the Richmond Regional Chamber of Commerce. This further strengthened the impact of VCU on the local — as well as the regional — economy. The president and high-level executives of the Florida Community College in Jacksonville serve on a number of local and regional business boards, giving them first-hand knowledge of employment trends.

6. Think long-term.

Colleges and universities have to contend with two major hurdles when engaging with local communities. First, they often encounter initial resistance and skepticism. Second, while there may be short-term, quick hits that help set relationships on the positive path, most economic development takes a long period to show results. To have meaningful impact, some university leaders interviewed suggested taking a 10-year view.

Mayors Can:

7. Incorporate colleges and universities in short-term and long-term economic development strategies of their cities.

Colleges and universities are often missing

from a local government's inner-city economic growth strategy. Mayors should incorporate college and university leadership to advise on future direction and bring to bear their considerable purchasing, employment, real estate development, business incubation, advising, and workforce development resources.

8. Convene college and university presidents and business leaders regularly to identify and further economic development partnerships and opportunities.

Our research showed that regular interaction between mayors and college and university presidents is the exception, rather than the rule. Regular interactions among public, private, and academic leaders accompany greater success in forging partnerships.

9. Establish a college- or university-liaison office to advance collaboration and economic development.

Aside from regular, high-level convening, mayoral-university liaison offices can be critical to identifying and acting upon economic development opportunities. For example, Boston's Mayor Menino recently established a Liaison to Schools of Higher Education office to ensure continuous dialogue and collaboration with the city's colleges and universities.

Community Group Leaders Can:

10. Seek out "win-win" partnerships with colleges and universities and acknowledge these institutions' economic interests.

Instead of focusing on charitable contributions, community leaders should look for leveraged and large-scale opportunities where an academic institution can deploy its assets for community economic growth while achieving its own goals. For example, community groups can help create land-use partnerships, identify

capable local vendors to meet university purchasing needs, and screen and refer local residents to open positions at universities. This approach to partnership has proved successful for community groups to attract larger amounts of foundation or public-sector funding.

Business Leaders Can:

11. Invest with colleges and universities in real estate development, supplier development, research commercialization, incubators, workforce development, and other economic development partnerships.

12. Involve institutions of higher education in business forums, associations, and public/private initiatives.

NOTES

1. This study does not examine the ways in which universities invest their endowment funds. Part of the revenues generated from investments of endowment funds support the capital and operating activities outlined in this report. Further analyses may elucidate the potential of channeling a greater share of these investments to local economic development.

2. Association of University Technology Managers, Licensing Survey (1999).

3. ICIC/PricewaterhouseCoopers, "Inner City Business Development: Benchmarking Federal Spending" (1999). The 1996 federal direct spending on urban job and business development amounted to $16 billion.

4. Appleseed, Inc., "Partners for the 21st Century: Brown University's Economic Contributions to Providence and Rhode Island" (2000).

5. Appleseed, Inc., "Investing in the Future: Harvard University's Contribution to the Boston Metropolitan Area Economy" (1999).

6. The dollar values here represent the "book value" of the assets. According to NCES reporting rules: "Book value for institutional plant assets is the purchase or construction cost of purchased or constructed assets or the market price at the time of the gift for donated assets."

7. Cluster Mapping Project, Institute of Strategy and Competitiveness, Harvard Business School (www.isc.hbs.edu).

CHAPTER 51

Citizens

John Esterle *and* Chris Gates

Overview

Service is increasingly important within the public, private, nonprofit and philanthropic sectors. Philanthropy for Active Civic Engagement (PACE), a collaborative of national foundations, has been exploring the role of foundations in advancing and rethinking service as private philanthropy has increasingly been supporting service and civic engagement over recent decades. Evidence of the continued expansion of the service and civic engagement arena is demonstrated in recently passed federal legislation that substantially expands the public service infrastructure, a growing spirit of voluntarism, and the institutionalization of service into the core of college and universities. Many have concluded that service and civic engagement can nurture a sense of purpose and provide "real world" experiences that develop potentially marketable skills. Additionally, service enhances educational performance. Active learning eases young people's progression along an education and employment pathway.

Community organizing remains an important expression of civic responsibility. Youth organizing in particular demonstrates the next generation's interest in making their voices heard around the issues and policies that shape their lives. Various manifestations of service, civic engagement, and organizing have been incorporated into a cross sector infrastructure. Numerous entities, from small grassroots non-profit organizations to larger youth development initiatives to well-funded federal programs collectively comprise a service and civic engagement field.

In a wider context, racial and economic inequities continue to persist, only exacerbated by a lengthy economic downturn. The nature of industry and work has shifted, with knowledge and technology driving the way. The educational system is not fully prepared to adapt to an increased demand for technical skills and the need for improved school performance across the board. Low-income people and communities of color are most vulnerable within these dynamics. Innovative strategies are required in order to expand opportunities for the next generation of vulnerable communities.

While service and civic engagement have not exactly been framed as potential solutions to economic and racial inequalities and the need to expand educational and employment opportunities for low-income youth and youth of color, with creative thinking, possibilities can emerge. Involvement in service brings extraordinary learning to participants and can improve school performance, sharpen skills, and increase employment opportunities. How can some marriage between the service and civic engagement infrastructure and the need to increase educational and workforce opportunities improve the life chances of low-income youth and youth of color?

Despite the increased popularity of service

Originally published as *Civic Pathways Out of Poverty and Into Opportunity*, November 2010, by PACE (Philanthropy for Active Civic Engagement), Washington, DC. Reprinted with permission of the publisher.

and civic engagement in discourse and action, the concepts have traditionally not been adequately tied to diminishing the effects of poverty. While the service field has involved many young people, it has not sufficiently increased opportunities for low-income young people and youth of color. The basic act of engagement is important in itself; however, the potential of the service field to expand opportunities and solve critical social challenges has not been fully tapped, nor has the ability of service to transition young people out of poverty.

Under the auspices of PACE, three major foundations, the W.K. Kellogg Foundation, the Bill and Melinda Gates Foundation, and the New World Foundation, found a common interest in wanting to more thoroughly understand how service and civic engagement can strengthen pathways into and through higher education and meaningful careers for young people from low-income families and communities of color. With the support of these three institutions, PACE has commissioned this report by Marga Incorporated to assess and analyze the state of the field and inform the future of service. *Civic Pathways Out of Poverty and into Opportunity* is this report's proposed reframing of the potential value of service and civic engagement to society.

The potential role in policy in service, education, and workforce development has been well documented; however, service's potential to expand life-changing opportunities for the poorest young people has not been sufficiently studied or discussed. This report is informed by an inclusive cross-sector dialogue focused on how civic engagement, youth organizing and national service expansion strategies can improve workforce development and access to and success throughout postsecondary education. Greater connections across established fields are necessary to bring about new civic pathways that increase opportunity. This paper captures insights from various stakeholders on how the fields of service, civic engagement, community organizing, workforce development and higher education can better connect with each other and low-income youth and youth of color. Three overarching messages emerge from this research:

1. Across the country, elements of effective civic pathways exist in the form of community-based organizations, national service programs, and civic engagement opportunities. Replicating, scaling-up, and connecting these elements is the work that lies ahead;

2. The importance of civic engagement transcends charitable acts of kindness — the skill development, increased content knowledge, and self empowerment resulting from civic engagement activities foster the necessary confidence and skills for success in higher education and the workforce; and

3. Civic opportunities like national service, community organizing and civic engagement can and should be more viable opportunities for young people on the road to success in education and careers, particularly within current economic and policy contexts.

In light of these observations, this chapter proposes a variety of recommendations relevant to particular stakeholders (youth, community-based organizations, philanthropy, all levels of education, the private sector, government entities, and others) to connect, promote, and scale-up existing efforts and concepts. Each stakeholder is situated within a larger interdependent context. Each can play critical simultaneous and collaborative roles in strengthening postsecondary success and workforce development. Various formal and informal programs, policies, and networks can shape opportunities available to youth at different stages in development, but these efforts will achieve greater impact if they are strategically connected.

Additionally, the impact of service and other civic opportunities should be promoted differently. Service must be reframed as an opportunity to develop content area knowledge, as well as professional, social, and personal skills. The importance of opportunities available through service should be promoted through both government and private channels, building on the cross-sector nature of effective civic pathways.

Finally, the field should scale-up existing initiatives to more adequately include and reflect the unique needs of low-income youth and youth of color. This includes a commitment to diversifying national senior level leadership, decreasing barriers to organizational participation in national service, increasing incentives for more inclusive participation, and crafting workforce development strategies around viable industries.

This chapter is a call to build a tighter pathway across relevant fields, incorporate innovative approaches, and respond to the urgent need and opportunity to provide structures for young people to leverage civic opportunities to build their communities and the skills necessary for success in college and meaningful employment.

Background

This research was driven by the need to address persistent barriers for low-income young people and young people of color in college access/completion and job readiness. This chapter proposes new and innovative ways to better pave civic pathways to success. Based on this work, it is clear that service,[1] civic engagement, and youth organizing can improve educational and employment opportunities. Federal policy, programs, and knowledge must be connected, promoted, and scaled-up to maximize engagement among low-income youth and youth of color.

Our pursuit is distinctive in its focus on low-income youth[2]—and largely youth of color—and their engagement with civic pathways leading to higher education and the workforce through service, civic engagement and youth organizing. Methods to leverage federal policy to reduce poverty[3] and to engage the nation in service activities[4] have been addressed. Other relevant reports highlight the anticipated leadership shortage in the nonprofit sector[5] and the nature of civic engagement patterns among disadvantaged youth.[6] None of them frame service as a means for disadvantaged youth and young adults to achieve postsecondary credentials *and* meaningful employment within or outside the field. Given substantial evidence of the positive impact of service on educational improvement, it is only logical to explore service and civic engagement as essential features

of strengthening the educational and employment pathways for youth.

The Research Process

This chapter's findings and recommendations are informed by a qualitative field scan. Interviewees represented components of what we see as a civic pathway. The research stimulated a cross-sector dialogue, incorporating the voice of thought leaders, experts, practitioners, and youth in the areas of civic engagement, youth and community organizing, national service, leadership development, social entrepreneurship, philanthropy, government, higher education and workforce development. Participating foundations developed an initial list of representatives in these fields. From this group, forty-nine individuals were interviewed. An in-person dialogue among eighteen leaders in the relevant fields was convened to discuss preliminary findings. We also conducted a focus group of twenty-four participants in the YouthBuild Young Leadership Council.[7] Throughout the process, researchers took careful note of the overarching lessons learned and compiled common messages and themes. Additional perspectives will influence continued research in the months and years to come.

The Road Forward

Its potential to increase college completion rates, reform education, and strengthen America's global competitiveness demonstrates the urgency of the civic pathways concept. Stronger civic pathways can enrich national conversations on a range of issues of critical significance. Many programs already provide civic pathways to opportunity, but often not on a large enough scale. Recent legislation has expanded service opportunities, increased investment in community colleges, and created jobs; yet sufficient strategic partnerships across fields are not in place to maximize impact.

Furthermore, a large base of research and resources on higher education offer solutions to challenges facing communities, though those connections are often unrealized. Even greater civic engagement through service and organizing, increased avenues for access to higher education with supports for student success, and more effective workforce development with a proven pipeline to meaningful careers is all desirable and still needed. To achieve these ends and ensure ideas on civic pathways expressed by practitioners in the field come to fruition, the following policy and systems innovations are recommended:

SYSTEMICALLY CONNECT EXISTING PUBLIC AND PRIVATE ENTITIES IN CIVIC PATHWAYS TO POSTSECONDARY EDUCATION, MEANINGFUL EMPLOYMENT AND POSITIVE CHANGES IN COMMUNITIES

Low-income youth and youth of color are not well represented among service participants in many of the more well-resourced programs. The act of service can strengthen school performance and overall enthusiasm around progressing along a civic pathway to higher education and the workforce. Every stage of completion along the civic pathway, from high school to postsecondary and beyond, from volunteering to organizing, increases employment opportunities and potential income. Institutions of higher education require a range of capacities to improve retention and matriculation. Greater clarity and commitment in policy and philanthropy around what it takes to strengthen the overall progression along civic pathways can enhance connections across various fragmented components.

Connect programs, communities, and young people through existing infrastructure. The significant budget increase of the Corporation for National and Community Service could bring opportunities to increase inclusivity in existing federal service program. Potential philosophical alignment with the idea of service as a means to strengthen communities may open doors to dialogue. Close communication and emerging collaborations between philanthropy and the federal government, as demonstrated in the Social Innovation Fund, opens doors to creative

approaches to rethinking and retooling the service infrastructure for greater opportunities for low-income youth and youth of color.

- Diversify participation in existing federal service initiatives. Increase the representation of organizing groups, civic engagement initiatives, and workforce development opportunities among federal service partnerships. Bring program participation closer to more communities, schools, and community-based organizations that participate in these activities and support low-income youth.
- Leverage the emerging connection between institutional philanthropy and the federal service infrastructure and the White House to bring innovation to existing programs that can diversify service participation and provide greater support for the progression of low-income youth and youth of color along civic pathways.

Institutionalized promising models of civic pathways into federal policies and programs. The magnitude of the challenge of strengthening civic pathways for low-income youth and youth of color, especially in an unstable economy, requires a level of investment that only the federal government can provide. Philanthropy can provide flexible and catalytic resources to strengthen connections and innovate to complement governmental support. The strengthening of civic pathways requires leveraging existing resources as well as developing new resource possibilities. It is important to build upon success in the field. The promotion of these advances could raise awareness around various possibilities.

- Integrate promising approaches designed to strengthen civic pathways for low-income young people and youth of color (some of which are featured in this report) into existing federal programs. This could include supporting any of the components in the civic pathways diagram with particular attention to the cross-cutting themes.
- Establish or promote initiatives that explicitly engage low-income youth and youth of color in service of meaning to their com-

munities, connect these experiences to progression through secondary and postsecondary education, and limit financial barriers to college attendance.

Establish strategy and purposeful cross-sector dialogue around potential ways to create linkages to enhance civic pathways. Connecting across sectors requires deliberate attention. If the civic pathways we envision are not fully developed due to fragmentation across relevant stakeholders, conversations explicitly intending to identify strategies to refine and solidify civic pathways could lead to a range of unexplored possibilities.

- Continually convene dialogue across public programs, philanthropy, youth, community-based organizations, schools, and higher education around the possibilities, barriers, and future opportunities in greater connectivity in their collaborative efforts to strengthen civic pathways.

PROMOTE THE IMPACT OF SERVICE

Shift the perception of the pathway: reframe the discussion around "service". The act and impact of true service is deeper than what is achieved by simply volunteering, but this reality has not transformed the image of service in the public eye or in federal, state, or local legislation. Many participants in this research recommend adjusting the way advocates discuss service so that the value of these programs is accurately conveyed.

Advocates believe that particular attention should be paid to the framing of the national service debate. Currently, national service is not explicitly viewed as a means to address national priorities. At a time when government agencies are cutting costs and payrolls, service corps programs can provide support in places where human capital is sorely needed. While the youth in service programs gain valuable skills, they can simultaneously fulfill needs identified by their communities but unmet by local, state, or federal government.

- Conduct advocacy at the federal level for national service reform that reframes service in a jobs and education context. Service

should not be regulated through the Corporation for National Service and service legislation exclusively. The skills acquired in service are relevant to all areas of the workforce and should be reflected through the work of multiple government agencies.

- Incorporate service into the jobs, juvenile justice, and higher education legislative initiatives to respond to the ways in which service relates to job creation, workforce development, dropout prevention, higher educational achievement, etc.
- Partner with comparatively untapped federal agencies such as the U.S. Departments of Labor, Justice and Education to ensure a deeper understanding of the importance of service in these sectors.
- Investigate how the impact of service can lighten the load of the federal government in areas where it is already deficient. In other words, what work could participants in service programs achieve that the federal government cannot currently accomplish, due to capacity and budgeting limitations? Examples could include building civic structures and parks, fighting wildfires, trail maintenance, and education and health services.

Prioritize increasing diversity at the senior leadership level in the service sector. As noted previously, diversity in the service field remains on ongoing concern. Most service, civic engagement and community organizing groups work extensively in communities of color, and some work in communities of color exclusively and by design of their mission; however, in many situations, the leadership of service organizations does not, at least in part, represent either participants or the communities where those participants serve and work. This can strain trust, damage credibility, and limit connection in low-income, racially diverse, and immigrant communities.

- Prioritize developing and engaging leadership reflective of the communities where their participants live and serve.
- Develop a carefully facilitated leadership pipeline streaming from community-based organizations, as well as the sector more

broadly, to provide high qualified and competitive senior level leadership positioned to successfully fill these roles in the long-term.

SET YOUNG PEOPLE ON THE PATHWAY EARLY: INCORPORATE THE SKILLS TAUGHT THROUGH SERVICE, CIVIC ENGAGEMENT AND ORGANIZING INTO THE CURRICULUM AT ALL LEVELS

Evaluations of youth-serving organizations suggest the skills acquired through youth involvement with service, organizing and civic engagement shape success in college and jobs for young people from low-income backgrounds. Although research acknowledges the importance of these skills, especially in the workplace, our public and higher education systems do not prioritize these skill sets.

• Provide real opportunities for meaningful civic engagement through the public school system by developing ways for students to engage in their community and reflect through readings and classroom teaching and learning.
• Develop national standards around civic engagement that reflect the "soft skills" students learn through service to enhance their value in education circles. These could include non-cognitive attributes that have been associated with nontraditional student success, such as knowledge acquired in or about a field, successful leadership experience, realistic self-appraisal, positive self-concept, understanding and knowledge of how to handle racism, and others.

SCALE-UP EXISTING PATHWAYS FOR DISCONNECTED YOUTH AND YOUNG ADULTS

Decrease the barriers to service. Often low-income youth are the most under-engaged group in their communities due to myriad pressures in their lives, especially when constraints are placed upon the organizations and systems offering service, civic engagement and organizing opportunities. While the country does not

have a comprehensive second-chance system for youth and young adults who have dropped out of school, are ex-offenders, or are leaving the foster care system, many strong second-chance programs have begun to figure out how to use service as a strategy for reengagement and success achievement for those that have been disconnected from pathways to higher education and employment. This approach should be a priority for state, federal and philanthropic investors, especially with national service funding. Current national service programs restrict organizational participation to those that can accommodate a minimal number of volunteers — leaving out what may be a substantial number of organizations providing critically needed work in communities but without the capacity to manage such a large number of volunteers at any given time. They may also not be able to generate the required matching dollars to implement such programs. Ineligibility of some effective community-based organizations may translate into a missed opportunity for their populations.

• Reduce the matching requirement of national service programs in order to be more inclusive of small community-based organizations and the populations they serve.
• Integrate the service experience gained in national service programs with the actual attainment of postsecondary credentials. Presently, participants work towards their desired degrees independent of the knowledge and skills gained during their service tenure. Additionally, the education award is underleveraged among AmeriCorps members who have not completed college.

Increased incentives to serve by providing more options for affordable access to college to those who serve in their communities. Considering that this study is concerned with pathways out of poverty, the cost of higher education has been a recurring concern. The U.S. has historically rewarded service to country with college assistance: the GI Bill, the Civilian Conservation Corps, the Segal AmeriCorps Education award, loan deferral during participation in the Peace Corps and similar full-time volunteer programs, etc.; however, it is clear to organizations that engage low-income youth in service, civic engagement and especially organizing, that these opportunities are not widely available. Even when they are available, they do not sufficiently increase the affordability of higher education for low-income communities.

- Provide support to increase the number and geographic spread of institutions that match the Segal AmeriCorps Education Award. Currently, less than 100 colleges and universities and only one community college (the Community College of Rhode Island) match the award.
- Decrease the threshold for determining economic need and, most importantly, attach that award to proven civic engagement or service in a student's life. Ensure that civic engagement or service is not limited to AmeriCorps approved programs, allowing for students to also serve at smaller, community-based organizations.
- Incentivize full-time paid service for national service participants who are recruited from low-income communities and establish a set of transitional opportunities that allow their members to transition successfully from paid full-time service into and through college.
- Support community colleges that engage young people in civic engagement by supporting greater numbers to match the Segal AmeriCorps Education award and by financially supporting those specific departments and programs that effectively develop opportunities for civic engagement.

Craft workforce development programs around viable industries. Too often workforce development programs are training young people for careers in field that do not offer viable career paths. Young people see programs that do not reflect their existing needs or personal goals and, as a result, become disengaged. Young people with the kinds of skills developed through service, civic engagement and organizing could find meaningful work and excel in a variety of fields. The nonprofit sector, for example, is rapidly growing, as it already represents 11 percent of the jobs in the U.S. A tran-

sition to the nonprofit sector is a natural fit for civic-minded young people who want to serve in their community and adapt transferable skills.

- Provide support for workforce development programs to scale up to their nonprofit sector skill building programming and placement process.
- Engage the nonprofit sector in further developing workforce development programs tailored to the nonprofit sector to ensure appropriate skills development, as has been done in the business sector.
- Identify other sectors where employment opportunities will likely grow, and align skill sets enhanced by service accordingly.

Overall, these recommendations can increase connectivity throughout civic pathways. They can increase access for low income youth and youth of color, as well as enhance the impact of service and civic engagement on issues of national concern. This is a critical opportunity to refine the continually expanding civic infrastructure, and, in effect, usher in a new era in the rich historical evolution of service in the United States. Ultimately, this strategic leveraging of service and civic engagement can result in greater opportunities for young people, and more stable and resilient communities.

NOTES

1. Throughout this paper the terms "service," "civic engagement," and "community organizing" are used repeatedly to describe the breadth of fields under consideration. In part, this is in response to the fact that language limitations around the single term "service" sell the concept short and does not incorporate all potential civic pathways available to young people.

2. Youth is broadly defined, but the key group in the paper is ages 16 to 25.

3. Center for American Progress. (2007). *From Poverty to Prosperity: A National Strategy to Cut Poverty in Half.*

4. Reimagining Service Task Force. (2009). *Reimagining Service: Converting Good Intentions into Great Impact.*

5. Ierney, T.J. (2006). *The Nonprofit Sector's Leadership Deficit.* The Bridgespan Group.

6. Spring, K., Dietz, N., and Grimm, R. (2007). *Youth Helping America: Leveling the Path to Participation: Volunteering and Civic Engagement among Youth from Disadvantages Circumstances.* Corporation for National and Community Service.

7. Participants ranged in age from 18 to 30 years and represented rural and urban communities in 11 states. Almost all indicated that their parents had not finished high school

and only three indicated that their parents had attended college. Five have a post-secondary degree or certificate, eight have completed some college, nine have a high school diploma or General Equivalency Diploma, and two had not yet completed high school.

EDITOR'S NOTES

1. This state-of-the-art "civic engagement" project is the product of two years of conversation, research, deliberation, and writing. This background information, along with information about the publisher, PACE, and this project's funding sources, are contained on this organization's website.

2. Several pages of "findings," based on this research are also contained in this report, including some detailed graphical presentations, and a section on "additional recommendations," that relate to various state governments, as well as to the Federal government.

3. To review this material, and related reports and resources, the PACE (Philanthropy for Active Civic Engagement) website is listed in Appendix C.

CHAPTER 52

Students and Change

Deborah McKoy, Ariel H. Bierbaum, April Suwalsky, Erica Boas *and* Alissa Kronovet

Operating out of the University of California, Berkeley Center for Cities & Schools, Y-PLAN (Youth — Plan, Learn, Act, Now!) is a model for youth civic engagement in city planning that uses urban space slated for redevelopment as a catalyst for community revitalization and education reform. Y-PLAN is also a form of Social Enterprise for Learning (SEfL) project methodology developed by Deborah McKoy and David Stern at the UC Berkeley Graduate School of Education. SEfLs are school-based community-driven enterprises in which young people identify a need in the community and develop a product or specific service to address that need.

Traditionally, Y-PLAN partners graduate and undergraduate student mentors, high school young people, government agencies, private interests, and other community members who work together on a real-world planning or community development problem. This handbook is designed to provide adult allies and other interested participants with resources to develop and implement Y-PLAN initiatives.

The Y-PLAN began in 1999 as an interdisciplinary course between the Department of City and Regional Planning and the Graduate School of Education. This work builds on a long tradition of UC students reaching outside the university walls to engage with young people, schools, and the communities in which they live.

Why Urban Planning?

The Y-PLAN situates itself in the urban planning field for several unique reasons:

- Planning projects are authentic, inquiry-based learning opportunities that have a real need for community engagement — especially that which values a youth perspective.
- City planning initiatives provide important professional context and give a professional trajectory to high school young people.
- Planning offers excellent vehicles to connecting cities, schools, and communities.

Goal, Theory of Change and Core Principles

THE GOAL

The goal of the Y-PLAN is not only to engage schools and young people in community development projects, but also to foster learning experiences for all participants. The name Y-PLAN is a play on words — why plan? Why planning? Why include youth in planning? The Y-PLAN experience shows that youth can effectively participate in the development of public buildings and spaces. Unencumbered by previous models or traditional views of "how things are done," young people use their inti-

Originally published as *Y-Plan Handbook: Learning to Plan, Planning to Learn, 2010,* by the Center for Cities & Schools, University of California, Berkeley. Reprinted with permission of the publisher.

mate knowledge of the environment to provide innovative and positive suggestions. The Y-PLAN also challenges professional planners to explain what they do in terms youth will understand. Uniting young people with local elected officials, private and nonprofit housing developers, and others seeking to improve their communities forms what Lave and Wenger (1991) call "a community of practice."

THEORY OF CHANGE

There are three central conditions that lead to successful youth participation in community revitalization via Y-PLAN:

1. Authentic problems engage diverse stakeholders and foster a "community of practice" that includes local elected officials, government agencies, planners, neighborhood residents, and young people;

2. Adults share decision making with young people, valuing their input and giving them a noticeable role in outcomes; and

3. Projects build individual and institutional success that together creates equitable, healthy, and sustainable communities.

Together these three conditions constitute a framework and a theory of change for involving young people and adult allies in community revitalization and social change.

CORE PRINCIPLES

The fields of urban planning and education cover a wide range of theories and foundational principles. Now entering its 10th year, Y-PLAN builds on both of these disciplines and focuses primarily on five core principles that together serve as a building block for Y-PLAN lessons and projects.

"Community of Practice." *Everyone* involved in the Y-PLAN become participants in various community-based planning/community development projects. In a "community of practice," participants learn from each other and see how their perspectives differ while recognizing that everyone contributes something of importance and value to the process. The Y-PLAN is structured to bring out the "expertise" in everyone, from developer to city official to high school youth and principals. Thus, the

participants all contribute their various expertise to enhance understanding of the issues and to use this knowledge with activity for the community benefit.

Connectivity. How do people and places connect to one another? The built environment connects people to other people as it connects people to buildings. In urban planning, one must consider the ways in which public space encourages or discourages such relationships.

"Eyes on the Street." Jane Jacobs coined this term in her 1961 book, *The Death and Life of Great American Cities.* "Eyes on the street" refers to the need for hustle and bustle in public spaces to ensure safety made possible by "the natural proprietors of the street." A vibrant space will attract people to it, and active places are safer and more welcoming for people of all ages.

People vs. Place. Engaging in analysis of and developing proposals for urban environments requires examination of both the people that use these spaces and the design of these places. While city planning often focuses on the "bricks and mortar" construction of houses, streets, and parks, we must balance that with investments in social infrastructure, such as community programs, education, and jobs. Striking a balance between investing in the physical places and the social relationships is critical to create vibrant cities.

Place Memory. The concept of place memory reveals the reciprocal effects of place and identity. Developed by Dolores Hayden, this concept tells us that people's identity is deeply rooted in places in which we live, work, and play. Thus, places hold "memory" of its inhabitants. Yet, rarely are individual and community identities and connections to place made explicit and seen as a resource when in planning for the transformation of public places.

"Mapping into Action"— The Y-PLAN Methodology at a Glance

Y-PLAN's portfolio of activities is divided into *five modules* that guide participants through their projects and ensure that students understand what they have done and how it relates to both their education and the community. When working with new partners, CC&S customizes its activities depending on existing resources, local context, and perceived needs.

Module 1: Start Up

- Introductions
- Agreements
- Y-PLAN Framework
- Creating a Timeline

Module 2: Making Sense of the City

- Introduction to Urban Planning
- Mapping People, Places and Power
- Preparing to Make the Case
- Making the Case

Module 3: Into Action — Re-visioning Our Future

- Sources of Inspiration
- Visioning
- Understanding Physical, Fiscal, and Political Constraints
- Making a Plan

Module 4: Going Public!

- Crafting a Proposal
- Public Presentation
- Proposing Next Steps for Shared Accountability

Module 5: Looking Forward, Looking Back

- Assessment and Evaluation
- Short- and Long-Term Next Steps

How to Use This Toolkit

Who Uses this Toolkit? As stated, this toolkit is designed to provide participants and partners in Y-PLAN initiatives with a portfolio of teaching resources to be adapted to local circumstances and contexts. We have taken steps to ensure readability and usability for educators, clients, and other stakeholders interested in developing Y-PLAN types of collaborative initiatives.

How Should this Toolkit Be Used? We have created this handbook to facilitate ease of implementation and to provide a clear trajectory for Y-PLAN project partnerships. It is intended to give insight into an urban planning project "big picture" focus as it breaks down the overarching objectives into smaller goals. This handbook and a Y-PLAN project can happen over one week, 12 weeks, a year, or longer! Therefore, please adjust according to your local context, orienting yourself to the lessons provided well before you set about implementing them. We do, in addition, recognize that all communities have variable circumstances, and we encourage educators and adult ally partners to adapt their work to the local context and goals.

EDITOR'S NOTE

For more information about the complete Y-PLAN methodology and tools, and related resources, case studies, and information, visit the website for the Center for Cities & Schools, University of California, Berkeley, which is listed in Appendix C.

CHAPTER 53

Public Service

Zach Friend *and* Scott Collins

Media coverage has highlighted the oft-ignored reality of burgeoning student debt. But one aspect that is generally ignored by policymakers and the media alike is the connection between student debt loads and career choices. The results are predictable: burdened with crushing debt loads, graduates seek higher-paying professions, often in the private sector. Put simply: if you are saddled with debt, you will shy away from lower-paying, entry-level public service positions.

Loan debt has skyrocketed over the past 10 years. According to the most recent data from the National Loan Survey, debt amounts for students in the United States increased by at least 66 percent in the past 10 years, with the average debt increasing by more than $7,000. Increasing tuition costs, reduced federal and state aid, and growth in higher-cost private loan debt have all contributed to this problem.

The California Office of Postsecondary Education estimates that fees for in-state students at the University of California are 350 percent higher than they were in 1990. Nationwide, similar upward trends have been met with relative apathy on the part of most federal policymakers. In fact, the past few years have seen steady attempts to attack federal education subsidies.

While tuition costs have increased at double and triple the rate of inflation, until recently federal aid in the form of Pell grants and loans

has flattened or been reduced. Most state policymakers have decreased allocations to state colleges and universities in an effort to balance their budgets. Stagnating federal and declining state aid has required that a growing number of students take out private loans with higher interest rates to supplement federal loans.

Concurrently, baby boomers are set to retire, which is expected to result in a human resource crises, but the knowledge of significant retirements in the public sector is not likely to be of great interest to talented young employees. Saddled with massive debt, those talented and well-educated young people are precluded from even considering a public interest position. Thus, a replacement gap started in 2006 and continues today. With an estimated 151 million jobs in the U.S. economy, the U.S. Bureau of Labor Statistics reports there are only about 141 million people in the workforce to fill them. While all sectors of our economy are feeling the pinch, it is especially evident in the public sector.

A 2006 report by the U.S. Government Accountability Office, titled "Human Capital: Selected Agencies Have Opportunities to Enhance Existing Succession Planning and Management Efforts," concluded that more than 50 percent of middle- and upper-level public sector managers will be eligible for retirement in 2007. It is estimated that there will not be sufficient Gen Xers or Millennials to fill the im-

Originally published as "Drowning in Debt: Why Graduates Are Choosing Money Over Public Service," *Public Management*, Vol. 89, No. 11, December 2007, by the International City/County Management Association, Washington, DC. Reprinted with permission of the publisher.

pending vacancies. This problem is exacerbated, in large part, by the fact that many Americans, particularly those of the younger generations, perceive government work as bureaucratic and dull.

Of those who find government work appealing, the number willing to take lower-paying jobs in the public sector in the face of growing student debt is declining.

More and More Debt

In today's competitive job market, those students interested in pursuing a career in the public sector feel just as compelled as their counterparts seeking private sector jobs to acquire graduate, professional, and law degrees. With advanced degrees, however, comes greater student loan debt.

According to the Partnership for Public Service, a federal program aimed at bolstering interest in federal jobs, debt loads for master's degree candidates have *tripled* since 1993, to $30,000; for Ph.D. candidates, debt has *quadrupled* to $45,000; and for those with professional degrees, it has more than *doubled* to $65,000. These increases have been met with federal loans that cover a mere $17,125 over four years.

To cover the remaining tuition and room and board, students turn to private loans that, unlike federal loans with their current 6.5 percent rate of interest, carry variable interest rates that can soar into the credit card range — 20 percent. A typical college graduate is $19,000 in debt; attending graduate school for a master's degree will add an additional $30,000.

After obtaining a master's degree, a typical student will have accumulated approximately $50,000 in loan debt; $10,000 of that, at a minimum, will be in private loans. Six months after graduation, that student will begin to owe approximately $700 per month — for the next 15 years! On an annual salary of $40,000 (average public sector, entry-level position), $700 is 28 percent of an average graduate's after-tax monthly income! The pre-tax number is 21 percent of income, and this percentage is even higher once taxes are factored in.

The Partnership for Public Service notes that 66 percent of law students graduate with more than $100,000 of debt. Policy and public administration graduates face similar levels of debt. No wonder elite policy and law schools across America are seeing a growing number of their students pursue private sector jobs. A generation ago, almost three-quarters of graduates of public policy and public administration programs went to work for government. In recent years, only about half have chosen public service.

Even the prestigious Kennedy School of Government at Harvard University has witnessed these trends. Overall, public sector employment for its graduates has steadily declined from 55 percent in 1988 to about 34 percent in 2000. At the state and local levels, the numbers are far more discouraging.

In 1988, 13.5 percent of Kennedy School graduates took state jobs while 10.4 percent accepted jobs with local governments. In a matter of 12 years, those numbers had declined to 1 percent and 6.5 percent, respectively. Quite simply, private sector positions offer greater financial rewards to students facing large debt payments.

Growing Wage Disparity

Phil Primack writes in "Private Gain, Public Loss" that many students have found other outlets for their public service orientation, many of which offer greater financial compensation. This is a function of the growing wage disparity between the public and the private sectors for entry-level jobs.

"In 1970, when starting teachers in New York City made just $2,000 less than starting Wall Street lawyers, people who wanted to teach, taught," Daniel Brook, a noted author on the subject, explains in *The Trap*. "Today, when starting teachers make $100,000 less than starting corporate lawyers and have been priced out of the region's homeownership market, the considerations are very different."

Joseph A. Ferrara, a professor from the Georgetown Public Policy Institute, notes that a master of public policy (MPP), master of public administration (MPA), or law graduate accepting a Presidential Management Fellowship in the federal government will start with an average salary around $40,000, with comparable salaries found in state or local government. That same graduate, however, might receive a starting salary offer of $60,000 from a private consulting firm or $125,000 from a private law firm.

The increase in graduates' debt load is a threat to federal, state, and local government's ability to recruit and retain top talented employees. Local governments, similar to state governments and the federal government, simply cannot compete with the private sector in the recruitment of talented employees. Paul Brinkley, career adviser for George Washington University's School of Public Policy and Public Administration, notes that choosing a higher-paying position in the private sector is a function of student debt loads.

This situation led Paul C. Light, author of *The New Public Service,* to lament: "Ultimately, effective governance is impossible if government cannot attract talented citizens to serve at all levels of the hierarchy."

Solutions

Fortunately, policy options exist that can help remedy this situation. The following are proposals that work within current policy parameters and do not create any new significant bureaucratic programs. From a recruitment — and economic — standpoint, incentives are the key.

The first method of expanding the public sector workforce would be a two-pronged approach: enhancing appropriations and improving tax incentives. Specifically, this option would expand appropriations for the student loan repayment program to cover state and local government employees as well as provide tax incentives that make public sector employment more attractive. The goal would be to cover as many public employees as possible, including police officers, firefighters, and teachers, while providing both an educational and financial incentive to join the public sector.

The tax incentive program would hinge on the ability of state and local governments to create tax-deferred compensation programs through section 457 of the U.S. tax code. This allows for money to be automatically deducted from an employee's paycheck on a pre-tax basis. The same model could be applied to federal student loan debt. All public sector employees would have the opportunity to pay off their federal student loans automatically with pre-tax money.

The resultant benefit is twofold: employees would receive a direct economic benefit from the reduction in taxable gross wages, and public agencies could advertise a significant financial recruitment benefit. In addition, it is conceivable that the default rate, although already low, would drop even lower as debtors would be less likely to default on automatic payments. Thus, lower tax revenues to the U.S. Treasury would be partly offset by the reduction in defaults.

The second proposal involves increased federal appropriations to cover loan repayments for public sector employees. Again, this does not need to be an expensive program, and it does not need to create any undue bureaucratic burden. Costs could be minimized by phasing out reimbursement rates as incomes encroach on private sector rates, but the tax incentive could be maintained regardless of income. It would be essential to work with currently established tax and educational incentive channels to minimize bureaucratic costs.

Reimbursement rates could be standardized for ease of distribution and to provide a relative incentive to accept lower-wage public positions. As with any programmatic expansion, there are bound to be economic costs and potential benefits. In this case, initial economic costs should be outweighed by the long-run benefits of well-educated workers entering the public sector and their increased disposable income.

The third policy concept focuses on universities shouldering more responsibility. Currently, some schools have loan forgiveness programs for students who enter public service or loan reimbursement programs for graduates who seek public interest careers. These programs are an excellent start but are neither common enough in number nor adequate enough in reimbursement rates.

Often these programs, the vast majority of which are at high-priced private institutions, have low phase-out rates, meaning unreasonably low salary caps preclude meaningful participation. Universities, public and private, need to make a commitment to students who work in public service.

Finally, income tax deduction caps, currently set on an annual income of $60,000 for a single and $120,000 for a family, need to be increased. As the wage gap between public and private employment grows, the income tax deduction of loan interest needs to be increased to lessen that gap — even at higher income levels. This will provide those in public service with a longer-term incentive to stay in the public sector, and middle-level and executive managers will not leave the field as their incomes increase.

It is our belief, and that of many experts, that student loan debt poses a threat to the continuity of leadership in governments at all levels. The federal, state, and local governments in the United States need to recruit top talent, particularly from top law, policy, and public administration schools, to ensure their viability.

More important, the country as a whole benefits when its government ranks are filled with the best and the brightest. This problem has no quick fixes; it will take a combination of solutions to make possible greater participation in the public sector by civic-minded young professionals.

CHAPTER 54

Technology

Maria H. Andersen

Humans have always been learning, but how we learn has changed over time. The earliest means of education were highly personal: Oral histories passed from adults to children, informal or formal apprenticeships, and one-on-one tutoring have all been used in the early history of most cultures. It's only been in the last two centuries that we've used formalized systems of mass public education (aka industrialized education).

Certainly, personalized learning is the more effective method. In 1984, educational researcher Benjamin Bloom found that average students who were tutored one-on-one outperformed 98 percent of students who were learning via conventional methods (this is referred to as Bloom's two-sigma problem). However, personal learning is not cost-effective, and so we currently educate students in batches of 20, 30, or even 200 students at a time. This is likely to get worse before it gets better, with prominent philanthropists like Bill Gates declaring that "the best lectures in the world" will be online within the next five years. Certainly we can use technology to deliver those lectures to thousands, or even millions, of students at a time, but a lecture does not automatically produce learning any more than attending a class does.

Mass education is adequate, as long as students are highly motivated to learn and get ahead of their peers. In developing countries, a student who is successful in education will be able to climb the ladder of personal economic prosperity faster than those who are not successful. But in industrialized countries, where prosperity is the norm, an education does not necessarily translate into a significantly higher standard of living. In these countries, there is no longer a large economic incentive to learn, so the motivation to learn must become intrinsic. As we redesign en masse education, we must address learners' intrinsic motivations, which means that education must circle back to being personal again.

The vision of a modern education built around personalized learning is not new, but it is definitely tantalizing. Neal Stephenson's novel *The Diamond Age* (Spectra, 1995) shares a vision of personalized learning in the future via an interactive book that possesses a conversational interface (CI) and "pseudo-intelligence," a kind of artificial intelligence (AI) that is inferior to human intelligence. It's likely that we'll see decent conversational interfaces within the next decade, and certainly applications like Google Voice are moving us much closer to this reality. AI that is capable of directing the learning needs of a human will take much longer, developing in the next 20–50 years, but we can't wait that long for the technology to catch up with education. The need for personalized learning exists in the here and now. So how does one bridge this vision of the future with the realities of the present?

Originally published as "The World is My School: Welcome to the Era of Personalized Learning," *The Futurist*, Vol. 45, No. 1, January/February 2011, by the World Future Society, Bethesda, Maryland. Reprinted with permission of the publisher.

Learning Technologies Today

Let's start by taking stock of the personalized technologies for information that we already have. We have software that stores the content we like (e.g., Evernote, Posterous) and software that merely stores the location of that content (e.g., Diigo or Delicious). Even traditional media, like books, now have parallel digital systems that allow for note taking, highlighting, and bookmarking (e.g., Kindle, Nook, or iPad). While it's useful to store and search information, I would venture that we rarely go back to look at the information we mark for storage.

This is a problem; for deep learning to occur, we need to have repeated exposure to the information, along with some time in between for reflection. We need to give our brains a repeated opportunity to process the information we take in so that it becomes knowledge, understanding, and wisdom. This means we're going to have to find time in our busy lives to reflect on the information that flows past us on a daily basis, and we're going to need some kind of technology that keeps us on track with our learning goals.

While it seems outrageous that we could find any more time in our busy lives, consider some of the disruptive changes we've seen quite recently that affect how we spend our free time. Facebook, now with 500 million users, has disrupted normal social interactions in a little over six years. Micro-blogging exploded when a Web site simply invited us to answer the question: What's on your mind? Twitter users now send more than 50 million tweets per day, and big news stories break first on Twitter — in real time and with eyewitness accounts. As big as Twitter is, there were more people playing Farmville (a social media game on Facebook) at its peak than there were active Twitter users — a fact that has not gone unnoticed by game designers and educators. These Farmville players are choosing to spend their free time for collaborative activities (their "cognitive surplus," as media scholar Clay Shirky puts it) plowing virtual soil and planting virtual crops.

These innovative social disruptions have happened quickly, but not from within the existing organizational structures. For example, Facebook did not disrupt phone communication by changing the nature of phone calls or phones. Facebook built an entirely new system that eventually circled back around to phones by the way of phone apps. In the same way, the trick to developing a personal learning system is to abandon thinking about how to build it from within the existing educational system and to begin pondering how such a system could be developed outside of education. Educational institutions form a vast interconnected network, and while small changes can occur within the system, individual parts only have the ability to flex within their existing boundaries. For a personalized learning system to take hold inside education, it will have to be built on the outside.

A Simple Idea: Learn This

Let me propose a realistic scenario of what a true personalized learning system might look like and how it would function. We first have to create (1) a new layer of learning media in the background of the existing Internet and (2) an ecosystem of software to easily manage the learning media we engage with. In the same way we've integrated buttons like Twitter's "Tweet this" and Facebook's "Like" at the end of videos, articles, and other media, imagine we now add a button for "Learn This." Clicking this button (anywhere you find it) would bring you into an interface to help you learn the content.

We don't need a humanlike artificial intelligence to begin this journey. The technology for such a journey already exists and is simple enough to use with traditional learning methods. In the first version, learning should simply be by way of Socratic questioning, where questions are used to analyze concepts, to prod at the depth of knowledge, and to focus on principles, issues, or problems. Socratic questions are elegant because, unlike with other formats (e.g., multiple choice), learners must self-generate the answers rather than rely heavily on the ability to recognize a correct answer when they see it. The personal learning system would use a spaced repetition algorithm (SRA) to reintroduce the Socratic questions over time so that biological memory is more likely to grasp onto the ideas and information. For now, let's call this system SOCRAIT (a play on "Socratic" that includes SOC for *social,* AI for *artificial intelligence,* and IT for *information technology* within its name).

For example, suppose I read an article about digital copyright in educational settings, and I decide that it's important for me to remember some of the details of this article. At the end of this article, I choose "Learn This" to add a question to my SOCRAIT question bank. Two options would appear: (1) write your own question or (2) choose from a list of questions written by others. If I choose the first option, I might write a simple question and answer for myself: "What are the allowable uses for copyrighted video in an educational setting?" Following this, I'd write a short summary or clip a few sentences of content from the article to summarize the answer to the question. Along with the question and answer, SOCRAIT would save the source URL (link to the content), and I could tag the question with metadata tags I indicate (e.g., *copyright, digital copyright,* and *education*).

Later in the day or the week, when I have some down time, I could reengage with SOCRAIT. Here's how it would work: I read or listen to a question, answer it in my head or out loud, view or listen to the answer, rate my understanding, and go to the next question. Since the learning is tailored to intrinsic motivations, learners could rate their own ability to answer a question (e.g., 1 = I have no clue, 2 = I knew some of it, and 3 = I nailed it!), and SOCRAIT could make decisions based on these ratings. If your rating of understanding is low or spotty, the system would offer to send you back to the source for another look. Notice that there is no need to develop software to verify the answers to questions — if you aren't good at rating your own understanding (we call this metacognition), this will come out later in the process, and you'll have to learn to get better at it.

With a rudimentary computer interface, like the one implemented in Google Voice, there's no reason why SOCRAIT couldn't be voice-based and available anywhere we interact with computers (e.g., cell phones, tablets, auto navigation systems). This would allow us to improve our learning while performing other tasks: commuting to work, making dinner, or walking the dogs.

Initially, the so-called "Pareto's Vital Few" (the 20 percent of people who get 80 percent of the work done) would be the ones who would be most interested in creating and engaging with questions. But as the connectedness of the system matures, the need to write your own Socratic questions would lessen. Authors and media creators would write their own questions, targeting comprehension of important ideas and facts. Media consumers would be able to choose from a list of questions, perhaps seeing a sorted list based on their indicated learning priorities. Two readers of the same article would see different questions at the top of their "suggested questions" based on tags of the content. In some cases, the user might choose to pay for curated or reputable content so that their learning can later be certified by an employer, educational body, or organization.

Personal Learning's Implications for Education

Now let's take a step back and look at the big picture. Any content that exists on the Internet (or is connected to the Internet) would be tagged with Socratic learning questions and metadata for subjects. Learners would have their own bank of questions, personalized to their own learning interests. As a result, instead of learning that is designed around a physical place (e.g., schools), an educational space (e.g., learning management systems), or a person of authority (e.g., instructor), this system is designed around the learner.

It goes without saying that the implications for education are huge. In the space of a few years, we could develop a completely separate content learning system that's incredibly flexible and personalized to the interests of the learner. The architecture needs to develop organically around Web-based content and grow tendrils into everything we produce in the future. It will take some time to go back and create a learning layer to integrate with all the content that we already have, but as we've seen from projects like Wikipedia, there are people willing to contribute their time and energy to these kinds of tasks. Wikipedia became the largest encyclopedia ever assembled within a mere six years after its creation, and was built using less than 1 percent of the time that Americans spend watching TV every year (as calculated by Clay Shirky).

A system like SOCRAIT has the potential to benefit other industries outside of education. For example, modern journalism has been struggling with a problem of income stream. While revenue has shifted to online advertising, it is not enough to shore up the industry. At present, the vast majority of Internet content is free and, as Chris Anderson argues in his book *Free* (Hyperion, 2009), it's not likely to change. How do you get readers (or viewers) to pay for something that they already get for free? The answer: Add something to the content that's not already there. If readers or viewers had the ability to quickly add reputable questions to their learning bank, this would be a value-added service. Cleverly, the media content would remain free, but access to the question bank would require a one-time payment or ongoing subscription by the consumer. This would certainly help modern journalism (or the textbook industry) to shore up their revenue stream.

A New Learning Ecosystem

Books like Nicholas Carr's *The Shallows* (W.W. Norton, 2010) cause us to question whether we might be trapped on the information superhighway — stuck on the line between data lanes and unable to scoot forward or backward. Twitter users regularly use the phrase "drink from the fire hose" when referring to their experience of dipping into the live data stream. Information, whether it be from radio, television, print, Web media, or social networks, is coming at us too quickly; all that most of us can do is surface-skim, rarely pausing to reflect or think deeply. To learn, to analyze, to

innovate, and to think creatively, we must internalize some of the information we process.

An entirely new ecosystem could grow up around this Socratic learning system. Certainly a ratings system for questions could be built using the technology developed by companies like Netflix. For example, "Your friends John and Iveta chose this question. Would you like to see other questions/media they chose for this topic?" If you choose to do so, the questions you see when you add content to your question bank could be filtered by your existing social networks. Rather than showing all the possible questions in existence for that media (which could become a fairly lengthy list), you could choose to see only the ones people in your social network have also used.

So far, I've discussed how the system would work if you engaged in reading and watching media as you do today. However, such a system could also shift how and when we seek out content. After all, a lot of time is wasted in modern education by re-teaching content that some of the learners already know. There is no incentive for students to get ahead when the reward is sitting through a lecture on something they've already learned.

Imagine: When you need to learn something new, you could subscribe to a curated collection of questions on that topic. For example, "Digital Copyright 101" might be a collection of questions developed by somebody who teaches digital copyright policy to beginners. The truly fascinating shift is that you wouldn't necessarily start by consuming the media that goes with the questions. Instead, you would simply start answering the questions in your bank. As you encounter learning questions that you can't answer, you could dive into the content at those points in time — this is the exact point between boredom (with things you already know) and frustration (with things you don't know), the point to engage in learning.

Testing Knowledge Acquisition

Almost immediately after the personalized learning architecture is in place, we will need a new educational industry tasked with certifying knowledge and understanding. For lack of a better name, let's call these folks "Socratic scholars." Their job will be to rate how well you know what you claim to have learned. For example, let's say I've engaged with and theoretically learned 500 tagged questions on biochemistry to prepare for teaching a new class. In order for this to count toward my professional development hours, my college asks me to certify the learning. I pay for a Socratic scholar who specializes in chemistry to rate my knowledge. We meet either in person or via the Web (more likely) and have a discussion about the questions in my learning bank on biochemistry.

The scholar has access to the 500 questions I say I've mastered and asks me to answer a random selection. Of course, this is where it would be valuable to have reputable questions in my learning bank (from authors, researchers, scientists, and leaders in the field). Since the scholar can see both my questions and the answers (linked back to original content), it should not be difficult to ascertain whether I have, in fact, mastered the knowledge and concepts as I have claimed. Because the certification is human-to-human, and not human-to-machine, the nuances of human language would be understood. So if the language of the verbal answer and the language of the written answer don't match up exactly, that wouldn't be a problem. At the end of the session, the scholar would "grade" my understanding of the 500 questions on biochemistry, and I could provide this certification to the human resources department.

In many respects, this is a much better system than what we have today. For most certification of learning, we simply look at a transcript. If the class is listed, we assume the learner has that knowledge. Of course, knowledge ages — sometimes it evolves into understanding or wisdom, and sometimes it fades out of existence. The fact that I earned a chemistry degree in 1996 does not mean you would want to hire me as a chemist today. Ideally, you'd want me to recertify before I entered the "chemist" job pool. Biological memory is not reflected in the metrics of transcripts or grade point averages.

I am not saying that this "certified" con-

tent knowledge equals the ability to function as a practitioner in the discipline. Even a diploma only indicates that the educational system has walked you through some series of appropriate paces for the discipline. Skills like critical thinking and creativity are often lost in education (especially in science and technology) because there is such an incredible amount of content to cover. However, if the content knowledge moved outside the educational system, then educators could focus on the learning that surrounds technical knowledge instead (e.g., problem solving, analysis, creativity, applications).

Let's imagine what would happen if a robust Socratic learning system was at the heart of the educational system. A learning coach (a more appropriate term for the teacher or instructor in this learner-centered environment) will designate some core material that he or she wants you to learn. For example, in calculus, I might use a set of 500 curated concept-oriented questions from a well-known calculus textbook author, with each question linking to supporting media. Every student would be working on those questions, and so, as a learning community, we'd all work on that together. I would hope that this doesn't sound like too radical a departure from normal.

This is where it changes: Because every student has different interests and career ambitions, I would also require that each student find an additional 100 questions tagged with both *calculus* and tags that are of interest to that student. For a student studying to be a doctor, questions tagged with *medicine* or *epidemiology* might be appropriate. For a student going into business, questions tagged with *marketing* or *management* might be more appropriate.

As the learning coach, my job is no longer to "deliver content" to the students. SOCRAIT does that. Now I can use my time to help students search for good questions, help them to understand the content they are learning, provide activities to help them work with the concepts or connect the material in an applied way, and foster discussion with other students on these topics.

When it comes time to certify the learning for each student, it is done by an oral interview in which I have access to the common questions and the personalized questions for each student. Even if I'm not an expert on all the personalized questions, the answers are provided and the content is related to a subject of my expertise. Again, I only have to ask about a random selection of questions to be able to assess understanding. At the end of the semester, all students have learned their own personal versions of calculus, while still learning a core of common material.

Such a system has implications for lifelong learning "on the job," too. Instead of holding mandatory training, a human resources department could push out a bank of Socratic questions to all their employees about safety, new initiatives, mission statements, etc. For example, to train employees on Occupational Safety and Health Administration (OSHA) compliance, the employees would be invited to add a curated list of 40 questions about OSHA policies. Each question would lead back to a source that provides the necessary content to answer the question. After two weeks, someone in HR can act as the Socratic scholar and spend five minutes with each employee to test his or her knowledge of the policies, using a random selection of questions.

A Game Layer for Learning

Futurist John Smart writes about a coming "valuecosm" within 10 to 20 years, when we'll be able to program our apps or avatars to make decisions for us based on what we say is our set of values. The real question is whether learning can become one of our new values, especially in the United States. In 2009, The U.S. Bureau of Labor Statistics estimated that the average American adult spent more than five hours per day on leisure activities (close to three of those leisure hours watching television) and about 30 minutes per day on educational activities. Given the 10:1 ratio of leisure to educational activities, is American culture likely to embrace learning as a choice? Initially my answer was no, but then I began to think about video-game design.

Entrepreneur Seth Priebatsch spoke at TEDxBoston (2010) about building a "game layer on top of the world." What if one of the game layers we create surrounds learning? The same game dynamics used to build successful video games (e.g., appointment dynamics, influence and status dynamics, and progression dynamics) could be deployed to make learning the game itself. While this might still be a hard sell for the average adult, there will be subpopulations, such as early technology adapters, who will see the immediate value in cultivating and learning from their own question banks. Children who grow up learning with a Socratic question system might gain learning values naturally and carry these to their adult lives.

A successful Spaced Repetition Socratic Learning System (SRSLS) would have to entice you to keep to specific goals, like answering 50 questions per week or answering 100 questions with a certain tag in the next month. Any of these goals could be incentivized with points (1 question answered correctly = 1 point), incentive rewards for meeting certain goals ("you've earned your Silver Calculus badge for 100 questions learned"), and social status levels ("Maria has just become a Calculus Master — can you do it too?").

Those engaged in formal education would participate with a far greater intensity of daily questions than those who are in the workforce. However, the wise worker would continue to learn, albeit at a slower pace. Résumés would boast levels of knowledge on particular topics and stats on the intensity at which you participate in learning.

Let's Build It

A diploma has become a social signal to stop learning. In today's world, where technical knowledge doubles every two years, this is absolutely the wrong thing to do. Careers shift overnight, and industries collapse rapidly. We have to learn, and learn faster than we ever have before, in order to stay ahead of the problems we are now creating.

The content for a system like SOCRAIT already exists; it is the architecture and interface we are missing. This new learning medium needs to be an interconnected network of user-generated, or author-generated, Socratic questions with a seamless question-management interface. The architecture needs to remain open so that anyone can create questions on any content, and any developer can build applications for the computing device of his or her choice.

A system for personalized learning will not grow from inside formal education. Education is like a field that's been overplanted with only small patches of fertile soil. Too many stake-holders (parents, unions, administration, faculty, etc.) compete to promote various ideas about how to change, acting like weeds or plagues that choke off plant growth. The fresh and fertile soil of the open Web can foster the quick growth of a personalized learning system. Then, like a good fertilizer, it can be used to replenish the soil of formal education and help us to reach that "Holy Grail" of education: personalized learning for all.

CHAPTER 55

Education

John Dew

In 1972, visionary futurists Robert Theobald and J. M. Scott wrote one of the most interesting works related to education in the field of future studies, *Teg's 1994: An Anticipation of the Near Future*. Like many significant studies of the future, *Teg's 1994* was written as a work of fiction, in this case about a college student named Teg and her experiences as an "Orwell Scholar" in the year 1994.

What makes *Teg's 1994* significant is the nature of the future of higher education that Theobald and Scott envisioned and how much of it has come to pass. In many ways, Teg's *1994* can also provide valuable insights into the future of higher education that this fictional student's own children and grandchildren might encounter over the next 25 years.

Theobald and Scott were able to fairly accurately describe many of the trends in higher education that have actually occurred over the intervening 37 years. This includes a description of a worldwide computer system that provides Teg with opportunities to conduct her own research, as well as communicate with her peers; campus locations around the world that enable her to conduct her studies in different geographical settings; a faculty member who serves as a mentor, with whom she corresponds by e-mail; and pharmaceuticals that stimulate concentration and reduce the effects of adolescent hormones.

If Theobald and Scott were writing today, they might craft a sequel to *Teg's 1994* around

the following trends that are shaping the future of higher education, also commonly referred to as tertiary education in other countries.

1. Globalization of education that leads students to study outside their home country and to respect various cultural settings. This globalized education embraces English as the world language of convenience, while still supporting and honoring other languages and cultures.

2. A growing, but frustrated, need to harmonize the framework, definitions, and subject matter content of higher education programs around the world.

3. Continuous changes in technology that impact learning, including the use of the Internet, the digitizing of all the world's books, the complete transition of all technical journals to electronic format, the ascendancy of online teaching and instructional designers over classroom teaching, and the use of ever changing technology, such as iPods and iPhones to deliver educational content.

4. The changing role of faculty that diminishes their engagement in classroom teaching.

5. The changing nature of students, most of whom are already working adults who want to further enhance their knowledge and skills.

6. A continued need but a changing role for residential campuses, as they become the headquarters for global educational enterprises

Originally published as "Global, Mobile, Virtual, and Social: The College Campus of tomorrow," *The Futurist*, Vol. 44, No. 2, March/April 2010, by the World Future Society, Bethesda, Maryland. Reprinted with permission of the publisher.

and the gathering places for academic rituals and tribal events.

Globalized Learning

Education is shrinking the world, and the world is shrinking the educational enterprise. On the one hand, universities in the United States, Australia, and Europe are increasingly enrolling students from other nations while also encouraging and enabling their students to study abroad. Many U.S. institutions are establishing partnerships with universities in other countries to offer U.S. degree programs in these countries. On the other hand, China is exporting the teaching of Chinese language and culture through the establishment of Confucius Institutes at universities all around the world and increasing the quality and quantity of tertiary institutions at a rapid pace.

Higher education institutions in South America are seeking accreditation with U.S. regional accrediting bodies. Many postsecondary institutions state that preparing their students for living in a global society is a key part of their educational mission. This growing emphasis on global interaction provides much of the pressure for the second major trend, harmonization.

Harmonizing International Educational Standards

In the increasingly global economy, multinational entities such as corporations and nongovernmental organizations demand more standardization in higher education's structure and content. Corporations are already actively guiding efforts to standardize the content of curricula in key fields such as engineering and business, exerting influence on specialized accrediting agencies whose approval colleges and universities must have for credibility.

The disparities in educational structure among different nations and regions is constantly creating headaches: There is no international standard for a baccalaureate or a master's degree, for instance, and there is also wide variation among nations in quality assurance of academic programs, faculty credentials, and educational support services. These discrepancies create problems for students as they move internationally to obtain a global education, as well as for employers in assuring their workforce is properly prepared.

Despite the barriers, the pressure for harmonization mounts. It is only a matter of time before governments and multinational entities begin to establish alliances that will impose global standards in terms of structure and definitions, if the higher education community does not work this out for itself. Colleges and universities are being challenged to reexamine their historical approaches and enter into discussions that create a great amount of discomfort and discord within the complex perspectives of different academic disciplines. Efforts such as the Bologna Process in Europe (implementing comparable degrees, credit systems, and other standards) are a harbinger of what is to come globally.

The drive to harmonize can also be seen in assessment of student learning, where objective evidence of student learning based on standardized examinations will become the global norm, rather than the subjective evaluations of faculty using hundreds of different assessment methods.

Technology's Impacts on Teaching and Learning

Technology that supports higher education continues to evolve at a rapid rate. The once-valued library stacks and reading rooms full of printed periodicals are being replaced by semantic search engines, online book collections, and electronic journals.

Technology will continue to transform teaching. Freshman math classes are already being replaced by computer-based math teaching labs on many campuses. Large lecture courses are being replaced by courses taught online. Small discussion-oriented courses are being replaced by online courses with live chat rooms or asynchronous discussion boards, taking advantage of social networking to turn learning into a cooperative activity.

All of these changes support the ability of students to pursue their higher education from anywhere and at any time. Faculty are already putting class lectures onto small files for students to play on iPods and listen to while they go jogging.

New technology for proctoring students' online exams now allow students to take tests from any location under supervision. Online delivery already takes college courses to the smallest rural communities in America and to students around the world. This trend will continue and grow as young people growing up in the homeschooling movement move directly into college programs without setting foot on a campus. Online courses are also providing new access for students with disabilities and for students who want to complete an undergraduate or graduate degree while serving in the military.

"Going to college" no longer means going to a particular place for a particular number of years. It increasingly means engaging in a structured approach to higher education in whatever physical environment is most suitable for the learner.

The Changing Demography of College Populations

While most people envision the traditional 18- to 22-year-old when they hear the term "college student," that image no longer reflects the actual demographics of college students. In the United States, the college student body increasingly comprises working adults.

Fewer and fewer young people and their families will have the economic capacity, or the willingness to assume large amounts of debt, required for full-time college study, unless supported by academic scholarships. Instead, they will opt for part-time study, combining community college and online university courses to complete most degrees. The exceptions will be in the performing arts, sciences, and engineering fields, which will continue to require significant amounts of time for laboratory work or performance that cannot yet be done online. But even in these areas, there will be technical

innovations that will open up new possibilities for students to study online.

A movement toward national service could further accelerate this trend, as young people would work first and then use their education-financing benefits after their service is complete. Such a movement would accelerate the trend toward an older student body and would significantly disrupt the current model for residential campuses. As the student population continues to change, metrics that are primarily based on the assumption of a full-time 18- to 22-year-old student population that are used to evaluate tertiary institutions, such as the *U.S. News and World Report* rankings, will become increasingly misleading.

New Roles for Educators

The faculty have always been the core of the college or university, but their role is rapidly changing. The full-time faculty of the future will reflect current trends in three ways.

First, full-time faculty will increasingly serve as the guardians of a body of knowledge in their discipline. They will engage in the international discussion about the content and equivalence of academic courses and programs, working with other practitioners in their field through the auspices of specialized accrediting bodies.

Second, full-time faculty will continue to devote more of their time to conducting research and publishing or performing in their field. They will thus contribute to the body of knowledge in their field and reinforce their role as the critical evaluators of what constitutes that body of knowledge.

Third, full-time faculty will spend more time as mentors, either in the face-to-face setting or online, as envisioned by Theobald and Scott. They will teach a combination of honors courses at the undergraduate level and mentor graduate students in advanced studies and learning to conduct research.

Large institutions will continue to utilize graduate students for teaching undergraduates, but will also increasingly deploy adjunct faculty who are scholar-practitioners. The overall content of academic degree programs and the content of most courses will be guided by curriculum committees consisting of full-time faculty. These committees will ensure that programs and courses meet the international expectations required by accrediting agencies; this will ensure harmonization and compatibility of course content with the body of knowledge, enabling students to pursue their education globally.

College Campuses and "Homecoming"

Despite these trends, the residential college or university will continue to exist, even though the enrollment on campus may become a shrinking percentage of an institution's total enrolled population. Affluent parents will still value the opportunity to send their young student "off to college" as a reliable way to help them mature.

Many academic programs in the performing arts, sciences, and engineering will still require study that is best accomplished on a campus, which will help keep residential halls occupied. Moreover, many institutions will use their residential campus as the organizational glue to hold the institution together (like a corporate headquarters) and as a place to gather a critical mass of fulltime faculty and administrators.

The campus will be the home base for popular athletic programs that promote national visibility and tribal identity; as such, there may always be a need for "homecoming," as campus provides a touchstone where students may come (often for the first time to set foot on the campus) to wear the school colors.

Teg's Children

By now, Theobald and Scott's character Teg would have had children of her own, and those children would most likely be headed for college by 2020. Unlike their fictional mother, this next generation of college students really will be living wherever they want and taking many (if not all) of their courses online. They will interact with other students from all around the planet and may even complete degrees that are accredited by international accrediting agencies, giving them even more maneuverability in the global workplace.

Teg's children — and their twenty-first-century peers — truly will be the global, mobile learners that education futurists have envisioned.

Appendices

Containing ***A.*** *Glossary of Terms for Cities and Schools;* ***B.*** *Regional Resource Directory;* ***C.*** *National Resource Directory;* ***D.*** *International Resource Directory;* ***E.*** *Bibliographic and Reference Sources;* ***F.*** *Model Agreements and Documents;* ***G.*** *State Municipal League Directory;* ***H.*** *State Library Directory;* ***I.*** *Distance Learning Resources*

A. Glossary of Terms for Cities and Schools

The following list reflects those common terms frequently used to describe the relationship between municipalities (e.g., cities, towns, townships, boroughs, etc.) and schools (e.g., grade schools, middle-schools, high schools, colleges, universities, etc). At the city level the people include public officials and citizens. At the school level the people include faculty, staff, and students.

Adversarial Relationship —The negative relationship that sometimes exists between the citizens of a city and the students of a college. The joint goal (e.g., cities and schools) is to turn such adversarial relationships into harmonious and positive ones.

Appointed Officials —This term usually refers to those individuals appointed by elected officials to serve on advisory boards and commissions for a specific term of office. Sometimes school administrators and officials are asked to recommend such individuals to serve on such bodies.

Branch Campus —A term used to describe a school's location that is not "on-campus," such as classrooms available in leased office space or other school-owned facilities that are located away from the "home" or "main" campus.

Civic Use —The occasional joint use of school facilities and grounds (e.g., classrooms and parking) by citizens, such as for voting, community meetings, special events, and/or emergency shelters. This also holds true for citizens that use school recreational areas when the schools are not in session (e.g., on evenings and weekends).

Code of Conduct —Some schools have adopted a "Code of Conduct" to govern student behavior, both on and off campus. Some schools have a "Code of Conduct" for students living in dormitories, fraternity houses, sorority houses, as well as private apartments.

Collaboration —A process where groups that disagree (e.g., students and citizens) come together to identify common areas of interest, define common problems, and seek solutions that reach beyond what either one of these groups could accomplish on their own.

Commuter Colleges —A term used to describe a school, typically a college or university, where most of the students commute from home to campus, and do not reside on or near the campus, like at some schools.

Computer Colleges —A term used to describe colleges and universities that provide on-line courses and degree programs that students can take from home. There is no need to attend classes on a "main" or "branch" college or university campus.

Elected Officials —Those public officials elected by the citizens to represent them at all levels of government (e.g., municipal, county, state, and federal). Relative to cities and schools, this term usually refers to the mayor and members of the city council of the community in which the school is located.

Form of Governance —Relates to the form of municipal government. The major forms include

255

the council-manager plan, the strong-mayor plan, and the mayor-council plan. The form of government used in depends upon existing state laws, and those municipal government charters approved by the voters.

Fraternity Houses — A term used to describe male student membership organizations that usually provide housing, and are typically located "off-campus." Some schools have adopted a "Code of Conduct" to regulate student behavior at such living locations and accommodations.

Governing Body — At the city level, this involves elected officials (e.g., typically referred to as the mayor and city council), and at the school level, if it is a public school, a Board of Governors appointed by state officials, and for private schools a Board of Directors appointed by the existing Board of Directors.

Gown — A term used to reflect the school community (e.g., the faculty, staff, students), particularly the transient student population. "Gown" refers to the traditional academic robes worn by the faculty and students in British universities throughout their early history.

Harmonious Relationship — The positive relationship that hopefully exists between citizens of a city and students of a college. The joint goal (e.g., for cities and schools) is to avoid an adversarial relationship and, if one exists, to turn it into a harmonious or positive relationship.

HEI — The initials that stand for Higher Education Institution. The term that embraces those institutions that deliver primarily higher education programs, such as those provided by colleges and universities.

Host Community — The community where the school is located is considered the "host community." If a school is located in an unincorporated area, outside of a city's political boundaries, the county government would the school's "host community."

Inner-City — A term used to describe the "downtown center" of a community, typically where the school was built many years ago, and the commercial areas around it have developed and evolved over the years.

Joint Development — Two or more entities (e.g., the city and school) that form a partnership to plan, site, design and/or build a joint facility or renovate an existing one, typically for a joint use facility that will be used by both citizens and students.

Joint Use — A facility that is jointly utilized by a municipality and a school, such as open spaces, parks, and walkways used by the citizens of the community and the faculty, students, and staff from the school.

Mutual Support — The relationship that hopefully exists between the local community and the school community, and is typically fostered by the elected and appointed officials at both institutions.

Night Classes — The term used to describe evening courses offered by an educational institution. Many public and private schools offer evening classes to working adult professionals, who cannot attend daytime courses. Such courses are usually taken by the residents of a community, due to the location of the school offering such classes.

Off-Campus — A term used to describe geographic areas and events that are not held on the school's "main" or "home" campus. Sometimes students live "off-campus," if they do not live in school dormitories.

On-Campus — A term used to describe those geographic areas, where events, are located/held on the school's "main" or "home" campus. Sometimes students live "on-campus" if they live in school dormitories.

On-Line Classes — The term used to refer to the existence of on-line school classes, and on-line degree programs, offered by an educational institution. The trend towards "on-line" classes facilitates "off-campus" living, since faculty and students do not have to be located on-campus to participate in such classes and degree programs.

Payment in Lieu of Taxes — A term used to describe the non-property tax payment negotiated between a school's officials and the public officials of the community where it is located, typically for services provided to the school by the community government.

President — The administrator appointed by either the Board of Directors (for a private college or university) or the Board of Trustees (for a public college or university). For private schools the appointment process would be set forth in the by-laws approved by the Board of Directors. For public schools the appointment process would be set forth by the appropriate state laws.

Primary Grade Schools — Typically include those schools that provide educational services to students in Grades K through 6. This type of school is commonly called an elementary school.

Private College or University — This type of educational institution is governed by a President who is appointed by the Board of Directors of the school. It is "governed" by the private Board of Directors, who follow the appointment process set forth in their school's by-laws, which can be changed by the Board of Directors.

Professional Associations — Membership organizations that professionals join to advance their knowledge in their respective career fields. As related to cities and schools, or to town and gown, two of the larger national associations in the U.S. include the International City/County Management Association and the International Town & Gown Association.

Public College or University — This type of educational institution is governed by a President who is appointed by the Board of Directors of the school. It is "governed" by a public Board of Trustees, typically appointed by the Governor, as set forth by the appropriate state laws.

Public Infrastructure — Those improvements to public real property approved and by public officials at any level of government (e.g., local, state, and federal) on their respective public property (e.g., public facilities, roadways, bridges, parks, and other improvements made to publicly-owned real property).

Residential Colleges — A term used to describe those schools where most students live "on-campus" in school-owned housing called dormitories. They also consume most of their meals "on-campus" at school eating facilities, such as cafeterias.

Rural — A term used to describe the less populated and developed areas of a community.

School District — The local government entity responsible for a public school system, generally Grades K through 12 (e.g., grades school, middle school, and high school). The boundaries of the typical public school district are the same as the municipal political boundaries in which they are located.

School Infrastructure — Those improvements to school property approved by school officials (e.g., public or private) on their respective school property (e.g., school facilities, roadways, walkways, parking lots, and other improvements, made on school-owned real property).

Secondary Grade Schools — Typically includes those schools that provide educational services to students in Grades 7 through 12. These types of schools include what are commonly called middle schools (for Grades 7 and 8, and sometimes including Grade 9) and high schools (for Grades 9 thru 12, and sometimes Grades 10 thru 12).

Sorority Houses — A term used to describe female student membership organizations that provide housing and are typically located "off-campus." Some schools have adopted a "Code of Conduct"

to regulate student behavior at such living locations and accommodations.

Superintendent — The title of the typical top-level administrator of a local public school district appointed by its elected officials to manage the central office and all of the schools located within the school district.

Tax Exemption — A term used to describe the tax status of educational institutions since they are non-profit in nature, and do not have to pay property taxes, a major source of revenue for local governments. Some schools make a "payment in lieu of taxes" based on negotiated agreements with their "host" municipality.

Town — A term used to reflect the geographic area and the non-academic population of a municipality with a school (e.g., the permanent citizen population).

Town and Gown — A term used to describe the relationship and interaction that exists between the inhabitants of municipality (Town) and the faculty, staff, and students of a college or university (Gown).

Urban — A term used to describe the more highly populated and developed areas of a community.

B. Regional Resource Directory

The following list represents the municipal governments and schools included in the best practices section. They are listed categorically below in alphabetical order by their name. Additional information, including personal contacts, may be obtained from their respective organizational websites.

CITIES

Amherst: http://www.amherstma.gov/
Aspen: http://www.aspenpitkin.com/
Boston: http://www.cityofboston.gov/
Bridgewater: http://www.bridgewaterma.org/
Canton: http://www.canton.ny.us/
Chapel Hill: http://www.ci.chapel-hill.nc.us/
Charlottesville: http://www.charlottesville.org/
Chicago: http://www.cityofchicago.org/
Cutler Bay: http://www.cutlerbay-fl.gov/
Elmira: http://www.cityofelmira.net/
Emeryville: http://www.ci.emeryville.ca.us/
Gainesville: http://www.cityofgainesville.org/
Greencastle: http://www.cityofgreencastle.com/
Hamilton: http://www.hamilton.ca/
Kannapolis: http://www.cityofkannapolis.com/
Kingston: http://www.cityofkingston.ca/
Los Angeles: http://www.lacity.org/
Mentor: http://cityofmentor.com/

Meredith: http://www.meredithnh.org/
Middletown: http://www.cityofmiddletown.com/
New York City: http://www.nyc.gov/
Newark: http://www.ci.newark.nj.us/
Orange: http://www.cityoforange.org/
Phoenix: http://phoenix.gov/
Pittsburgh: http://www.city.pittsburgh.pa.us/
Plano: http://www.planotx.gov/
Portland: http://www.portlandonline.com/
Richmond CA: http://www.ci.richmond.ca.us/
Richmond VA: http://www.richmondgov.com/
Roanoke: http://www.roanokeva.gov/
Rockland: http://www.townofrocklandny.com/
Sacramento: http://www.cityofsacramento.org/
St. Paul: http://www.stpaul.gov/
San Francisco: http://www.ci.sf.ca.us/
San Jose: http://www.sanjoseca.gov/
San Pablo: http://www.ci.san-pablo.ca.us/
State College: http://www.statecollegepa.us/
Sugar Land: http://www.sugarlandtx.gov/
Tampa: http://www.tampagov.net/
Warrensburgh: http://www.warrensburgh-mo.com/
Washington, DC: http://www.dc.gov/
Williamsburg: http://www.williamsburghva.gov/

SCHOOLS

Arizona State University: http://www.asu.edu/
Bridgewater State University: http://www.bridgew.edu/
Chapman University: http://www.chapman.edu/
College of William and Mary: http://www.wm.edu/
Collin College: http://www.colinl.edu/
Columbia University: http://www.columbia.edu/
DePauw University: http://www.depauw.edu/
Elmira College: http://www.elmira.edu/
Emery Unified School District: http://www.emeryusd.k12.ca.us/
Georgetown University: http://www.georgetown.edu/
Hampshire College: http://www.hampshire.edu/
McMaster University: http://www.mcmaster.ca/
Mentor Public School District: http://www.mentorschools.org/
Miami–Dade County Public Schools: http://www.dadeschools.net/
Newark Public School District: http://www.nps.k12.nj.us/
Northeastern University: http://www.northeastern.edu/
Pearl River School: http://www.pearlriver.org/
Pennsylvania State University: http://www.psu.edu/

Plymouth State University: http://www.plymouth.edu/
Portland State University: http://www.pdx.edu/
Queen's University: http://www.queensu.ca/
Roanoke City Public Schools: http://www.rcps.info/
Sacramento City Unified School District: http://www.scusd.edu/
St. Lawrence University: http://www.stlawu.edu/
San Jose State University: http://www.sjsu.edu/
University of California: http://berkeley.edu/
University of Central Missouri: http://www.ucmo.edu/
University of Florida: http://www.ufl.edu/
University of Houston: http://www.uh.edu/
University of Illinois: http://www.uic.edu/
University of Michigan: http://www.umich.edu/
University of Minnesota: http://www.umn.edu/
University of North Carolina: http://www.unc.edu/
University of Pittsburgh: http://www.pitt.edu/
University of South Florida: http://www.usf.edu/
University of Southern California: http://www.usc.edu/
University of Virginia: http://www.virginia.edu/
Virginia Commonwealth University: http://www.vcu.edu/
Wesleyan University: http://www.wesleyan.edu/
West Contra Costa Unified School District: http://www.wccusd.net/

C. *National Resource Directory*

The following list represents major national professional associations, foundations, research organizations, and citizen associations, focusing on issues and problems relating to local governments, including their city and school related issues and problems.

Academy for State and Local Government: http://www.usa.gov/
Advisory Council on Historic Preservation: http://www.achp.gov/
Alliance for Regional Stewardship: http://www.regionalstewardship.org/
American Economic Development Council: http://www.aedc.org/
American Educational Research Association: http://www.aera.net/
American Planning Association: http://www.planning.org/
American Public Works Association: http://www.apwa.net/

American Real Estate and Urban Economics Association: http://www.areuea.org/

American Society for Public Administration: http://www.aspanet.org/

American Water Resources Association: http://www.awra.org/

American Water Works Association: http://www.awwa.org/

Association of Collegiate Schools of Planning: http://www.acslp.org/

Association for Enterprise Opportunity: http://www.microenterpriseworks.org/

Association of University Research Parks: http://www.aurrp.org/

Center for Cities & Schools: http://citiesandschools.berkeley.edu/

Center for Community Partnerships: http://www.centralfloridapartnershipcenter.org/

CEO's for Cities: http://www.ceosforcities.org/

Community Associations Institute: http://www.caionline.org/

Community Development Society International: http://comm-dev.org/

Congress of New Urbanism: http://www.cnu.org/

Corporation for Enterprise Development: http://www.cfed.org/

Council for Urban Economic Development: http://www.cued.org/

Distance Learning Resource Network: http://www.dlrn.org/

Downtown Development and Research Center: http://www.DowntownDevelopment.com/

Environmental Assessment Association: http://www.iami.org/eaa.html/

Government Finance Officers Association: http://www.gfoa.org/

Government Research Association, Stanford University: http://www.graonline.org/

Initiative for a Competitive Inner City: http://www.icic.org/

Inside Higher Ed: http://www.insidehigher ed.com/

Institute of Public Administration, University of Delaware: http://www.ipa.udel.edu/

International Municipal Lawyers Association: http://www.imla.org/

Lincoln Institute of Land Policy: http://www.lincolninst.edu/

Livable Streets Initiative: http://www.livablestreets.com/

Local Government Center, University of Wisconsin: http://lgc.uwex.edu/

Local Government Commission: http://www.lgc.org/

National Association of Counties: http://www.naco.org/

National Association of Development Organizations: http://www.nado.org/

National Association of Housing and Redevelopment Officials: http://www.nahro.org/

National Association of Local Government Environmental Professionals: http://www.nalget.org/

National Association of Planning Councils: http://www.communityplanning.org/

National Association of Regional Councils: http://www.narc.org/

National Association of Towns and Townships: http://www.natat.org/

National Association for Environmental Management: http://www.naem.org/

National Center for Safe Routes to School: http://www.saferoutesinfo.org/

National Civic League: http://www.ncl.org/

National Community Development Association: http://www.ncdaonline.org/

National Congress for Community Economic Development: http://www.ncced.org/

National Council for Urban Economic Development: http://www.ncued.org/

National League of Cities: http://www.nlc.org/

National Main Street Center: http://www.mainst.org/

National Trust for Historic Preservation: http://www.preservationnation.org/

New Partners for Smart Growth: http://www.newpartners.org/

New Urbanism: http://www.newurbanism.org/

Partners for Livable Communities: http://www.livable.com/

Partnership for a Walkable America: http://www.walkableamerica.org/

Philanthropy for Active Civic Engagement: http://www.pacefunders.org/

Regional Plan Association: http://www.rpa.org/

Smart Growth America: http://www.smartgrowthamerica.org/

Society for College and University Planning: http://www.scup.org/

Trust for Public Land: http://www.tpl.org/

Twenty-First Century School Fund: http://www.21csf.org/

Urban Affairs Association, University of Delaware: http://www.udel.edu/uaa/

The Urban Institute: http://www.urban.org/

Urban Land Institute: http://www.uli.org/

U.S. Conference of Mayors: http://www.usmayors.org/

U.S. Department of Energy: http://www.energy.gov/

U.S. Department of Housing and Urban Development, Office of University Partnerships: http://www.oup.gov/

U.S. Department of the Interior: http://www.doi.gov/

U.S. Department of Transportation: http://www.dot.gov/

U.S. Distance Learning Association: http://www.usdla.org/

U.S. Environmental Protection Agency, University-Community Collaboration: http://www.epa.gov/dced/univ-collaboration.htm/

U.S. Green Building Council: http://www.usgbc.org/

Walkable Communities: http://www.walkable.org/

D. International Resource Directory

The following list represents major international professional associations, research institutes, and resource centers focusing on issues and problems relating to local governments, including their city and school related issues and problems.

Communities & Local Government: http://www.communities.gov.uk/

International City/County Management Association: http://www.icma.org/

International Downtown Association: http://www.ida-downtown.org/

International Municipal Lawyers Association: http://www.imla.org

International Town & Gown Association, The College Town Resource Center: http://www.itgau.org/

Local Governments for Sustainability: http://www.iclei.org/

Town and Gown Association of Ontario: http://www.tgao.ca/

TownGown World: http://www.townandgownworld.com/

University Communities Council: http://www.nlc.org/

University Neighborhoods Association: http://www.myuna.ca/

Urban Land Institute: http://www.uli.org/

World Carfree Network: http://www.worldcarfree.net/

World Future Society: http://www.wfs.org/

E. Bibliographic and Reference Sources

The following subjects relate to cities and schools, or town and gown relationships, by general subject matter areas. This information was summarized from the town-gown knowledge base, The College Town Resource Center, International Town & Gown Association, which is listed in the Appendix C.

Alcohol (Cities/Towns and Schools/Gowns)

Best Practices (Cities/Towns and Schools/Gowns)

Bookstores (Cities/Towns and Schools/Gowns)

Budget and Economy (Cities/Towns and Schools/Gowns)

Campus Ministries (Schools/Gowns)

Campus Planning/Master Plans (Cities/Towns and Schools/Gowns)

Campus Safety (Cities/Towns and Schools/Gowns)

Civic Engagement (Cities/Towns and Schools/Gowns)

Community Colleges (Schools/Gowns)

Conferences (Cities/Towns and Schools/Gowns)

Economic Development (Cities/Towns and Schools/Gowns)

Economic Impacts (Cities/Towns and Schools/Gowns)

Elected Officials (newly) (Cities/Towns)

Events (Cities/Towns and Schools/Gowns)

General Information (Cities/Towns and Schools/Gowns)

Greek Life (Sorority and Fraternity Communities)

HBCU's (Historically Black Colleges and Universities)

Housing and Community Development (Cities/Towns and Schools/Gowns)

International Outreach (Schools/Gowns)

Jobs/Employment (Cities/Towns and Schools/Gowns)

Joint University-City Projects (Cities/Towns and Schools/Gowns)

Law Enforcement and Policing (Cities/Towns and Schools/Gowns)

Leadership (Cities/Towns and Schools/Gowns)

Legislation (All levels — Federal, State, County, and City)

Neighborhood Associations (Cities/Towns)

News Updates (Cities/Towns and Schools/Gowns)

Off-Campus Issues (Cities/Towns and Schools/Gowns)

Parking Issues/Problems (Cities/Towns and Schools/Gowns)

Planning and Development (Cities/Towns and Schools/Gowns)

Preservation & Revitalization (Cities/Towns and Schools/Gowns)

Service Learning (Cities/Towns and Schools/Gowns)

Social Media (Cities/Towns and Schools/Gowns)

Students (Cities/Towns and Schools/Gowns)

Sustainability and the Environment (Cities/Towns and Schools/Gowns)

Tailgating and Other Vehicular Issues (Cities/Towns and Schools/Gowns)

Technology Solution Centers (Schools/Gowns)

Traffic Issues and Problems (Cities/Towns and Schools/Gowns)

Transportation Projects (Cities/Towns and Schools/Gowns)

F. Model Agreements and Documents

The following list includes model agreements and documents. Agreements generally relate to those arrangements negotiated between municipalities and schools for joint planning, the joint discussion of issues, the provision and payment for services, the relationship between the local government and a school, and related agreements. Documents relate to important reports that contain facts relevant to city and school relationships and mutual cooperation.

Center for Cities & Schools
Institute of Urban & Regional Development
University of California at Berkeley
(http://citiesandschools.berkeley.edu/)

Program Guidelines, Policy Suggestions, and Webinars on getting schools involved in smart growth and sustainable communities

Models and Guidelines for campus-community partnerships, including the joint use of public schools

City of Burlington
(http://www.burlingtonvt.gov/)

Fee for Services Agreement between the City of Burlington and the University of Vermont

City of Clemson
(http://www.cityofclemson.org/)

Operating Agreements between the City of Clemson and Clemson University for fire suppression services, transit services, jail services, and street maintenance.

Approved agreement that created the Joint City-University Advisory Board.

City of Fort Collins
(http://www.fcgov.com/)

Proposal for a Community Liaison Program between the City of Fort Collins and Colorado State University

Job Description for Assistant Director of Community Liaison Programs, a joint program between the City of Fort Collins and Colorado State University

City of Gainesville
(http://www.cityofgainesville.org)

Agreement that formed the City of Gainesville Economic Development/University Community Committee with the University of Florida

Campus Development Agreement with the University of Florida, Alachua County, and the City of Gainesville

Reimbursement Agreement for football games with the University of Florida Athletic Association between the University of Florida and the City of Gainesville

Town/Gown Task Force Neighborhood Action Plan approved by the City of Gainesville, Alachua County, and the University of Florida

International Town & Gown Association
The College Town Resource Center
(http://www.itgau.org/)

School Reports, Papers, and Speeches on city and school topics ranging from alcohol to transportation from throughout the nation

School Reports and Papers on Civic Engagement and Best Practices from throughout the nation

Michigan Municipal League
(http://www.mml.org/)

Model State Legislation for the Creation of Educational Economic Opportunity Districts

North Carolina Association of Campus Law Enforcement Administrators
(http://www.ncaclea.org/)

Agreement for Police Cooperation and Mutual Aid between North Carolina State University and the City of Raleigh

Pennsylvania State University
(http://www.safeguardoldstate.org/)

Proposed Agreement for a Joint Student Relations Committee for the State College Borough Council and Pennsylvania State University

TownGown World
Town and Gown University Communities
(http://www.townandgownworld.com/)

Reports from City and School Officials on College Town Economics, Community Planning, and Community Reports from throughout the nation

University of Connecticut
(http://www.uconn.edu/uconnomy/)
Reports from the University of Connecticut titled UCONNOMY, that described the economic impact of the university on the State of Connecticut's economy

University of Vermont
(http://www.uvm.edu/communityrelations/)
Fire Safety Response Protocol Agreement between the City of Burlington and the University of Vermont
Payment for Services Annual Report for the payment of services provided by the City of Burlington to the University of Vermont

Virginia Polytechnic Institute and State University
(http://www.vt.edu/)
Guide for Students titled As You Move Off-Campus prepared and issued by the Virginia Polytechnic Institute and State University
Information on the Joint Town/Gown Community Relations Committee between the City of Blacksburg and the Virginia Polytechnic Institute and State University

Wikipedia Encyclopedia
(http://en.wikipedia.org/wiki/Town_and_gown/)
Brief history of the international term commonly referred to as "town and gown," including sources, references, bibliography, and website links

G. State Municipal League Directory

Most states have a municipal league, which serves as a valuable source of information about city government innovations and programs. Additional information on city and school practices is available from the various state municipal league websites, which are shown below in alphabetical order by state name (not all organization names start with the state name).

Alabama League of Municipalities: http://www.alalm.org/
Alaska Municipal League: http://www.akml.org/
League of Arizona Cities and Towns: http://www.azleague.org/
Arkansas Municipal League: http://www.arml.org/
League of California Cities: http://www.cacities.org/

Colorado Municipal League: http://www.cml.org/
Connecticut Conference of Municipalities: http://www.ccm-ct.org/
Delaware League of Local Governments: http://www.ipa.udel.edu/localgovt/dllg/
Florida League of Cities: http://www.flcities.com/
Georgia Municipal Association: http://www.gmanet.com/
Association of Idaho Cities: http://www.idahocities.org/
Illinois Municipal League: http://www.iml.org/
Indiana Association of Cities and Towns: http://www.citiesandtowns.org/
Iowa League of Cities: http://www.iowaleague.org/
League of Kansas Municipalities: http://www.lkm.org/
Kentucky League of Cities: http://www.klc.org/
Louisiana Municipal Association: http://www.lamunis.org/
Maine Municipal Association: http://www.memum.org/
Maryland Municipal League: http://www.mdmunicipal.org/
Massachusetts Municipal Association: http://www.mma.org/
Michigan Municipal League: http://www.mml.org/
League of Minnesota Cities: http://www.lmnc.org/
Mississippi Municipal League: http://www.mmlonline.com/
Missouri Municipal League: http://www.mocities.com/
Montana League of Cities: http://www.mlct.org/
League of Nebraska Municipalities: http://www.lonm.org/
Nevada League of Cities and Municipalities: http://www.nvleague.org/
New Hampshire Local Government Center: http://www.nhmunicipal.org/
New Jersey State League of Municipalities: http://www.njslom.com/
New Mexico Municipal League: http://www.nmml.org/
New York Conference of Mayors and Municipal Officials: http://www.nycom.org/
North Carolina League of Municipalities: http://www.nclm.org/
North Dakota League of Cities: http://www.ndlc.org/
Ohio Municipal League: http://www.omunileague.org/

Oklahoma Municipal League: http://www.oml.org/

League of Oregon Cities: http://www.orcities.org/

Pennsylvania League of Cities and Municipalities: http://www.plcm.org/

Rhode Island League of Cities and Towns: http://www.rileague.org/

Municipal Association of South Carolina: http://www.masc.sc/

South Dakota Municipal League: http://www.sdmunicipalleague.org/

Tennessee Municipal League: http://www.tml1.org/

Texas Municipal League: http://www.tml.org/

Utah League of Cities and Towns: http://www.ulct.org/

Vermont League of Cities and Towns: http://www.vlct.org/

Virginia Municipal League: http://www.vml.org/

Association of Washington Cities: http://www.awcnet.org/

West Virginia Municipal League: http://www.wvml.org/

League of Wisconsin Municipalities: http://www.lwm-info.org/

Wyoming Association of Municipalities: http://www.wyomuni.org/

H. State Library Directory

Most state libraries have copies of state laws relating to the various tax and revenue options available to the local governments within their jurisdiction. The amount of state funds allocated to cities is also available. The contact information for the various state libraries is shown below.

Alabama: http://www.apls.state.la.us/

Alaska: http://www.www.library.state.ak.us/

Arizona: http://www.www.lib.az.us/

Arkansas: http://www.www.asl.lib.ar.us/

California: http://www.www.library.ca.gov/

Colorado: http://www.cde.state.co.us/

Connecticut: http://www.cslib.org/

Delaware: http://www.state.lib.de.us/

District of Columbia: http://delibrary.org/

Florida: http://dlis.dos.state.fl.us/

Georgia: http://www.georgialibraries.org/

Hawaii: http://www.librarieshawaii.org/

Idaho: http://www.lili.org/

Illinois: http://www.cyberdriveillinois.com/departments/library/

Indiana: http://www.statelib.lib.in.us/

Iowa: http://www.silo.lib.ia.us/

Kansas: http://www.skyways.org/KSL/

Kentucky: http://www.kdla.ky.gov/

Louisiana: http://www.state.lib.la.us/

Maine: http://www.state.me.us/msl/

Maryland: http://www.sailor.lib.med.us/

Massachusetts: http://www.mass.gov/mblc/

Michigan: http://www.michigan.gov/hal/

Minnesota: http://www.state.mn.us/libraries/

Mississippi: http://www.mlc.lib.ms.us/

Missouri: http://www.sos.mo.gov/library/

Montana: http://msl.state.mt.us/

Nebraska: http://www.nlc.state.ne.us/

Nevada: http://dmla.clan.lib.nv.us/

New Hampshire: http://www.state.nh.us/nhls/

New Jersey: http://www.njstatelib.org/

New Mexico: http://www.stlib.state.mn.us/

New York: http://www.nysl.nysed.gov/

North Carolina: http://statelibrary.dcr.state.nc.us/

North Dakota: http://ndsl.lib.state.nd.us/

Ohio: http://winslo.state.oh.us/

Oklahoma: http://www.odl.state.ok.us/

Oregon: http://oregon.gov/OSL/

Pennsylvania: http://www.statelibrary.state.pa.us/libraries/

Rhode Island: http://www.olis.ri.gov/

South Carolina: http://www.statelibrary.sc.gov/

South Dakota: http://www.sdstatelibrary.com/

Tennessee: http://www.tennessee.gov/tsla/

Texas: http://www.tsl.state.tx.us/

Utah: http://library.ut.gov/index.html/

Vermont: http://dol.state.vt.us/

Virginia: http://www.lva.lib.va.us/

Washington: http://www.secstate.was.gov/library/

West Virginia: http://librarycommission/lib.wv.us/

Wisconsin: http://www.dpi.state.wi.us/dltcl/pld/

Wyoming: http://www-wsl.state.wy.us/

I. Distance Learning Resources

The following list reflects those organizations that provide on-line distance-learning information and resources to the public from their respective websites. This information was obtained from the U. S. Distance Learning Association and the Distance Learning Resource Network, both of which are listed in the National Resource Directory.

The Babbage Net School (www.babbagenetschool.com)
Is a virtual high school offering courses taught in a highly interactive classroom by certified teachers.

Distance Learning Exchange (www.dle.state.pa.us)
Is a free Web-based clearinghouse of distance learning and Internet project opportunities. It in-

cludes a directory listing individuals or groups who provide distance-learning activities.

The Internet Academy (www.iacademy.org)
Provides learning opportunities meeting state standards for students anywhere.

Jefferson County, Colorado, Public School District (www.jeffcoweb.jeffco.k12.co.us)
Offers online courses nationwide. Students participate in numerous group interactions in real time with other students, teachers, and mentors.

Laurel Springs School (www.laurelsprings.com)
Integrates home schooling, independent study, distance learning, and virtual schooling into a personalized educational experience.

Issues to consider when selecting an online program include the parent organization's credentials, qualifications of the teaching staff, assignment and assessment of student work, course structure and administration, and whether the college of your choice will recognize courses.

About the Contributors

The affiliations of the contributors are as of the time the articles were written.

Bob Adebayo, director of institutional research, University of Central Missouri, Warrensburg.

Steve Alexander, town manager, town of Cutler Bay, Florida.

Marni Allen, member, board of directors, 21st Century School Fund, Washington, D.C.

Maria H. Andersen, learning futurist, the LIFT Institute, Muskegon Community College, Muskegon, Michigan.

Rob Baker, professor of political science, Wittenberg University, Springfield, Ohio.

Luke Beasley, media fellow, Center for Contemporary Media, DePauw College, Greencastle, Indiana.

Ariel H. Bierbaum, senior researcher, Center for Cities and Schools, University of California, Berkeley.

Erica Boas, doctoral candidate, Graduate School of Education, and graduate fellow, Center for Research on Social Change, University of California, Berkeley.

Allen Bogard, city manager, city of Sugar Land, Texas.

Kara Brandeisky, student and features editor, *Georgetown Voice*, Georgetown University, Washington, D.C.

Laura Brown, executive editor, *The Wesleyan Argus*, Wesleyan University, Middletown, Connecticut.

Irving H. Buchen, business and education consultant, Fort Myers, Florida.

Tracy Clemmons, general assignment reporter, NBC News (WVIR-TV), Charlottesville, Virginia.

Scott Collins, budget analyst, Budget and Management Analysis Division, Administrative Services Department, Jefferson County, Golden, Colorado.

John Dew, associate vice chancellor for institutional research, planning, and effectiveness, Troy University, Troy, Alabama.

John Esterle, board president, PACE (Philanthropy for Active Civic Engagement), Washington, DC.

Mary Filardo, executive director, 21st Century School Fund, Washington, D.C.

Anthony Flint, fellow and director of public affairs, Lincoln Institute of Land Policy, Cambridge, Massachusetts.

Michael Fox, professor and head, Department of Geography and Environment, Mount Allison University, Sackville, New Brunswick, Canada.

Jason Franklin, deputy director, 21st Century School Fund, Washington, D.C.

Debra Friedman, professor of public affairs and dean, College of Public Programs, Arizona State University, Phoenix.

Zach Friend, principal administrative analyst, Police Department, city of Santa Cruz, California.

Chris Gates, executive director, PACE (Philanthropy for Active Civic Engagement), Washington, DC.

Carol Granfield, town manager, town of Meredith, New Hampshire.

Paul Grogan, chief executive officer, president, and founder, CEO's for Cities, Boston, Massachusetts.

Roger L. Kemp has been a city manager on both coasts of the United States. He is now a practitioner in residence, Department of Public Management, University of New Haven, Connecticut, and a distinguished adjunct professor, Executive MPA Program, Golden Gate University, San Francisco, California.

Alissa Kronovet, research associate, Center for Cities and Schools, University of California, Berkeley.

Christine Legere, correspondent, *The Boston Globe*, Boston, Massachusetts.

Mike Legg, city manager, City of Kannapolis, North Carolina.

Carrie Makarewicz, doctoral candidate, Department of City and Regional Planning, and graduate student researcher, Transportation Center, University of California, Berkeley.

James Martin, professor, English and Humanities, School of Arts and Sciences, Mount Ida College, Newton, Massachusetts.

Deborah McKoy, executive director, Center for Cities and Schools, University of California, Berkeley.

Carrie Menendez, PhD candidate, Urban Planning and Policy Program, and research assistant, Great Cities Institute, University of Illinois, Chicago.

Mary Jane Nirdlinger, special projects coordinator, Planning Department, town of Chapel Hill, North Carolina.

Lorraine Oback, marketing communications director, Public Library, city of San Jose, California.

P. Michael Paules, city manager, city of San Gabriel, California.

David C. Perry, director, Great Cities Institute, and professor of urban planning and policy, University of Illinois, Chicago.

Robin Popik, supervisor, Volunteer Resource Group, city of Plano, Texas.

Michael Porter, chief executive officer, chairman, and founder, Initiative for a Competitive Inner City (ICIC), Boston, Massachusetts.

Adam Prestopnik, assistant director of distance learning, Onondaga Community College, Syracuse, New York.

Gregory S. Prince, Jr., president, Hampshire College, Amherst, Massachusetts.

Paree Roper, industry specialist, Public Risk Management Association (PRIMA), Alexandria, Virginia.

James E. Samels, president and chief executive officer, the Education Alliance, New York.

Carissa Schively Slotterback, assistant professor and director, Urban and Regional Planning Program, Humphrey School of Public Affairs, University of Minnesota, Minneapolis.

Ann H. Shawver, director of finance, city of Roanoke, Virginia.

John W. Sibley, city manager, City of Orange, California.

Adam Smeltz, senior editor and news reporter, student newspaper, Pennsylvania State University, State College.

Laurence Sprecher, former city manager, Beaverton, Oregon.

Roger Stancil, town manager, town of Chapel Hill, North Carolina.

David Stern, professor of policy, organization, measurement, and evaluation, Graduate School of Education, University of California, Berkeley, California.

Jake Sticka, student and commissioner, Advisory Neighborhood Commission, Washington, DC.

Daniel F. Sullivan, president, St. Lawrence University, Canton, New York.

Yesim Sungu-Eryilmaz, research associate, Lincoln Institute of Land Policy, Cambridge, Massachusetts.

April Suwalsky, director, community engagement, Nystrom United ReVitalization Effort (NURVE), Richmond, California.

Erika Tate, PLUS (Planning and Learning United for Systems change) research fellow, Center for Cities and Schools, University of California, Berkeley.

Jeffrey M. Vincent, deputy director, Center for Cities and Schools, University of California, Berkeley.

Brian Whitson, director of university relations, the College of William and Mary, Williamsburg, Virginia.

Wim Wiewel, president, Portland State University, Portland, Oregon.

Todd Wilkinson, free-lance writer, Bozeman, Montana.

Daniel L. Wilson, chief financial officer, Mentor Public Schools, Mentor, Ohio.

Phil Wood, dean of students, McMaster University, Hamilton, Ontario, Canada.

Charles E. Young, president, University of Florida, Gainesville.

Joshua Zaffos, free-lance writer, Collins, Colorado.

Index